BUYER'S

clocks & barometers

DEREK ROBERTS CONSULTANT

MTTER'S

Acknowledgements

The publishers would like to acknowledge the great assistance given by our consultants.

Contributing Editor

Derek Roberts has run his antique clocks business in Tonbridge, Kent, since 1967. He gained his Freedom of the Worshipful Company of Clockmakers in 1977 and was elected to the Livery the following year. His publications include British Skeleton Clocks, Continental and American Skeleton Clocks, The British Longcase Clock, Collectors Guide to Clocks and Carriage Clocks. He has held several exhibitions, notably Precision Pendulum Clocks and Amazing Clocks, and The Art and Craft of the Clockmaker, accompanied by publications.

Longcase Clocks

Brian Loomes has been buying and selling British clocks since 1966. He is the author of 20 books on clocks including Painted Dial Clocks (a new edition was published in 1995), Grandfather Clocks and their Cases, and the companion volume to Baillie's dictionary Watchmakers and Clockmakers of the World. He has contributed many articles to major antique and specialist publications.

Bracket Clocks

Ben Wright has been head of the clock department at Christie's salerooms in London since 1991. As an autioneer he has sold several important collections of clocks, including the Vitale collection in 1996, which achieved a world record for any clock sale.

Mantel Clocks & Garnitures

Roderick Mee bought his first clock at the age of 12, and later began his career in his mother's antique shop. However, within a year he had started up on his own, first at Chelsea Antique Market, then at Antiquarius in London's King's Road. He moved to his current premises in Kensington in 1989. His special interest is in 19th-century clocks.

Carriage Clocks

Oliver Saunders is manager of the clock and watch department at Bonhams in London. He trained as a clockmaker, taking the British Horological Institute's exams in the history, theory and making of clocks and parts of watches. He gained experience in the clock department at Harrods, followed by eight years selling clocks and watches at Mappin & Webb and Garrard's before moving to Bonhams.

Wall & Cartel Clocks

Michael Turner began his career with the firm of Camerer Cuss and Co in London in 1965. Later he worked for John Keil Ltd, the English furniture specialists, introducing antique clocks into the stock. He joined Sotheby's London in 1978, where he is now a director of the clock and watch department and auctioneer for the London horological sales.

Skeleton & Lantern Clocks

M. D. Tooke is a member of the Worshipful Company of Clockmakers as well as the British Antique Dealers' Association. He does not classify himself as a dealer but rather as a horologist.

Regulators

Gerard Campbell combined a career as a physicist with a passion for collecting clocks. He started dealing in clocks 22 years ago, with particular interest in early Vienna Regulators.

American Clocks

Bob Schmitt began collecting clocks in 1969, while working for the Ford Motor Company. In 1979 he left Ford to pursue the clock business full time. In 1985 he moved to New Hampshire, where he and his wife, Tricia, conduct semi-annual clock and watch auctions. He is a life member of the National Association of Watch and Clock Collectors, based in Columbia, Pennsylvania, USA.

Barometers

With 40 years experience, Derek and Tina Rayment are acknowledged in the trade as the leading specialists in English and Continental Antique Barometers, Thermometers and Barographs, including restoration undertaken for Europe and the USA. They are members of The London & Provincial Antique Dealers' Association and the British Antique Dealers' Association and exhibit at major London Antique Fairs.

Electric Clocks

Alan Shenton is the author of The Eureka Clock, Pocket Watches 19th and 20th Century, and co-author with his wife, Rita, of Collectable Clocks 1840–1940.
Rita Shenton has published a monograph on the 18th-century clockmaking family of Christopher Pinchbeck and has contributed articles on horology to many journals and periodicals. She has run a horological book business for over 22 years. Both Alan and Rita Shenton have been actively involved with the Antiquarian Horological Society and are members of the British Horological Institute. James Nye started repairing clocks at school at the age of 14, and trained as a clock repairer between school and university. Later he developed an exclusive interest in electrical horology, building a comprehensive knowledge of Continental and English electric clocks.

Miscellaneous Clocks

John Denvir collected clocks from an early age, with a particular interest in unusual models. About ten years ago he started his own business in Portobello Road, specialising in novelty, mystery and electric clocks. This has led one of his customers to dub him 'the King of Quirky Clocks' – a title with which he is very happy.

clocks &
barometers

MILLER'S CLOCKS & BAROMETERS BUYER'S GUIDE

Created and designed by
Miller's
The Cellars, High Street,
Tenterden, Kent TN30 6BN
Tel: 01580 766411
Fax: 01580 766100

Consultant: Derek Roberts

Project Editor: Léonie Sidgwick, Jo Wood
Editorial Assistants: Maureen Horner, Deborah Wanstall
Production Assistant: Ethne Tragett
Advertising Executive: Jill Jackson
Advertising Assistants: Jo Hill, Melinda Williams
Design: K & S Promotions, Kari Reeves
Index compiled by: Hilary Bird
Additional photography: Ian Booth, Robin Saker

First published in Great Britain in 1997
by Miller's, a division of Mitchell Beazley,
imprints of Octopus Publishing Group Ltd,
2–4 Heron Quays, London E14 4JP

© 1997, 2001 Octopus Publishing Group Ltd

A CIP catalogue record for this book is
available from the British Library

ISBN 1-84000-499-1

Miller's Clocks & Barometers Buyer's Guide

Some images have appeared in previous editions of
Miller's Antiques Price Guide

Film output by CK Litho, Whitstable, Kent
Illustrations by G. H. Graphics, St. Leonard's-on-Sea
Colour origination by Scantrans, Singapore
Printed in Great Britain by Butler and Tanner Ltd., Frome and London

A Louis XVI gilt-bronze mantel clock, the dial signed Jean Baptiste Baillon, late 18thC, with later movement signed Payne & Co, London, 15¾in (40cm) high. **£6,000–9,000 $8,700–13,000** ⚡ S

Miller's is a registered trademark of
Octopus Publishing Group Ltd

Contents

MILLER'S

Key to Illustrations

Each illustration and descriptive caption is accompanied by a letter code. By referring to the following list of auctioneers (denoted by *) and dealers (•) the source of any item may be immediately determined. Please note that inclusion of an item in this book does not guarantee that the item, or any similar item, is available for sale from the contributor. Advertisers are denoted by †.

If you require a valuation for an item, it is advisable to check whether the dealer or specialist will carry out this service and if there is a charge. Please mention Miller's when making an enquiry. Having found a specialist who will carry out your valuation it is best to send a photograph and description of the item to the specialist together with a stamped addressed envelope for the reply. A valuation by telephone is not possible. Most dealers are only too happy to help you with your enquiry. However, they are very busy people and consideration of the above points would be welcomed.

AG * Anderson & Garland, Marlborough House, Marlborough Crescent, Newcastle-upon-Tyne, Tyne & Wear NE1 4EE Tel: 0191 232 6278

AGr * Andrew Grant, St Mark's House, St Mark's Close, Worcester, Worcestershire WR5 3DJ Tel: 01905 357547

AH * Andrew Hartley, Victoria Hall Salerooms, Little Lane, Ilkley, Yorkshire LS29 8EA Tel: 01943 816363

AHL • Adrian Hornsey Ltd, Brook Manor, Buckfastleigh, Devon TQ11 0HR Tel: 01364 642324

ALL * Allen & Harris, Bristol Auction Rooms See **Bri**

ALS • † Allan Smith Clocks, Amity Cottage, 162 Beechcroft Road, Upper Stratton, Swindon, Wiltshire SN2 6QE Tel: 01793 822977

ARE • Arenski, 185 Westbourne Grove, London W11 2SB Tel: 020 7727 8599

ASA • A. S. Antiques, 26 Broad Street, Pendleton, Salford, Greater Manchester M6 5BY Tel: 0161 737 5938

B * Boardman Fine Art Auctioneers, Station Road Corner, Haverhill, Suffolk CB9 0EY Tel: 01440 730414

BD • Private Collection

Bea * Bearnes, Avenue Road, Torquay, Devon TQ2 5TG Tel: 01803 296277

Bea(E) * Bearnes, St Edmund's Court, Okehampton Street, Exeter, Devon EX4 1DU Tel: 01392 422800

BEL • Bell Antiques, 68 Harold Street, Grimsby, South Humberside Tel: 01472 695110

BF • No longer trading

BH • Bob Hoare Pine Antiques, Unit Q, Phoenix Place, North Street, Lewes, Sussex Tel: 01273 480557

BL • † Brian Loomes, Calf Haugh Farm, Pateley Bridge, Yorkshire HG3 5HW Tel: 01423 711163

Bon * Bonhams, Montpelier Street, Knightsbridge, London SW7 1HH Tel: 020 7393 3900

Bri * Bristol Auction Rooms, St John's Place, Apsley Road, Clifton, Bristol, Avon BS8 2ST Tel: 0117 973 7201

BS • Private Collection

BWA • Bow-Well Antiques, 103 West Bow, Edinburgh, Scotland EH1 2JP Tel: 0131 225 3335

BWe * Biddle and Webb Ltd, Ladywood Middleway, Birmingham, West Midlands B16 0PP Tel: 0121 455 8042

C * Christie's, Manson & Woods Ltd, 8 King Street, St James's, London SW1Y 6QT Tel: 020 7839 9060

C(S) * Christie's Scotland Ltd, 164–166 Bath Street, Glasgow, Scotland G2 4TG Tel: 0141 332 8134

CAG * Canterbury Auction Galleries, 40 Station Road West, Canterbury, Kent CT2 8AN Tel: 01227 763337

C(Am) * Christie's Amsterdam, Cornelis Schuystraat 57, Amsterdam 107150 Tel: (3120) 57 55 255

CBS * C. B. Sheppard & Son, Auction Galleries, Chatsworth Street, Sutton-in-Ashfield, Notts NG17 4GG Tel: 01773 872419

CDC * Capes Dunn & Co, The Auction Galleries, 38 Charles Street, off Princess Street, Gtr Manchester M1 7DB Tel: 0161 273 6060/1911

CeD * Christie's & Edmiston's, Glasgow, see **C(S)**

CER • Private Collection

CLC • † The Clock Clinic Ltd, 85 Lower Richmond Road, London SW15 1EU Tel: 020 8788 1407

CNY * Christie Manson & Woods International Inc, (including Christie's East), 502 Park Avenue, New York, NY 10022, USA Tel: 001 212 546 1000

CoH * Cooper Hirst, The Granary Saleroom, Victoria Road, Chelmsford, Essex CM2 6LH Tel: 01245 260535

CRY • No longer trading

CS • Private Collection

CSK * Christie's South Kensington Ltd, 85 Old Brompton Road, London SW7 3LD Tel: 020 7581 7611

DA * Dee, Atkinson & Harrison, The Exchange Saleroom, Driffield, Yorkshire YO25 7LJ Tel: 01377 253151

DaD * David Dockree, 224 Moss Lane, Bramhall, Stockport, Cheshire SK7 1BD Tel: 0161 485 1258

DDM * Dickinson, Davy & Markham, Wrawby Street, Brigg, Humberside DN20 8JJ Tel: 01652 653666

DHa • David Harriman, 25 Nightingale Road, Rickmansworth, Hertfordshire WD3 2DE Tel: 01923 776919

DJM • Private Collection

DN/ * Dreweatt Neate, Donnington Priory,
DWB Donnington, Newbury, Berkshire RG13 2JE Tel: 01635 31234

DRA • † Derek Roberts Antiques, 24–25 Shipbourne Road, Tonbridge, Kent TN10 3DN Tel: 01732 358986

DSH * Dacre Son & Hartley, see **AH**

E * Ewbank Auctioneers, Burnt Common Auction Rooms, London Road, Send, Woking, Surrey GU23 7LN Tel: 01483 223101

EA • No longer trading

EHL/ • E. Hollander, 1 Bennetts Castle, 89 The Street,
HOL Capel, Dorking, Surrey RH5 5JX Tel: 01306 713377

FHF * Frank H. Fellows & Sons, Augusta House, 19 Augusta Street, Hockley, Birmingham, West Midlands B18 6JA Tel: 0121 212 2131

FLE • No longer trading

GA(W)• Private Collection

GAK * G. A. Key, Aylsham Salerooms, 8 Market Place, Aylsham, Norfolk NR11 6EH Tel: 01263 733195

Gam * Clarke Gammon, Guildford Auction Rooms, Bedford Road, Guildford, Surrey GU1 4SJ Tel: 01483 566458

GC • Private Collection

GD • Gilbert & Dale Antiques, The Old Chapel, Church Street, Ilchester, Nr Yeovil, Somerset BA22 8ZA Tel: 01935 840464

GeC • † Campbell & Archard Ltd, Lychgate House, Church Street, Seal, Kent TN15 0AR Tel: 01732 761153

GH • No longer trading

GIB • David Gibson, 4 Wood Street, Queen Square, Bath, Avon BA1 2JQ Tel: 01225 446646

GIL * Gildings, 64 Roman Way, Market Harborough, Leicestershire LE16 7PQ Tel: 01858 410414

GM	*	Mealys, Chatsworth St, Castle Comer, Co Kilkenny, S. Ireland Tel: 0035356 41229
GSP	*	Graves, Son & Pilcher, Hove Auction Rooms, Hove, Sussex BN3 2GL Tel: 01273 735266
GUN	• †	Gaby Gunst Antique Clocks & Barometers, 140 High Street, Tenterden, Kent TN30 6HT Tel: 01580 765818
HAM	*	Hamptons Auctioneers and Valuers, Baverstock House, 93 High Street, Godalming, Surrey GU7 1AL Tel: 01483 423567
HAW	•	No longer trading
HCH	*	Hobbs & Chambers, Market Place, Cirencester, Gloucestershire GL7 1QQ Tel: 01285 654736
HOD	•	Private Collection
HSS/ P(HSS)	*	Henry Spencer and Sons (Phillips), 20 The Square, Retford, Notts DN22 6BX Tel: 01777 708633
IAT	• †	It's About Time, 863 London Road, Westcliff-on-Sea, Essex SS0 9SZ Tel: 01702 472574
IM	*	Ibbett Mosely, 125 High Street, Sevenoaks, Kent TN13 1UT Tel: 01732 452246
JD	*	Lewes Auction Rooms (Julian Dawson), 56 High Street, Lewes, Sussex BN7 1XE Tel: 01273 478221
JeB	•	Private Collection
JL	*	Joy Luke, The Gallery, 300E Grove Street, Bloomington, IL 61701, USA Tel: 001 309 828 5533
JH	*	Jacobs & Hunt, 26 Lavant Street, Petersfield, Hampshire GU32 3EF Tel: 01730 233933
JMW	•	Private Collection
JRB	•	Private Collection
L	*	Lawrence Fine Art Auctioneers, South Street, Crewkerne, Somerset TA18 8AB Tel: 01460 73041
LANG	*	Bonhams & Langlois, Westaway Chambers, 39 Don Street, St Helier, Jersey JE2 4TR Tel: 01534 22441
L&E	*	Locke & England, Black Horse Agencies, 18 Guy Street, Leamington Spa, Warwickshire CV32 4RT Tel: 01926 889100
LBP	•	Private Collection
LRG	*	Lots Road Auction Galleries, 71 Lots Road, London SW10 0RN Tel: 020 7351 7771
LT	*	Louis Taylor Auctioneers & Valuers, Britannia House, 10 Town Road, Hanley, Stoke-on-Trent, Staffordshire ST1 2QG Tel: 01782 214111
M	*	Morphets of Harrogate, 6 Albert Street, Harrogate, Yorkshire HG1 1JL Tel: 01423 502282
MAT	*	Christopher Matthews, 23 Mount Street, Harrogate, Yorkshire HG2 8DQ Tel: 01423 871756
MAW	•	No longer trading
MCA	*	Mervyn Carey, Twysden Cottage, Benenden, Cranbrook, Kent TN17 4LD Tel: 01580 240283
McC	*	McCartney's, Ox Pasture, Overture Road, Ludlow, Shropshire SY8 4AA Tel: 01584 872251
MERT	•	Barometer World, Quicksilver Barn, Merton, Okehampton, Devon EX20 3DS Tel: 01805 603443
MGM	•	Private Collection
MIL	•	No longer trading
Mit	*	Mitchells, Fairfield House, Station Road, Cockermouth, Cumbria CA13 9PY Tel: 01900 827800
MJB	*	Michael J Bowman, 6 Haccombe House, Netherton, Newton Abbot, Devon TQ12 4SJ Tel: 01626 872890
MN	•	Private Collection
MSL	*	Michael Stainer Ltd, St Andrew's Hall, Wolverton Road, Boscombe, Bournemouth, Dorset BH7 6HT Tel: 01202 309999
MSW	*	Marilyn Swain Auctions, The Old Barracks, Sandon Road, Grantham, Lincolnshire NG31 9AS Tel: 01476 568861
N	*	Neales, 192–194 Mansfield Road, Nottingham, Notts NG1 3HU Tel: 0115 962 4141
OFT	• †	Old Father Time Clock Centre, 101 Portobello Road, London, W11 2BQ Tel: 020 8546 6299
OL	*	Outhwaite & Litherland, Kingsway Galleries, Fontenoy Street, Liverpool, Merseyside L3 2BE Tel: 0151 236 6561
P	*	Phillips, 101 New Bond Street, London, W1Y 0AS Tel: 020 7629 6602
P(EA)	*	Phillips, 32 Boss Hall Road, Ipswich, Suffolk IP1 5DJ Tel: 01473 740494

P(M)	*	Phillips, Trinity House, 114 Washway Road, Sale, Gtr Manchester M33 1RF Tel: 0161 962 9237
P(PWC)	•	Private Collection
P(Re)	•	Private Collection
P(S)	*	Phillips, 49 London Road, Sevenoaks, Kent TN13 1AR Tel: 01732 740310
PAO	• †	P. A. Oxley, The Old Rectory, Cherhill, Calne, Wilts SN11 8UX Tel: 01249 816227
PB	*	Phillips inc Brooks
PC	•	Private Collection
PCh	*	Peter Cheney, Western Road Auction Rooms, Littlehampton, Sussex BN17 5NP Tel: 01903 722264
PHA	•	Paul Hopwell Antiques, 30 High Street, West Haddon, Northants NN6 7AP Tel: 01788 510636
PWC	•	Private Collection
RBB	*	Russell, Baldwin & Bright, Ryelands Road, Leominster, Hereford & Worcestershire HR6 8NZ Tel: 01568 611166
Re	•	Private Collection
RFA	• †	Gem Antiques, 10 Gabriels Hill, Maidstone, Kent ME15 6JG Tel: 01622 763344 28 London Road, Sevenoaks, Kent TN13 1AP Tel: 01732 743540
RID	*	Riddetts of Bournemouth, 26 Richmond Hill, The Square, Bournemouth, Dorset BH2 6EJ Tel: 01202 555686
RSch	* †	R. O. Schmitt Fine Art, Box 1941, Salem, NH 03079, USA Tel: 603 893 5915
S	•	Sotheby's, 34–35 New Bond Street, London W1A 2AA Tel: 020 7493 8080
S(C)	*	Sotheby's, Booth Mansion, 28 Watergate Street, Chester, Cheshire CH1 2LA Tel: 01244 315531
S(NY)	*	Sotheby's, 1334 York Avenue, New York, NY 10021, USA Tel: 212 606 7000
S(S)	*	Sotheby's Sussex, Summers Place, Billingshurst, Sussex RH14 9AD Tel: 01403 783933
SBA	•	Private Collection
SH	•	Private Collection
SHO	•	Private Collection
Sim	*	Simmons & Sons, 32 Bell Street, Henley-on-Thames, Oxfordshire RG9 2BH Tel: 01491 571111
SK	*	Skinner Inc, The Heritage on the Garden, 63 Park Plaza, Boston, MA 02116, USA Tel: 001 617 350 5400
SK(B)	*	Skinner Inc, 357 Main Street, Bolton, MA 01740, USA Tel: 001 508 779 6241
SO	•	Samuel Orr Antique Clocks, 36 High St, Hurstpierpoint, Brighton, Sussex BN6 9RG Tel: 01273 83208
STW	•	Private Collection
SWO	*	G. E. Sworder & Sons, 14 Cambridge Road, Stansted Mountfitchet, Essex CM24 8BZ Tel: 01279 817778
TCW	• †	The Clock Workshop, 17 Prospect Street, Caversham, Reading, Berkshire RT4 8JB Tel: 0118 947 0741
TEN	*	Tennants, 34 Montpellier Parade, Harrogate, Yorkshire HG1 2TG Tel: 01423 531661
THG	•	Private Collection
TKN	•	Private Collection
TL	•	No longer trading
TM	*	Thomas Mawer & Son, Lincoln Saleroom, 63 Monks Road, Lincoln, Lincolnshire LN2 5HP Tel: 01522 524984
TW	*	Thomas Watson & Son, Northumberland Street, Darlington, Co Durham DL3 7HJ Tel: 01325 462559/463485
V	•	Private Collection
W&W	• †	Alan Walker, Halfway Manor, Halfway, Nr Newbury, Berkshire RG20 8NR Tel: 01488 657670 Weather House Antiques, Foster Clough, Hebden Bridge, West Yorkshire HX7 5QZ Tel: 01422 882808
WHB	*	William H. Brown, Ashford House, Saxmundham, Suffolk IP17 1AB Tel: 01728 603232
WL	*	Wintertons Ltd, Lichfield Auction Centre, Wood End Lane, Fradley, Lichfield, Staffords WS13 8NF Tel: 01543 263256
Wor	*	See **CAG**
WW	*	Woolley & Wallis, Salisbury Salerooms, 51–61 Castle Street, Salisbury, Wiltshire, SP1 3SU Tel: 01722 411422

Introduction

Since the first edition of *Miller's Clocks & Barometers Buyer's Guide* some four years ago, the economies of the western world have changed appreciably. Rapidly declining interest rates, which appear to be set to remain low for the foreseeable future, mean that people are getting a poor return on money they deposit with a bank or building society. The problem for investors is compounded by the rapid fall in the value of stocks and shares, virtually worldwide over the last 18 months, which means they are often sitting on substantial losses. Although investments will no doubt recover in the medium to long term as confidence returns, and also because of the the substantial sums of money piling up waiting to be invested, investors, particularly small ones, for instance those running their own businesses, will be far more cautious than in the past and many will be searching for alternative avenues for their money.

Unfortunately, similar problems arise with pension funds. The heady forecast of 10–12 years ago has now been nearly halved, with those who have poured money into this avenue for many years now finding that they will be in difficulties when they retire.

An avenue open to small rather than major investors are antiques. They are in many ways an ideal investment area as they have consistently in the long term provided excellent returns and have the big bonus that they also give pleasure to their owners, which is indeed a happy state of affairs.

Several friends and customers have expressed the sentiment that it is far more pleasurable to surround oneself with objects which constantly give one pleasure, but can be disposed of in later life should the need arise, rather than always being worried by fluctuations which take place in interest rates or on the stock exchange and which one is assailed daily in the newspapers and on television.

The natural course is to acquire objects you know about and have an interest in. Clock collectors are particularly fortunate because mechanical devices attract no capital gains tax.

So far as clocks and indeed antiques in general are concerned, it is always best to buy good examples in as original a condition as possible. A poor example of a fine or rare item will never sell as well as an excellent example of a somewhat lesser piece. In our experience serious collectors will always, if possible, find the money for that special piece they want to have in their collection, and for the same reason they will always find it easy to resell.

A good example is the Cole Tripod clock, a highly individual clock with several unusual features of which only about 70 were made. The last example we sold in August 1996 reached £6,400 ($9,000). A few months ago one fetched over £16,000 ($23,000) at auction. Special items such as Condliff's superb skeleton clocks and complex, rare mystery and novelty clocks are also much in demand.

One of the problems for clock collectors is the scarcity of fine items. When they do appear there is strong competition, particularly because it is not unusual, even in a major London specialist sale, for there to be more than five, or at the outside, ten clocks which would be considered desirable.

The top names are inevitably much sought after; a month-duration walnut longcase by Tompion fetched £315,000 ($455,000) in Christie's sale, and an early unnumbered table clock by the same maker achieved around £250,000 ($360,000) in Paris recently.

Some five years ago we sold what might be termed a very good but standard striking and repeating table clock by Tompion for £88,000 ($128,000) and in recent months have disposed of another similar clock by the same maker for £138,000 ($200,000).

Good regulators have been in strong demand in recent times as increasingly collectors appreciate their superb quality, and prices have gone up by maybe 50 per cent in the last four to five years. The Victorian arched-top regulator was made in appreciable numbers because it has never attracted the prices achieved by its earlier brethren; however, good examples are now in short supply and they are being increasingly sought after because of their superb movements, usually of appreciably better quality than those seen in the earlier clocks. A good example, maybe 72–74in (183–188cm) high will now fetch around £14,000–15,000 ($20,300–22,000) fully restored with a premium for additional refinements on the movement and the case, such as glazed sides.

Apart from specialized items such as those already mentioned, good furnishing clocks are also much in demand, again with the best examples leading the way. A slim, small and well-proportioned Scottish mahogany longcase clock, preferably with moonphases, will now fetch £8,500–9,500 ($12,500–13,500) fully restored, whereas a large and poorly proportioned 8-day clock will probably struggle to make £2,000 ($3,000) in auction. This pattern holds true throughout the various other types of clocks. The demand and hence price of clocks is affected by many variables, some of which are age, size, amount of repair, restoration and, finally, fakes.

Age

The age of a clock is of far less importance than its quality, aesthetic appeal and originality. Black bracket clocks for instance, unless they are early examples, by famous makers, or have some particularly interesting technical feature, are still out of favour, more so if they have silvered or painted dials, and will fetch only half that of one with a good mahogany case.

Size

Size is often an important factor, particularly with longcase clocks, but is sometimes counterbalanced by the superb quality of some of the taller examples, usually made in London.

The same holds true of bracket clocks, a substantial premium being required for the smaller examples, particularly those only 8–10in (20.5–25.5cm) high. Conversely, the large Victorian bracket clocks, often of superb quality, are still much undervalued when related to their original cost of manufacture.

Repairs, Restorations and Rebuilds

Virtually all clocks have had some restoration in their lifetime, and provided this is limited and has been done well it will have little effect on their value, and indeed may well be beneficial. Examples which spring to mind are the regilding of carriage clock cases (other than possibly the early ones), the careful touching in of a painted dial (much as one would restore a picture), and the cleaning of a brass dial and resilvering of the chapter ring, which may have been done many times in the life of a clock.

What is far less acceptable is the fitting of a modern escapement on a carriage clock, usually because the original is badly worn and difficult to repair, and the complete repainting of a longcase dial, which takes away much of its character.

As far as longcase clocks are concerned, the rebuilding of the base of a clock, usually necessitated by woodworm and damp coming up from the floor or wall, is a serious problem as it means that an appreciable portion of the original case has been lost. Other defects are the reveneering of the case and, particularly on early clocks, the loss of its patination and colour through stripping and repolishing.

Reproduction clock cases housing old movements are not usually a problem as they are fairly obvious. However, with the more valuable early clocks the problem could be more serious as the case may have been made to deceive.

Fakes

Fake signatures are relatively uncommon and have little effect on the value of less expensive clocks. With early and rare clocks fake signatures can be a problem, but are usually fairly obvious as the work of the best makers is highly individual, and known to dedicated dealers and collectors.   **Derek Roberts**

The kind of longcase clock which attracts a substantial premium. It stands just 78in (198cm) high, has a finely figured mahogany case with good patination and an attractive brass dial with moonphases.

A classic example of the Victorian arched-top regulator, now much in demand because of the superb quality of the movement, small size, usually between 72in (183cm) and 76in (193cm) high, and fine case with glazed door displaying the mercury compensated pendulum.

General Information

The different categories of clock vary enormously in appearance and mechanism. However, there are certain key factors common to all clocks, an understanding of which is useful in assessing the age and authenticity of any piece, and should be considered before a purchase is made. The principal elements of any clock are the mechanism, or movement, the case, which houses the clock, and the hands and dial, showing the time.

Movements

Power

Clocks are powered in three ways:

• weight-driven, by the pull of hanging weights – lantern, longcase and some wall clocks.
• spring-driven, by the release of energy in a coiled spring – bracket, carriage, skeleton, novelty and some wall clocks. The use of a spring instead of a weight made clocks more portable than they had been previously. Most English spring-driven clocks have a device known as a fusee, a conical-shaped spool used to even out the pull of the spring that provides the motive force, thus spreading power over the running time of the clock, allowing more accurate timekeeping.
• electricity, both from the mains and a battery. Clocks powered by electricity date from the mid-19th century and are increasingly popular today.

Escapements

All mechanical clocks have an escapement, a device that releases at set intervals a train of wheels and pinions to which the clock hands are attached, thus enabling the clock to keep time. The two main types are the **verge**, used initially with the foliot or balance wheel, and later in conjunction with the pendulum after 1658, and the **anchor**, which replaced the verge and was used in longcase clocks from c1670, and in bracket and wall clocks from c1800.

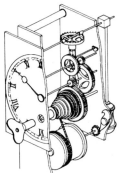 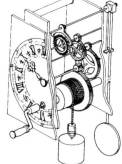

Verge escapement   *Anchor escapement*

It is possible to distinguish between the verge and the anchor escapement as the arc of the pendulum's swing in an anchor escapement is far less than in the verge pendulum, and instead of a small pendulum bob a large lenticular bob will have been used on the anchor escapement. Many clocks have been converted from a verge to an anchor escapement. The backplate of a bracket clock fitted with a verge escapement was often ornately engraved. If such engraving is concealed by a large pendulum bob, then it is likely that a conversion from verge to anchor escapement has taken place.

Other types of escapement include:

• the **cylinder** escapement, found in inexpensive late 19th-century French carriage clocks.
• the **deadbeat** escapement, used in good-quality longcase clocks and regulators, usually combined with a compensated pendulum to give accurate timekeeping.

Platform lever escapement

• the **chronometer** escapement, found mainly in chronometers.
• the **lever** escapement, with balance wheel, used in many carriage clocks (*see above*).
• the **pinwheel**, a form of anchor escapement used by French clockmakers.
• the **Brocot** escapement, frequently found in French and marble-cased clocks, often visible on the front of the clock.

The pendulum

Most weight- and spring-driven clocks from the mid-17th century have a pendulum to control the clock's speed and accuracy. The pendulum is a brass or steel rod, with a metal disc or bob at the bottom, usually lead cased in brass, and the bob's position alters timekeeping. It swings in a regular arc and is connected, directly or indirectly, to the same arbor, or shaft, on which the escape wheel turns.

On a verge escapement the bob is usually on a threaded rod, and on an anchor escapement the bob slides on the rod and can be adjusted by a rating nut. The length of the rod varies with temperature, affecting timekeeping. The longer the rod the slower its swing, and so the slower the clock. To avoid variations, two types of compensating pendulums were developed, the mercurial and the gridiron pendulums.

Until c1790 London-made clocks and many of those made in the provinces have a brass-faced lead pendulum bob. A small number of bobs were painted and decorated – these were often made in Scotland. American clocks usually have brass or tin pendulums.

Cases

Careful examination of the materials and fittings used in the making of a clock case provides a useful indication of age, value and condition.

Wooden cases

Wooden cases were introduced c1660 to house the movement, weights and pendulum. The frame or carcase of the longcase is oak, overlaid with very thin layers of wood, or veneers, the most common of which are:

• **ebony** – a dense wood, dark when polished, used on early longcase clocks c1660–80, and on bracket clocks c1660–1715.
• **ebonized wood** – pale fruitwood stained black and less desirable than ebony cases.
• **walnut** – used on most early longcases, often finely figured, depending on how it is cut.
• **mahogany** – a dark wood, often finely figured, imported from the Caribbean, widely used 1730–1840.
• **oak** – solid, not veneered, used mainly by English provincial makers c1710–1810.
• **rosewood** – a dark, strongly figured wood, often with black streaks, widely used in the early 19th century.
• **oyster veneer** – wood cut from olive and other trees in round forms, across the grain.

Decoration

• **marquetry** – wood inlaid in decorative patterns, popular on longcases in the late 17th and early 18th century.
• **lacquer** – fashionable from 1710–60, longcases may have a black, green, red or yellow ground, and tend

to have chinoiserie motifs painted over a *gesso* (raised work) ground, with extensive use of gold leaf. Later examples may have applied prints. Lacquer is also found on bracket and tavern clocks.
- **applied metal mounts** – usually of brass, often found on English bracket clock cases.
- **brass inlay** – common on mahogany or rosewood-veneered bracket clocks from the Regency period and on some ebonized cases.
- **tortoiseshell** – used by some French makers, or combinations of pewter, brass, tortoiseshell and wood veneer.

Metal cases

Brass is the most common metal. Although English lantern clocks have an all-brass case, metal cases are associated with French bracket and carriage clocks. Most carriage clocks are brass-cased. Old brass is uneven, with marks left by the casting process, whereas modern rolled brass is of uniform thickness. Bronze was used on some English carriage clocks and for the components of some French clocks.

Hinges and locks

Hinges and locks should be original. Replacements will be evident from spare screw or pin holes, or from the outline of the original hinge. Gaps around the lock on the trunk door may indicate a replacement lock.

The Hands and Dial

Hands

Early lantern clocks have only one hand, for the hours, but from c1600 most clocks have separate hour and minute hands. There are many different designs of hands, with variations in detail according to the type of clock they were made for. Although some clocks have a centre seconds hand, it is common to show seconds on a subsidiary dial.

Hands are usually made of blued steel, although gilded brass is found from c1790, particularly on Continental clocks. Steel hands are 'blued' by heating rather than painting, a process which protects them and makes them easier to see. The hour hand is secured to a brass pipe projecting through the dial centre, the minute hand fitting on to a concentric shaft in the centre of the pipe. Hands can break, usually through careless handling, but are easily repaired. If lost, a replacement in the correct style is acceptable.

Dials

The dial, or 'face', of a clock consists of a square, arched or round metal or wooden plate. Dials can be dated by their material and shape:
- **square** – used from the early 17th to early 18th century, popular with English provincial makers until the 1840s, usually in painted metal rather than brass.
- **arched** – from c1715, and standard on London-made longcase and bracket clocks from 1720–25.
- **round** – used especially in France, very common in the 19th century.
- **brass** – with applied chapter ring. The earliest type of dial, used on lantern clocks and most early longcases. From 1780 one-piece brass is more common.
- **painted wood** – common on 18th-century Continental clocks, English wall clocks, and some American clocks.
- **painted metal** – very common during the 19th century.
- **enamelled metal** – also known as porcelain, used on most French clocks and most carriage clocks.

With the advent of arched tops to dials from the early 18th century, moon dials can be found, particularly on longcase clocks, showing the time it takes for a full cycle of the moon. Dials showing tides either at London or other major ports may be found after 1756.

Parts of the dial

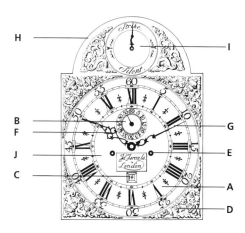

The basic parts of the dial, as on the 18th-century example, *above*, include:

A chapter ring	**F** hour hand
B subsidiary dial	**G** minute hand
C calendar aperture	**H** dial arch
D applied corner spandrels	**I** strike/silent lever
E winding holes	**J** dial centre

Other elements to consider when buying a clock are the following:

Signatures

Most clocks are signed by the clockmaker. Although a signature can help to date a clock, it does not guarantee that a clock was made in the stated period, or by the man whose name it bears. During the 19th century it was common for a clock to be signed by the retailer rather than the maker. The position of the signature varies with the type of clock, but usually appears on the dial and/or the backplate. Occasionally a fake signature has been added, usually to a clock that was not signed by its maker. This can usually be detected by feel – old engraving will be smooth, whereas new work can feel sharp.

Condition

All clocks should have their original finish and decorative featues intact. Some restoration is acceptable, if carried out sympathetically. Changes in temperature and humidity cause veneers to lift and, on longcase clocks, the trunk door to warp. All mouldings may loosen as the original glue dries out. On lacquered cases, bubbles caused by excessive heat and humidity may appear under the lacquer. No clock should be kept in direct sunlight, as this causes the finish to bleach. Other problems include: missing finials, damaged mouldings, broken glass on the hood, scratching or damage to polish.

Care and Attention

Cleaning of the movement should always be left to a specialist clockmaker. Cases should be dusted and polished regularly, using traditional wax polish.

Transporting a Clock

Never transport a clock by its handle, always hold it from underneath. The spring from which the pendulum is suspended is fragile and may break when a clock is moved. Spring-driven clocks with a short pendulum, such as English bracket clocks and most 19th-century French clocks, should be held upright when carried. When transporting a bracket clock, take out the pendulum, if it is detachable, or pack the back with tissue paper. Remove the weights and pendulum from a longcase clock. The hood should be taken off, and the dial and movement packed separately.

Dates	British Monarch	British Period	French Period
1558–1603	Elizabeth I	Elizabethan	Renaissance
1603–1625	James I	Jacobean	
1625–1649	Charles I	Carolean	Louis XIII (1610–1643)
1649–1660	Commonwealth	Cromwellian	Louis XIV (1643–1715)
1660–1685	Charles II	Restoration	
1685–1689	James II	Restoration	
1689–1694	William & Mary	William & Mary	
1694–1702	William III	William III	
1702–1714	Anne	Queen Anne	
1714–1727	George I	Early Georgian	Régence (1715–1723)
1727–1760	George II	Early Georgian	Louis XV (1723–1774)
1760–1811	George III	Late Georgian	Louis XVI (1774–1793) Directoire (1793–1799) Empire (1799–1815)
1812–1820	George III	Regency	Restauration Charles X (1815–1830)
1820–1830	George IV	Regency	
1830–1837	William IV	William IV	Louis Philippe (1830–1848)
1837–1901	Victoria	Victorian	2nd Empire Napoleon III (1848–1870) 3rd Republic (1871–1940)
1901–1910	Edward VII	Edwardian	

German Period	U.S. Period	Style	Woods
Renaissance	Early Colonial	Gothic	Oak Period (to c1670)
Renaissance/ Baroque (c1650–1700)		Baroque (c1620–1700)	Walnut period (c1670–1735)
	William & Mary		
	Dutch Colonial	Rococo (c1695–1760)	
Baroque (c1700–1730)	Queen Anne		
Rococo (c1730–1760)	Chippendale (from 1750)		Early mahogany period (c1735–1770)
Neo–classicism (c1760–1800)		Neo–classical (c1755–1805)	Late mahogany period (c1770–1810)
	Early Federal (1790–1810)		
Empire (c1800–1815)	American Directoire (1798–1804)	Empire (c1799–1815)	
	American Empire (1804–1815)		
Biedermeier (c1815–1848)	Late Federal (1810–1830)	Regency (c1812–1830)	
Revivale (c1830–1880)		Eclectic (c1830–1880)	
	Victorian		
Jugendstil (c1880–1920)		Arts & Crafts (c1880–1900)	
	Art Nouveau (c1900–1920)	Art Nouveau (c1900–1920)	

Longcase Clocks

For many people the dignified appearance and mellow sound of a longcase clock gives life to a home, as well as it being a good investment. As decorative objects they cover a large variety of styles, from the early country examples to those with extremely sophisticated dials, movements and cases.

The earliest longcase clocks were made in 1658 with the invention of the pendulum. The long case was a practical solution to the problem encountered with the weight-driven lantern clock, that of protecting the weights and pulleys from dust and from interfering children or animals. The first examples had short pendulums and verge escapements, housed in narrow, ebony cases. By the 1670s the verge escapement was discontinued in favour of the anchor escapement, a much simpler process which increased the accuracy of the clocks. From this date the cases became wider to accommodate the longer pendulum, and the dial size increased in proportion, first to about 10in (25.5cm), then 11in (28cm), and to 12in (30.5cm) by the early 18th century. The majority of 8-day clocks made in the cities from 1710 have arched dials, whereas arched-dial cottage clocks are rare. However, some early clocks were modernized at this date to acknowledge the new fashion and had an arched dial added to their square dial plates. Dials became increasingly sophisticated, with automated scenes, landscapes or seascapes, phases of the moon and other calendar information all variously incorporated. In the 18th century, the dial was normally flanked by columns and crowned by a pediment.

The buyer should recognize that the longcase clock is a marriage of engineering and craftsmanship. Occasionally, however, divorces and remarriages have taken place somewhere along the line. Many things can be altered in a clock, which is acceptable as long as the buyer is aware of the alterations when considering the price. If the clock has not got its original combination of features it will significantly affect its value. Dealer Michael Oxley points out: 'Between 1670–1870 you have 200 years of evolution of longcase clocks. After 1870 you begin to get copies of previous styles. The Victorians tended to go for big grand things and copied the 18th-century style of case, as well as going back to the brass dial of 100 years earlier.' He makes the point that someone who was not an expert would not necessarily be able to spot these differences, hence the importance of going to a specialist dealer so that you have recourse to a third party if the clock turns out to be wrong.

Brian Loomes, author and dealer of clocks, is well aware of the dangers: 'A great many clocks have been put in different cases, the works altered, abused, chopped, changed or married up.' Basically it is hard nowadays to get a genuine bargain – you get what you pay for and usually an inexpensive price tag means that the clock has undergone a great deal of alteration. You are unlikely to get a good longcase clock for less than £1,500 ($2,200), and at that price it is likely be a very simple, modest one and in need of complete restoration. Generally an 8-day, oak longcase clock of about 1820–30 with painted dial would cost in the region of £3,500–4,000 ($5,000–5,800). Brass dials are earlier and tend to be more expensive. Interestingly, in the recession it was the less expensive items that tended to remain unsold, with the better pieces in good condition continuing to increase in price.

So what are the main criteria affecting the price? Authenticity, first and foremost, followed by shape, size, condition, complexity of movement and unusual features. Clocks by famous makers such as Tompion, Quare, Knibb or East fetch very high prices. A fine clock by Tompian or Knibb is likely to fetch £125,000–150,000 ($180,000–218,000). These makers would have had a large number of apprentices who were working to their masters' high standards and who are worthy of investigation. In the upper middle range of the market the collectable London makers of the mid- to late 18th century include Robert Allam, John Shelton, Matthew Dutton and Thomas Mudge. A Holmes mahogany longcase achieved a bid of £70,000 ($102,000) at Bonhams recently in contrast with its pre-sale estimate of £10,000–12,000 ($14,500–17,500). Clocks by named makers will always be more valuable, but buyers should be aware that at the lower end of the market it was common for 19th-century clocks to be signed by the retailer rather than the maker.

Clock cases vary in style from region to region. A good start for a prospective buyer is to do some research into the production of longcases in their own region. Many collectors concentrate on clocks from a particular county, and there are often two or three makers from each county who are truly outstanding. In the past, country longcases were considered second-best to their smarter London cousins, but prices for country examples have been catching up and even, sometimes, exceeding those achieved by their London counterparts. A good Liverpool longcase with moonphase is now more than likely to reach a bid of £8,000 ($11,600).

Once a longcase clock is bought it should only be cleaned and overhauled by a specialist clock restorer. Never attempt to try and clean or repair an antique clock yourself. If you keep a longcase clock purely for decorative reasons without winding it, make sure it is not placed in damp conditions because it may pick up rust; it is a good idea to run it for a week or so once a year to keep the wheels turning. Finally, when transporting a longcase clock, remove the weights and pendulum. The hood should be taken off, and the dial and movement packed separately.

◄ A George II blue japanned longcase clock, the 12in (30.5cm) dial signed Thomas Atherton, London, the 5 pillar movement with rack and bell striking, silvered wood finials and decorated throughout in gilt chinoiserie against a blue ground, 95in (241.5cm) high.
£5,000–6,000
$7,000–8,700 ⚒ S

A Scottish mahogany longcase clock, the 12in (30.5cm) painted dial signed W. Alexander, Aberdeen, 19thC, 85in (216cm) high.
£6,500–7,000
$9,400–10,200
⊞ TL

A George III oak longcase clock, the brass dial inscribed Jn. Agar & Son, York, with 8-day movement.
£4,500–5,000
$6,500–7,500 ⚒ GSP

A mahogany longcase clock, the silvered 12in (30.5cm) break-arch dial signed Henry Adams, Hackney, subsidiary seconds and date dials, strike/silent dial in the arch, 8-day movement striking on a bell, c1800, 85½in (217cm) high.
£6,000–7,000
$8,700–10,200 ⚒ S(S)

A mahogany longcase clock, by Wm. Aitken, Haddington, c1840.
£7,500–8,000 $10,800–11,600 ⊞ CLC

A George III dark green japanned longcase clock, the dial signed Thomas Allen, Deptford, with strike/silent ring above the silvered chapter ring, 5 pillar movement with rack strike and anchor escapement, 90in (230cm) high.
£6,000–7,000
$8,700–10,200 ⚒ C

A late Stuart period stained burr maple longcase clock, signed M. F. Aubert, London, with 11in (28cm) square dial, the inside count-wheel striking movement with 5 ringed pillars and anchor escapement, the hood with brass capped ebonized columns and caddy top, 94in (239cm) high.
£12,000–14,000
$17,400–20,300 ⚒ C

A small country oak longcase clock, by R. Alexander, Chippenham, the white dial showing both seconds and date, with 8-day movement striking the hours on a bell, plain oak case with canted corners to the trunk veneered with mahogany, the hood with swan's neck top and brass finial, c1830, 82in (208cm) high.
£4,500–5,500
$6,500–8,000 ⊞ PAO

A small mahogany longcase clock, by Thomas Aldridge, Deal, the engraved brass silvered dial with sunken seconds and square date aperture, with 8-day 5 pillar movement striking the hours on a bell, the case with long trunk door and double plinth to base, the hood with reeded pillars, brass capitals and blind fret, c1785, 76½in (194.5cm) high.
£7,500–8,500
$10,800–12,300 ⊞ PAO
Small mahogany clocks are very rare and desirable.

An oak and mahogany crossbanded longcase clock, by John Baker of Hull, with shell motif inlays, moonwork and tidal dial for high water, 8-day movement, fully restored, c1770, 92in (233.7cm) high.
£5,500–7,500
$8,000–11,000 ⊞ BL

A black lacquer chinoiserie decorated longcase clock, signed William Barron, London, the brass break-arch dial with subsidiary seconds dial and date aperture, 8-day movement with bell striking, internal count wheel, c1740, 84½in (214.5cm) high.
£4,000–5,000
$5,800–7,000 🔨 S(S)

► **A longcase clock,** by John Barron, with arabesque marquetry, London, early 18thC.
£15,500–16,000
$22,500–24,500 ⊞ CLC

◄ **A Regency mahogany longcase clock,** signed Barrauds, Cornhill, London, 1140, the 11in (28cm) painted dial with subsidiary seconds, the 5 pillared movement with signed, shaped plates, maintaining power, and deadbeat escapement, the wood rod pendulum with calibrated rating nut, 76in (193cm) high.
£10,000–11,000
$14,500–16,000 🔨 P

A red lacquer pine longcase clock, by J. Barron, London, with 5 pillar rack striking movement and brass dial, c1720, 85in (216cm) high.
£6,500–8,000
$9,400–11,600 ⊞ DRA

A carved oak longcase clock, by James B. Banks, with arched brass dial and second hand, 8-day movement, c1800.
£2,500–3,000
$3,600–4,400 ⊞ MGM

Miller's is a price GUIDE not a price LIST

► **A walnut longcase clock,** signed on a cartouche Hen. Batterson, London, the arched brass dial with engraved wheatsheaf border and silvered chapter ring, subsidiary seconds and date aperture, strike/silent in the arch, the movement with internal rack striking and anchor escapement, 18thC, later gilt mounts to the hood, 90in (228cm) high.
£6,000–7,000
$8,700–10,200 🔨 P

◄ **A Georgian oak longcase clock,** by John Baddeley of Tong, 83in (211cm) high.
£4,500–5,000
$6,500–7,500 🔨 FHF

► **A heavily carved longcase clock,** signed Thos Bartholomew, London, with arched brass dial, silvered chapter ring, matt centre with seconds dial, strike/silent and Westminster chimes/chime on 10 bells/chime on 8 bells dials, 110in (279.5cm) high.
£4,000–4,500
$5,800–6,500 🔨 Bea

An automaton longcase clock, by Aquila Barber, Bristol, with white dial painted with roses to the corners, Father Time automaton to the arch, 8-day movement striking the hours on a bell, c1795, 92in (233.5cm) high.
£10,000–11,000
$14,500–16,000 ⊞ PAO

A mid-Georgian mahogany longcase clock, with raised brass chapter ring and rococo scrolled spandrels, the centre decorated with Masonic emblems, inscribed Benjamin Barlow, Oldham, the long pendulum door with shaped ogee moulded edge, 2 quartered reeded pilasters, moulded shoulder, plinth base, the 8-day movement with a phases of the moon dial, second hand and date aperture.
£6,500–7,000
$9,400–10,200 ⚒ L&E

A mahogany longcase clock, by Henry Baker of Mallin (now West Malling), the 8-day 5 pillar movement with raised chapter ring, 88in (223.5cm) high.
£7,000–8,000
$10,200–11,600
⊞ DRA
Henry Baker worked from 1768 to 1784.

A walnut longcase clock, the 12in (30.5cm) dial with silvered chapter ring, signed in the engraved arch Tho. Baker, Portsmouth, the matted centre with subsidiary seconds, date, double cherub and crown spandrels, the 5 ringed pillar movement striking on a bell, c1740, 91in (231cm) high.
£6,000–7,000
$8,700–10,200 ⚒ Bon

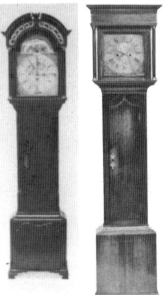

◀ **An oak longcase clock,** the face inscribed, the rear of the movement marked W. Barnard, Newark, No. 473, the brass dial with pierced spandrels, the 8-day movement with seconds and date dials, 18thC, 78in (198cm) high.
£6,000–7,000
$8,700–10,200 ⚒ DDM

Longcase/ Tallcase Clocks

In the United States longcase clocks are commonly referred to as 'tallcase'. Both terms are equally correct and are interchangeable.

◀ **An oak longcase clock,** with canted corners, the 12in (30.5cm) brass dial signed around the arch John Bagnall, Dudley, subsidiary seconds and calendar sector in the scroll engraved centre, the break-arch hood with pagoda pediment and giltwood finials, 4 pillar movement.
£5,000–6,000
$7,000–8,700 ⚒ Bon

A mahogany longcase clock, by William Barnish of Rochdale, the arch with calendar and lunar aperture painted with faces of the moon and figures in rural and coastal scenes, inscribed 'I am Moving Whilst thou art Sleeping', the 3 train movement with later comb and cylinder strike on 6 graduated bells, anchor escapement, late 18thC, 89in (226cm) high.
£6,000–6,500
$8,700–9,400 ⚒ HSS

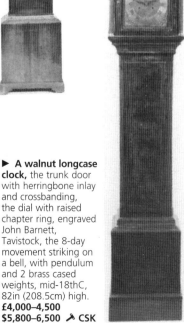

▶ **A walnut longcase clock,** the trunk door with herringbone inlay and crossbanding, the dial with raised chapter ring, engraved John Barnett, Tavistock, the 8-day movement striking on a bell, with pendulum and 2 brass cased weights, mid-18thC, 82in (208.5cm) high.
£4,000–4,500
$5,800–6,500 ⚒ CSK

◄ A George III mahogany longcase clock, the 12in (30.5cm) painted dial signed Bentley & Beck, Royal Exchange, London, with subsidiary seconds and calendar dials, rack and bell striking movement, c1810, 87in (221cm) high.
£6,500–7,000
$9,400–10,200 🔨 S

An oak and mahogany longcase clock, by Thos. Bembow, Newport, late 18thC, 94in (238cm) high.
£5,000–5,500
$7,000–8,000 🔨 P(M)

An oak and mahogany longcase clock, by William Bellman of Broughton, with white dial, c1790, 78in (198cm) high.
£3,000–3,500
$4,400–5,000 ⊞ BL

A George III mahogany longcase clock, the dial signed John Berry, London, with 5 pillar rack striking movement with anchor escapement and alarm pulley to one side, with securing bracket to the back-board, case restored, 95in (242cm) high.
£8,000–9,000
$11,600–13,000 🔨 C

A George II burr walnut longcase clock, the flat top case with brass capped hood pilasters, the dial signed Jno. Berry, London, with seconds dial, calendar aperture, mask and leaf spandrels, strike/silent dial in the arch, the movement with rack and bell striking, restored, 84½in (214.5cm) high.
£6,000–7,000
$8,700–10,200 🔨 S

An oak and mahogany longcase clock, the arched painted dial inscribed Border, Sleaford, with 8-day striking movement, the broken swan neck pedimented hood flanked by reeded columns, 19thC.
£4,000–4,500
$5,800–6,500 🔨 TM

A lacquered longcase clock, by John Berry, London, chinoiserie decorated on a tortoiseshell back-ground, the 8-day 5 pillar movement with brass dial showing seconds, date and with strike/silent, c1750, 86in (218.5cm) high.
£8,000–9,000
$11,600–13,000 ⊞ PAO

◄ A George III mahogany longcase clock, with arched dial, signed Thomas Barton, Manchester on a silvered arc above the moonphase in the arch, silvered chapter ring with silvered matted centre having subsidiary seconds and calendar aperture, pierced black painted hands, the 4 pillar rack striking movement with anchor escapement, 89in (226cm) high.
£6,500–7,250
$9,400–10,500 🔨 C

► A George III longcase clock, by Bertler & Eggert of Bristol, the painted dial with automaton swans in a lake in the arch, the main dial painted with Admiral Lord Nelson, 8-day movement striking on a bell, 87in (221cm) high.
£5,000–6,000
$7,000–8,700 🔨 Bea

A mahogany longcase clock, by Beverley, Caistor, the white painted dial showing both seconds and date, with 8-day duration movement striking the hours on a bell, c1795, 84in (213cm) high.
£6,000–7,000
$8,700–10,200 ⊞ PAO

A mahogany longcase clock, by John Berry, London, with 12in (33cm) brass dial, calendar aperture, seconds hand, strike/silent dial, the 2 train 8-day movement with anchor escapement, 18thC, 84in (213cm) high.
£8,500–9,500
$12,300–13,800 ⚒ AGr

A George III mahogany quarter chiming longcase clock, the dial signed Brandreth, Middlewich, moonphase in the arch, the 6 pillar rack striking movement chiming on 6 bells with hour strike on further bell, anchor escapement, 90in (228.5cm) high.
£8,000–10,000
$11,600–14,500 ⚒ C

A George III oak longcase clock, by Thomas Bridge, Wigan, with 12in (30.5cm) brass dial, 8-day movement and anchor escapement, 80in (203cm) high.
£4,000–4,500
$5,800–6,500 ⚒ P(M)

An inlaid mahogany longcase clock, by Blurton, Stourbridge, with painted arch dial, restored 8-day bell striking movement, early 19thC, 93in (236cm) high.
£3,200–4,200
$4,700–6,100 ⚒ MJB

An oak longcase clock, by H. Blake of Appleby, with mahogany cross-banding, c1830.
£1,300–1,700
$1,900–2,400 ⊞ STW

An oak and mahogany longcase clock, signed D. Bowen, Alfreton, with 8-day movement, rack striking, mid-19thC, 90in (228.5cm) high.
£2,800–3,400
$4,000–4,500 ⚒ **L**

A mahogany longcase clock, inscribed Bouffler, London, with silvered dial, Roman numerals, seconds and date dials engraved with floral sprays, strike/silent dial to the arch, 8-day striking movement, the arched hood surmounted by brass pineapple finials flanked by fluted pilasters, on bracket feet, 19thC, 93in (236cm) high.
£5,000–6,000
$7,500–8,700 ⚒ **AG**

A mahogany longcase clock, by Joseph Brown, Worcester, with 8-day striking movement, c1780, 79in (200.5cm) high.
£4,500–5,000
$6,500–7,500 ⊞ **SBA**

A dark Cuban mahogany longcase clock, by Nathaniel Brown, Manchester, the brass dial with moon, 8-day movement, c1750, 97in (246.5cm) high.
£8,000–10,000
$11,600–14,500 ⊞ **BL**

A George III mahogany longcase clock, signed John Brand, London, the brass dial with raised chapter ring and foliate spandrels, subsidiary seconds, date aperture and strike/silent ring in the arch, the 8-day movement striking on a bell, 100in (254cm) high.
£10,000–11,000
$14,500–16,000 ⚒ **CSK**

A George III mahogany longcase clock, signed Philip Bromyard, with painted dial, subsidiary seconds ring, Roman and Arabic chapter ring, rolling moonphase in the arch, 4 pillar rack striking movement with anchor escapement, 97in (246.5cm) high.
£5,700–6,700
$8,300–9,600 ⚒ **C**

A walnut longcase clock, by Joseph Bosley, London, with hourly strike on a bell, 14in (35.5cm) arch brass dial, 5 pillar, 8-day movement, strike/silent in arch, c1720, 96in (243.5cm) high.
£20,850–22,000
$30,000–32,000 ⊞ **SBA**

A mahogany longcase clock, inlaid with rosewood, tulipwood and satinwood, signed Nichs. Blondel, Guernsey, with break-arch dial and strike/silent, raised chapter ring, recessed seconds dial and date aperture, 5 pillar movement, 81in (205.5cm) high.
£7,000–8,000
$10,200–11,600 ⊞ **DRA**

An oak longcase clock, by Matthew Bold, 30-hour movement, c1740, 90in (228.5cm) high.
£3,500–4,000
$5,000–5,800 ⊞ **BL**

◀ **An oak longcase clock,** by Nathaniel Brown, Manchester, late 18thC.
£7,000–7,500
$10,200–11,000 ⊞ **CLC**

◄ **A George III mahogany and oak longcase clock,** by Emmanuel Burton of Kendal, the hood with a swan neck pediment set with a central finial above the arched glazed door, with arched painted dial, 8-day movement, second and date hand, gilt spandrels against a blue ground, flanked by turned columns above the shaped oak and mahogany-banded trunk door, with reeded quarter column corners and conforming base.
£3,250–4,000
$4,700–5,900 ⚒ Mit

An inlaid mahogany longcase clock, by Wm. Bullock, Bath, late 18thC.
£6,000–6,500
$8,700–9,400 ⊞ CLC

A mahogany longcase clock, signed Nathaniel Brown, Manchester, the 13in (33cm) dial with painted rolling moon in the arch, centre sweep seconds and date pointer, 8-day 4 pillar rack striking movement with deadbeat escapement, c1780, 95½in (241cm) high.
£5,500–6,500
$8,000–9,400 ⊞ Re

A mahogany longcase clock, signed Thos. Bruton, Bow, with brass dial, subsidiaries for seconds and date, and strike/silent, the 5 pillared movement with anchor escapement, 18thC, 102in (257.5cm) high.
£9,500–11,000
$13,800–16,000 ⚒ P

► **An oak longcase clock,** signed Samuel Bryan, London, with 12in (30.5cm) brass dial, 8-day bell striking movement, the associated case applied with a garland and spiral columns, with plain trunk and plinth, 82½in (209.5cm) high.
£2,500–3,000
$3,600–4,400 ⚒ S(S)

A mahogany longcase clock with barometer, by Brysons, Edinburgh, the 8-day movement with deadbeat escapement and maintaining power, c1860, 85in (216cm) high.
£12,000–14,000
$17,400–20,300 ⊞ PAO

A Scottish mahogany longcase clock, by John Bryson, Dalkeith, with 8-day movement striking the hours on a bell, painted dial with both seconds and date, c1840, 85in (216cm) high.
£2,700–3,300
$3,900–4,800 ⊞ PAO

An oak longcase clock, by Thos. Brown, Birmingham, the brass dial with black Roman numerals and engraved decoration, altered, 19thC.
£1,200–1,500
$1,700–2,200 ⚒ BWe

◄ **A walnut and marquetry longcase clock,** signed Jno. Buffett, Colchester, the dial with matted centre, engraving to the calendar aperture, subsidiary seconds, urn and scroll spandrels, the 5 pillar rack striking movement with anchor escapement, the altered case with marquetry to the skirted plinth and panels, associated, 80in (203cm) high.
£6,000–7,000
$8,700–10,200 ⚒ C

A pine longcase clock, signed John Carne, Penzance, with brass dial, subsidiary seconds and date aperture, 8-day movement, 84in (213.5cm) high.
£2,000–2,500
$2,900–3,600 ⚒ Bon

A mahogany longcase clock, signed Jno. Chambley, W. Hampton, 14in (35.5cm) painted dial, calendar dial and central moon disc, 92½in (234cm) high.
£3,250–4,000
$4,700–5,800 ⚒ S

◀ **An oak longcase clock,** inscribed Thos. Carswell, Hastings, with brass dial, silvered chapter ring, 30-hour birdcage movement, hour hand only, mid-18thC, 78in (198cm) high.
£2,200–3,000
$3,200–4,400 ⚒ DDM

A mahogany longcase clock, signed Christie of Perth, 19thC, 88in (224cm) high.
£3,000–4,000
$4,400–5,800 ⊞ TL

A mahogany longcase clock, by Carter, Salisbury, with signed brass dial with Roman numerals, subsidiary seconds dial with Arabic quarter hour intervals, strike/silent lever in the arch and engraved spandrels, the 4 pillar 3 train movement with anchor escapement, 88½in (225cm) high.
£4,000–5,000
$5,800–7,000 ⚒ L

A Georgian oak longcase clock, by John Clark, with brass dial, moonphase, second hand, date aperture, silvered chapter ring and 8-day movement, quarter striking with either 4 or 8 bells, flanked on either side by turned columns, with conforming trunk door and base, 86in (218.5cm) high.
£5,000–6,000
$7,500–8,700 ⚒ Mit

▶ **A black lacquered and chinoiserie decorated longcase clock,** signed Joseph Cayre, St Neots, brass dial, subsidiary seconds and date aperture, strike/silent in the arch, 5 pillared movement with anchor escapement, 18thC, 99in (250cm) high.
£5,000–6,000
$7,500–8,700 ⚒ P

◀ **A George III oak longcase clock,** engraved Geo. Clapham, Brigg, with silvered chapter ring and Roman numerals, 8-day striking movement, decorated with applied gilt spandrels and a boss to the arch, 86in (218cm) high.
£3,000–3,500
$4,400–5,000 ⚒ AG

A 30-hour longcase clock, by Humphrey Clarke, c1680.
£6,000–7,000
$8,700–10,200 ⊞ MAW

An oak longcase clock, signed Chaffey, Sherborne, engraved and silvered dial, c1770, 76in (193cm) high.
£3,000–3,500
$4,400–5,000 ⊞ ALS

A satin birchwood longcase clock, by James Common, Coldstream, the dial showing date and seconds, with 8-day movement striking the hours on a bell, c1810, 81in (205.5cm) high.
£8,000–9,000
$11,600–13,000 ⊞ PAO

A mahogany longcase clock, by W. B. Cornforth, Macclesfield, early 19thC, 93in (236cm) high.
£3,000–3,500
$4,400–5,000 ✗ P(M)

► **A George III red walnut longcase clock,** signed Richard Corless, Stockport, the 13in (33cm) dial with calendar aperture, seconds dial, mask and leaf spandrels, rack and bell striking movement, c1770, 99in (251.5cm) high.
£4,500–5,500
$6,500–8,000 ✗ S

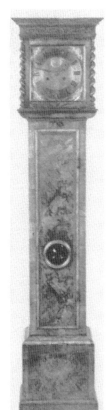

◄ **A James II longcase clock,** signed James Clowes, Londini Fecit, the square dial with brass chapter ring, the matted centre with subsidiary seconds and calendar aperture, pierced blued steel hands, latches to the 5 ringed pillar movement with anchor escapement and outside countwheel strike, the purpose-built convex moulded walnut case with skirted plinth, lenticle to the trunk door, associated, late 17thC, 71in (180cm) high.
£5,000–6,000
$7,000–8,700 ✗ C

A George III mahogany longcase clock, inscribed Thos. Conley, Whitby, the 8-day movement with anchor escapement and striking on a single bell.
£4,000–4,500
$5,800–6,500 ✗ HSS

◄ **A mahogany longcase clock,** signed John Cooke, Runcorn, with 14in (35.5cm) break-arch painted dial, subsidiary seconds dial and date aperture, moonphase in the arch, the 8-day movement with bell striking, Wilson falseplate, the case with blind swan's neck pediment, double fluted columns, shaped trunk door and freestanding columns, inlaid trunk and base, c1790, 96in (243.5cm) high.
£4,000–4,750
$5,800–6,900 ✗ S(S)

◀ A mahogany veneered longcase clock, signed Cottell, Crewkerne, subsidiary seconds dial, the 8-day movement rack striking, c1800, 92½in (233cm) high.
£4,000–4,500
$5,800–6,500 ⚒ L

An early George III oak longcase clock, inscribed Richd. Corless, Stockport, with brass dial, the movement with anchor escapement and rack striking on a bell, restored, mid-18thC, 88in (224cm) high.
£3,000–3,500
$4,400–5,000 ⚒ S(C)

An oak longcase clock, signed Creighton B-Mena No. 120, the dial with applied chapter ring and spandrels, ringed date aperture and winding holes, phases of the moon in the arch with lunar calendar and time of high tide scale, c1780, 91in (231cm) high.
£3,000–3,500
$4,400–5,500 ⚒ CSK

A George III musical longcase clock, by Corba Cranefield, Sheringham, with 3 train movement.
£7,000–8,000
$10,200–11,600 ⚒ DN

A walnut and floral marquetry month going longcase clock, signed Daniel Le Count, London, brass dial with winged cherub head spandrels and silvered chapter ring, subsidiary seconds, date aperture and ringed winding holes, 5 ring turned pillar movement, one replaced, with outside countwheel strike and anchor escapement, restored, late 17thC, 82in (208cm).
£11,000–12,000
$16,000–17,400 ⚒ P

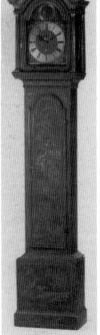

A Georgian mahogany longcase clock, by Alexander Crawford, Scarborough, with painted dial and 8-day movement, c1790, 90in (229cm) high.
£6,000–7,000
$8,700–10,200 ⊞ PAO

An oak longcase clock, inscribed Courter, Ruthin, with 8-day movement, 87in (222cm) high.
£1,800–2,500
$2,600–3,600 ⚒ OL

◀ A late George III mahogany longcase clock, by John Criddle, Bridgwater, 95½in (244cm) high.
£3,000–3,500
$4,400–5,000 ⚒ DWB

◀ A green lacquered longcase clock, signed John Cotsworth, London, the arched dial with silvered chapter ring, subsidiary seconds dial and date aperture, the 8-day 6 pillar movement with external locking plate and striking on a bell, the associated case with pagoda top and break-arch trunk door, part late 17thC, 96½in (244cm) high.
£4,000–5,000
$5,800–7,000 ⚒ S(S)

An oak and crossbanded longcase clock, signed Wlm. Davison, London, the 12in (30.5cm) brass dial with engraved chapter ring, date ring and seconds dial, the 8-day bell striking movement with inside countwheel and cut-out backplate, the associated oak case with crossbanded trunk door and plinth, c1700, 79½in (201cm) high.
£3,000–3,500
$4,400–5,000 ⚒ S(S)

An oak and mahogany longcase clock, signed Thos. Dickinson, Boston, with arched painted dial and 8-day striking movement, c1828.
£3,250–4,000
$4,700–5,800 ⚒ TM

An oak longcase clock, by Samuel Deacon of Barton, the white dial with a blue ground, with 8-day movement, 1806, 87in (221cm) high.
£4,500–5,500
$6,500–8,000 ⊞ BL

A 30-hour oak and mahogany longcase clock, by Samuel Deacon, with painted dial, together with original bill of sale, c1800, 88in (222.5cm) high.
£2,000–2,800
$2,900–4,000 ⊞ BL

An Edwardian chiming longcase clock, by C. S. Davies, Haverfordwest, the brass and silvered dial with scrolling foliate mounts, subsidiary chime/silent, Whittington/ Westminster and seconds dials, the movement chiming and striking on 9 tubes, brass cased weights, in a mahogany case with bevelled glass trunk door, 93in (236cm) high.
£5,000–6,000
$7,500–8,700 ⚒ Bea

A mahogany longcase clock, by John Deacon, London, with early white dial, strike/silent and centre sweep hand for the calendar, subsidiary dial for seconds, 8-day movement, c1760, the case in pagoda design, with inlaid brass columns, all brasswork original.
£7,500–8,500
$10,500–12,300 ⊞ SBA

An Irish mahogany longcase clock, signed Barny Delahoyde, Dublin, the brass dial with date aperture and seconds dial, putto spandrels, 8-day bell striking movement, hood with lion mask carved mantling, c1800, 92½in (235cm) high.
£4,000–4,500
$5,800–6,500 ⚒ S

◀ **A walnut marquetry longcase clock,** by Robert Dingley, London, the 10in (25.5cm) brass dial with silvered chapter ring, the movement with 6 ringed pillars, of month duration, anchor escapement and striking locking plate on the backplate, with later bottom moulding and bun feet, with Equation of Time table inside the door, late 17thC, 83in (211cm) high.
£30,000–35,000
$43,500–50,500
🔨 Bon

A Queen Anne walnut and marquetry longcase clock, signed Fra. Dorrell, London, ringed winding holes, cast gilt metal cherub's head spandrels, 8-day movement, striking on 7 bells, restored, 93in (236cm) high.
£10,000–12,000
$14,500–17,400 🔨 N

A George III longcase clock, by Joseph Denton of Hull, with brass dial, moonphase and tidal indicators.
£7,000–8,000
$10,200–11,600
🔨 SWO

A walnut longcase clock, by Francis Dorrell, London, 8-day duration, detachable caddy top, c1730, 94in (239cm) high.
£10,000–13,000
$14,500–18,500
⊞ SO

▶ **A walnut longcase clock,** the 12in (30.5cm) brass dial with silvered chapter ring and date aperture, signed James Dury, London, the 5 ringed pillared movement with anchor escapement, 18thC, 88in (223.5cm) high.
£6,500–8,000
$9,400–11,600 🔨 P

◀ **A George III 8-day longcase clock,** by John Darke, Barnstaple, with 12in (30.5cm) brass dial, signed silvered chapter ring, seconds dial, calendar aperture, phase of the moon in the arch and High Water at Barnstaple Key, the 4 pillar movement with anchor escapement, striking on a bell, with pendulum and weights in mahogany case, 89in (226cm) high.
£4,500–5,500
$6,500–8,000 🔨 Bea

An oak longcase clock, the brass dial with the maker's name William Downie, Edinburgh, strike/silent, the trunk with quartered reeded columns, the hood with scroll pediment and blind frets, c1770, 83in (211cm) high.
£5,000–6,000
$7,500–8,700 ⊞ CLC

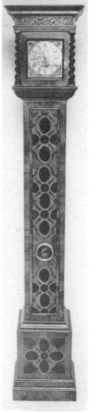

A Queen Anne-style marquetry grandmother clock, signed Thomas Durman.
£6,500–7,000
$9,400–10,200 🔨 GIL

A mahogany longcase clock, by John Duffet, Bristol, with High Water at Bristol Key (*sic*), c1770.
£13,000–15,000
$18,850–21,750
⊞ PAO

◀ **A Georgian japanned longcase clock,** now with dial signed John Dewe, Monde Lane, Southwark, the 5 pillar rack striking movement with anchor escapement, 102in (259cm) high.
£3,000–4,000
$4,400–5,800 🔨 C

▶ **A walnut longcase clock,** signed W. Donald, Glasgow, with 13in (33cm) painted dial, subsidiary seconds and calendar dials, 8-day movement with anchor escapement, rack striking, 85½in (215cm) high.
£2,200–2,800
$3,200–4,000 🔨 L

A George III-style mahogany and inlaid longcase clock, signed William Dobbie, Falkirk, with painted dial, lunar and subsidiary dials, 19thC, 90½in (230cm) high.
£6,000–7,000
$8,700–10,200 🔨 SK(B)

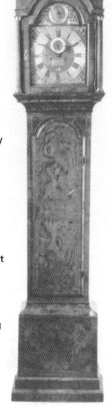

▶ **A mid-Georgian burr walnut longcase clock,** signed Arl. Dobson, London, the dial with matted centre with subsidiary seconds and calendar aperture, silvered chapter ring, urn and scroll spandrels, strike/silent ring in the arch, the 5 pillar movement with rack strike and anchor escapement, 90in (228.5cm) high.
£11,000–12,000
$16,000–17,400 🔨 C

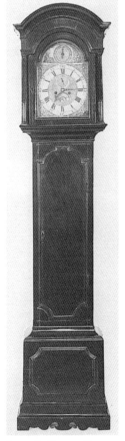

An early George III mahogany longcase clock, by Dudds of London, the arched brass dial with wide silvered chapter ring, curved date aperture, seconds dial and strike/silent dial to arch, 8-day striking movement, 94in (238cm) high.
£7,000–8,000
$10,200–11,600 🔨 CAG

A walnut longcase clock, inscribed Dan Delander, London, the brass dial with subsidiary dial and date aperture, silvered chapter ring and chased spandrels, the 8-day striking movement with anchor escapement, early 18thC, 90in (228cm) high.
£10,000–12,000
$14,500–17,400 ⊞ GC

A mahogany longcase clock, by W. D. Fenwick, Dundee, with 8-day movement striking the hours on a bell, the mahogany veneered case with quarter columns to the trunk with panelled door and base, the hood with swan's neck top and brass central finial, c1850, 85½in (216.5cm) high.
£7,000–8,000
$10,200–11,600 ⊞ PAO

A walnut and marquetry longcase clock, by John Finch of London, 17thC.
£16,000–18,000
$23,200–26,000 ⚒ HSS

▶ **A George II mahogany tavern longcase clock,** signed Finch, London, with 20in (51cm) green painted wood dial, gilt numerals and hands, 5 pillar weight driven movement with deadbeat escapement, the case with architectural broken pediment, waisted trunk enclosing a similarly painted fielded panel inscribed 'Donum convivii vice Jacobi Hill. Hujus Societatis Gardiani Anno 1744', 94in (238cm) high.
£10,000–12,000
$14,500–17,400 ⚒ S

A George III mahogany and boxwood strung longcase clock, signed Finney, Liverpool, the 13in (33cm) arched brass dial with silvered chapter ring, centre date (hand missing) and subsidiary seconds, the twin-train movement with anchor escapement, 94in (239cm) high.
£7,000–8,000
$10,200–11,600 ⚒ P

A mahogany chiming longcase clock, signed Finnigans Ltd, Manchester, the silvered dial with applied gilt Arabic numerals, overlaid with a gilt filigree mask, with seconds dial, strike/silent lever and subsidiary dials in the arch, substantial 3 train movement with deadbeat escapement maintaining power and playing one of 3 chimes on 8 tubular bells with a further hour bell, c1910, 98½in (250.5cm) high.
£7,000–8,000
$10,200–11,600 ⚒ S

Miller's is a price GUIDE not a price LIST

◀ **An oak and mahogany crossbanded longcase clock,** by Ebenezer Fisler of Ellesmere, the dial with rolling moon by Wright, Birmingham, with 8-day movement, c1835.
£1,000–1,200
$1,500–1,750 ⊞ STW

A mahogany and chequer strung longcase clock, signed R. Fox, Pontypool, with arched ring and date aperture, the 8-day movement striking on a bell, with weights and pendulum, mid-19thC, 86½in (219cm) high.
£3,500–4,000
$5,000–5,800 ⚒ CSK

A mahogany longcase clock, signed John Galbraith, Falkirk, with 13in (33cm) brass dial, with date aperture and seconds subsidiary dial, the movement with anchor escapement rack striking on a bell, c1770, 87in (221cm) high.
£6,000–6,500
$8,700–9,400 ⚒ DN

Further examples of Longcase Clocks will be found in the Colour Reviews.

An oak longcase clock, crossbanded with mahogany, by John Fothergill of Knaresborough, with 30-hour movement, c1825, 90in (228.5cm) high.
£2,000–2,600
$2,900–3,800 ⊞ BL

▶ **A mahogany longcase clock,** by John Fladgate, London, with 8-day movement, c1775, 85in (216cm) high.
£7,000–9,000
$10,200–13,000 ⊞ BL

A Federal inlaid mahogany longcase clock, inscribed Thomas Gardner, London, the hood with pierced fretwork surmounted by brass finials above an arched glazed door opening to a brass dial with Roman and Arabic chapter ring, enclosing a sweep second hand, on bracket feet, damaged and restored, c1863, 90in (228.5cm) high.
£5,000–6,000
$7,500–8,700 ⚒ CNY

A Victorian mahogany longcase clock, by J. Galloway, Leeds, with 8-day movement.
£1,200–1,800
$1,500–2,500 ⚒ TW

◀ **A mahogany longcase clock,** by B. French, Upwell, the enamelled face with subsidiary date and seconds dials, painted figure spandrels and a rolling moon in the arch, with 8-day striking movement, early 19thC, 90in (228.5cm) high.
£5,000–6,000
$7,000–8,700 ⚒ MAT

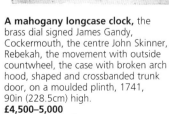

A mahogany longcase clock, the brass dial signed James Gandy, Cockermouth, the centre John Skinner, Rebekah, the movement with outside countwheel, the case with broken arch hood, shaped and crossbanded trunk door, on a moulded plinth, 1741, 90in (228.5cm) high.
£4,500–5,000
$6,500–7,500 ⚒ S

A mahogany longcase clock, by Henry Fish, Royal Exchange, London, with 3 train movement, quarter striking on 8 bells, c1760, 101in (256.5cm) high.
£20,000–25,000
$29,000–36,000 ⊞ PAO

An oak longcase clock, with mahogany trim, by C. Fletcher, Rotherham, with painted dial, 8-day movement, c1790, 87in (221cm) high.
£3,250–4,250
$4,700–6,000 ⊞ BL

A mahogany longcase clock, by Paul Ganter, Huddersfield, with painted dial, 8-day movement, c1845, 96in (244cm) high.
£2,000–2,500
$2,900–3,600 ⊞ BL

An oak longcase clock, by Gardner of Birmingham, with brass dial, 8-day movement, restored, c1750, 80in (203cm) high.
£3,800–4,800
$5,500–7,000 ⊞ BL

▶ **A George III mahogany brass-inlaid longcase clock,** silvered metal dial, inscribed Grant, Fleet Street, London, 8-day striking movement with anchor escapement, 85in (216cm) high.
£6,500–7,500
$9,500–10,500 ⊞ GC
John Grant of Fleet Street, London, was an eminent clockmaker. He was freeman of the Clockmakers' Company in 1781, and was warden. He died in 1810.

▶ **A walnut longcase clock,** signed L. Gray Westover, the 8in (20.5cm) brass dial with raised chapter ring, scallop shell spandrels and matted centre, 18thC, with later 8-day movement striking on a bell, 65in (165cm) high.
£2,500–3,000
$3,600–4,400 ⚒ CSK

A Georgian mahogany longcase clock, with brass dial, inset seconds subsidiary and date aperture, signed Jerem'h Garbett, London, the 5 pillar movement with anchor escapement, 91in (231cm) high.
£7,000–8,000
$10,200–11,600 ⚒ P

An oak pagoda style longcase clock, by Godfrey of Winterton, with white dial, restored, c1790, 86in (219cm) high.
£4,250–4,950
$6,000–7,000 ⊞ BL

A George II oak and mahogany longcase clock, by Charles Edward Gillett, Manchester, with 8-day movement, and inside pinned locking plate, c1760, 86in (219cm) high.
£4,000–4,500
$5,800–6,500 ⊞ GIB

◀ **A Victorian mahogany longcase clock,** arch signed Edmond Gibbs, London, the brass dial with subsidiary seconds ring and date aperture, the 8-day movement striking on a bell, 81in (206cm) high.
£3,250–3,800
$4,700–5,500 ⚒ CSK

A Georgian mahogany and shell inlaid longcase clock, inscribed James Garvis, Darlington, the arched brass dial with pergoda style pediment, 95in (241.5cm) high.
£5,000–6,000
$7,250–8,700 ⚒ BWe

An oak longcase clock, signed James Green, Nantwich, the brass dial with subsidiary seconds and date aperture, the 8-day movement rack striking, 84in (213cm) high.
£4,000–5,000
$5,800–7,000 ⚒ L

◄ **A Queen Anne japanned longcase clock,** signed Wm. Grimes, Hatton Garden fecit, with 12in (30.5cm) dial, 6 pillar latched movement with inside countwheel, in a flat topped case with hood pilasters, trunk door with a lenticle and altered plinth, the whole decorated with gilt chinoiserie against a black ground, c1705, 84in (213cm) high.
£5,000–6,000
$7,500–8,700 ⚒ S

► **A Regency mahogany longcase clock,** signed Grant, London, the 12in (30.5cm) silvered dial with subsidiaries for seconds and date, 5 pillared movement with anchor escapement, 84in (214cm) high.
£7,000–8,000
$10,200–11,600 ⚒ P

A Charles II walnut and floral marquetry longcase clock, signed Chas. Gretton in Fleet Street, the square dial with silvered chapter ring, the matted centre with ringed winding holes, decorated calendar aperture and subsidiary seconds ring, pierced blued hands, foliate winged cherub spandrels, 6 ringed-pillar movement with outside countwheel strike and anchor escapement, associated and restored, 78in (198cm) high.
£10,000–15,000
$14,500–21,500 ⚒ C

A walnut and marquetry longcase clock, inscribed Chas. Gretton Londini Fecit, the dial with silvered chapter ring, the 5 ringed pillar rack striking movement with anchor escapement, the hood with later parcel gilt angle columns, associated and adapted, 82in (208cm) high.
£6,000–7,000
$8,700–10,200 ⚒ C

A mahogany longcase clock, inscribed Daniel & Thomas Grignion, 3 train movement, c1740.
£9,000–10,000
$13,000–14,500 ⚒ DN

► **A walnut longcase clock,** signed Robt. Henderson, London, the brass dial with silvered chapter ring, seconds dial, calendar aperture, strike/silent in the arch, 4 pillar movement with anchor escapement, rack striking on a bell, c1800, 99in (251cm) high.
£9,000–10,000
$13,000–14,500 ⚒ L

A walnut longcase clock, signed at the base Christopher Gould Londini fecit, with brass dial and chapter ring, the centre with subsidiary seconds, date aperture and harboured winding holes, the 7 ring pillared 30-day movement with outside countwheel and anchor escapement, 18thC, with later arch to dial, 82in (208cm) high.
£5,000–6,000
$7,000–8,700 ⚒ P

◀ **A George III Lancashire-style longcase clock,** the dial signed Hadwen, Liverpool on the chapter ring, with cherub and scroll spandrels, rack striking movement with anchor escapement, 93in (236cm) high.
£6,000–7,000
$8,700–10,200 ⚒ C

▶ **A mahogany granddaughter clock,** the 6in (15cm) brass dial signed on the chapter ring Jan de Groot, with 8-day bell striking movement with rolling moon, restored, 1751, 52in (132cm) high.
£3,000–4,000
$4,400–5,800 ⚒ S(S)

An oak 30-hour longcase clock, by John Hocker, Reading, with 10in (25.5cm) dial, Roman numeral chapter ring, birdcage movement striking on a bell, in a case with flat pediment and door flanked by plain columns, on a plinth, c1750, 84½in (214.5cm) high.
£2,000–2,500
$2,900–3,600 ⚒ Bon

A George III mahogany longcase clock, by Thomas Grignion, London, 95in (241cm) high.
£10,000–12,000
$14,500–17,400
⚒ RBB

◀ **An Edwardian Sheraton-style satinwood longcase clock,** the dial signed John Hill, King St, Covent Garden, inlaid with ovals, ribbon ties and paterae, the 3 train movement quarter striking on 8 bells with anchor escapement, with added arch, 96in (244cm) high.
£5,000–6,000
$7,500–8,700 ⚒ C

A mahogany longcase clock, by Hampson, Bolton, with 8-day movement and brass dial, c1780, 94in (239cm) high.
£5,500–6,750
$8,000–9,800 ⊞ BL

A mahogany longcase clock, the brass dial signed Jas Heron, New Town, with subsidiary dial for seconds, date aperture, the 8-day movement striking on a bell, 87in (221cm) high.
£4,500–6,000
$6,500–7,000 ⚒ CSK

▶ **A Georgian mahogany longcase clock,** signed William Haughton, London, with brass dial, silvered chapter ring, subsidiary seconds and date aperture, strike/silent in the arch, chiming the quarters on 8 bells, 97in (246cm) high.
£10,000–12,000
$14,500–17,400 ⚒ P

An oak and mahogany crossbanded longcase clock, the brass dial inscribed Thos. Hauxwell, Brompton, with swan neck pediment and plain pillars to the hood, pierced spandrels, seconds and date dials, 30-hour movement, late 18thC, 83in (211cm) high.
£3,000–3,500
$4,400–5,000 ⚒ DDM

◀ **An oak longcase clock,** by Richard Houton, Oversley Green, the square brass dial with urn pierced spandrels, circular chapter ring with Roman numerals, floral engraved centre with date indicator and seconds hand, with key, with 8-day movement, early 18thC, 87in (221cm) high.
£3,500–4,000
$5,000–5,800 ⊞ GH

A Georgian mahogany longcase clock, signed C. W. Hooke, London, the painted dial with subsidiaries for seconds and date, the 5 pillar movement with anchor escapement, 92in (232cm) high
£7,000–8,000
$10,200–11,600 ⚒ P

A mahogany longcase clock, by Thomas Holmes, Cheadle, the painted dial with moon in the arch, 8-day movement, c1800, 87in (221cm) high.
£3,800–4,500
$5,500–6,500 ⊞ BL

▶ **A George III mahogany longcase clock,** inscribed Robert Hood, London, with brass break-arch dial, the 8-day, 5 pillar 3 train movement with rack striking on an hour bell and quarter-hour chiming on 8 bells, late 18thC, 94in (239cm) high.
£12,000–15,000
$17,400–21,500 ⚒ S(S)

An oak longcase clock, inscribed Peter Horner, Ripon, the brass dial with subsidiary seconds and date aperture, 8-day bell striking movement and a pair of brass-cased weights, 18thC, 81in (206cm) high.
£3,000–3,500
$4,400–5,000 ⚒ MJB

An oak longcase clock, by John Horsnaile, Warfield, 30-hour striking movement, 18thC, 74in (188cm) high.
£1,500–2,000
$2,000–2,900 ⚒ CDC

A George III mahogany longcase clock, signed Wm. Howells, Bristol, the brass dial with moving ship in the arch, the 8-day movement with anchor escapement and rack strike, 92in (234cm) high.
£7,000–8,000
$10,200–11,600 ⚒ C

A mahogany veneered longcase clock, by Hudson, Otley, with painted dial, 8-day movement, c1850, 96in (244cm) high.
£2,500–3,000
$3,600–4,400 ⊞ BL

A longcase clock, by Hudson & Son, Otley, the dial with painted landscape decoration, 8-day movement, c1830, 93½in (237cm) high.
£1,800–2,000
$2,600–2,900 ⚒ AH

A mahogany longcase clock, by William Hughes, London, the brass dial with seconds, date and strike/silent, the 8-day movement striking on a bell, c1765, 93in (236cm) high.
£11,000–12,000
$16,000–17,400 ⊞ PAO

A mahogany longcase clock, by James Ivory, London, the brass dial with subsidiary seconds, date aperture and strike/silent, with brass-cased weights and pendulum, 8-day movement, c1765, 97in (246cm) high.
£10,000–12,000
$14,500–17,400 ⚒ M

An oak and mahogany-banded longcase clock, by Jonathon Ivison, the arched brass dial with pierced foliate spandrels and silvered chapter ring, with 8-day movement, 86in (218cm) high.
£3,000–3,500
$4,400–5,000 ⚒ OL

▶ **A mahogany, satinwood and boxwood strung longcase clock,** signed Petr. Keir, Falkirk, with painted dial depicting Commerce in Art, with seconds and date rings, the 8-day movement striking on a bell, with pendulum and 2 weights, 85in (216cm) high.
£4,500–5,000
$6,500–7,000
⚒ CSK

A walnut longcase clock, by James Jenkins, the dial with a silvered Roman and Arabic chapter ring, matted centre with subsidiary seconds and calendar aperture, double cherub and crown spandrels in the corner, 5 ringed pillar movement with inside locking plate and striking on a bell, the later purpose-made case with a flat top, plain columns and gilt capitals in the corners, on a trunk veneered in burr walnut, 19thC, 85in (216cm) high.
£2,500–3,000
$3,600–4,400 ⚒ Bon

An oak longcase clock, by John Kent, Monmouth, with hand-painted dial, and 30-hour movement, c1790, 19in (48cm) wide.
£2,000–2,750
$2,900–3,900 ⊞ GH

An inlaid mahogany longcase clock, the brass dial with trade plate, of Kemp Brothers, Union St, Bristol, the 3 train movement with anchor escapement, 93in (236cm) high.
£4,500–5,000
$6,500–7,000 ⚒ L

◀ **A George II black japanned longcase clock,** signed Thomas Johnson, Richmond, with subsidiary seconds ring and calendar aperture, pierced blued hands, the 5 pillar rack striking movement with anchor escapement, 88in (223cm) high.
£5,500–7,000
$8,000–10,200 ⚒ C

▶ **A mahogany longcase clock,** signed Jas and W. Kelley, Glasgow, the dial with Roman numerals, rack and bell striking movement, the case with carved pediment, c1830, 81in (206cm) high.
£2,250–2,750
$3,250–4,000 ⚒ Bon

A carved oak long case clock, by Ben Kimberly, Catshill, with 8-day striking movement, 18thC, 90in (228cm) high.
£2,000–2,250
$2,900–3,500 ⊞ GH

A George II walnut longcase clock, signed Wm. Kipling, London, with arched dial, silvered chapter ring, subsidiary seconds, date aperture, bell striking movement with anchor escapement, c1730, 86in (218cm) high.
£9,000–10,500
$13,000–15,000 ⚒ S

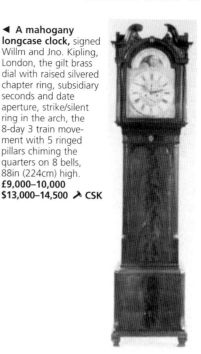

◀ **A mahogany longcase clock,** signed Willm and Jno. Kipling, London, the gilt brass dial with raised silvered chapter ring, subsidiary seconds and date aperture, strike/silent ring in the arch, the 8-day 3 train movement with 5 ringed pillars chiming the quarters on 8 bells, 88in (224cm) high.
£9,000–10,000
$13,000–14,500 ⚒ CSK

◀ **A mahogany longcase clock,** by John Kirkwood, Melrose, with brass dial and 8-day movement, c1770, 87in (221cm) high.
£8,000–10,000
$11,600–14,500 ⊞ SO

A mahogany longcase clock, by William Lawson, Newton, with 14in (35.5cm) brass dial, rolling moon, 8-day 4 pillar movement and anchor escapement, c1770, 89in (226cm) high.
£3,000–4,500
$4,400–6,500 ⚒ Bon

A George III mahogany longcase clock, by William Lassell, Toxteth Park, Liverpool, the 8-day movement with rack striking bell, with break-arch hood, and shaped trunk, c1720, 90in (228cm) high.
£7,500–9,000
$11,000–13,000 ⊞ GIB

A mahogany longcase clock, by Knight of Chichester, the brass dial with raised chapter ring, with 5 pillar movement, the trunk door and base with figured veneers, 83in (211cm) high.
£7,500–8,500
$10,500–12,300 ⊞ DRA

An oak longcase clock, by Lawson, Newton, with 8-day movement, c1770.
£3,500–4,500
$5,000–6,500 ⚒ **DaD**

A mahogany longcase clock, by Lister, Bolton, with 14½in (37cm) painted dial, 8-day movement, c1770.
£3,500–4,500
$5,000–6,500 ⚒ **DaD**

A George II longcase clock, walnut veneered with feather crossbanding, by Samuel Lee, London, with 12in (30.5cm) dial, the movement with anchor escapement and rack striking mechanism, damaged, 87in (221cm) high.
£9,000–10,000
$13,000–14,500 ⚒ **Bea**

A George III figured mahogany longcase clock, with 8-day movement by James Lomax of Blackburn, having additional musical movement, 88in (223cm) high.
£2,800–3,500
$4,000–5,000 ⚒ **CDC**

► **An oak and mahogany chiming longcase clock,** signed Hugh Lough, Penrith, with Roman numerals, half-hour divisions and Arabic 5 minute numerals, sweep centre calendar, the 8-day movement playing a tune every 3 hours on 8 bells with hammers and changing automatically every 24 hours, late 18thC, 93in (236cm) high.
£7,000–8,000
$10,200–11,600 ⚒ **CSK**

◄ **A mahogany longcase clock,** signed Philip Lloyd, Bristol, the brass dial with engraved border and brass chapter ring, the engraved centre with subsidiary seconds and date aperture, with moonphase in the arch, the twin train movement with anchor escapement, 18thC, 88in (224cm) high.
£7,000–8,000
$10,200–11,600 ⚒ **P**

A George III mahogany longcase clock, the engraved giltwood dial signed Jas Wilson Loop, with Roman and Arabic chapter ring, pierced blued hands, subsidiary spandrels, with added arch, the 5 pillar rack striking movement with anchor escapement, the pagoda top surmounted by associated carved giltwood figures, restored and composite, 72in (183cm) high.
£3,000–3,500
$4,400–5,000 ⚒ **C**

► **A walnut veneered longcase clock,** early 18thC style, the brass dial with silvered chapter ring inscribed Tho Lee, London, calendar aperture, the 4 pillar 8-day movement striking on a bell, 70in (179cm) high.
£1,800–2,500
$2,600–3,600 ⚒ **Bea**

◀ **A walnut longcase clock,** inscribed Jonat. Lowndes, London, with brass dial, 5 ring pillar movement with inside countwheel strike and anchor escapement, early 18thC, 93in (236cm) high.
£10,000–12,000
$14,500–17,400 ⚒ P

A mahogany longcase clock, signed Macrossan, Glasgow, the painted break-arch dial with subsidiary seconds and date dials, the spandrels depicting the 4 continents, the arch with a cameo of Sir William Wallace between Liberty and Justice, c1850, 85½in (217cm) high.
£3,000–3,500
$4,400–5,000 ⚒ S(S)

A walnut and marquetry longcase clock, by F. G. Lubert of Amsterdam, 18thC, 94in (239m) high.
£7,000–8,000
$10,200–11,600 ⚒ LRG

▶ **A walnut longcase clock,** by Thos. Martin, Cloake Lane, London, c1714, 85½in (217cm) high.
£6,000–7,000
$8,700–10,200 ⚒ DWB

A William III ebonized longcase clock, signed Charles Lowndes, Pall Mall, London, the 5 pillar movement with inside countwheel and external detent, the case with domed caddy cresting, c1680, 91in (231cm) high.
£8,000–10,000
$11,600–14,500 ⚒ S

A Scottish mahogany longcase clock, by Charles Lyon, Hamilton, the brass dial with seconds, date and phases of the moon in the arch, with 8-day movement striking the hours on a bell, the case with rosewood and boxwood inlay, c1780, 87in (221cm) high.
£9,000–11,000
$13,000–16,000 ⊞ PAO

A mahogany longcase clock, by J. Lum, London, the brass dial with seesaw in the arch, with 8-day movement, c1760, 90in (228cm) high.
£8,000–10,000
$11,600–14,500 ⊞ BL

A George II figured walnut longcase clock, by Jonathan Marsh, London, the 8-day rack striking movement with 5 scribed pillars, latched to centre, anchor escapement, 97in (246cm) high.
£6,000–7,000
$8,700–10,200 ⊞ Re

A mahogany longcase clock, by Richard Maggs, Wells, the white dial with seconds, date and phases of the moon in the arch, the 8-day movement striking the hours on a bell, the hood with cresting and 3 brass finials, the case inlaid with boxwood and stringing, c1840, 92in (234cm) high.
£8,000–9,000
$11,600–13,000 ⊞ PAO

◄ **A burr walnut longcase clock,** inscribed Robt. Maisley, London, the silvered dial with seconds, date aperture and strike/silent in the arch, 18thC, 90in (228cm) high.
£9,000–10,000
$13,000–14,500 ⊞ P(PWC)

A carved walnut long-case clock, signed Maple & Co, London, the movement with massive pillars, anchor escapement, and quarter chiming on 8 bells and 4 gongs.
£4,000–5,000
$5,800–7,000 ⚹ L

A mahogany longcase clock, inscribed Maple & Co. Ltd, London, the brass dial with silvered chapter ring, seconds and chime/silent ring in the arch, gilt metal cherub head and dolphin spandrels, the 8-day 3 train chiming movement with brass coated weights, early 20thC, 95in (241cm) high.
£2,500–3,000
$3,600–4,400 ⊞ P(PWC)

A black and gilt softwood longcase clock, by William B. Marsh, the steel dial with calendar and chapter rings, and brass spandrels, with 8-day striking movement, early 19thC.
£5,500–6,500
$8,000–9,400 ⊞ V

A George III mahogany longcase clock, signed Jno. Manley, Chatham, with brass dial, the 8-day movement with anchor escapement and rack striking on a bell, 83in (211cm) high.
£4,000–4,500
$5,800–6,500 ⚹ CSK

An oak longcase clock, signed Humphrey Mason, Gosport, the brass dial with seconds, date aperture, and applied spandrels symbolising the 4 seasons, with 8-day movement striking on a bell, the pagoda topped hood with brass ball and spire finials, 85in (216cm) high.
£3,250–4,000
$4,700–5,800 ⚹ S(S)

► **A Queen Anne green japanned longcase clock,** signed Markwick, London, with square dial, and 5 ring pillar movement with anchor escapement and rack strike, possibly associated, 95in (241cm) high.
£5,000–6,000
$7,000–8,700 ⚹ C

A George III longcase clock, inscribed John Mansfield, London, the arched brass and silvered dial with subsidiary seconds dial and calendar, the movement with a chime of 8 bells, strike/silent regulator to the lunette, 90in (229cm) high.
£8,000–10,000
$11,600–14,500 🔨 WW

A mahogany musical longcase clock, signed by Jonathan Marsh, London, c1780, 90in (229cm) high.
£12,000–14,000
$17,400–20,300 🔨 L

A Scottish longcase clock, by Joseph McIntyre, Crieff, the painted dial showing chinoiserie scenes to the arch and corners, with 8-day movement striking the hours on a bell, with seconds and date, c1835, 82in (209cm) high.
£6,000–7,000
$8,700–10,200 ⊞ PAO

◄ **An oak longcase clock,** by McGregor of Ayton, Scotland, with white dial, 8-day movement, c1810, 79in (201cm) high.
£3,500–4,500
$5,000–6,500 ⊞ BL

A mahogany longcase clock, the break-arch silvered 12in (30.5cm) dial signed Robt Mawley, London, subsidiary seconds dial, date aperture, 8-day movement striking on a bell, strike/silent arch, c1780, 95in (241cm) high.
£8,000–9,000
$11,600–13,000 🔨 S(S)

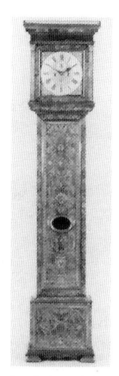

A walnut marquetry brass-inlaid longcase clock, with chequered stringing, the dial signed Jonat Marsh, London, seconds dial, calendar aperture, double cherub and crown spandrels, movement with inside countwheel, restored, c1705, 87in (221cm) high.
£8,000–9,000
$11,600–13,000 🔨 S

Hints to dating Longcase Clocks

Dials

8in square	to c1669	Carolean
10in square	c1665–1800	
11in square	1690–1800	
12in square	from c1700	from Queen Anne
14in square	from c1740	Georgian
Break-arch dial	from c1715	Georgian
Round dial	from c1760	Georgian
Silvered dial	from c1760	Georgian
Painted dial	from c1770	Georgian
Hour hand only	to 1820	
Minute hand introduced	c1663	
Second hand introduced	from 1675	post-Restoration
Matching hands	from c1775	George III

Case Finish

Ebony veneer	up to c1725	to early Georgian
Walnut veneer	c1670 to c1770	to mid-Georgian
Lacquer	c1700 to c1790	to late Georgian
Mahogany	from 1730	mid-Georgian
Softwood	from c1690	William & Mary
Mahogany inlay	from c1750	mid-Georgian
Marquetry	c1680–c1760	to mid-Georgian
Oak	throughout	

◀ **A mahogany longcase clock,** signed Chas. Merrilies, Edinburgh, the silvered dial with subsidiary and date dials, 8-day movement striking on a bell, the drum hood with concave brass bezel, 80½in (204cm) high.
£4,200–4,800
$6,100–7,000 ⚒ S(S)

An oak longcase clock, by Francis Mitten, Chichester, the 8-day movement striking on a single bell, c1711, 82in (208cm) high.
£4,000–4,500
$5,800–6,500 ⚒ HSS

A Scottish red walnut longcase clock, by John Mearns, Aberdeen, subsidiary dial for seconds, hourly striking on a bell, with brass moon-phase movement, sunburst inlay to the trunk, 8-day duration, 31-day calendar, c1760, 82in (208cm) high.
£7,500–8,500
$10,800–12,300
⊞ SBA

A mahogany and brass inlaid longcase clock, signed Thos. Milner, London, the arched brass dial with silvered chapter ring, subsidiary seconds and date aperture, 8-day bell striking movement, the altered hood with broken arch pediment, c1750, 92in (234cm) high.
£7,000–8,000
$10,200–11,600
⚒ S(S)

A mahogany longcase clock, by Morgan, London, married, 99in (251cm) high.
£4,000–5,000
$5,800–7,000 ⚒ L

An oak longcase clock, by P. Millar, Alloa, the painted arched dial with subsidiary seconds, 8-day movement striking hourly on a bell, 31-day calendar, c1800, 85in (216cm) high.
£3,750–4,500
$5,400–6,500 ⊞ SBA

A Scottish mahogany longcase clock, signed W. McEwan, Auchterarder, the arched painted dial with 2 subsidiary dials, 8-day striking movement with anchor escapement, the case with decorative stringing, c1850, 82in (208cm) high.
£4,500–5,500
$6,500–8,000 ⚒ MCA

◀ **A Queen Anne walnut longcase clock,** the 12in (30.5cm) dial signed Rich. Medhurst, London, on the silvered chapter ring, the matted centre with subsidiary seconds ring and decorated calendar aperture, ringed winding holes, pierced blued hands, crown and putti spandrels, 5 ringed pillar movement with anchor escapement and inside countwheel strike on bell, 96in (243cm) high.
£9,000–10,000
$13,000–14,500 ⚒ C

◀ **An oak longcase clock,** by Rob Murray, Lauder, c1850.
£3,500–4,500
$5,000–6,500 ⊞ CLC

A mahogany long-case clock, signed in the arch Zak Mountford, London, the brass dial with silvered chapter ring, mask and scroll spandrels, 8-day bell striking movement, c1685, 86in (219cm) high.
£6,750–7,750
$9,800–11,200
⚒ S(S)

◄ **A Scottish George III mahogany longcase clock,** with brass and silvered dial and date aperture, inscribed Will Morvat, Aberdeen and with the motto 'Keep your end in view', Corinthian columns and door with marquetry Britannia, lion and plumes in angles, 84in (213cm) high.
£6,500–7,500
$9,400–10,500
⚒ **GSP**

A mahogany longcase clock, by Neath, with painted dial, 8-day movement, boxwood strung case flanked with ropetwist columns, early 18thC, 86in (218cm) high.
£3,800–4,500
$5,500–6,500 ⊞ **MGM**

A walnut longcase clock, by Andreas Mülner, Eisenstadt, the dial with calendar, arcaded minutes, engraved arch with signed silvered boss, flanked by subsidiary dials for repetirt/nicht and schlagt/nicht, 3 train weight driven movement with anchor escapement, front mounted pendulum and striking on 2 bells, c1800, 95in (241cm) high.
£5,500–6,500
$8,000–9,400 ⚒ **S**

A walnut longcase clock, with silvered chapter ring, engraved with Roman numerals, seconds dial and date aperture, engraved John Miller, London, 8-day striking movement, early 18thC, 84in (214cm) high.
£9,000–10,000
$13,000–14,500 ⚒ **AG**

► **A mahogany crossbanded and boxwood stung longcase clock,** the painted dial with floral decorations, signed D. Norrie, Leith, c1795, 84in (213cm) high.
£6,000–7,000
$8,700–10,200 ⊞ **CLC**

► **A mahogany inlaid longcase clock,** by Denton Northgraves of Hull, with 8-day movement, c1800, 96in (244cm) high.
£6,500–7,000
$9,400–10,200 ⚒ **AH**

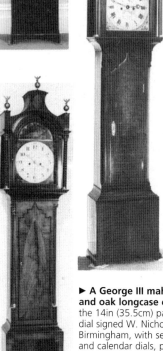

◄ **A pagoda-style oak longcase clock,** by Denton Northgraves, Hull, with white dial, c1825, 88in (223cm) high.
£4,250–4,950
$6,150–7,150 ⊞ **BL**

◄ **An oak and crossbanded longcase clock,** the silvered dial signed Nicklin, Birmingham, with date aperture, subsidiary seconds dial and engraved foliate spandrels, with 8-day bell striking movement, 99in (252cm) high.
£3,750–4,500
$5,500–6,500 ⚒ **S(S)**

► **A George III mahogany and oak longcase clock,** the 14in (35.5cm) painted dial signed W. Nicholas, Birmingham, with seconds and calendar dials, painted shell spandrels and decorated arch, 4 pillar rack striking movement, 89in (226cm) high.
£3,750–4,750
$5,500–7,000 ⚒ **Bon**

◀ **A walnut longcase clock,** signed David Paine, London, No. 104, the brass dial with raised silvered chapter ring, the moulded centre with raised silvered seconds ring, date aperture, and strike/silent, mechanism missing, gilt Indian head spandrels, the 5 ring pillar movement striking on a bell, restored, c1735, 91in (231cm) high.
£8,000–9,000
$11,600–13,000
🔨 CSK

An oak longcase clock, signed Pattison, Halifax, with brass dial, the 30-hour bell striking movement with outside countwheel, the hood with swan-neck pediment, and fluted columns, c1790, 86in (219cm) high.
£2,750–3,250
$4,000–4,800 🔨 S

A Victorian mahogany and satinwood longcase clock, engraved William Patterson of Hamilton, the brass dial and silver chapter ring with Roman numerals, seconds dial and date aperture, with 8-day movement, 81in (206cm) high.
£4,500–5,000
$6,500–7,500 🔨 AG

An Edwardian mahogany longcase clock, signed Ollivant & Botsford, Manchester, the 2 train quarter striking movement with 4 pillars and deadbeat escapement, c1910, 77in (195cm) high.
£2,500–3,000
$3,600–4,400 ⊞ Re

A Regency mahogany longcase clock, by J. A. Paterson, Edinburgh, the 8-day chiming movement with anchor escapement.
£2,500–3,000
$3,600–4,400
🔨 BWe

An oak longcase clock, by Richard Lear Pinhey, Plymouth Dock, the arched brass dial with a ship in a harbour, 8-day bell striking movement, c1795, 94in (238cm) high.
£3,500–4,500
$5,000–6,500 🔨 P(S)

An oak and mahogany longcase clock, by John Parton, Worksop, the white enamelled arched dial with hand-painted floral spandrels, vignette scene in arch, second hand, date aperture, hands original, 18thC, 90in (228cm) high.
£3,500–4,500
$5,000–6,500 ⊞ GH

A George III mahogany longcase clock, by James Pike, Newton Abbot, with subsidiary dial for seconds, 8-day movement, striking on a bell, playing one tune of 7 bells every 4 hours, the case inlaid with Sheraton shells, c1790, 83in (211cm) high
£9,000–10,000
$13,000–14,500 ⊞ SBA

▶ **A mahogany longcase clock,** by Richard Peyton, Gloucester, the brass dial showing the phases of the moon, calendar aperture and subsidiary dial for seconds, the 8 day movement striking on a bell, c1760, 94in (239cm) high.
£8,500–9,500
$12,300–13,800 ⊞ SBA

A green and gilt lacquered longcase clock, signed Thos. Palmer, London, the brass dial with raised silvered chapter ring, recessed seconds disc and date aperture, strike/silent in the arch, the 8-day movement striking on a bell, 93in (236cm) high.
£5,500–6,500
$8,000–9,400 ⚒ CSK

A George III mahogany longcase clock, signed Jno. Price, Chichester, the dial with engraved centre, seconds dial, calendar aperture, strike/silent in the arch, the 5 pillar movement with rack and bell striking and star wheel mounted snail, 90in (229cm) high.
£6,000–6,500
$8,700–9,400 ⚒ S

◀ **A walnut longcase clock,** signed Robt. Pattison, Greenwich, with seconds dial and calendar aperture, the movement with 5 well latched pillars and inside countwheel, the flat-topped case with repoussé brass cornice fret, c1700, 85½in (217cm) high.
£11,000–12,000
$16,000–17,400 ⚒ S

▶ **A late Stuart burr walnut longcase clock,** signed Tho. Power at Wellingborough, the movement with latches to 4 of the 5 ring pillars, outside countwheel strike and anchor escapement, restored, 78in (198cm) high.
£8,000–9,000
$11,600–13,000 ⚒ C

A mahogany longcase clock, by W. Podger of Bridgwater, the arched brass dial with rocking ship automaton, subsidiary dial for seconds and date aperture, the 8-day movement striking on a bell, the case edged in boxwood stringing, c1830.
£4,500–5,500
$6,500–8,000 ⊞ SBA

▶ **A George III oak longcase clock,** by Thomas Pringle, St. Ninians, with 8-day movement.
£3,500–4,000
$5,000–5,800 ⊞ FLE

◀ **A George III mahogany longcase clock,** engraved Puckridge, Snow Hill, London, the brass dial with seconds, calendar and strike/silent dials, 5 pillar movement with rack and bell striking, c1800, 84in (213cm) high.
£6,000–7,000
$8,700–10,200 ⚒ S

A figured walnut longcase clock, by Robert Potts of Patrington, the arched brass dial with silvered chapter ring and seconds hand, 18thC, 88in (223cm) high.
£5,500–6,500
$8,000–9,400 ⚒ DA

An oak longcase clock, by S. & J. Porter, Oakingham, the painted dial with Roman numerals, the movement striking on a bell, c1830, 78in (198cm) high.
£2,750–3,500
$4,000–5,000 ⚒ Bon

◄ **A simulated tortoiseshell longcase clock,** the dial signed Richard Purratt, Newport Pagnell, c1750, 88in (224cm) high.
£4,000–4,750
$5,800–6,900 ⚒ C

► **A green stained and chinoiserie longcase clock,** by Rich. Rayment, Bury, with 8-day movement, early 18thC, 90in (227cm) high.
£4,500–5,000
$6,500–7,500 PC

A Georgian longcase clock, by Richard Reed, Chelmsford, with blue lacquer case and gilt chinoiserie decoration, 8-day movement, c1765, 85in (216cm) high.
£8,000–9,000
$11,600–13,000 ⊞ PAO

A George III walnut longcase clock, the dial signed Richard Peckover, London, subsidiary seconds ring and calendar aperture, pierced blued hands, female mask and foliate spandrels, subsidiary strike/silent ring in the arch, the 5 pillar rack striking movement with anchor escapement, 92½in (238cm) high.
£8,000–9,000
$11,600–13,000 ⚒ C

A late Georgian oak and mahogany banded longcase clock, the brass dial with plaque inscribed Benjamin Ratcliffe of Welshpool, rococo spandrels, 30-hour movement, bell strike, 83in (210cm) high.
£3,000–3,500
$4,400–5,000 ⚒ WL

◄ **A late Georgian mahogany Scottish longcase clock,** by J. Ramage, Edinburgh, with brass dial, 8-day movement, the case with shell motif inlay, satinwood stringing and fluted pilasters, 84in (213cm) high.
£3,000–3,500
$4,400–5,000 ⚒ RBB

► **A walnut and mulberry longcase clock,** the brass dial inscribed Joseph Rasher, London, the 5 ringed pillared movement with anchor escapement, 18thC, 99in (251cm) high.
£6,000–7,000
$8,700–10,200
⚒ P

A mahogany longcase clock, signed T. Pyke, Bridgwater, Somerset, with white dial, 8-day movement, the corners painted with representations of the Empire, the arch with a rampant eagle and a banner inscribed 'Tempus Fugit', original pendulum, weights and winder, c1820, 89in (226cm) high.
£5,000–6,000
$7,500–8,700 ⊞ GIB

A walnut and marquetry longcase clock, the dial signed George Raby, Falmouth, subsidiary seconds dial and date aperture, later 8-day movement, wheat-ear border, part early 18thC, 82in (208cm) high.
£7,000–8,000
$10,200–11,600 ⚒ S(S)

◀ A mahogany longcase clock, by Roberts of Otley, the painted dial with moon and centre seconds, with 8-day movement, c1790, 92in (234cm) high.
£4,500–5,000
$6,500–7,500 ⊞ BL

◀ A mahogany longcase clock, signed Richd. Rooker, London, the 12in (30.5cm) dial with seconds, calendar aperture and mask and leaf spandrels, the movement with inside countwheel and later gong striking, the hood with a bronzed girl finial, movement c1730, case c1780, 90in (228cm) high.
£6,000–7,000
$8,700–10,200 ⚒ S

A mahogany longcase clock, signed Jno. Roberts, Bath, the 13in (33cm) painted break-arch dial, with subsidiary seconds and date aperture, moonphase in the arch, sea shell spandrels, the dial plate, date and moon phase rings stamped Wright, Birmingham, the 8-day movement with bell striking, c1835, 88in (223cm) high.
£5,000–6,000
$7,500–8,700 ⚒ S(S)

A Scottish mahogany longcase clock, by D. Robinson, Airdrie, the painted dial with seconds and date, with 8-day movement, 19thC, 84in (213cm) high.
£2,000–2,500
$2,900–3,600 ⚒ CoH

A William IV mahogany longcase clock, signed And'w. Rich, Bridgwater, with seconds dial, calendar sector, the arch with automaton scene of Adam and Eve, with rack and bell striking movement, the trunk door crossbanded with rosewood and flanked by similar pillars, 91in (231cm) high.
£3,000–3,500
$4,400–5,000 ⚒ S

A mahogany longcase clock, signed Roberts, Burnley, the painted dial with Roman numerals and Arabic 5 minute divisions, the centre painted with Masonic symbols, subsidiary dials for seconds and date, rolling moon in the arch with lunar calendar, the 8-day movement striking on a bell, 94½in (240cm) high.
£6,000–6,500
$8,700–9,400 ⚒ CSK

◀ **A Victorian longcase clock,** the silvered dial signed W. Ransone, London, with Roman numerals and blued steel hands, the weight-driven timepiece movement with 4 ring pillars and anchor movement, 69in (175cm) high.
£4,500–5,000
$6,500–7,500 ⚒ CSK

An oak and mahogany longcase clock, by Richards of Uttoxeter, 8-day movement, c1830, 86in (218cm) high.
£3,250–3,950
$4,700–5,700 ⊞ BL

◀ **A Sheraton inlaid figured mahogany longcase clock,** by Richardson of Paisley, 8-day duration, c1805.
£2,000–2,500
$2,900–3,600 ⊞ PHA

An oak and mahogany cross-banded longcase clock, by Richardson, Weaverham, the frieze signed J. Andrews, Cabinet Maker, the square brass dial with subsidiary seconds and date crescent, 4 pillar, 8-day movement with anchor escapement, late 18thC, 80in (203cm) high.
£3,000–4,000
$4,400–5,800 ⚒ P(M)

A mahogany longcase clock, signed Recordon, Greek Street, London, the 13in (33cm) dial with Roman numerals, subsidiary seconds, bell and rack striking movement, c1790, 92in (234cm) high.
£4,500–5,000
$6,500–7,500 ⚒ Bon

A Georgian mahogany longcase clock, the arched painted dial with subsidiary seconds and date, signed Geo. Ritchie, Arbroath, the twin train movement with anchor escapement, with swan neck pediment and spirally turned columns, c1830, 82in (208cm) high.
£5,500–6,000
$8,000–8,700 ⚒ P

A flame mahogany longcase clock, the dial signed F. B. Roberts, London, the trunk with brass inserts to the reeded angles, and reeded columns, surmounted by a pagoda pediment with pierced sound fret, c1790, 83in (211cm) high.
£10,000–12,000
$14,500–17,400 ⊞ CLC

A mahogany longcase clock, by Rowden, Stapleford, with 8-day duration, c1820, 78in (198cm) high.
£3,750–4,750
$5,500–7,000 ⊞ SO

A mahogany inlaid longcase clock, by Samuel Ritchie, Forfar, with dial showing seconds and date, with 8-day duration movement striking the hours on a bell, with swan's neck top, c1830, 82in (208cm) high.
£7,000–8,000
$10,200–11,600 ⊞ PAO

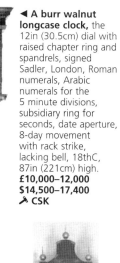

◄ **A burr walnut longcase clock,** the 12in (30.5cm) dial with raised chapter ring and spandrels, signed Sadler, London, Roman numerals, Arabic numerals for the 5 minute divisions, subsidiary ring for seconds, date aperture, 8-day movement with rack strike, lacking bell, 18thC, 87in (221cm) high.
£10,000–12,000
$14,500–17,400
🔨 CSK

A mahogany longcase clock, by Colin Salmon, Dundee, subsidiary dial for seconds, 8-day movement with 31-day calendar, strike on a bell, c1811, 84in (213cm) high.
£5,500–6,500
$8,000–9,400 🎩 SBA

► **A mahogany brass inlaid longcase clock,** by William Scott, London, subsidiary dial, 8-day duration, 31-day calendar, c1780, 102in (259cm) high.
£10,000–12,000
$14,500–17,400 🎩 SBA

A German walnut cased pedestal longcase clock, the pedestal fitted with a polyphon metal disc player, stamped Schütz-Marke, c1900, 102in (259cm) high.
£7,000–7,500
$10,200–10,900
🎩 HOD

A walnut and inlaid longcase clock, the 11in (27.5cm) brass dial inscribed Tho. Savage, London, the 5 ring pillar movement with inside countwheel strike and anchor escapement, 80in (203cm) high.
£6,500–7,000
$9,400–10,200 🔨 P

► **A Dutch-style walnut veneered longcase clock,** the later arched brass dial with moonphase aperture, the movement striking on a bell, with the engraved centre with a calendar aperture, the chapter ring inscribed J. Schofield, Rochdale, 18thC, 88in (224cm) high.
£6,000–7,000
$8,700–10,200 🔨 WW

◄ **A Georgian walnut and inlaid longcase clock,** signed Jon Sales, Dublin, with an age of the moon dial in the added arch, subsidiary seconds, date aperture and harboured winding holes, the twin train movement with inside countwheel and anchor escapement, 102in (259cm) high.
£5,000–6,000
$7,500–8,700 🔨 P

Condition of clock cases

All clocks should have their original finish and decorative features intact. Some restoration is acceptable, if carried out sympathetically. Cases in need of extensive repair and reconstruction should be avoided. Changes in temperature and humidity cause veneers to lift and longcase clock trunk doors to warp. All mouldings may loosen as the original glue dries out, and bubbles may appear under the lacquer on lacquered cases. This is caused by excessive heat and humidity. No clock should be kept in direct sunlight, as this causes the finish to bleach.

Other problems include:
• Missing finials
• Damaged mouldings
• Broken glass on the hood
• Scratching or damage to polish

An oak longcase clock, by John Seddon, Frodsham, the brass dial with silvered chapter, subsidiary seconds and date aperture, pointer and penny moon in the arch, with spandrels and incised engraving to the dial centre, the 8-day, 3 train movement with 4 finned pillars, striking on a carillon of 8 bells, with anchor escapement, c1790, 100in (254cm) high.
£4,500–5,000
$6,500–7,500 ⚒ P(M)

A late Georgian mahogany longcase clock, signed Samuel Shepley, Stockport, the brass dial with moonphase in the arch, the 8-day movement with anchor escapement and rack strike, 96in (244cm) high.
£6,000–7,000
$8,700–10,200 ⚒ C

A mahogany longcase clock, signed Shuttleworth, London, the 12in (30.5cm) painted dial with subsidiary seconds, with 8-day movement striking on a bell, the hood with scalloped pediment, on bracket feet, 89in (226cm) high.
£5,000–5,500
$7,000–8,000 ⚒ S(S)

A mahogany longcase clock, by Thomas Shaw of Lancaster, the brass dial with centre calendar and fixed arch landscape scene, with 8-day movement, the case attributed to Gillows of Lancaster, dated 1777, 90in (228cm) high.
£8,500–9,500
$12,300–13,800 ⊞ BL

◀ A mahogany longcase clock, by J. Slade, Trowbridge, the dial with seconds, date and moonphase to the arch, the 8-day movement striking the hours on a bell, c1825, 92in (234cm) high.
£8,000–9,000
$11,600–13,000 ⊞ PAO

◀ A mahogany longcase clock, signed James Sandiford, Manchester, the 13in (33cm) brass dial with rolling moon, subsidiary seconds and date aperture, the 8-day movement striking on a bell, the hood with swan neck pediment, the trunk with broken arch, scroll frieze, moulded door and plinth, c1775, 84½in (214cm) high.
£5,500–6,500
$8,000–9,400 ⚒ S(S)

An oak longcase clock, signed Peter Selby, Wareham, with brass dial, the 30-hour movement striking on a bell, with outside countwheel, the hood with baluster columns, plain trunk and plinth, c1780.
£1,500–2,500
$2,200–3,600 ⚒ S(S)

A George III oak longcase clock, signed John Smith, Chester, with 13in (33cm) brass dial, 8-day movement striking on a bell, 91in (231cm) high.
£4,750–5,750
$6,900–8,000 ⚒ S(S)

◀ An oak panelled longcase clock, with 10in (25.5cm) dial, subsidiary seconds and date aperture, the arch signed James Smith, London, with 8-day, 4 pillar movement with anchor escapement, the break-arch hood with brass ball finials, c1875, 85in (216cm) high.
£3,500–4,500
$5,000–6,500 ⚒ Bon

A Georgian mahogany clock, by James Smith, King's Lynn, with moonphases, c1774.
£6,000–6,500
$8,700–9,400 ⚒ JD

A walnut marquetry longcase clock, the 11in (28cm) brass dial signed William Sharp, London, the movement with 5 ring pillars, inside locking plate striking, late 17thC, 79in (201cm) high.
£12,000–14,000
$17,400–20,300 ⚒ Bon

A mahogany longcase clock, by Alexander Sim of Aberdeen, with white dial, 8-day movement, fully restored, c1800, 87in (221cm) high.
£4,500–5,000
$6,500–7,200 ⊞ BL

Longcase Clocks

The term 'longcase' was adopted after the invention of the short pendulum, which needed to be boxed to protect and conceal the pulleys and weights. At this stage the pendulum was only about 9in long, cases were therefore narrow and only around 75in (190cm) high. In 1670, however, with the invention of the anchor escapement, a much longer 39in (99cm) seconds-beating pendulum was required and longcase clocks gradually got larger.

Dials also became larger, growing from 10in (25.5cm) on early clocks, to 11in (28cm) and finally to 12in (30.5cm), which is still a popular size today.

A walnut longcase clock, with 12in (30.5cm) brass dial with brass chapter ring, signed G. A. Smith, Bartholmey, with subsidiary and date aperture, the 6 ring pillar movement with inside countwheel strike and anchor escapement, the case restored, 18thC, 84in (213cm) high.
£5,000–6,000
$7,250–8,700 ⚒ P

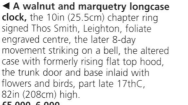

◀ A walnut and marquetry longcase clock, the 10in (25.5cm) chapter ring signed Thos Smith, Leighton, foliate engraved centre, the later 8-day movement striking on a bell, the altered case with formerly rising flat top hood, the trunk door and base inlaid with flowers and birds, part late 17thC, 82in (208cm) high.
£5,000–6,000
$7,250–8,700 ⚒ S(S)

▶ A mahogany longcase clock, by Smith of Chester, with brass dial, moon phases, 8-day movement, c1770, 82in (208cm) high.
£6,000–7,500
$8,700–11,000 ⊞ BL

◀ **An inlaid mahogany longcase clock,** by S. Smith & Son, Strand, London, the silvered dial with subsidiary seconds, leaf and flower engraved centre, engraved spandrels representing music and subsidiary dials in the arch for music selection, chime, chime and music/silent, massive 4 train 6 pillar movement with deadbeat escapement, mercury pendulum and maintaining power, one of 2 chimes sounding at the quarters on 8 tubular bells with a large hour gong and one of 6 tunes played by a 14in (36cm) pinned cylinder on 12 tubular bells, c1900, 106in (269cm) high.
£10,000–12,000
$14,500–17,400 ⚒ S

A mahogany longcase clock, signed Joseph Smith, Chester, with 12in (30.5cm) brass dial, associated movement, the hood with broken arch, *verre eglomisé* frieze, trunk with shaped door and chamfered plinth, c1740, 83½in (212cm) high.
£3,000–3,500
$4,400–5,000 ⚒ S(S)

An Irish George III mahogany longcase clock, signed Adam Somervill, Dublin, with brass dial, the case labelled P. J. Walsh & Son, 20 Batchelors Walk, Dublin, 95in (241cm) high.
£3,500–4,000
$5,000–5,800 ⚒ C

▶ **A George III mahogany longcase clock,** signed Francis Shuttleworth, Salisbury, the dial with brass chapter ring, subsidiary seconds ring, calendar aperture, pierced blued hands, painted moonphase in the arch and floral spandrels, the 5 pillar rack striking movement with anchor escapement, 88in (223cm) high.
£8,000–9,000
$11,600–13,000 ⚒ C

A Queen Anne walnut longcase clock, by Edward Speakman, London, the 30-day movement with 5 ringed pillars, rack strike and anchor escapement, restored, 108in (274cm) high.
£12,000–15,000
$17,400–21,750 ⚒ C

◀ **A mahogany longcase clock,** signed John Smith, Chester, the dial with silvered chapter ring engraved 'Our days on earth are as a shadow and there is no abiding', chime control levers at IX and III, the 3 train movement chiming on 8 bells or 4 gongs with a further massive bell for the hour, and with wood rod pendulum, late 19thC with some 18thC components, 97in (246cm) high.
£7,500–9,000
$11,000–13,000 ⚒ S

An oak longcase clock, by William Snow, Padside, with 30-hour movment, c1780, 92in (234cm) high.
£3,250–4,250
$4,700–6,000 ⊞ BL

▶ **A mahogany longcase clock,** by Snowden of Grimsby, with painted dial, 8-day movement, c1800, 96in (244cm) high.
£4,950–5,950
$7,200–8,600 ⊞ BL

◀ **An oak longcase clock,** by Joshua Squire, with arched brass dial, silvered sunburst between dolphin spandrels in the arch, 8-day movement with date and second hand, the hood with moulded pediment and arched window sides, 18thC, 88in (224cm) high.
£3,500–4,000
$5,000–5,800 ✿ **DA**

◀ **A mahogany longcase clock,** by Samuel Stevens of London, the 12in (30.5cm) brass dial with silvered name-plate to arch, 8-day striking 5 pillar movement, 18thC, 92in (234cm) high.
£8,000–9,000
$11,600–13,000 ✿ **CAG**

A mahogany longcase clock, by James Smythe, Woodbridge, the brass dial with raised chapter ring and spandrels, recessed seconds ring, 8-day movement, c1784, 77in (196cm) high.
£5,500–6,500
$8,000–9,400 ⊞ **DRA**

▶ **An oak with walnut trim longcase clock,** by William Stumbels, Totnes, the brass dial with lunar and universal tidal dials in arch, 8-day movement, c1740, 96in (244cm) high.
£5,000–6,500
$7,000–9,400 ⊞ **BL**

▶ **An oak longcase clock,** the brass arch dial signed Sutton, Stafford, subsidiary seconds dial, moonphase in the arch with altered motion work, the 8-day movement with bell striking, c1785, 86in (218cm) high.
£4,500–5,000
$6,500–7,500 ✿ **S(S)**

A George II oak longcase clock, signed Archd. Strachan, with brass dial, the silver calendar dial framed by dolphin spandrels, 8-day movement, c1760, 84in (213cm) high.
£5,500–6,000
$8,000–8,700 ⊞ **GIB**

An oak musical longcase clock, the 12in (30.5cm) brass dial with silvered chapter ring, subsidiary seconds and date aperture with engraved centre and ringed winding holes, signed Josiah Stringer, Stockport, the 3 train movement with inside countwheel strike and anchor escapement playing on 6 bells, 18thC, 85in (216cm) high.
£6,000–6,500
$8,700–9,400 ✿ **P**

► An ebonized longcase clock, signed W. Tomlinson, London, the dial with silvered chapter ring, matted centre, pierced blued hands, subsidiary seconds ring, ringed winding holes and calendar aperture, cherub and crown spandrels, the 5 ringed pillar movement with anchor escapement and inside countwheel strike on a bell, movement c1700, in later case, 87in (221cm) high.
£3,000–4,000
$4,400–5,800 ⚒ C

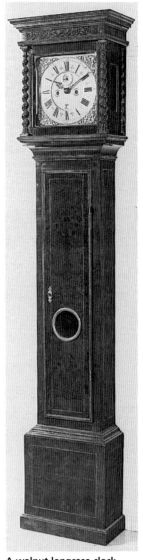

An oak longcase clock, signed Paul Thackwell, Ross, the brass dial with scroll spandrels, the 30-hour posted movement with outside countwheel striking on a bell, the case with 3 urn finials, c1776, 83in (211cm) high.
£2,450–3,250
$3,000–4,700 ⚒ DN

An oak and mahogany longcase clock, signed W. Toleman, Caernarvon, the 13in (33cm) dark blue painted dial with gilt Arabic numerals, subsidiary seconds and calendar, a painted sunburst in the arch, the 4 pillar movement striking on a bell, c1780, 86in (218cm) high.
£2,750–3,250
$4,000–4,700 ⚒ Bon

A walnut longcase clock, inscribed W. Tomlinson, London, the brass dial with silvered chapter ring, subsidiary seconds, and date aperture, 8-day movement, early 18thC.
£10,000–12,000
$14,500–17,400 ⚒ RBB

A walnut longcase clock, signed Thomas Tompion, Londini, the brass dial with silvered chapter ring, the 30-hour lantern form movement originally designed for verge escapement, now with anchor and long pendulum, c1680, in later restored case, 92in (234cm) high.
£12,000–14,000
$17,400–20,300 ⚒ P
Thomas Tompion could be described as the father of British clockmaking and was a supreme craftsman. Charles II commissioned him to make 2 clocks for Greenwich Observatory in 1676.

◄ A mahogany longcase clock, by James Thomas, Chester, the brass dial with silvered chapter ring, moonphase in the arch, with pagoda hood, flanked by fluted columns, c1780.
£6,000–6,500
$8,700–9,400 ⚒ BWe

◄ An 18thC-style fruit-wood longcase clock, signed Tompion, London, the dial with an automaton ship in the arch, the 8-day 2 train movement striking on bell, with anchor escapement, c1880, 69in (175cm) high.
£4,500–5,000
$6,500–7,500 ⚒ S

► A mahogany longcase clock, by John Todd, Glasgow, the painted dial with subsidiary seconds, and 31-day calendar, the movement striking on a bell, c1825, 78in (198cm) high.
£6,000–7,000
$8,700–10,200 ⊞ SBA

◄ A walnut marquetry longcase clock, the 11in (28cm) brass dial inscribed Thos. Taylor in Holborn, London, with 8-day pillar movement, 17thC, 85in (216cm) high.
£10,000–12,000
$14,500–17,400 🔨 S(S)

A George III inlaid mahogany longcase clock, by Thomas Millsom, the brass dial with seconds, date, moonphase and high water at Bristol, c1780, 91in (231cm) high.
£7,500–8,500
$11,000–12,300 ⊞ ALS

A Scottish longcase clock, by Thomas Taylor of Anstruther, the 8-day movement with rack striking, c1840, 85in (216cm) high.
£5,000–6,000
$7,000–8,700 ⊞ IAT

A George II inlaid oak longcase clock, inscribed John Tickle, Crediton, the brass dial with single hand and date aperture, the 30-hour birdcage movement striking on a bell, the case door and plinth base with star inlay, c1730, 79in (201cm) high.
£2,750–3,250
$4,000–4,700 🔨 MJB

LOCATE THE SOURCE

The source of each illustration in Miller's can be found by checking the code letters below each caption with the Key to Illustrations, pages 6–7.

◀ **A mahogany longcase clock,** by Thomas Upjohn, Exeter, the brass dial with strike/silent in the arch, recessed subsidiary seconds and date aperture, the 8-day 5 pillar rack striking movement with anchor escapement, 18thC, now in an early 19thC inlaid and crossbanded case with swan neck pediment, above freestanding spirally fluted columns, 81½in (207cm) high.
£3,500–4,000
$5,000–5,800 ⚒ P(M)

An oak and mahogany longcase clock, by Thomas Vurley of Wisbech, with white dial and 8-day movement, 1791, 80in (203cm) high.
£3,500–4,000
$5,000–5,800 ⊞ BL

A George III mahogany longcase clock, inscribed Vale, Birmingham, the arched brass dial with moonphase, with 8-day striking movement, carved panel and fluted pilasters to the trunk, on bracket feet, 86in (218cm) high.
£4,000–4,500
$5,800–6,500 ⚒ AG

A mahogany longcase clock, inscribed Turnbull and Aitchison, Edinburgh, with 8-day movement striking on a bell, the trunk with 2 panels veneered in burrwood, Corinthian columns at the corners, c1770, 89in (226cm) high.
£6,000–6,500
$8,700–9,400 ⚒ P(S)

▶ **An inlaid mahogany longcase clock,** signed Peter Walker, London, the 8-day movement with inside countwheel, c1720, 92in (234cm) high.
£3,500–4,000
$5,000–5,800 ⚒ L

A walnut and floral marquetry longcase clock, signed John Wainwright, Welling-boro', No. 1132, the brass dial with subsidiary seconds and date aperture, the 5 pillar movement with anchor escapement, c1745, 84in (213cm) high.
£11,000–12,500
$16,000–18,000 ⚒ P

An oak Night-watchman's clock, signed Vulliamy, London, No. 1835, A.D. 1848, with 5in (12.5cm) silvered dial, the outer dial with lever operated time pegs, the movement with 4 baluster pillars, 73½in (187cm) high.
£3,000–4,000
$4,400–5,800 ⚒ S(S)
Clocks of this type were in service at the Houses of Parliament, c1835–50.

◀ **An oak longcase clock,** inscribed John Varley, the brass arched dial, with subsidiary seconds, date and lunar ring, mid-18thC, 82in (208cm) high.
£4,000–5,000
$5,800–7,000 ⚒ HCH

◀ **An oak cross-banded longcase clock,** by Walker, Preston, the brass dial with Roman numerals and cherub head spandrels, with 8-day striking movement, the hood supported on tapering columns, the trunk door with brass escutcheon and key, 18thC, 78in (198cm) high.
£4,000–4,500
$5,800–6,500 ⊞ GH

A walnut longcase clock, signed in the arch Will Upjohn, Exon., the dial with silvered chapter ring, 8-day movement, 18thC, 87in (221cm) high.
£10,000–11,000
$14,500–16,000 🔨 S(S)

A George III green chinoiserie decorated longcase clock, by Vidion, Faversham, c1780, 96in (244cm) high.
£5,500–6,500
$8,000–9,400 ⊞ ALS

A mahogany inlaid longcase clock, signed M. Walker, Bolton, with painted dial, 8-day bell striking movement, the case with borders and stringing, c1820.
£3,500–4,500
$5,000–6,500 🔨 S(S)

A Georgian mahogany long-case clock, the 12in (30.5cm) brass dial signed Willm. Wasbrough, Bristol, inscribed around arch High Water at Bristol Key (sic), c1766, 100in (254cm).
£7,500–8,500
$11,000–12,300 🔨 P

An oak and mahogany longcase clock, by Ward of Evesham, with painted dial, 8-day movement, c1840, 84in (213cm) high.
£3,250–3,950
$4,700–5,700 ⊞ BL

▶ **A mahogany longcase clock,** the 12in (30.5cm) arched brass dial signed on a plate Warburton, W. Hampton, with 8-day bell striking movement, c1760, 93in (236cm) high.
£4,500–5,500
$6,500–8,000 🔨 S(S)

◀ **A mahogany longcase clock,** the arch boss inscribed William Warren, London, with 8-day striking movement, c1770.
£4,000–5,000
$5,800–7,000 🔨 WW

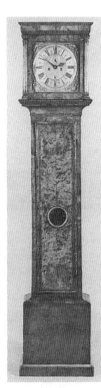

◄ **A walnut veneered longcase clock,** signed James Walker, London, the 12in (30.5cm) dial with subsidiary seconds and calendar aperture, gilt double cherub and crown spandrels in the corners, the 5 ring pillar movement with inside countwheel striking on a bell, c1700, 84in (213cm) high.
£5,000–6,000
$7,200–8,700 ⚒ Bon

► **A William & Mary walnut and floral marquetry longcase clock,** signed Ben Wright Londini Fecit, with silvered chapter ring, calendar aperture, the movement with latches to the 4 ringed pillars, inside countwheel striking on bell above, anchor escapement, 82in (208cm) high.
£12,000–14,000
$17,400–20,300 ⚒ C

A mahogany longcase clock, by Webb & Sons, Frome, with 8-day movement, c1810, 87½in (222cm) high.
£6,000–7,000
$8,700–10,200 ⊞ ALS

A George III longcase clock, engraved Jn. Walker, Newcastle, with silvered chapter ring, Roman numerals, subsidiary seconds, date aperture and gilt spandrels, with 8-day striking movement, 89in (226cm) high.
£4,500–5,500
$6,500–8,000 ⚒ AG

◄ **A Queen Anne black lacquer longcase clock,** signed Brouncker Watts, London, with silvered chapter ring, pierced blued hands, mask and foliate spandrels, the 5 pillar movement with anchor escapement and inside countwheel strike on a bell, 76in (193cm) high.
£2,500–2,800
$3,600–4,000 ⚒ C

A mahogany and marquetry longcase clock, signed Brouncker Watts, London, the brass dial with raised silvered chapter ring, the 4 ringed pillar movement with inside countwheel striking on a bell, c1700, 83in (211cm) high.
£5,000–6,000
$7,200–8,700 ⚒ CSK

A George III oak and mahogany longcase clock, by John Warrone, Kirkbymoorside, 96in (244cm) high.
£2,500–3,000
$3,600–4,400 ⚒ P(M)

► **An oak longcase clock,** by William Webb, Wellington, the 10in (25.5cm) engraved brass dial with chapter ring, 4 season spandrels with date indicator, with 8-day movement, mid-17thC, 78in (198cm) high.
£2,500–3,000
$3,600–4,400 ⊞ GH

A mahogany longcase clock, by James Walker, Montrose, the painted dial with subsidiary seconds and date, with a painted fisherman in the arch, the 8-day movement striking on a bell, the case with flame veneers, rosewood crossbanding and boxwood stringing, c1810, 91in (231cm) high.
£6,500–7,500
$9,400–11,000 ⊞ PAO

◀ **A George III oak and mahogany longcase clock,** signed Walker, Liverpool, the cream enamelled dial with black Roman numerals and Arabic minutes, with subsidiary seconds and calendar aperture, moon dial, the 8-day movement striking on a bell, together with 2 weights, pendulum and winding key, 90in (228cm) high.
£3,800–4,500
$5,500–6,500 ⚒ HSS

A Georgian mahogany longcase clock, stamped Webbs, Gorey, with divided dentil moulded pediment and carved frieze.
£2,500–3,250
$3,600–4,700 ⚒ GM

◀ **A George III mahogany chiming longcase clock,** signed Robt. Welsh, Dalkeith, with 13in (33cm) dial, substantial 3 train movement with anchor escapement, chiming the quarters on 6 bells with a further bell for the hour, 91in (231cm) high.
£6,000–7,000
$8,700–10,200 ⚒ S

A mahogany longcase clock, inscribed James West, London, with brass dial and 30-day movement, 18thC, 13½in (34cm) wide.
£4,500–5,500
$6,500–8,000 ⚒ GSP

A mahogany veneered longcase clock, inscribed Geo. White, Glasgow, the painted dial with subsidiary seconds and calendar, the 8-day movement striking on a bell, domed hood, reeded pilasters, early 19thC, 86in (218cm) high.
£2,500–3,000
$3,600–4,400 ⚒ WW

A carved oak longcase clock, signed Edw. Whitehead, Wetherby, the dial with subsidiary seconds and engraved silvered centre, the 8-day movement striking on a bell, c1780, 86in (218cm) high.
£2,500–3,000
$3,600–4,400 ⚒ CSK

An inlaid mahogany longcase clock, inscribed Wenham, Dereham, with brass dial and 8-day 2 train movement striking on a bell, late 18thC, 90½in (230cm) high.
£3,500–4,500
$5,000–6,500 ⚒ HSS

A mahogany longcase clock, inscribed Weslake, Southwark, the silvered dial with subsidiary seconds, with 8-day movement striking on a bell, early 19thC, 81in (206cm) high.
£4,500–5,000
$6,500–7,200 ⚒ P(S)

▶ **A chinoiserie lacquered longcase clock,** by William Webster, Exchange Alley, London, the arched brass and silvered dial with subsidiary seconds, strike/silent and calendar aperture, with 8-day movement striking on a bell, 18thC, 104in (264cm) high.
£5,500–6,500
$8,000–9,400 ⚒ Bea

◀ **A Regency mahogany and ebonized longcase clock,** signed Widenham, No. 13 Lombard Street, London, the silvered dial with Roman numerals and seconds ring, c1832, 83in (211cm) high.
£7,000–8,000
$10,200–11,600 ⚒ CSK

▶ **A mahogany longcase clock,** the silvered chapter ring signed Thomas Wightman, London, the brass dial with later break-arch, altered 8-day movement with bell striking, in later case, c1800, 99in (252cm) high.
£3,000–3,500
$4,400–5,000 ⚒ S(S)

A Victorian mahogany longcase clock, by Hugh Williams, Caernarvon, with rocking ship arch, 8-day movement.
£1,500–1,800
$2,000–2,600 ⚒ DaD

A Cuban mahogany longcase clock, by Samuel Whalley, Manchester, with brass dial and moonphases, c1770.
£7,500–8,500
$11,000–12,300 ⊞ ALS

◀ **A mahogany longcase clock,** by James Whitelaw, Edinburgh, with silvered dial, 8-day movement striking the hours on a bell, the case with round drumhead hood and brass concave bezel, the trunk door and base with mahogany flame veneers, c1830, 82in (208cm) high.
£6,000–7,000
$8,700–10,200 ⊞ PAO

◀ **A walnut longcase clock,** the silvered chapter ring signed E. Williamson, London, with subsidiary seconds, date aperture, recessed winding holes, the 5 ring pillar movement with inside countwheel strike and anchor escapement, late 17thC, restored, 81in (206cm) high.
£8,000–10,000
$11,600–14,500 ⚒ P

A George II elm 30-hour longcase clock, by Wilks of Wolverton, c1735.
£2,000–3,000
$2,900–4,400 ⊞ PHA

▶ **A marquetry long-case clock,** by J. Wiles, with Transitional hood moulding and original frets, the movement with internal count-wheel and single latched pillar, c1695, 88in (224cm) high.
£12,000–16,000
$17,400–23,200 ⊞ RFA

A Georgian mahogany longcase clock, the arch signed Williams, Preston, the brass dial with silvered chapter ring, subsidiary seconds and date aperture, twin train movement with anchor escapement, 90in (229cm) high.
£5,000–6,000
$7,200–8,700 ⚒ P

An oak longcase clock, signed Winstanley, Holywell, with 13in (33cm) brass dial, the movement with anchor escapement and rack striking on a bell, c1800, 83in (211cm) high.
£3,000–3,500
$4,400–5,000 ⚒ S(C)

◄ **A mahogany longcase clock,** by Witheridge, Bridgwater, with 8-day movement, c1830, 80in (203cm) high.
£3,500–4,000
$5,000–5,800 ⊞ ALS

A mahogany longcase clock, signed Robert Windsor, Newport, the brass dial with strike/silent feature, surmounted by shaped cresting, c1780.
£9,000–10,000
$13,000–14,500 ⊞ CLC

A walnut longcase clock, by Windmills, London, with brass dial, the 8-day movement with anchor escapement, 18thC, 91in (231cm) high.
£4,000–5,000
$5,800–7,200 ⚒ AGr

A George III black and gilt japanned longcase clock, by John Wimble, Ashford, with 8-day movement, 90in (228cm) high.
£6,000–7,000
$8,700–10,200 ⚒ PB

An oak and mahogany longcase clock, signed William Winder, with arched painted dial, and 8-day movement striking on a bell, with chamfered trunk, 19thC, 81½in (207cm) high.
£3,000–3,500
$4,400–5,000 ⚒ S

A marquetry longcase clock, by John Wise, London, with brass dial, 8-day movement with anchor escapement and outside locking plate, striking the hours on a bell, c1700, 87in (221cm) high.
£6,000–7,000
$8,700–10,200 ⚒ Bea

◄ A George III mahogany longcase clock, signed William Withers, London, the brass dial with subsidiary seconds and date aperture, the arch containing strike/silent, foliate spandrels, the 5 pillar movement in a case with brass inlaid Corinthian pilasters, 95in (241cm) high.
£7,500–8,500
$10,500–12,300
⚒ **Bon**

An oak and mahogany longcase clock, by John Woolley of Codnor, with brass dial and 30-hour movement, c1780, 80in (203cm) high.
£3,500–4,500
$5,000–6,500 ⊞ **BL**

A George III mahogany longcase clock, signed Thomas Willshire, Bristol, the silvered dial with subsidiary seconds and calendar, the arch with moon and tidal disc indicating High Water at Bristol Key, with rack and bell striking movement, feet replaced, c1790, 102in (259cm) high
£6,500–7,500
$9,400–11,000 ⚒ **S**

A Scottish mahogany longcase clock, signed J. Wiseman, Hamilton, with 8-day movement striking on a bell, the arched hood with baluster columns, c1840, 83½in (212cm) high.
£2,500–3,000
$3,600–4,400 ⚒ **S(S)**

◄ An oak longcase clock, by Michael Wilde of Wakefield, with a reeded flower-painted dial, 8-day movement, c1780, 94in (239cm) high.
£1,800–2,500
$2,600–3,600 ⚒ **AH**

A mahogany longcase clock, signed Edwd. Woodyear, Salisbury, c1830, 82½in (209cm) high.
£4,000–5,000
$5,800–7,200 ⚒ **S(S)**

A George III mahogany 8-day longcase clock, by Scotchmer, Islington, with striking movement, the painted dial with strike/silent to the arch, with subsidiary date and second hand, the hood and trunk flanked by fluted columns with brass inlay, 91in (231cm) high.
£7,500–9,000
$10,800–13,000 ⚒ **Mit**

A walnut longcase clock, by Windmills, London, the brass dial with silvered brass chapter ring, and subsidiary seconds, date in the arch, the 8-day 5 pillar movement striking on a bell, c1730, 90in (228cm) high.
£20,000–25,000
$29,000–36,000 ⊞ **PAO**

A late Georgian green and gilt Japanese lacquered longcase clock, by C. Woller, Birmingham, with brass dial and 8 day movement, the arched hood with swan neck pediment, flanked on either side by columns with brass capitals, 88½in (225cm) high.
£4,500–5,500
$6,500–8,000 ⚒ **Mit**

An inlaid mahogany longcase clock, by L. Wyatt, Macclesfield, enamel dial gilt calendar aperture and hands, with 8-day duration, case decorated with boxwood stringing and feather banding, early 19thC, 90in (229cm) high.
£3,000–3,750
$4,400–5,450 ⚬ CoH

◄ **A walnut longcase clock,** signed Jno Wise, London, the 11in (28cm) brass dial with replaced winged cherub spandrels, brass chapter ring, subsidiary seconds, date aperture and harboured winding holes, the movement with outside count-wheel and later wheelwork, with restorations and alterations, 18thC, 83in (211cm) high.
£3,000–4,000
$4,400–5,800 ⚬ P

An oak and crossbanded month-going longcase clock, signed Saml L. Young, Nantwich, with brass dial, the 4 pillar movement with latched plates and anchor escapement, case reduced, movement repaired, 85in (216cm) high.
£4,500–5,000
$6,500–7,200 ⚬ Bea

A marquetry longcase clock, the dial signed Ben Wright, Londini Fecit, with calendar aperture, seconds dial, the 8-day latched movement with inside countwheel, the flat-topped case with formerly rising hood, c1695, 81in (206cm).
£20,000–24,000
$29,000–34,800 ⚬ S(S)

A mahogany longcase clock, the painted dial signed Jas. Young, Dundee, subsidiary seconds and date dials, the spandrels and arch depicting various Scottish battles, stamped Laudale & Tod, Edinburgh, the 8-day movement with bell striking, c1825, 83in (211cm) high.
£4,500–5,000
$6,500–7,200 ⚬ S(S)

Parts of a clock

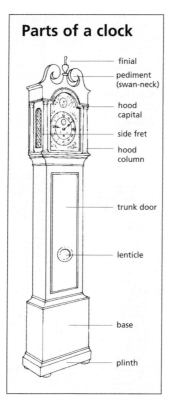

- finial
- pediment (swan-neck)
- hood capital
- side fret
- hood column
- trunk door
- lenticle
- base
- plinth

▶ **A walnut and marquetry longcase clock,** the brass dial signed Wm. Wright, Londini Fecit, with subsidiary seconds and date aperture, 5 ring pillar movement with anchor escapement and inside countwheel strike, early 18thC, 98in (249cm) high.
£18,000–20,000
$26,000–29,000 ⚬ P

A George III mahogany longcase clock, by W. Yardley, Bishops Stortford, with brass inlaid reeded columns, and quarter columns c1690, 96in (244cm) high.
£3,500–4,500
$5,000–6,500 ⊞ CRY

A William & Mary marquetry inlaid longcase clock, with later movement.
£5,000–6,000
$7,200–8,700 ↗ SWO

An ebonized oak longcase clock, with brass dial, the movement with anchor escapement chiming on 8 bells and striking on a gong, c1890, 91in (231cm) high.
£2,000–2,500
$2,900–3,600 ↗ S(C)

◄ **A mahogany longcase clock,** the enamelled dial with subsidiary seconds and calendar aperture, painted rotating moonphase in the arch, with 8-day 2 train movement striking on a bell, c1800, 84in (213cm) high.
£3,000–3,750
$4,400–5,450 ⊞ LBP

► **A late Georgian oak longcase clock,** crossbanded in mahogany, with 8-day movement, 89in (226cm) high.
£3,000–3,500
$4,400–5,000 ⊞ JRB

► **A mahogany longcase clock,** the brass dial with raised chapter ring, Roman numerals, matted centre and applied spandrels, inscribed 'Tempus Fugit', the 8-day spring-wound 3 train movement chiming quarter hours on 5 rods, 59½in (151cm) high.
£2,000–2,500
$2,900–3,600 ↗ CSK

An inlaid mahogany longcase clock, with 3 train movement, quarter chiming and playing 7 named tunes, late 18thC, 96in (244cm) high.
£5,000–6,000
$7,250–8,700 ⊞ LBP

A 19thC-style inlaid mahogany longcase clock, the brass dial with Westminster/8 bells dial, the 8-day 3 train movement with anchor escapement, 100in (254cm) high.
£5,500–6,500
$8,000–9,400 ↗ AGr

◄ **A mahogany longcase clock,** the brass dial with half and quarter-hour divisions and blued steel hands, the early added arch with silvered plaque flanked by dolphin spandrels, the 8-day movement with 5 ringed pillars, internal countwheel striking on a bell, the case with stringing and boxwood inlay, 96½in (245cm) high.
£4,000–4,500
$5,800–6,500 ↗ CSK

An oak longcase clock, with 14in (35cm) brass dial, the movement with anchor escapement and rack striking on a bell, c1820, 88in (223cm) high.
£1,800–2,200
$2,600–3,200 ↗ S(C)

A French longcase clock, with shaped trunk embellished with ormolu mounts and inlaid with floral and foliate marquetry, 90in (228cm) high.
£5,000–6,000
$7,200–8,700 🔨 GSP

A seaweed panel marquetry longcase clock, on a replaced base, with a later twin-train movement with anchor escapement, 18thC, 85in (216cm) high.
£3,000–4,000
$4,400–5,800 🔨 P

◄ **A Lincolnshire oak longcase clock,** the painted dial moon in the arch, 8-day movement, the case with original brass fittings, late 18thC, 82in (208cm) high.
£2,700–3,300
$3,900–4,900 ⊞ BL

► **A Scottish mahogany longcase clock,** with painted dial and 8-day movement, c1840, 89in (226cm) high.
£3,000–4,000
$4,400–5,800 ⊞ BL

An Edwardian mahogany longcase clock, the arched brass and silvered dial with regulator to the lunette, gilt leaf spray spandrels, the 8-day movement with tubular chimes, 86in (218cm) high.
£3,500–4,000
$5,000–5,800 🔨 WW

◄ **An Edwardian mahogany and inlaid combination longcase clock,** the brass dial with silvered chapter ring, the movement with alternative electric motor and 8-day chain fusee going train, striking the hours and the quarter hours on 9 gongs, with concealed spirit level, strike/silent lever and glazed trunk door, with pendulum brass cased weight and 4 keys, 72in (183cm) high.
£2,500–3,000
$3,600–4,400 🔨 Bea

► **A lacquered longcase clock,** the dial with raised chapter ring, inner quarter hour ring, the 30-hour posted frame movement with countwheel striking on a bell, the case with stylized pagoda top surmounted by a gilt cockerel finial, 85in (216cm) high.
£2,000–2,500
$2,900–3,600 🔨 CSK

An oak and mahogany longcase clock, the 14in (35.5cm) dial with subsidiary seconds and date dials, the spandrels painted with the Evangelists, moonphase in the arch, the movement with false plate and anchor escapement rack striking on a bell, 90in (229cm) high.
£2,250–2,750
$3,250–4,000 🔨 DN

◄ **An oak and crossbanded longcase clock,** the arched brass dial indistinctly signed, 8-day bell striking movement, 86in (219cm) high.
£3,000–3,500
$4,400–5,000 🔨 S(S)

A mahogany longcase clock, with lunar painted dial, the case with swan-neck pediment, rope-twist columns, Gothic arched door, on a plinth base, 90in (230cm) high.
£3,000–4,000
$4,400–5,800 ⊞ MGM

A mahogany and inlaid longcase clock, the brass break-arch dial with silvered chapter ring, subsidiary seconds dial, chime/ silent dial in the arch, the 8-day 3 train movement chiming on a nest of 8 bells and striking the hours on a gong, c1900, 94in (239cm) high.
£4,000–4,500
$5,800–6,500 🔨 S(S)

An Edwardian Chippendale Revival longcase clock, Whittington with Westminster chimes, 3 train movement, chiming on tubular bells, c1905, 102in (259cm) high.
£8,000–9,000
$11,600–13,000 🔨 N

A walnut longcase clock, 18thC.
£6,000–7,000
$8,700–10,200 🔨 DMM

◄ **A George III miniature mahogany longcase clock,** with arched painted dial, the weight-driven movement with anchor escapement, the hood with swan-neck pediment and reeded columns, the trunk enclosed by an arched panel door between reeded quarter columns, the door and base inlaid with fan corner motifs, hood door missing, 65in (165cm) high.
£3,000–3,500
$4,400–5,000 🔨 P

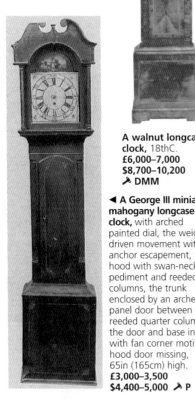

A pine longcase clock, c1840, 82in (208cm) high.
£2,000–2,500
$2,900–3,600 ⊞ BH

A Dutch floral marquetry longcase clock, 18thC.
£7,000–8,000
$10,200–11,600 🔨 LRG

A mahogany longcase clock, the brass and silvered dial with subsidiary seconds dial and cast gilt mask scroll corner spandrels, late 19thC, 88in (223cm) high.
£2,000–3,500
$2,900–5,000 🔨 WW

A George III mahogany regulator, the dial signed Holmes, London, later movement, 72in (183cm) high.
£12,000–14,000
$17,400–20,300 🔨 P

A walnut longcase clock, the 10in (25.5cm) dial signed Bird, London, restored, late 17thC, 81in (206cm) high.
£18,000–22,000
$26,000–32,000 🔨 P

A longcase clock, signed David Wood, Newbury-Port, Mass., c1790, 90in (229cm) high.
£20,000–25,000
$29,000–36,000 🔨 CNY

A walnut longcase clock, by Jacob Lovelace, Exeter, c1730, 101in (257cm) high.
£8,500–9,000
$12,300–13,000
⊞ DJM

A walnut and marquetry longcase clock, the dial signed Jona. Spencer, London, early 18thC, 84in (213.5cm) high.
£10,000–12,000
$14,500–17,400 🔨 P

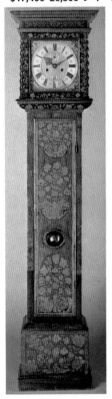

A floral marquetry longcase clock, the 11in (28cm) dial signed Thos. Bradford Londoni fecit, restored, c1690, 78in (198cm) high.
£12,000–14,000
$17,400–20,300 🔨 CNY

A mahogany longcase regulator, the dial signed Ollivant & Son, Manchester, mid-19thC, 75in (190.5cm) high.
£15,000–18,000
$22,000–26,000 🔨 C

A walnut and panel marquetry longcase clock, the 11in (28cm) dial signed J. Windmills, London, early 18thC, with later pierced fret, 86in (218.5cm) high.
£20,000–25,000
$29,000–36,000 🔨 P

A mahogany longcase sidereal regulator, with break circuit work, signed Wm. Bond & Sons, Boston, c1858, 64½in (163cm) high.
£20,000–25,000
$29,000–36,000 🔨 CNY

A walnut and marquetry longcase clock, the dial signed Wm. Sharpe, Londini fecit, late 17thC, 85in (216cm) high.
£20,000–22,000
$29,000–32,000 🔨 L

A Regency longcase regulator, with 12in (30.5cm) silvered dial signed A. Samuel & Son, City London, No. 8388, 78½in (199.5cm) high.
£18,000–20,000
$26,000–29,000 ⊞ DRA

A Queen Anne twin-train month-going mean and sidereal longcase movement, by Daniel Quare and Stephen Horseman, London, No. 148, now in a Regency pale mahogany case, 82½in (209.5cm) high.
£40,000–50,000 $58,000–72,500 ⚥ C

Two American longcase clocks, l. by Jacob Godschalk, c1771, 96in (244cm) high. **£7,000–9,000 $10,200–13,000, r.** by David Rittenhouse, c1770, 80in (203cm) high. **£6,000–8,000 $8,700–11,600** ⚥ CNY

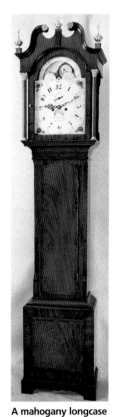

A mahogany longcase clock, the dial signed by Wm. Fletcher of Gainsboro', c1800, 91in (231cm) high.
£7,000–7,500
$10,200–11,000 ⊞ DRA

A gilt-metal mounted Sèvres pattern vase clock and pedestal, late 19thC, 69½in (176.5cm) high overall.
£5,000–6,000
$7,250–8,700 ⚥ C

A Black Forest Biedermeier organ automaton clock, mid-19thC, 106in (270cm) high.
£12,000–14,000
$17,400–20,300 ⚥ C

▶ **A Federal maple and *eglomisé* clock,** by Aaron Willard, Boston, Mass., No. 508, c1815, 35½in (90cm) high.
£8,000–10,000
$11,600–14,500 ⚥ CNY

◀ **A burr walnut longcase clock,** with brass dial, by Thomas Tompion, c1705.
£95,000–110,000
$137,000–159,000 ⚥ Bon

A walnut and marquetry longcase clock, the dial signed by James Wightman, London, 17thC, 78½in (199.5cm) high.
£24,000–28,000
$34,800–40,600 ⊞ DRA

◄ **A George III mahogany longcase clock,** the dial signed Feniller Liverpool, the gilt centre engraved with foliage and dragons' heads, 95in (242cm) high.
£7,500–8,500
$10,500–12,300 ⚒ C

► **A burr walnut longcase clock,** the dial inscribed Dan. Quare, London, composite and restored, 103in (262cm) high.
£4,500–5,000
$6,500–7,500 ⚒ C

► **A William & Mary walnut and seaweed marquetry longcase clock,** the dial signed John Finch, London, 76in (193cm) high.
£11,000–12,000
$16,000–17,500 ⚒ C

A George III mahogany and satinwood inlaid longcase clock, the dial signed John Snow, Frome Fecit, restored, 87in (221cm) high.
£8,000–9,000
$11,600–13,000 ⚒ C

◄ **A Queen Anne marquetry inlaid walnut and ebony month-going longcase clock,** the dial signed Dan. Quare, London, 99in (250cm) high.
£30,000–35,000
$43,500–50,500 ⚒ C

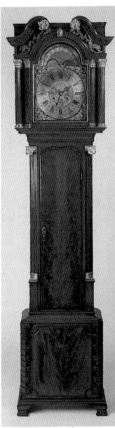

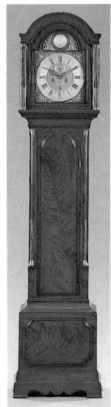

A mahogany longcase clock, by Blackwood, North Shields, c1820.
£5,000–6,000
$7,000–8,700 ⊞ PAO

An oak longcase clock, by Friend, Lyme Regis, 8-day movement striking on a bell, c1830.
£4,500–5,000
$6,500–7,500 ⊞ PAO

A mahogany longcase clock, signed Samuel Guy, London, c1770.
£9,000–10,000
$13,000–14,500 ⚒ S

A George III mahogany longcase clock.
£7,000–8,000
$10,200–11,600 ⚒ C

A Charles II ebonized longcase clock, by Henry Jones, c1685.
£30,000–35,000
$43,500–50,500 ⚒ S

A mahogany longcase clock, c1830.
£10,000–12,000
$14,500–17,400 ⊞ SO

A George II walnut longcase clock, by John Ellicott, c1740.
£40,000–50,000
$58,000–72,500 ⚒ S

An Edwardian mahogany longcase clock, c1905.
£22,000–25,000
$32,000–36,000 ⚒ S

A burr elm longcase clock, the brass dial signed Jno Clowes, Russell St, Covent Garden, the 6 ringed pillar movement with bolt and shutter maintaining power, late 17thC.
£20,000–25,000
$29,000–36,000 ⚒ Bon

◀ **A William & Mary marquetry longcase clock.**
£7,000–8,000
$10,200–11,600 ⚒ S(NY)

A burr walnut longcase clock, signed Chas. Blanchard, London, c1750, 104in (264cm) high.
£12,000–15,000
$17,400–21,700 ⚒ CSK

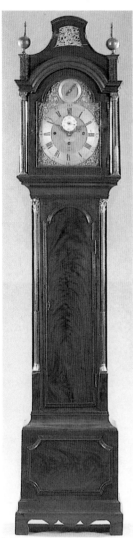

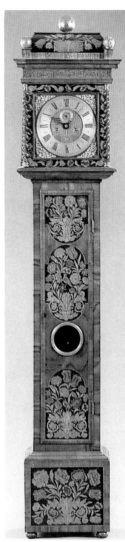

A mahogany longcase clock, by William Scott, London, c1770.
£15,000–16,000
$21,000–23,200 ⊞ PAO

A George III longcase clock, by Thos. Wilkinson, c1770.
£10,000–11,000
$14,500–16,000 🔨 S

A Charles II walnut longcase clock, 78in (198cm) high.
£35,000–40,000
$51,000–58,000 🔨 C

A walnut marquetry longcase clock, by J. Wise, c1700.
£20,000–23,000
$29,000–33,300 🔨 S

An oak and mahogany longcase clock, c1820.
£6,000–7,000
$8,700–10,200 ⊞ PAO

A William & Mary walnut longcase clock, late 17thC.
£14,000–16,000
$20,300–23,200 🔨 S(NY)

A miniature oak and mahogany month-going longcase clock, signed J. Windmills, London, early 18thC, 66in (168cm) high.
£10,000–12,000
$14,500–17,400 🔨 S

A mahogany longcase clock, by James Robertson, c1800.
£6,000–7,000
$8,700–10,200 ⊞ PAO

◄ An oak long-case clock, the brass dial with moonphase, c1770.
£6,000–7,000
$8,700–10,200
⊞ CLC

◄ A burr yew longcase clock, London, c1695.
£15,000–18,000
$21,750–26,000
⊞ CLC

◄ A mahogany longcase clock, with moonphase and calendar, c1770.
£10,000–12,000
$14,500–17,400
⊞ CLC

A gilt-bronze-mounted and brass-inlaid rosewood longcase clock, signed John Jones, London, 18thC.
£14,000–16,000
$20,300–23,200   ⚒ S(NY)

A German neo-classical ormolu-mounted long-case clock, late 18thC.
£17,500–20,000
$25,400–29,000
⚒ S(NY)

A Scottish miniature long-case clock, c1810.
£4,500–5,500
$6,500–8,000
⊞ CLC

An oak longcase clock, with painted dial, c1810.
£3,000–4,000
$4,400–5,800
⊞ CLC

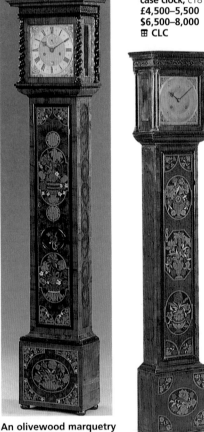

A burr walnut month-going longcase clock, by Daniel Quare, London, c1705.
£60,000–80,000
$87,000–116,000   ⚒ S

◄ A mahogany longcase clock, London, c1790.
£12,000–15,000
$17,400–21,700   ⊞ CLC

An olivewood marquetry longcase clock, by Thomas Tompion, London, c1680.
£100,000–120,000
$145,000–174,000   ⚒ S

An olivewood month-going striking long-case clock, by Joseph Knibb, London, c1680.
£75,000–100,000
$108,750–145,000
⚒ S

An ebonized longcase clock, by Thomas Tompion, London, No. 533, c1710.
£75,000–85,000
$108,500–123,500
⚒ S

A walnut longcase clock, by
Nicholas Lambert, c1730.
£20,000–22,000
$29,000–32,000 ⚷ S

**A Scottish mahogany longcase
clock,** with 13½in (34.3cm) dial,
signed John Johnson, Galway.
£5,000–6,000
$7,200–8,700 ⚷ S

**A mahogany electric longcase
clock,** by Alexander Bain, London,
c1845, 82½in (209cm) high.
£40,000–50,000
$58,000–72,500 ⚷ S

**A quarter striking
longcase clock,** by Isaac
Nickals, Wells, c1750.
£25,000–30,000
$36,000–43,500 ⚷ S

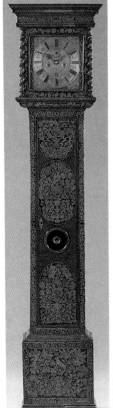

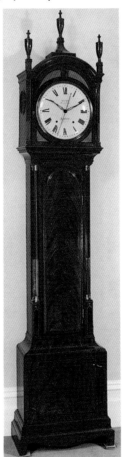

**A lacquered long-
case clock,** 18thC.
£10,000–11,000
$14,500–16,000
⚷ S(NY)

**A chiming and musical
longcase clock,** by
Claudius Du Chesne,
restored c1720.
£8,000–9,000
$11,600–13,000 ⚷ S(NY)

◀ **A walnut
marquetry long-
case clock** c1695.
£11,000–12,000
$16,000–17,400
⚷ S

**A 3 train long-
case clock,** 18thC.
£7,000–8,000
$10,200–11,600
⚷ Bea

◀ **A Regency mahogany
longcase clock,** dial
signed Massey, 1803.
£15,000–18,000
$21,000–26,000 ⊞ CLC

A walnut and marquetry longcase clock, by George Tyler, c1705, 83in (211cm) high.
£12,000–14,000
$17,400–20,300
⊞ ALS

A Chippendale carved walnut longcase clock, by Jacob Hostetter, c1810, 104in (264cm) high.
£18,000–20,000
$26,000–29,000
🔨 S(NY)

A mahogany and shell inlaid longcase clock, by Sainsbury, Bridgwater, c1810, 84in (213cm) high.
£5,750–6,750
$8,300–9,800 ⊞ ALS

A mahogany longcase clock, by Aaron Willard, c1800, 100in (254cm) high.
£30,000–35,000
$43,500–50,000
🔨 S(NY)

An 8-day long-case clock, by Charles Merrilies, c1825.
£6,000–7,000
$8,700–10,200
⊞ PAO

An oak longcase clock, by A. Buchan, Perth, with 8-day move-ment, c1790, 83in (210cm) high.
£6,000–7,000
$8,700–10,200 ⊞ PAO

A Dutch rococo walnut longcase clock, by Johannes Logge, early 18thC.
£9,000–10,000
$13,000–14,500
🔨 S(NY)

An oak long-case clock, by Isaac Nickall, Wells, 18thC.
£3,000–3,500
$4,400–5,000
⊞ ALS

A George III oak and mahogany longcase clock, c1795.
£4,000–4,500
$5,800–6,500
⊞ ALS

A flame mahogany and inlaid longcase clock, by Cox, Devizes, late 18thC, 90in (228cm) high.
£6,500–7,000
$9,400–10,200 ⊞ ALS

A flame mahogany longcase clock, by Bellzoni, Shaftesbury, the arch having a lion with moving eyes, early 19thC, 83in (210.5cm) high.
£5,500–6,500
$8,000–9,400 ⊞ ALS

A mahogany and boxwood strung longcase clock, by Pitt, Tetbury, early 19thC, 86in (210.5cm) high
£5,750–6,500
$8,300–9,400 ⊞ ALS

A figured walnut case longcase clock, with brass dial and silvered chapter ring, early 20thC.
£850–1,000
$1,250–1,500 🔨 PCh

A mahogany 8-day longcase clock, by R. Summerhays, Ilminster, striking the hours on a bell, c1840.
£5,000–6,000
$7,200–8,700 ⊞ PAO

KEITH LAWSON LBHI

Purveyors of antiquarian horology
Probably the largest stock in the UK
As featured on Anglia Television
Hundreds of antique clocks of all types in stock
Full price or more paid back in part exchange
5 years guarantee on all
longcase and bracket clocks

ASK ABOUT OUR INVESTMENT GUARANTEE

Above: A small area of one of our showrooms

OPEN 7 DAYS A WEEK

01493 730950

Scratby Garden Centre
Beach Road, Scratby, Great Yarmouth
Norfolk NR29 3AJ
www.antiqueclocks.co.uk

A mahogany longcase clock, London, c1790.
£11,000–13,000
$16,000–18,800 ⊞ CLC

A mahogany longcase clock, by Morse & Tanner, Malmesbury, 8-day striking movement, c1840, 90in (228cm) high.
£5,000–6,000
$7,200–8,700 ⊞ PAO

A mahogany longcase clock, by Chas. Price, Wiveliscombe, with 8-day repeating movement, 86in (218.5cm) high.
£6,500–7,500
$9,400–10,800 ⚒ SWO

A mahogany longcase clock, by Howse, Marlborough, c1830, 82in (208cm) high.
£4,750–5,500
$6,900–8,000 ⊞ ALS

An oak and mahogany 8-day longcase clock, by Harlett & Dursley, striking hours on a bell, c1810, 78in (198cm) high.
£4,500–5,500
$6,500–8,000 ⊞ PAO

◀ **A George III longcase clock,** by William Rout, 18thC.
£5,750–6,750
$8,300–9,800 ⚒ S(NY)

An 8-day longcase clock, by Robert Seagrave, c1770, 97in (246cm) high.
£15,000–16,000
$21,500–23,200 ⊞ PAO

A mahogany longcase clock, by Aynesworth Thwaites, late 18thC.
£9,000–10,000
$13,000–14,500 ⚒ SWO

A Scottish mahogany longcase clock, c1790.
£7,000–8,000
$10,200–11,600 ⊞ CLC

An oak longcase clock, by Maurice, Haverfordwest, late 18thC, 83in (211cm) high.
£3,850–4,850
$5,600–7,000 ⊞ ALS

A George II gilt decorated scarlet japanned longcase clock, signed Henry Fish, 18thC, 98in (249cm) high.
£9,000–10,000
$13,000–14,500 ⚒ S(NY)

An oak and mahogany longcase clock, by Richard Herring, with Adam and Eve automata, c1810.
£7,000–8,000
$10,200–11,600 ⊞ PAO

A mahogany and oak 8-day longcase clock, by Thomas Johns, c1830.
£4,500–5,500
$6,500–8,000 ⊞ PAO

◄ **An oak 8-day longcase clock,** by Philip Avenell, Farnham, with engraved silvered brass dial, c1770, 79in (201cm) high.
£5,500–6,500
$8,000–9,400 ⊞ PAO

A mahogany 8-day longcase clock, by S. Passmore, Plymouth, brass silvered dial, with flame veneers and boxwood stringing, c1840, 87in (221cm) high.
£4,500–5,500
$6,500–8,000 ⊞ PAO

A George III mahogany longcase clock, with 8-day rocking ship movement.
£7,750–8,750
$11,200–12,700 ⚒ SWO

A mahogany 8-day longcase clock, by J. MacGregor, Edinburgh, with flame veneers and boxwood inlay, the painted dial with seconds and date, c1830, 79½in (201cm) high.
£6,000–7,000
$8,700–10,200 ⊞ PAO

A mahogany longcase clock, by John Richardson, London, with brass dial, the 8-day 5 pillar movement striking the hours on a bell, c1765, 100in (254cm) high.
£12,500–13,500
$18,000–19,600 ⊞ PAO

A mahogany 8-day longcase clock, by Francis Hobler, London, the brass dial with silvered chapter ring, 5 pillar movement striking the hours on a bell, c1770, 95in (241cm) high.
£14,000–15,000
$20,300–21,700 ⊞ PAO

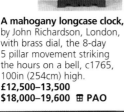

A mahogany 8-day longcase clock, by William Carter, Hampstead, with brass dial, silvered brass chapter ring, c1790, 84in (213cm) high.
£14,000–15,000
$20,300–22,000 ⊞ PAO

An oak 8-day longcase clock, by Thomas Mear, Dursley, with mahogany banding, painted dial, striking the hours on a bell, c1820, 78in (198cm) high.
£4,250–5,000
$6,150–7,250 ⊞ PAO

An oak 8-day longcase clock, by Thomas Furnival, Taunton, with brass dial and silvered brass chapter ring, 5 pillar movement, c1750, 80in (203cm) high.
£6,500–7,500
$9,400–10,800 ⊞ PAO

A mahogany 8-day longcase clock, by M. Michael, Bristol, the white dial painted with shells to the corners and flowers to the arch, striking the hours on a bell, c1820, 88in (224cm) high.
£6,000–6,750
$8,700–9,800 ⊞ PAO

► **An oak 8-day longcase clock,** by Martin, Faversham, with painted dial, c1810, 84in (213cm) high.
£5,000–6,000
$7,200–8,700 ⊞ PAO

A mahogany 8-day longcase clock, by John Anderson, 5 pillar movement striking on a bell, strike/silent in the arch, c1765, 101in (256.5cm) high.
£12,500–13,500
$18,000–19,600 ⊞ **PAO**

A mahogany longcase clock, by James McCabe, London, with 3 train movement on 4 graduated bells, early 19thC.
£10,500–12,500
$15,250–18,150 ⚒ **BWe**

An olivewood parquetry month-going longcase clock, signed Robert Thompson, with 5 ringed pillar movement, restored, 78in (198cm) high.
£20,000–22,000
$29,000–32,000 ⚒ **C**

A mahogany longcase clock, signed Saml. Collier, Eccles, c1790, 93in (236cm) high.
£6,500–7,500
$9,400–11,000
⚒ **S**

A George III 8-day longcase clock, signed Thomas Blundell, Dublin, 94in (238cm) high.
£1,500–2,000
$2,170–2,900 ⚒ **AH**

An Edwardian quarter chiming longcase clock, the 4 pillar 3 train movement with deadbeat escapement and mercury pendulum, 93in (236cm) high.
£5,000–7,000
$7,200–10,200 ⚒ **C**

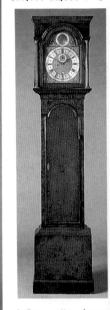

A George II walnut and burr walnut longcase clock, signed Michael Gibbs, London, with gilt metal mounted dial, and silvered chapter ring, associated, 87in (221cm) high.
£7,000–8,000
$10,200–11,600 ⚒ **C**

An inlaid mahogany longcase clock, signed George White, Bristol, c1790, 100in (254cm) high.
£7,500–8,500
$10,500–12,500
⚒ **S(S)**

A William & Mary walnut marquetry and ebony longcase clock, signed Thomas Lumpkin, London, 77in (195cm) high.
£11,000–13,000
$16,000–18,000 ⚒ **C**

A George III mahogany and rosewood crossbanded longcase clock, signed J. Dankin, Grassington, 93in (236cm) high.
£6,000–6,750
$8,700–9,800 ⚒ **AH**

◄ **An oak longcase clock,** by John Sterland, Nottingham, the arched brass dial with silvered chapter and well, 8-day movement striking the hours on a bell, the engraved centre with both date and seconds, maker's name on a cartouche in the arch, long trunk door, c1780, 81in (205.5cm) high.
£7,000–8,000
$10,200–11,600 ⊞ PAO

A mahogany 8-day longcase clock, by John Breakenrig, Edinburgh, engraved dial, c1790, 85in (216cm) high without finial.
£8,500–9,000
$12,300–13,000 ⊞ PAO

A mahogany 8-day longcase clock, by Bell, St. Andrews, striking the hours on a bell, c1790, 87in (221cm) high.
£7,000–8,000
$10,200–11,600 ⊞ PAO

► **A mahogany 8-day longcase clock,** by James Rowland, Bristol, striking the hours on a bell, white dial showing seconds, date and phases of the moon in the arch, c1790 and later, 88in (223.5cm) high.
£8,000–9,000
$11,600–13,000 ⊞ PAO

◄ **An oak 8-day longcase clock,** by John Stokes, St Ives, the brass dial with silvered chapter ring, date, strike/silent in the arch, striking the hour on a bell, long trunk door, c1750, 83in (210.5cm) high.
£7,500–8,500
$11,000–12,300 ⊞ PAO

◀ **A walnut 8-day longcase clock,** the brass dial with silvered Roman and Arabic chapter ring, inscribed Dan. Quare, London, 88in (224cm) high.
£6,000–8,000
$8,700–11,600
🔨 **CSK**

A Dutch walnut and marquetry longcase clock, the dial signed Garrit Bramer, Amsterdam, mid-18thC, 114in (289.5cm) high.
£8,500–9,500
$12,300–13,800 🔨 **C**

A Charles II burr walnut month-going longcase cloc the dial signed Daniel Quare, London, 86in (218cm) high.
£22,000–25000
$32,000–36,000 🔨 (

A Regency mahogany 8-day longcase clock, the brass dial with Roman and Arabic chapter ring, foliate engraved centre, the trunk with fluted canted angles, on a stepped panelled plinth, 92½in (235cm) high.
£2,000–2,500
$2,900–3,600 🔨 **CSK**

An Edwardian mahogany quarter chiming longcase clock, 4 pillar movement with jewelled deadbeat escapement, 113in (287cm) high.
£8,500–9,500
$12,300–13,800 🔨 **C**

◀ **A walnut month-going longcase clock,** the dial signed 234 Dan. Quare & Ste. Horseman, London, the case with domed caddy cresting and 2 ball and spire finials above a fret, 100in (254cm) high.
£35,000–38,000
$50,700–55,000 🔨 **S**

A William & Mary walnut and marque longcase clock, the dial signed Luke Wise, Reading, 83in (211cm) high.
£10,000–12,000
$14,500–17,400 🔨

A Charles II olivewood oyster and floral marquetry grande sonnerie quarter striking longcase clock, the dial signed Eduardus East Londini, the case on bun feet, 73½in (186cm) high.
£14,000–16,000
$20,300–23,200 🔨 **C**

▶ **A japanned longcase clock,** the dial signed William Kipling, London, the oval boss engraved 'Tempus Fugit', c1715, 103in (262cm) high.
£15,000–16,000
$21,700–23,200 🔨 **S**

Lantern Clocks

As the oldest English domestic clock, dating from the late 16th century, the lantern is probably the clock that has been most vulnerable to alterations and reproductions. The Victorians liked its appearance and so copied the earlier designs, but they also wanted an efficiency of time-keeping which the older models could not provide. All the 19th-century examples are therefore spring-driven rather than weight-driven. Original lantern clocks have generally undergone many repairs; replaced or faked parts appear brighter than the originals, or may be artificially distressed to look old.

Developed from the German Gothic wall clock, lantern clocks were originally made to hang from a sturdy hook on the wall by means of an iron hoop at the back of the clock. Being weight-driven, one or two weights hung on ropes through holes in the bottom of the clock, held in place either by spikes protruding from the bottom of the backplate, or the back feet. Alternatively, the clocks were placed on an oak wall bracket, but were not expected to be accurate timekeepers and only marked time in units of a quarter of an hour, registered by a single hand. The few that exist with two hands probably had only one originally. The details of a lantern clock – the engraving, the design of the hand or the frets – may change subtly, but the overall shape remains much the same.

By about 1710 lantern clocks were going out of fashion, supplanted by the longcase clock. However, production did not cease, in fact the arched-dial lantern clock appeared c1750, made almost exclusively by provincial makers with the maker's signature usually appearing in the arch. In the 19th century many were converted to table clocks and had their movements replaced with Victorian ones.

A lantern clock will need oiling periodically and if it has ropes they must be checked for fraying. Dealer Brian Loomes suggests not running the very old examples continuously in order to avoid wearing the mechanics out completely. A major overhaul should only be necessary once every 15 years.

Prices of lantern clocks have been relatively stable in the last few years. A mid-18th-century clock with minimal restoration would fetch anything between £2,500–4,000 ($3,600–5,800) – William Bower and Henry Ireland are makers to look out for – whereas one made around 1900 would achieve around £1,500 ($2,170). A notable retailer of the time was Payne & Co. of Bond Street. Clock dealer M. D. Tooke and Oliver Saunders from Bonhams both cite the problem of the many fake lantern clocks that came to England from eastern Europe 20 or 30 years ago. To the uninitiated these would look old, and many were even marked with the names of actual 18th-century makers such as Thomas Moore of Ipswich. Only buy from a reputable source that can provide a detailed description of the clock, so that you can have some recourse if it proves to be a fake.

◀ **A brass lantern clock,** the 6½in (16.5cm) chapter ring with fleur-de-lys half-hour marks, the engraved centre signed Christopher Carter, the 2 train movement in a posted case of typical form, dolphin frets beneath the bell, anchor escapement, now with an oak bracket, c1730, 15in (38cm) high.
£3,500–4,000
$5,000–5,800 ⚒ Bon

A silver-plated lantern clock, the 6½in (16.5cm) silvered chapter ring with engraved Roman numerals, engraved centre signed Andrew Allan in Grabb St Londini fecit, the movement stamped W & H sch, striking on a bell mounted above, German, c1890, 15½in (39.5cm) high.
£1,200–1,400
$1,700–2,000 ⚒ Bon

▶ **A brass-cased balance wheel lantern clock,** with 6¼in (16cm) silvered chapter ring, signed on the dial Nicholas Coxeter, Neer (sic) Goldsmiths Hall, Londini, Fecit, the movement with outside countwheel, vertical verge for alarm and balance wheel escapement, hoop and spurs, c1650, 15in (38cm) high.
£5,000–6,000
$7,200–8,700 ⚒ S

A brass striking lantern clock, the dial signed Gerardus Brand, Fecit, Amstelodamj, the 2 train movement with verge escapement and bob pendulum, on brass ball feet, 9½in (24cm) high.
£5,500–6,500
$8,000–9,400 ⚒ Bon

A George II lantern timepiece, the dial signed John Belling, Bodmyn, 1753, with central alarm disc, pierced blued single hand, the movement with verge escapement and alarm striking on bell above, within engraved pierced gallery frets, spurs to back feet, 9in (23cm) high.
£4,000–4,750
$5,800–6,900 ⚒ C

▶ **A lantern clock,** by Barnard Dammant of Colchester, the engraved dial with raised chapter ring, now fitted with 2 train chain fusee movement, early 18thC, 15in (38cm) high.
£1,500–1,800
$2,000–2,600 ⊞ DRA

◀ **A brass lantern clock,** the dial signed Peter Closon, Neere (sic) Holbourne Bridge Londini Fecit, the posted framed movement with balance wheel and verge escapement, countwheel and alarm on bell, with restorations, c1650, 15in (38cm) high.
£7,500–9,500
$10,800–13,800 ⚒ C

A brass winged lantern clock, with 6½in (16.5cm) chapter ring, engraved dial, and central alarm disc, the central fret signed Peter Closon at London fecit, the movement now with verge escapement, outside countwheel and central anchor pendulum, with an oak bracket and weight, with alterations and replacements, c1650.
£4,500–5,000
$6,500–7,500 ⚒ S(S)

A late Stuart brass lantern clock, signed Nicholas Coxeter Londini fecit, within the florally engraved centre, with anchor escapement and countwheel strike on bell above, with dolphin pierced frets above the dial, 16in (40.5cm) high.
£3,500–4,000
$5,000–5,800 ⚒ C(Am)

A brass lantern clock, with 7in (18cm) silvered chapter ring, the centre signed Wm. Goodwin, Stowmarket, single hour hand, the posted movement with anchor escapement, outside countwheel, iron hanging hoop and wall spikes, c1710, 15½in (39.5cm) high.
£3,750–4,750
$5,450–6,900 ⚒ S(S)

LOCATE THE SOURCE
The source of each illustration in Miller's can be found by checking the code letters below each caption with the Key to Illustrations, pages 6–7.

A brass lantern clock, by Francis Forman, the 6in (15cm) chapter ring set on an engraved dial plate, central alarm disc, posted weight-driven movement with verge and balance wheel escapement, later chains, the case with metamorphic frets, the front one signed Francis Forman at St. Paules' Gate, restored, alarm removed, c1635, 14in (35.5cm) high.
£8,000–10,000
$11,600–14,500 ⚒ S

A brass wall lantern and alarm clock, by Robt. Higgs London, the 30-hour weight-driven movement with verge escapement, mid-18thC, 8in (20.5cm) high.
£4,500–5,000
$6,500–7,500 ⚒ DN

◀ **A brass lantern clock,** with anchor escapement, seconds pendulum and brass-cased weight hoop and spikes to the rear, chapter ring inscribed Dan L. Hoskins, the single steel hand indicates hours only, lacking side and back doors, c1630, 15½in (39.5cm) high.
£7,000–8,000
$10,200–11,600 ⚒ P(S)

◄ A Georgian brass lantern clock, made for the Turkish market, with brass dial and chapter ring, signed on a cartouche in the arch Jno. Parks, London, the posted frame surrounded by a bell, the movement with verge bob pendulum escapement, 14½in (37cm) high.
£700–800
$1,000–1,200 ⚒ P

A hooded lantern clock, the 7in (18cm) brass break-arch dial signed Geo. Lumley, Bury, the 30-hour movement of conventional posted construction with anchor escapement, top mounted bell, with associated mahogany bracket and hood with pagoda top, part 18thC, 30in (76cm) high.
£1,400–1,800
$2,000–2,600 ⚒ S(S)
This lantern clock would appear to have been converted to hooded form as there is evidence of side frets and a rear hanging hoop. The feet are later replacements, leaving no sign of spurs.

A Charles II striking lantern clock, the dial signed James Delance Froome Fecit, within the centre with tulip engraving, silvered Roman chapter ring with pierced steel hand, the movement with verge escapement and short bob pendulum, countwheel strike on bell above, with iron straps to the 4 corner finials, with pierced frets, 15½in (39.5cm) high.
£5,000–6,000
$7,200–8,700 ⚒ C

► A brass lantern clock, with silvered chapter ring, half and quarter-hour divisions, engraved central field with single steel hand, signed Ninyan Burleigh, Durham, the weight-driven movement with anchor escapement striking on a bell, early 18thC, 15½in (39.5cm) high.
£2,200–2,400
$3,200–3,500 ⚒ CSK

A George I miniature brass lantern timepiece, by Massey London, with verge escapement and bob pendulum, lacking gallery frets and one side door, 8in (20.5cm) high.
£1,500–2,000
$2,100–2,900 ⚒ C

◄ A brass lantern clock, signed R. Rayment, Clare, the pierced cresting with interlaced adorsed dolphins and foliage, on bun feet, c1750, 13½in (34.5cm) high.
£2,000–2,500
$2,900–3,600 ⚒ C

A Charles II brass striking lantern clock, with brass Roman chapter ring and single steel hand, foliate engraved centre with alarm disc, the movement with verge escapement, countwheel strike on bell above, pierced and engraved dolphin frets, the front fret signed Henry Montlon London, alarm assembly lacking, 15in (38cm) high.
£6,000–8,000
$8,700–11,600 ⚒ C

A brass lantern clock, the dial engraved R. L. beneath the alarm disc, now fixed, with 17thC posted frame, with 19thC twin fusee movement, earlier case, 13in (33cm) high.
£1,200–1,500
$1,700–2,100 ⚒ P

A Charles II brass-cased lantern clock, with 30-hour striking verge movement, inscribed Jos. Norris Abingdon, c1670.
£5,500–6,500 $8,000–9,400 ⚒ WW

A George III lantern clock, made for the Turkish market, the 9in (23cm) dial with scroll and flower spandrels, signed Isaac Rogers, London, in the arch above, the posted movement with verge and short pendulum escapement and countwheel bell striking, c1770, 14in (35.5cm) high.
£1,800–2,400
$2,600–3,500 ✗ S

A Georgian brass miniature lantern clock, made for the Turkish market, signed on the cartouche in the arch Robt. Ward, London, with verge escapement, the bell, bell cage, pallet arbor and bob pendulum missing, 5½in (14cm) high.
£1,800–2,400
$2,600–3,500 ✗ P

A brass striking lantern clock, the dial with silvered chapter ring signed Thos. Savidge, Exeter Fecit, with anchor escapement, countwheel strike on a bell, c1600, 15in (38cm) high.
£2,400–3,000
$3,500–4,400 ✗ C

▶ **A small alarm lantern clock,** the 2½in (6.5cm) dial signed Tho. Tamkin de Bedforde fecit, the movement with verge escapement, pendulum lacking, 8½in (21.5cm) high.
£7,000–9,800
$10,200–14,200 ✗ S

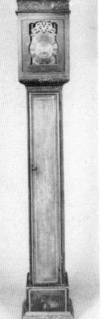

◀ **A Queen Anne oak longcased striking lantern clock,** the dial signed William Speakman Londini Fecit on the brass chapter ring, with steel hour hand, lacking alarm disc, with later decorated case, the clock with verge escapement and centre swinging bob pendulum, countwheel strike on bell above, damaged, 67in (170cm) high.
£2,400–3,600
$3,500–5,200 ✗ C

A brass 30-hour lantern clock, by Robert Watts, with 6in (15cm) brass Roman numeral chapter ring, signed on the foliage engraved centre Robt. Watts, Stamford, with a single hand, post weight-driven movement and verge, short bob pendulum, outside locking, plate striking on a bell mounted above the case, with slender columns and turned finials, c1760, 14in (35.5cm) high.
£1,800–2,400
$2,600–3,500 ✗ Bon

▶ **A brass lantern clock,** the dial with brass chapter, signed Wilmshurst, Odiham, with engraved centre, the posted frame surmounted by a bell, the movement with verge bob pendulum escapement and countwheel strike, mid-18thC, 15in (38cm) high.
£1,800–2,400
$2,600–3,500 ✗ P

A lantern timepiece, by Smith, c1920, 10½in (26.5cm) high.
£140–200
$200–300 ⊞ SBA

◄ **A brass lantern clock,** the dial inscribed J. Windmills, London, with single steel hand, the 30-hour movement with anchor escapement and countwheel strike, 15in (38cm) high.
£2,400–3,000
$3,500–4,400 ⚒ P

▶ **A 17thC-style brass lantern clock,** with central alarm disc, verge escapement and bob pendulum, 8in (20.5cm) high, on a stained oak bracket.
£1,200–1,450
$1,750–2,100 ⚒ S(S)

A brass lantern alarm clock, the 5½in (14cm) chapter ring set on a leaf- and flower-engraved plate, signed John Snow Ano Do 1630, the reverse also signed John Snow 1630, with central alarm disc and single hand, the posted movement with reconverted balance and verge escapement, outside countwheel and replaced alarm work mounted on the iron backplate, the frame with slender one-piece corner columns with turned feet and finials, part 17thC, 15in (38cm) high.
£4,800–6,000
$6,900–8,700 ⚒ S

▶ **A lantern clock,** unsigned, with original verge escapement and alarmwork, c1700, 16in (40.5cm) high.
£4,500–5,000
$6,500–7,200 ⊞ BL

◄ **A brass lantern clock,** the movement with verge and double foliot escapement, European hour count-wheel strike on pork pie bell, fixed chapter ring with 12 Japanese hours twice, central alarm disc with pierced blued steel hand, side doors engraved, on lacquered wood stand and wood framed canopy with side doors, old damage, 18thC.
£6,600–7,800
$9,500–11,300 ⚒ C

A lantern alarm clock, by John Welsh of Chesham, with original anchor escapement, c1700, 7in (18cm) high.
£2,200–2,800
$3,200–4,000 ⊞ RFA

A brass lantern clock, with foliate-engraved dial, c1730, with Victorian movement, 16½in (42cm) high.
£900–1,150 $1,300–1,650 ⊞ SBA

A Continental grande sonnerie lantern clock, the 10in (25.5cm) dial with engraved centre, 3 train weight-driven movement with verge escapement and cow tail pendulum, inside countwheel for the quarters, nag's head detent to release the double 6-hour striking train with outside countwheel, the frame with iron corner posts, the bells mounted above, frets lacking, mid-18thC, 20in (51cm) high.
£2,400–3,600
$3,500–5,200 ⚒ S

A miniature winged brass lantern clock, with verge escapement and pendulum bob in the form of an anchor, the dial centre engraved with tulips, the arrow-shaped steel hand indicating hours only, 9½in (24cm) high.
£2,400–3,000
$3,500–4,400 ⚒ P(S)

A brass lantern clock, with 6¾in (17cm) brass chapter ring, twin fusee movement striking the hours and quarters on 2 bells, in a case with turned corner columns and finials, pierced frets, on ball feet, c1870, 16in (40.5cm) high.
£1,200–1,500
$1,700–2,200 ⚒ Bon

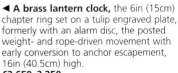

A brass striking lantern clock, with pierced blued hand, the movement with anchor escapement and countwheel strike on bell above, enclosed within pierced brass frets, 15in (38cm) high.
£950–1,200
$1,400–1,800 ⚒ C

◄ **A brass lantern clock,** the 6in (15cm) chapter ring set on a tulip engraved plate, formerly with an alarm disc, the posted weight- and rope-driven movement with early conversion to anchor escapement, 16in (40.5cm) high.
£2,650–3,250
$3,850–4,700 ⚒ S

A brass-cased balance wheel lantern clock, with 6½in (16.5cm) silvered chapter ring, engraved dial, the movement with brass pillars, 16in (40.5cm) high.
£2,650–3,250
$3,850–4,700 ⚒ S

A spring-driven lantern clock, with 2 train movement, ting tang quarter strike on 2 bells, late 19thC, 15½in (39.5cm) high.
£1,650–1,850
$2,400–2,700 ⊞ DRA

Lantern Clocks

The lantern clock was the earliest wall clock, made initially in Europe, particularly in southern Germany and northern Italy, around 1500. English clockmakers made lantern clocks from about 1620. The verge escapement used in the early German examples gradually gave way to the balance wheel, which was employed in most English lantern clocks. Many have similar features and it is sometimes only possible to date them if the maker's name appears on the front.

After the discovery of the pendulum in 1657, most lantern clocks were converted to this method, thus ensuring greater accuracy. By c1720, lantern clocks were no longer made, having been almost completely replaced by the longcase clock.

◀ **A brass open-case lantern clock,** the engraved dial with silvered chapter ring, the verge balance escapement with bell strike and alarm mechanism, 17thC, 13in (33cm) high.
£2,050–2,400
$2,950–3,500 ⚒ WW

Miller's is a price GUIDE not a price LIST

An iron and brass lantern clock, the 6½in (16.5cm) chapter ring set on a tulip engraved surround with a single hand, early conversion to verge and pendulum escapement, 17thC, 15¾in (40cm) high.
£2,900–3,350 $4,200–4,850 ⚒ S

▶ **A lantern clock movement,** the brass dial with Roman chapters and Arabic quarters, the movement with anchor escapement and countwheel strike on bell, 19thC, 13½in (34cm) high.
£300–350 $440–500 ⚒ CSK

A brass lantern clock, the 6¼in (16cm) silvered chapter ring signed John Wawne, single hand and matted centre, weight-driven movement with verge and balance wheel escapement, early 18thC, 14in (35.5cm) high.
£3,000–4,200
$4,400–7,000 ⚒ S

Bracket Clocks

The term 'bracket' clock describes a spring-driven clock with a short pendulum, housed in a wooden case and designed to stand on a table, sideboard, mantelpiece or wall bracket. They were developed from c1660, roughly the same time as the longcase clock, but had the advantage over the longcase of being reasonably portable. The principal variety has a square-fronted case, with a domed top fitted with a metal handle in order to facilitate carrying.

There are several parallels between the development of the bracket clock and the longcase in terms of shape, colour and decoration. The hood of a longcase clock was virtually the same design as that of a bracket clock, and many makers would have applied their skills to both types. The first examples were well proportioned, with pillars at each corner, beautifully detailed mouldings and occasionally gilt-metal mounts. These did not have the carrying handle at the top but were flat or portico-shaped. In common with longcases, they were made of ebony-veneered oak, with walnut, mahogany and rosewood cases following later. Marquetry bracket clocks are rare. From the late 17th century there were also lacquered cases, some decorated with chinoiserie motifs, others in imitation tortoiseshell. Seventeenth-century lacquer was mostly black or dark green, but by 1700 other colours such as red and light green were introduced. Some cases of this period also feature complex applied metal-work, and the backplates were often beautifully engraved. In the Regency period, rosewood became fashionable, and British makers produced a greater variety of case shapes.

Early bracket clocks have square brass dials, typically with an applied chapter ring. The arched dial became increasingly common and decorative from about 1720 and necessitated a taller case, thus producing a more impressive-looking clock. Silvered brass dials were used from c1760, and painted metal dials were introduced between 1780 and 1790. The circular dial is a feature of bracket clocks from the late 18th century and the Regency period. The late 18th century is an interesting transitional period for bracket clocks, with the introduction of the flat brass dial and then the popular round dial.

Unlike longcases, few English bracket clocks were produced in country districts or towns outside London. Some examples exist from East Anglia and the west country but hardly any from the north. Makers such as Adam Travers, who initially worked in Liverpool in the 1770s, tended to move to London once they had established themselves. Edinburgh was an exception, producing from the mid-18th century fine clockmakers such as Andrew Dickie and Alexander Cumming. Many bracket clocks sold in the provinces bear the retailer's name when, in fact, they were made in London. It was only in the 19th century that these clocks were made in large numbers; previously only the wealthy had been able to afford them.

From the 1850s inexpensive bracket or shelf clocks were imported from America. Mass production resulted in cheaper clocks which helped lead to the decline of the English bracket clock.

Ben Wright of Christie's cites early ebony-veneered bracket clocks as the best sellers during the last few years. They began to appear around 1670, contemporary with walnut and olivewood cases. Very often, rather than use expensive ebony, pale fruitwood veneers were used and ebonized, or stained black. Typical features of ebonized bracket clocks include a brass carrying handle, side frets and mounts, and a brass dial with applied chapter ring and spandrels.

Generally less expensive, and a good buy, according to Ben Wright, are the late 18th-century mahogany clocks. Mahogany was used for cases from c1730 until the end of the century and these clocks are usually larger than the walnut or ebony variety. Cases do vary considerably – some are more elaborate than others – but one can buy an attractive mahogany bracket clock made in London c1780 in good condition for around £8,000 ($11,600). Michael Turner of Sotheby's agrees that a mahogany bracket clock in that price range is a good investment. On the whole the smaller ones with good colouring fetch more. Bracket clocks such as these should be cleaned carefully, preferably by a professional. Unfortunately, some restorers have been over zealous, wanting to make the wood look 'as good as new' and thereby destroying the subtlety of the clock's colour. Ideally all clocks should have their original finish and decorative features intact. Considering their age, it is not unusual to come across problems such as missing finials, damaged mouldings or scratched wood. Prices are influenced by condition and by how much restoration they have undergone. Michael Turner cites a beautiful tortoiseshell clock of c1695 at a recent Sotheby's sale which, because the movement had been considerably altered, only made the low estimate of £9,450 ($13,700). If it had been in perfect order without much restoration it could have made between £20,250 ($29,350) and £27,000 ($39,000). If a clock has had a major rebuild it will affect the price, whereas some minor alterations and restorations are acceptable.

In terms of restoration there is obviously a difference between making essential replacements in the correct style and deliberately faking a piece in order to pass it off as original. There are people who try to re-sign a clock with a better maker's name, those who come across an interesting movement and try and case it up, or who find a damaged movement without a dial and have one made, but generally it is unusual for someone to fake an entire bracket clock. The best advice, which applies to buying any type of clock, is to do some research, be vigilant, go to a reputable dealer or auction house, and always use a professional restorer to carry out any cleaning or repairs.

A French Louis XV-style green-lacquered bracket clock, the gilt dial inscribed Balthazard, Paris, the case surmounted by an allegorical figure and outlined with gilt-metal mounts, late 19thC, 38in (96.5cm) high.
£2,900–3,850
$4,200–5,600 ⚒ S(S)

► **An early Victorian mahogany bracket clock,** the enamelled dial inscribed John Bentley, London, 8-day striking movement, on brass ball feet, 21in (53.5cm) high.
£1,900–2,900
$2,700–4,200 ⚒ AG

A George I ebonized striking bracket clock, the dial signed Ed. Bayley, London, twin fusee movement with verge escapement, the scroll-engraved backplate with securing brackets to the case, later mounts and finials, 19in (48.5cm) high.
£2,700–3,500
$3,900–5,000 ⚒ C

► **An ebony single fusee bracket clock,** by John Berry of London, with 8-day movement, c1690, 14in (35.5cm) high.
£8,700–9,700
$12,600–14,000 ⊞ SBA

◄ **An ebonized and gilt-brass mounted quarter chiming bracket clock,** the brass dial with silvered chapter ring, signed J. W. Benson, Ludgate Hill, with subsidiaries for regulation and chime/silent above, the triple fusee movement with anchor escapement striking on gongs, together with matching wall bracket, late 19thC, 43in (109cm) high.
£2,900–3,800
$4,200–5,600 ⚒ P

► **A Victorian brass-inlaid rosewood chiming bracket clock,** the 7in (18cm) dial signed Benson, London, the massive 3 train fusee and chain movement with anchor escapement and chiming on 8 bells and a gong, the front inlaid with brass leaves and stringing, c1885, 29in (73.5cm) high.
£3,850–5,800
$5,600–8,400 ⚒ S

A George II ebonized bracket clock, by John Berry, London, with pull quarter repeat, verge escapement and calendar to the arch, c1720.
£7,000–8,500
$10,200–12,300 ⊞ TCW

A Regency rosewood and brass-inlaid bracket clock, by Brugger, Holborn, London, with 8-day movement.
£1,900–2,900 $2,750–4,200 🔨 Mit

A Regency Gothic mahogany bracket clock, the repainted dial signed Bentley & Beck, Royal Exchange, London, the movement by Handley & Moore, No. 4167, chiming on 8 bells and hour strike on further bell, with strike/silent, anchor escapement with micrometer regulated pendulum, the case with brass and ebony line inlay, adapted, 23in (58.5cm) high.
£5,800–6,750
$8,400–9,800 🔨 C

A Louis XV _première_ and _contre partie_ boulle bracket clock, signed Calon à Paris, stamped with crowned C, the associated cresting with a figure of Victory, lacking trumpet, 48in (122cm) high, with bracket.
£11,500–15,500
$16,700–22,500 🔨 C

An ebonized quarter chiming bracket clock, signed on an inset plaque Dan L. Catlin, Lynn, the 3 train 5 pillar fusee movement now with anchor escapement, with bell striking, chiming the quarters on 6 bells actuated by a pin drum, with pull repeat, c1784, 20in (51cm) high.
£3,850–5,800
$5,600–8,400 🔨 L

A verge bracket clock, by Charles Cabrier of London, with applied gilt spandrels, c1740, 34in (86.5cm) high.
£19,300–28,950
$28,000–42,000 ⊞ SBA

▶ **A George III ebony-veneered striking bracket clock,** the 7in (18cm) brass dial with silvered chapter ring, mock pendulum aperture and date in the matted centre, signed on a plaque between the dials and on backplate Thomas Carrington, London, the movement now with striking train removed and replaced with one at the hour strike, with verge escapement, the case with pineapple finials and carrying handle, 19in (48.5cm) high.
£2,900–3,850
$4,200–5,600 🔨 Bon

A Regency brass-inlaid mahogany bracket clock, with 8in (20.5cm) convex painted dial, signed Brugger, London, the 5 pillar bell striking fusee movement with unusual pin wheel escapement, c1820, 18in (45.5cm) high.
£2,900–3,850
$4,200–5,600 🔨 S

A mahogany bracket clock, with 6½in (16.5cm) brass break-arch dial, signed Rich. Collins, Margate, with silvered chapter ring, date aperture and false pendulum aperture, with strike/silent, the twin fusee movement with verge escapement, c1790, 19in (48.5cm) high.
£5,800–7,700
$8,400–11,000 ⚒ S(S)

An ebony and gilt brass-mounted bracket clock, the brass dial with silvered chapter ring, signed Claudius du Chesne, London, with date aperture and ringed winding holes, with strike/silent, early 18thC, 17½in (44.5cm) high.
£6,500–8,000
$9,400–11,600 ⚒ P

A Victorian ebonized chiming bracket clock, the dial signed Cook Bros, London, on silvered chapter ring with pierced blued hands, Indian mask and foliate spandrels, subsidiary chime/silent ring in the arch, the 5 pillar triple chain fusee movement with anchor escapement chiming on 4 bells with hour strike on gong, pendulum holdfast to the foliate engraved backplate, 36½in (92.5cm) high.
£2,900–3,850
$4,200–5,600 ⚒ C

◄ **A bracket clock,** signed George Davis, Halifax, in ebonized case with gilt-metal mounts and chiming action, 19thC, 24in (61cm) high.
£750–950
$1,100–1,300 ⚒ LRG

A George III ebonized bracket clock, the brass dial with silvered chapter ring and date aperture, signed Thos Clements, London, with subsidiary strike/silent, the twin fusee movement with verge escapement, 19in (48.5cm) high.
£3,850–5,800
$5,600–8,400 ⚒ P

An early Louis XV ormolu-mounted polychrome contre-partie boulle bracket clock, signed on dial and backplate Chastelain à Paris, distressed, 38½in (98cm) high.
£5,800–6,750
$8,400–9,800 ⚒ C

◄ **An ebonized bracket clock,** by Benj. Cotton, repeating on 6 bells, c1760, 22½in (57cm) high.
£4,500–5,500
$6,500–8,000 ⊞ RFA

An early George III mahogany striking bracket clock, the dial signed Ellicott, London, twin fusee movement, ringed pillars, converted to wire lines and anchor escapement, with later hour hand, later additions to feet, 16in (40.5cm) high.
£5,800–7,700
$8,400–11,000 ⚒ C

A George II walnut striking bracket clock, by John Ellicott, London, now converted to anchor escapement, a pull quarter repeat train removed, case with some restoration, 19in (48.5cm) high.
£11,600–15,500
$16,500–22,500 ⚒ C

A George III ebonized bracket clock, the brass dial signed John Ellicott, London, with date aperture and subsidiary strike/silent in the arch, the 5 pillar movement originally with verge escapement and pull quarter repeating, now fitted with deadbeat escapement, 18thC, 20in (51cm) high.
£2,300–2,900
$3,300–4,200 ⚒ P

A double fusee bracket clock, by T. Farr, Bristol, with 8-day movement, hourly strike on the bell, in mahogany with fish-scale brass fretwork, c1830, 16in (40.5cm) high.
£4,800–5,000
$6,950–7,250 ⊞ SBA

A Georgian mahogany bracket clock, the painted dial signed D. Evans, London, with subsidiaries for date and strike/silent, the twin fusee movement now converted to anchor escapement, 20½in (52cm) high.
£2,900–3,850
$4,200–5,600 ⚒ P

A Georgian fruitwood striking bracket clock, the dial inscribed John Ellicott, London, the twin fusee movement now wire lines, with pull quarter repeat on 6 bells, alarm now converted to anchor escapement, 15½in (39.5cm) high.
£6,750–8,700
$9,800–12,600 ⚒ C

◄ **An ebonized bracket clock,** signed on a plate John Ellicott, London, the brass dial with silvered chapter ring and mock pendulum aperture, with subsidiary strike/silent in the arch, the 5 pillared movement with verge escapement and pull quarter repeat on 6 bells, with signed and scroll-engraved backplate, 18thC, 16½in (42cm) high.
£7,700–11,600
$11,000–16,800 ⚒ P

▶ **A George III mahogany striking balloon bracket clock,** the white painted dial signed Evans, Royal Exchange, London, with satinwood crossbanded case and gilt ball and eagle finial to bell top, pierced gilt hands, 5 ringed pillar twin fusee movement, wire lines, with anchor escapement and pendulum holdfast, the similarly signed backplate with securing brackets to case, 33in (84cm) high.
£3,850–5,000
$5,600–7,500 ⚒ C

An ebonized bracket clock, by Thomas Gardner, London, with brass dial, the verge movement with 6 bell quarter repeating movement and strike/silent, with engraved backplate, requires repairing, early 18thC, 18½in (47cm) high.
£4,800–6,750
$7,000–9,800 ⚒ GSP

A George III mahogany verge bracket clock, signed William Gatford, Uxbridge, the twin fusee movement striking and repeating on a bell, c1770, 17in (43cm) high.
£12,000–15,000
$17,400–22,000 ⊞ DRA

A George III mahogany bracket clock, the enamelled dial signed Gardner, London, the fusee movement converted to anchor escapement, 15in (38cm) high.
£5,000–6,750
$7,250–9,800 ⚒ P

An ebonized and brass-inlaid bracket clock, signed below the chapter ring Gillett & Co, Croydon, the gong striking movement with twin fusees, with presentation inscription dated October 1892, c1890, 27½in (70cm) high.
£2,900–3,850
$4,200–5,600 ⚒ S(S)

A mahogany and brass-inlaid bracket clock, the painted dial signed Thos. Glaze, Bridgnorth, with twin fusee movement and anchor escapement, 19thC, 19in (48.5cm) high, with wall bracket.
£2,900–3,850
$4,200–5,600 ⚒ P

A Regency mahogany bracket clock, the white enamelled dial inscribed Gibbs, London, 8-day bell striking fusee movement, 20in (51cm) high.
£3,850–5,000
$5,600–7,000 ⚒ P(S)

▶ **A late Victorian walnut-cased chiming bracket clock,** with silvered chapter ring and ormolu dial, stamped Goldsmiths Co, Regent St, London, 35in (89cm) high including bracket.
£2,900–3,850
$4,200–5,600 ⚒ GM

◀ **A walnut-cased bracket clock,** by Garrard, the dial with silvered chapter ring and gilt metal mask spandrels, with Westminster chimes movement, c1920, 15½in (39.5cm) high.
£800–1,200
$1,150–1,750 ⚒ GAK

◄ **A mahogany striking bracket clock,** the 8in (20.5cm) white painted dial with subsidiary date, strike/silent in the arch, with anchor escapement, the backplate signed Green, Liverpool, 20½in (52cm) high.
£2,900–3,850
$4,200–5,600 ⚒ Bon

A green-painted and gilt bronze bracket clock, the dial signed Guiot A Paris, the movement with anchor escapement and outside numbered countwheel, c1720, 39in (99cm) high.
£3,850–5,000
$5,600–7,000 ⚒ S

A Regency mahogany bracket clock, the painted dial signed P. Grimalde, London, the twin fusee movement with arched plates and engraved border, with anchor escapement, 17in (43cm) high.
£3,850–5,000
$5,600–7,000 ⚒ P

A Regency fruitwood striking bracket clock, signed John Harper, 65 Goswell Street, London, with blued steel pierced spade hands, the 5 pillar twin fusee movement with anchor escapement, with steel suspended calibrated pendulum, strike on bell, with border engraved securing brackets to case, 16½in (42cm) high.
£1,950–2,900
$2,800–4,200 ⚒ C

A George III ebonized striking bracket clock, signed Haley & Son, London, the dial with white enamel chapter disc and blued steel hands, the 5 pillar twin fusee movement now wire lines, with anchor escapement, adapted and associated, 13½in (34.5cm) high.
£3,850–4,800
$5,600–7,000 ⚒ C

An ebony cased bracket clock, with 7in (18cm) brass dial, inscribed Robert Halsted, London, the 5 pillar 8-day movement with anchor escapement and chain fusee gong and striking the hours on a bell, restored and altered, early 18thC, 13½in (34.5cm) high.
£3,850–5,000
$5,600–7,000 ⚒ Bea

A George III mahogany stiking bracket clock, the dial signed John Green, London, with false pendulum and calendar apertures, pierced blued hands, foliate scroll spandrels, subsidiary strike/silent ring to the arch, the 5 pillar twin gut fusee movement with anchor escapement, restored and possibly associated, 23in (58.5cm) high.
£3,850–5,000
$5,600–7,000 ⚒ C

A bird's-eye maple four-glass mantel clock, by William Hardy, with fusee movement, 8-day duration, c1830, 11in (28cm) high.
£1,550–2,300 $2,250–3,350 ⊞ SO

A Regency ebonized bracket clock, signed Handley & Moore, London, the white painted dial with Roman numerals and subsidiary date ring, with strike/ silent ring in the arch, the 8-day repeating fusee movement striking on a bell, with engraved borders to the backplates, the pendulum with lock, 16in (40.5cm) high.
£1,950–2,900
$2,800–4,200 ⚒ CSK

An ebonized bracket timepiece, signed Jeffery Harris, London, the 5 pillar movement with verge escapement, 18thC, 17in (43cm) high.
£3,850–5,000 $5,600–7,000 ⚒ P

► **An ebonized bracket clock,** by Wm. Hatton, 12in (30.5cm) high.
£1,950–2,900
$2,800–4,200 ⊞ SBA

◄ **An ebonized bracket clock,** the dial inscribed Robert Henderson, London, with automaton depicting 4 blacksmiths with moving arms in the arch, with verge movement, 18thC, 18½in (47cm) high.
£9,650–13,500
$14,000–19,600 ⊞ PWC

◄ **An ebonized bracket clock,** the 6in (15cm) brass dial signed Robt. Henderson, London, with date aperture and strike/silent, the movement with verge escapement, c1760, 16in (40.5cm) high.
£3,850–5,000
$5,600–7,000 ⚒ S

► **A William IV mahogany bracket clock,** the white dial inscribed Henderson, Brigg, with 8-day single fusee non-striking movement, 19½in (49.5cm) high.
£950–1,350
$1,380–1,950 ⚒ DDM

◄ **A late Stuart ebonized striking bracket clock,** the 7in (18cm) dial signed John Harris, London, the striking movement with 5 ringed pillars, pull quarter repeat on 5 bells and now converted to anchor escapement, 14½in (37cm) high.
£11,600–15,500
$16,800–22,500 ⚒ C

A Queen Anne ebony-veneered table clock, signed Jacobus Hassenuis, Londini, on engraved backplate, calendar aperture and strike/not strike lever above XII, 6 pillar bell striking fusee movement, with verge escapement, c1705, 13in (33cm) high.
£8,700–9,650
$12,600–14,000 ⚒ S

A George II ebonized bracket clock, the 7in (18cm) dial signed in the stopped pendulum aperture Geo Hide, with calendar aperture, the 5 pillar movement with rack and bell striking and now with anchor escapement, in an inverted bell top case, shell and leaf cast brass door frets and ball-and-claw feet, one pillar missing, c1740, 19in (48.5cm) high.
£1,950–2,900
$2,800–4,200 🔨 S(S)

A George III ebonized striking bracket clock, signed Hindley, York, the movement with 6 baluster pillars to the arched plates, inverted chain fusees, rack strike, now incomplete, quarter repeat on 2 bells, anchor escapement, some alterations, 21in (53.5cm) high.
£5,000–9,650
$7,250–14,000 🔨 C

A William & Mary ebonized striking bracket clock, the 8in (20.5cm) square dial signed A. L. Irving, London, with cast gilt mask and foliate sound frets to the sides and foliate handle to basket top, with later finials, on later turned brass feet, 16½in (42cm) high.
£3,850–4,800
$5,600–7,000 🔨 C

An ebonized fruitwood bracket clock, with white enamel Arabic dial, brass fish-scale sound frets to the sides, the fusee with verge escapement striking a bell, the foliate incised backplate signed Holliwell & Son, Derby, 18thC, 7in (18cm) high.
£2,900–3,500
$4,200–5,600 🔨 C

A George III ebonized musical bracket clock, by Charles Howse, London, the enamelled and brass dial with chime/ not chime and gavot/hornpipe/air/gavot/ song/cotillion, the 8-day 3 train fusee movement with a 3in (7.5cm) cylinder and 13 bells, 2 repeat pulls, 19in (48.5cm) high.
£7,700–11,600
$11,000–16,800 🔨 E
Charles Howse produced clocks at 5 Great Tower Street between 1768 and 1794, and was Master of the Clockmakers Company in 1787.

An Irish bracket clock, the arched brass and silvered dial inscribed Chas. Hull, Dublin, the single fusee movement with anchor escapement and rise and fall to the pendulum, with an engraved backplate, late 18thC.
£2,900–3,850
$4,200–5,600 🔨 WW

◄ **A Regency mahogany bracket clock,** the white painted dial with Roman numerals signed Hyman Dass & Co, Louth, with a single fusee non-striking 8-day movement, with a fluted pediment, brass-inlaid dial surround on platform base, the case with gilded metal ring handles and pineapple finial, together with a mahogany wall bracket, 18½in (47cm) high.
£1,150–1,550
$1,650–2,250 🔨 DDM

A brass Atmos bracket clock, by Jaeger-LeCoultre, inscribed 'Cary (Grant) – Because of you we have each other Rosalind (Russell) and Freddie (Brisson), 10.25.41', 9in (23cm) high.
£950–1,550
$1,380–2,250 🔨 P(G)

A mahogany bracket clock, inscribed George Jamison, Charing Cross, London, with strike/silent dial and subsidiary seconds, 2 train movement, early 19thC, 20½in (52cm) high.
£3,850–5,000 $5,600–7,000 ⚒ HAM

A bracket clock, by Johnson, Grays Inn Passage, the brass dial with silvered-brass chapter ring, spandrels and strike/silent to the arch, the 8-day movement striking the hours on a bell and repeating at will, the verge escapement with bob pendulum and with backplate engraved with maker's name, in mahogany broken-arched case, c1775, 15in (38cm) high.
£7,000–8,000
$10,200–11,600 ⊞ PAO

An ebonized musical table clock, with 8in (20.5cm) foliate engraved silvered dial signed Johnson, London, in the arch below a tune selection dial, the bell-top case with flambeau finials, scale side frets and bracket feet, c1790, 20in (51cm) high.
£5,000–7,700
$7,250–11,150 ⚒ S

An early Victorian mahogany bracket timepiece, signed Wm. Johnson, 4 Hercules Passage, Stock Exchange, London, within foliate engraving, 10½in (26.5cm) high.
£1,350–1,950
$2,000–2,800 ⚒ C

A Charles II ebonized striking bracket clock, the 6in (15cm) dial signed Joseph Knibb, London, with finely pierced and sculpted blued steel hands, the matted centre with calendar aperture and foliate spandrels, the movement with latches to the 5 pillars of tapering baluster form, with rebuilt knife edge verge escapement, twin fusees and wire lines, with numbered countwheel strike on bell via Knibb's pulley system, the phase II case with handle and gilt-metal foliate mount to the cushion moulded top, 12in (30.5cm) high.
£28,950–38,600
$41,950–55,950 ⚒ C

A Regency mahogany bracket clock, with 8in (20.5cm) silvered dial signed Joseph Johnson, Liverpool, twin fusee movement with pull repeat and engraved backplate, with pierced gilt hands, 17in (43cm) high.
£1,950–2,900
$2,800–4,200 ⚒ S

An ebonized bracket clock, the silvered dial with foliate scroll engraved spandrels, inscribed Kleyser & Co, 66 High St., Southwark, London, the bell striking fusee movement with pull repeat, 19thC, 12½in (32cm) high.
£1,550–1,950
$2,250–2,800 ⚒ P(S)

▶ **A mahogany fusee bracket clock,** by John Kemp, Oxford, with silvered-brass dial incorporating strike/silent in the arch, strikes the hour on a bell and repeats at will, the original verge movement with engraved backplate, c1790.
£3,000–4,000
$4,400–5,800 ⊞ PAO

A Regency ebonized break-arch brass-inlaid bracket clock, the dial signed H. Knight, numbered 2243, the 2 train movement striking and repeating on a bell, with strike/silent regulation, 17in (43cm) high.
£2,250–2,500
$3,250–3,600 ⊞ DRA

A French bracket clock, veneered with arabesque green boulle, supplied by Lee & Son, Belfast, mid-19thC, 12in (30.5cm) high.
£950–1,150 $1,380–1,650 ⚒ HSS

A George III bracket clock, the 8-day repeater movement with silvered dial and ormolu spandrels, inscribed De Lasalle, London, in a mahogany case with brass loop handle on arched moulded top, grille sides, glazed back revealing chased backplate, moulded base and bracket feet, 18½in (47cm) high.
£5,800–9,000
$8,400–14,000 ⚒ AH

A Regency brass-inlaid rosewood bracket clock, by Benjamin Lautier, Bath, the 8-day movement with double fusee, early 19thC, 17½in (44.5cm) high.
£6,750–8,700
$9,800–12,600 ⚒ AGr

A Regency mahogany lancet bracket clock, by In. Lamb, London, with brass inlay, silver dial with strike, on 4 brass feet, 19½in (49.5cm) high.
£1,950–2,900 $2,800–4,200 ⚒ IM

A George III mahogany striking bracket clock, the painted dial signed Leplastrier, London, with pierced blued hands, the 5 pillar twin fusee movement with anchor escapement, 15in (38cm) high.
£4,800–5,800
$7,000–8,400 ⚒ C

An ebonized balloon bracket clock, signed J. Leroux, London, the fusee movement with verge escapement, late 18thC, 19in (48.5cm) high.
£2,900–3,500 $4,200–5,600 ⚒ L

An ebonized bracket clock, the 6½in (16.5cm) brass square dial inscribed Jonathan Lowndes, Pall Mall, London, the double fusee movement with stop work, crown wheel escapement, striking the hours on a single bell and chiming the quarters on 2 graduated bells, 18thC, 16in (40.5cm) high.
£13,500–15,500
$19,500–22,500 ⚒ HSS

A George III ebonized bracket clock, inscribed Philip Lloyd, Bristol, the bell striking repeating movement with anchor escapement, 21in (53.5cm) high.
£2,900–3,500 $4,200–5,600 ⊞ PWC

A late Louis XIV scarlet boulle miniature bracket clock, the silvered chapter ring signed Margotin à Paris, the sides with Bérainesque panels inlaid with pewter and brass, the movement with shaped plates, rack strike and now converted to anchor escapement, later canopy and finial figure, c1800, 14½in (37cm) high.
£2,000–2,900
$2,800–4,200 🔨 **C**

A mahogany and brass-inlaid bracket clock, the 7in (18cm) enamelled dial signed Marriott, London, the associated twin fusee movement quarter striking on 2 bells, early 19thC, 14½in (37cm) high.
£2,000–2,900
$2,800–4,200 🔨 **S(S)**

A George III mahogany striking bracket clock, the painted dial signed Thos. Logan, Maybole, with Roman and Arabic chapters, pierced blued hands and calendar aperture, the spandrels painted with wild roses and strawberries, the 4 pillar twin fusee movement with knife edge verge escapement and strike on bell, the similarly signed backplate with centrally engraved Prince of Wales' feathers, 20in (51cm) high.
£5,000–6,000
$7,000–9,800 🔨 **C**

A George III mahogany bracket clock, the 6¾in (17cm) dial signed Jno. Matthews, Leighton, with leaf spandrels and a strike/silent dial in the arch, c1800, 15½in (39.5cm) high.
£4,800–5,800
$7,000–8,400 🔨 **S**

An ebonized fruitwood bracket clock, the brass dial with silvered Roman and Arabic chapter ring enclosing a matted centre, the fusee movement with pull repeat, anchor escapement striking a bell, the foliate engraved backplate signed Jacobus Markwick, Londini, with pendulum and key, mid-18thC, 11in (28cm) high.
£8,700–9,650
$12,600–14,000 🔨 **C**

A George III mahogany musical bracket clock, the dial with original cream-painted Roman and Arabic chapter disc, signed Marriott, Fleet Street, the upper spandrels with subsidiary dials for chime/silent and 6 tune selection, the arch with a later painted cut-out of Chronos automated to the escapement, the 6 pillar triple fusee, chain lines, movement now with anchor escapement, the music playing on a nest of 9 bells with hour strike on a further bell, 26in (66cm) high.
£8,700–9,650
$12,600–14,000 🔨 **C**

Hints on dating Bracket Clocks

Dials

Square dial	to c1760	pre-George III
Break-arch dial	from c1720	George I or later
Round/painted/silvered	from c1760	George III or later

Case finish

Ebony veneer	from c1660 to c1850	Carolean to mid-Victorian
Walnut	from c1670 to c1870	Carolean to Victorian
Marquetry	from c1680 to c1740	Carolean to early Georgian
Rosewood	from c1790	from mid-Georgian
Lacquered	from c1700 to c1760	Queen Anne to early Georgian
Mahogany	from c1730	from early Georgian

A Regency mahogany striking bracket clock, the glazed painted dial signed James McCabe, Royal Exchange, London, 1410, with brass-lined quarter mouldings, pierced Breguet hands and strike/silent above XII, 19½in (49.5cm) high.
£3,850–5,800
$5,600–8,400 ⚒ C

A mahogany bracket clock, the 9½in (24cm) silvered dial signed James McCabe, Royal Exchange, London, with moon hands and strike/silent at XII, the twin chain fusee movement gong striking and with signed backplate, the case with outline leafy scrolls and pierced foliate rear door, c1840, 22in (56cm) high.
£2,900–3,500
$4,200–5,600 ⚒ ALL

◄ **A bracket clock,** by Moginie of Pimlico, with painted dial and raised brass decoration to the front, the 2 train movement striking and repeating on a bell, with brass carrying handles and surmounted by a brass ball finial, c1830, 20½in (51cm) high.
£3,500–4,000
$5,000–5,800 ⊞ DRA

A mahogany quarter striking bracket clock, the repainted dial signed Jas. McCabe, London, the signed twin fusee movement with shaped plates and anchor escapement chiming on 8 bells, the movement with some alterations, together with a brass-mounted mahogany wall bracket with sliding base, 19thC, 32in (81.5cm) high.
£1,950–2,900
$2,800–4,200 ⚒ P

A Regency brass-mounted mahogany bracket clock, the painted dial signed James Murray, Royal Exchange, London, the movement with anchor escapement, 19½in (49.5cm) high.
£2,900–5,800
$4,200–8,400 ⚒ P

► **A mahogany bracket clock,** by Wm. Morgan, London, with silvered chapter ring, double fusee movement and strikes on a bell, with glass side panels, c1760, 17in (43cm) high.
£7,700–9,500
$11,000–14,000 ⚒ IM

A Regency mahogany bracket clock, the painted convex dial signed Jas. McCabe, Royal Exchange, London, No. 881, with strike/silent lever above, similarly signed fusee and chain movement No. 6084, with anchor escapement, bell striking, pull repeat, c1820, 16in (40.5cm) high.
£1,950–2,900
$2,800–4,200 ⚒ S

An ebony and gilt-brass-mounted bracket clock, the 7in (18cm) brass dial signed J. Mondehare, Londini Fecit, the 5 tulip pillared movement with latched dial and plates, with replaced verge escapement and pull quarter repeating on 3 bells, 18thC, 15in (38cm) high.
£11,600–15,500
$16,800–22,500 ⚒ P

A red-lacquered and chinoiserie-decorated bracket clock, inscribed Wm. Page, London, converted to anchor escapement, 18thC, 18in (45.5cm) high.
£4,800–6,000
$7,000–9,800 ⚒ P

A George III mahogany bracket clock, the arched brass dial signed John Newton, London, with subsidiary strike/silent ring to the arch, the movement with verge escapement and bob pendulum, and an associated oak bracket, c1790, 16½in (42cm) high.
£8,700–9,650
$12,600–14,000 ⚒ N

A Continental ebonized striking bracket clock, the 6½in (16.5cm) dial with Roman and arabic chapter ring now signed E. Norton, London, plain steel hands, the pounced centre with mock pendulum aperture engraved I.G.E. on the background, lacking alarm disc in the centre, the 4 pillar single going barrel movement with strike on bell above, verge escapement with crown wheel extended above the plates, pull wind alarm, early 18thC, 14in (35.5cm) high.
£1,350–1,750
$2,000–2,500 ⚒ C

A Regency mahogany bracket timepiece, by John Nicholls, London, converted to anchor escapement, c1770, 15in (38cm) high.
£3,500–4,000
$5,000–5,500 ⊞ BL

◀ **A George III mahogany bracket clock,** by S. Norris, London, with painted dial, 8-day duration, 15in (38cm) high.
£4,800–6,000
$7,000–9,800 ⊞ SBA

▶ **A mahogany bracket alarm clock,** by Perigal, Coventry Street, London, c1775, 9½in (24cm) high.
£8,000–9,000
$11,600–13,000 ⊞ TCW

A late Victorian oak quarter chiming bracket clock, the dial signed Parkinson & Frodsham, Exchange Alley, London, with Gothic chapter ring and blued fleur-de-lys hands, subsidiary rings above for chime/silent regulation, the chime on 8 bells/Westminster chimes, the 5 pillar twin chain fusee movement with anchor escapement, 39in (99cm) high.
£2,900–3,500
$4,200–5,600 ⚷ C

A late Victorian oak quarter chiming bracket clock, the dial signed Joseph Penlington, Liverpool, within the Arabic chapter ring, with blued hands, subsidiary rings above for chime/silent regulation and chime on 8 bells/Westminster chimes, the 5 pillar triple chain fusee movement with anchor escapement and chime on 8 bells or 4 gongs with hour strike on further gong, pendulum securing piece to the plain backplate, 33½in (85cm) high.
£1,950–2,900
$2,800–4,200 ⚷ C

An Edwardian bracket clock, inscribed Pearce & Sons, Leeds, with 8-day chiming movement, the chased and brass dial with silvered chapter ring, 18in (45.5cm) high.
£1,950–2,900
$2,800–4,200 ⚷ AH

A late George III mahogany miniature bracket timepiece alarm, the engraved silvered dial signed Perigal, Coventry Street, London, with central alarm disc, chain fusee movement with verge escapement, pull wind alarm on bell, 9½in (24cm) high.
£4,800–6,750
$7,000–9,800 ⚷ C

An ebonized bracket clock, signed John Pepys, London, with striking brass movement, anchor escapement and engraved backplate, on brass ball feet, with pendulum and key, 18thC, 16in (40.5cm) high.
£2,900–4,800
$4,200–6,500 ⚷ RID

A Louis XV ormolu-mounted poly-chrome boulle bracket clock, stamped A. G. Peridiez, with glazed enamel dial, the bracket with floral spray and pierced foliate boss, 42½in (108cm) high.
£7,700–11,600
$11,000–16,800 ⚷ C

◄ **A George III ebonized quarter chiming bracket clock,** the brass dial signed Perigal, London, with moonphases, fusee movement with verge escapement, striking the quarters on 8 bells, 21in (53.5cm) high.
£8,700–11,600
$12,600–16,800 ⚷ P

A Regency mahogany bracket clock, with 4in (10cm) enamel dial and brass hands, the 5 pillar fusee movement signed Perigal & Duterrau, London, with shouldered stepped plates bordered by engraving, the front plate stamped Thwaites and numbered 4835, c1812, 11½in (29cm) high.
£1,750–2,300
$2,500–3,300 ⚒ S

A Regency bracket clock, by Perigal & Duterrau, Bond Street, London, the circular painted dial with Roman numerals, the twin fusee repeating movement striking on a bell, in brass-mounted mahogany case, on ball feet, 16in (40.5cm) high.
£3,800–4,800
$5,500–7,000 ⚒ Bea

A late Regency rosewood striking bracket clock, the engraved silvered dial signed in the arch G. Philcox Patentee, London, No. 13, with blued Breguet hands, the 4 pillar twin fusee movement with shaped plates and anchor escapement, with brass-inlaid side angles, on wood bun feet, 11½in (29cm) high.
£1,950–2,900
$2,800–4,200 ⚒ C

An ebonized bracket clock, the dial inscribed Chris Pinchbeck Senior, London, with automaton in the arch, the 6 pillar hour striking fusee movement with original verge escapement, 6 bell pull quarter repeat, 18thC, 21½in (54.5cm) high.
£9,650–15,500
$14,000–22,500 ⊞ PWC

A mahogany bracket clock, the 7½in (19cm) silvered break-arch dial signed John Pollard, Plymouth Dock, with date aperture, strike/silent dial in the arch, the 5 pillar movement with twin fusees and verge escapement, c1795, 20in (51cm) high.
£4,800–6,750
$7,000–9,800 ⚒ S(S)

A Regency walnut cased bracket clock, by Raw Brothers, 31 Duke Street, Grosvenor Square, London, with double chain fusee movement.
£1,150–1,550
$1,700–2,250 ⚒ M

◀ **A gilt-brass-mounted ebonized musical bracket clock,** the 8in (20.5cm) dial with silvered and patterned chapter ring, with calendar aperture to the matted centre, the arch inset with a plaque signed Prior, London, below a tune selection arc and flanked by subsidiary dials for strike/silent and chime/silent, the 3 train fusee and chain movement with verge escapement, bell striking and playing one of the 4 tunes at every hour, or at will, on 10 bells, c1780, 24in (61cm) high.
£11,600–15,500
$16,800–22,500 ⚒ S

A George III ebonized bracket clock, the 8in (20.5cm) silvered dial signed Wm. Ray, Sudbury, with central calendar and strike/silent dial in the arch, the 5 pillar bell striking repeating fusee movement with deadbeat escapement, c1800, 17½in (44.5cm) high.
£2,900–3,850
$4,200–5,600 ⚒ S

A mahogany bracket clock, the 5in (12.5cm) painted dial signed Robt. Roskell, Liverpool, with alarm dial in the arch, similarly signed fusee movement with anchor escapement, pull/wind alarm and engraved border to the backplate, c1820, 13in (33cm) high.
£1,950–2,900
$2,800–4,200 ⚒ S

An early Victorian brass-inlaid mahogany striking bracket clock, signed Smith, St. Peters, with glazed brass bezel to the cream painted Roman dial and with blued spade hands, the 5 pillar twin fusee movement with anchor escapement and strike/trip repeat on bell, with plain backplate, lacking feet, 20½in (52cm) high.
£2,900–3,850
$4,200–5,600 ⚒ C

A George III faded mahogany striking bracket clock, the 7in (18cm) dial signed John Rycutt, London, the matted centre with false pendulum and date aperture, with silvered chapter rings and strike/silent in the arch, the 5 pillar fusee movement with verge escapement, 8in (45.5cm) high.
£8,700–11,600
$12,600–16,800 ⚒ Bon

A mahogany bracket clock, by Edward Scales, London, the brass dial with date and strike/silent, the 8-day movement with verge escapement, striking the hour on a bell, engraved backplate, c1765.
£11,500–12,500
$16,700–18,000 ⊞ PAO

A bracket clock in a mahogany case, the brass and silvered dial signed Wm. Smith, London, c1770.
£9,000–11,000
$13,000–16,000 ⊞ HOL

▶ **A walnut bracket timepiece,** signed Smallwood, Litchfield, the ringed pillar movement with verge escapement, pull quarter repeat, now missing, 18thC, 18in (45.5cm) high.
£2,900–3,850
$4,200–5,600 ⚒ P

◀ **A George III mahogany bracket clock,** inscribed John Scott, London, the brass and silver dial with subsidiary month and strike/silent regulation, the centre with bob aperture and calendar, the 8-day movement with verge escapement, engraved backplate, bob pendulum, 15½in (39.5cm) high.
£7,700–9,650
$11,000–14,000 ⚒ WW

An Austrian ebonized bracket clock, with 7in (18cm) dial signed Johan Schreibmayr, Wien, and 2 selection dials, with dummy pendulum and date aperture, the triple train fusee movement with *grande sonnerie* striking on 2 bells, the case with caddy top, c1770.
£2,900–3,850
$4,200–5,600 ⚒ S(S)

A walnut bracket clock, signed Wm. Smith, London, with 8in (20.5cm) brass dial, silvered chapter ring and matted centre, the movement with replaced verge escapement, pull repeat, c1770, 20in (51cm) high.
£7,700–9,650
$11,000–14,000 ➤ S(S)

A George II green-lacquered striking bracket clock, the dial signed Ralph Tolson, London, with mock pendulum and calendar aperture, silvered chapter ring and pierced blued steel hands, the arch with strike/silent ring, the 5 pillar movement with twin fusees, wire lines, knife edge verge escapement, 18½in (47cm) high.
£2,900–5,800
$4,200–8,400 ➤ C

An inlaid mahogany bracket clock, by Thompson, Ashford, with 6in (15cm) square dial, 8-day striking movement, 24in (61cm) high.
£600–800
$850–1,200 ⊞ V

A George III bracket clock, signed Tinker and Edmondson, Leeds, the brass and silvered dial with an automaton, the 8-day striking double fusee movement with anchor escapement, c1800, 22½in (57cm) high.
£6,750–8,700
$9,800–12,600 ➤ DN

A George III ebonized bracket clock, the brass dial engraved Jasper Taylor, Holborn, London, the 5 pillar movement with verge escapement, hour strike and engraved backplate, 16in (40.5cm) high.
£4,500–6,000
$6,500–8,700 ⊞ IAT

▶ **A mahogany bracket clock,** by John Tucker, Exeter, with silvered arched dial, the 8-day movement with verge escapement, 19thC, 20in (51cm) high.
£1,950–2,900
$2,800–4,200 ➤ E

A Regency brass-inlaid mahogany and ebonized striking bracket clock, the painted dial signed Trendell, Reading, with blued spade hands, the 5 pillar twin fusee, wire lines, movement with anchor escapement and strike on bell, 17in (43cm) high.
£2,900–3,850
$4,200–5,600 ➤ C

◀ **A Georgian mahogany bracket clock,** by W. Tomlinson, London, with silvered dial, date dial and phases of the moon to the arch, the 8-day movement with repeat mechanism, 15in (38cm) high.
£11,600–13,500
$16,800–19,600 ➤ AG

A George III mahogany bracket clock, signed W. Turnbull, Darlington, with mock pendulum and twin chain fusee movement, 19½in (49.5cm) high.
£8,700–10,600
$12,600–15,500 ⚲ C

A Regency mahogany bracket clock, the 8in (20.5cm) dial inscribed T. Verley, Fakenham, c1825.
£1,350–1,750 $2,000–2,500 ⚲ GAK

A Regency mahogany bracket clock, with white painted dial, signed Viner, London, the twin fusee with anchor escapement, 10in (25.5cm) high.
£5,800–7,700
$8,400–11,000 ⚲ C

A George III ebonized quarter striking bracket clock, by Justin Vulliamy, London, with verge escapement, 14½in (37cm) high.
£10,000–15,000
$14,500–22,000 ⚲ C

A mahogany bracket clock, by Vulliamy, London, with gilt embellishment, 8-day duration, hourly strike on bell/pull repeat strike, c1830, 15in (38cm) high.
£4,000–6,000
$5,800–8,700 ⊞ SBA

A Regency mahogany bracket clock, in Egyptian style, by John Wakefield, London, the 8-day fusee movement with anchor escapement and striking hours on a bell, c1820.
£6,000–7,000 $8,700–10,200 ⊞ PAO

A George III mahogany striking bracket clock, the dial signed Thos. Wagstaffe, London, the twin fusee movement with verge escapement, 19in (48.5cm) high.
£8,700–10,600 $12,600–15,000 ⚲ C

A miniature ebony bracket clock, by Samuel Watson, London, with 14-day duration, c1680, 13in (33cm) high.
£9,650–11,600 $14,000–16,800 ⊞ SBA

An ebonized verge bracket clock, by Wasborn, London, with date aperture and 2 train striking movement, c1740, 15in (38cm) high.
£10,000–11,000
$14,500–16,000 ⊞ DRA

A rosewood and brass-inlaid bracket clock, signed T. J. Wood, Barbican, London, the painted dial set within a pierced and engraved mask, the 5 pillar bell striking fusee movement with anchor escapement and signed backplate, c1850, 16in (40.5cm) high.
£4,850–6,750
$7,000–9,800 ⚒ S(S)

A mahogany bracket clock, the 7in (18cm) arched brass dial signed on a shield Widenham, London, with scroll spandrels, twin fusee bell striking movement, the case in the style of the late 18thC, c1850, 15in (38cm) high.
£2,300–2,900
$3,350–4,200 ⚒ S(S)

▶ **A Regency rosewood-veneered bracket clock,** by Thomas Woolfield, Liverpool, the 6in (15cm) white dial with matching steel hands, the 8-day duration double fusee movement striking the hours on a bell and repeating, c1820, 14in (35.5cm) high.
£6,000–7,000
$8,700–10,200 ⊞ PAO

▶ **A George III musical ormolu-mounted mahogany bracket clock,** signed S. Williams, London, the 3 train chain fusee movement with anchor escapement, chiming on 9 bells and 9 hammers, with chime selector in the arch for Song, Minuet, Cotillion and Air, 20in (51cm) high.
£8,700–11,600
$12,600–16,800 ⚒ L

A Georgian walnut bracket clock, signed Sam Whichcote, London, with verge escapement, 19in (48.5cm) high.
£5,000–9,650
$7,250–14,000 ⚒ P

▶ **An Edwardian bracket clock,** with fusee movement.
£2,000–2,800
$2,900–4,000 ⊞ CLC

A Victorian ormolu-mounted mahogany bracket clock, strike/silent, chime selection and anchor escapement, 27in (68.5cm) high.
£2,900–3,850 $4,200–5,600 ⚒ Wor

A late Victorian chiming bracket clock, with 7½in (19cm) dial and subsidiary dials for chime/silent and chime selection for Westminster/8 bells/ 10 bells, the movement with a further 4 gongs and one other for the hour, 28in (71cm) high.
£3,850–4,850
$5,600–7,000 ⚒ Bea

A South German automaton quarter striking bracket clock, with painted dial, the 3 train skeletonized movement striking the quarters on 2 bells, with nun appearing at the quarters and monk at the hours, late 19thC, 30in (76cm) high.
£2,900–3,850
$4,200–5,600 ⚒ CSK

An ebonized and inlaid bracket clock, the white enamel dial with gilt brass engraving, flowers and scrolling foliate, the wire gong striking 8-day movement with side winding, 19thC, 16in (40.5cm) high.
£4,850–6,750
$7,000–9,800 ⚒ P(S)

A mahogany bracket clock, with 7in (18cm) arched brass dial, the triple chain fusee movement quarter chiming on coil gongs, the case carved with leafy scrolls, c1900, 21in (53.5cm) high.
£2,900–3,850
$4,200–5,600 ⚒ S(S)

▶ **A rosewood and inlaid bracket clock,** with circular silvered dial, wire gong striking movement and rounded arch pediment, c1890, 14½in (37cm) high.
£1,350–1,550
$1,950–2,250 ⚒ P(S)

A Victorian walnut quarter chiming bracket clock, with subsidiaries at the top for chime/silent regulation and Westminster/8 bells, the triple fusee movement with anchor escapement, 31in (78.5cm) high.
£2,900–3,850
$4,200–5,600 ⚒ P

◀ **A Victorian oak chiming bracket clock,** the dial with silvered chapter ring, matted centre and subsidiary rings in the arch for regulation, with chime/silent and chime on 8 bells/Westminster chime, the triple chain fusee movement with anchor escapement and chiming on 8 bells with hour strike on gong, 24in (61cm) high.
£1,950–2,900
$2,800–4,200 ⚒ C

A brass-mounted mahogany bracket clock, the French 8-day movement with half-hour striking on gongs, late 19thC, 17½in (44.5cm) high.
£600–700
$870–1,000 ⊞ TKN

A late Victorian chiming bracket clock, the arched brass and silvered dial with subsidiary dials for chime/silent and chime on 8 bells/Cambridge chimes, the repeating movement chiming on the quarter hours, in gilt-brass-mounted ebonized case, 24in (61cm) high.
£2,900–4,250
$4,200–6,000 ⚒ Bea

A late Victorian 3 train brass-inlaid rosewood bracket clock with matching bracket, the fusee movement chiming the quarters on 8 bells and striking the hours on a gong, with Cambridge/Westminster selector, 43in (109cm) high.
£4,850–6,750
$7,000–9,800 ⚒ TEN

A mid-Victorian bracket clock, with 8-day movement, Whittington and Westminster chimes, 25in (63.5cm) high.
£1,950–2,900
$2,800–4,200 ⚒ DSH

A French red boulle bracket clock, with 12-piece enamel cartouche dial, gong striking movement with anchor escapement, the waisted case veneered with brass and tortoiseshell, outlined with ormolu mounts, putto finial, c1880, 16in (40.5cm) high.
£1,550–1,950
$2,250–2,800 ⚒ S

A satinwood bracket clock, the 8-day repeating 3 train movement with 6 screwed plate pillars, striking the quarters on a choice of 4 or 8 bells with a gong for the hour, 21in (53.5cm) high.
£3,000–4,000
$4,400–5,800 ⊞ PAO

◄ **A Victorian bracket clock,** with rosewood case and ormolu mountings, chime on bells and Westminster, c1880, 30in (76cm) high.
£4,250–5,400
$6,150–7,800 ⚒ FHF

▶ **A Regency brass-inlaid mahogany bracket clock,** with 8in (20.5cm) painted dial, the fusee and chain movement with anchor escapement, c1815, 19in (48.5cm) high.
£1,350–1,950
$2,000–2,800 ⚒ S

Dating Bracket Clocks

Bracket clocks were developed from c1660, roughly the same time as longcase clocks. Many makers of longcases probably also made bracket clocks, and developments in the style, shape and size of both cases and dials largely follow the longcase pattern. Woods used include ebony, walnut, mahogany and rosewood. Some cases also feature lacquer decoration or complex applied metalwork.

Early bracket clocks have a square brass dial, typically with an applied chapter ring (the ring on the dial, on which the hours and minutes are engraved, attached or painted). The arched dial became increasingly common from c1715.

Silvered brass dials were used from c1760 and painted dials from c1780. The round dial, sometimes enamelled, is a feature of bracket clocks from the late 18thC and the Regency period.

In the 1840s, the advent of the American bracket, or shelf clock, with its mass-produced stamped components, led to the gradual decline of the English bracket clock. Mass-production meant that American clocks were considerably less expensive than English ones.

Both American and European bracket clocks are popular today, and French bracket clocks in particular represent good value for money.

Walnut c1675
19in (48cm) high

Ebony c1665–80
15in (38.5cm) high

Ebony c1685
11¼in (29cm) high

Ebony c1685
13½in (34cm) high

Walnut c1685
14in (35.5cm) high

Ebony c1695
16in (41cm) high

Ebony c1720
17½in (44cm) high

Ebony c1760
19½in (49.5cm) high

Mahogany c1765
18in (46cm) high

Lacquer c1770
25in (63.5cm) high

Mahogany c1780
19½in (49.5cm) high

Ebonized c1780
17in (43cm) high

Mahogany c1780
15¾in (40cm) high

Ebonized c1790
21in (53cm) high

Mahogany c1790
20½in (52cm) high

Ebonized c1800
15in (38cm) high

Ebonized c1810
19in (48cm) high

Mahogany c1810
16in (40.5cm) high

Mahogany c1827
26in (66cm) high

Gilt bronze c1840
18¾in (47.5cm) high

Mahogany c1840
13in (33.5cm) high

Mahogany c1840
19in (48cm) high

Mahogany c1850
18in (46cm) high

Ormolu c1875
18¾in (46.5cm) high

A mahogany bracket clock, the white painted dial with Roman numerals, enclosing an 8-day double fusee repeater movement striking on a single bell, early 19thC, 16in (40.5cm) high.
£2,900–3,850 $4,200–5,600 🔨 DDM

A George III fruitwood striking bracket clock, with silvered chapter ring, calendar arc in centre, converted to anchor escapement, associated, 20in (51cm) high.
£2,900–3,850 $4,200–5,600 🔨 C

A William IV bronze bracket clock, with 5in (12.5cm) silvered dial, the bell striking fusee movement with anchor escapement, on scroll bracket feet, c1830, 16in (40.5cm) high.
£950–1,350 $1,380–1,950 🔨 S

A Regency brass-inlaid mahogany striking bracket clock, the Roman dial with black painted moon hands, 5 pillar twin wire fusee movement with anchor escapement, strike on bell above, plain backplate, 19in (48.5cm) high.
£1,550–2,300 $2,250–3,350 🔨 C

A rosewood bracket clock, the 7½in (19cm) silvered dial signed 75 Old Broad St, Royal Exchange, London, with fast/slow and strike/silent subsidiary dials in the arch, the fusee movement with anchor escapement and shaped brass plates, striking on a bell, early 19thC, 16in (40.5cm) high.
£2,900–4,850
$4,200–7,000 🔨 DN

A Regency mahogany bracket clock, the white enamel dial in arched case with brass stringing, with 8-day striking movement, Gothic side grilles and ring handles, ball feet, and matching bracket, dial requires restoration, 15in (38cm) high.
£3,300–4,650
$4,800–6,750 🔨 L&E

▶ **A Neuchatel bracket clock,** with 9in (23cm) enamelled dial, painted with putti at a fountain, the movement rack striking on 2 gongs, the waisted case with *verre églomisé* panels and painted with garlands, 28in (71cm) high.
£1,550–2,300
$2,250–3,350 🔨 S(S)

◀ **A George III red japanned striking bracket clock,** restored, possibly associated, 18½in (47cm) high.
£5,800–9,650
$8,400–14,000 🔨 C

A George II ebonized striking bracket clock, the 6 pillar twin fusee movement with verge escapement, pull quarter repeat on 6 bells, repeat pulley to foliate engraved backplate, with securing brackets to case, 17in (43cm) high.
£5,800–9,650
$8,400–14,000 ✕ C
The dial layout for this clock is similar to work by William Scafe, 1749–64.

A George III mahogany bracket clock, with 7in (18cm) painted dial and anchor escapement, 13½in (34.5cm) high.
£4,850–6,750 $7,000–9,800 ✕ Bon

A French tortoiseshell and brass boulle bracket clock, with 9½in (24cm) cast dial, bell striking movement with outside countwheel, 35in (89cm) high.
£2,900–3,850 $4,200–5,600 ✕ S(S)

A French tortoiseshell boulle and ormolu-mounted bracket clock, the 5 tulip pillared movement converted to anchor escapement, with rectangular plates and countwheel strike, with matching wall bracket, 18thC, 48in (122cm) high.
£5,800–7,700
$8,400–11,000 ✕ P

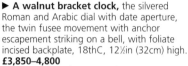

► **A walnut bracket clock,** the silvered Roman and Arabic dial with date aperture, the twin fusee movement with anchor escapement striking on a bell, with foliate incised backplate, 18thC, 12½in (32cm) high.
£3,850–4,800
$5,600–7,000 ✕ C

A George III ebonized chiming bracket clock, with 5in (12.5cm) re-painted dial on brass plate, with strike/silent lever above XII and subsidiary dials in the arch for date and regulation, the 5 pillar 3 train fusee movement with anchor escapement and chiming on 8 bells with a further bell for the hour, c1800, 12in (30.5cm) high.
£4,800–6,750
$7,000–9,800 ✕ S

A Louis XV tortoiseshell boulle striking bracket clock, the 4 pillar twin going barrel movement with silk suspended verge escapement and countwheel, restored, 36½in (92.5cm) high.
£4,800–6,750
$7,000–9,800 ✕ C

A burr walnut 8-day longcase clock, by Philip Abbot, London, c1725, 85in (216cm) high.
£14,000–15,000
$20,300–22,000 ⊞ ALS

A mahogany 8-day striking longcase clock, by William Avenell, Farnham, with silvered brass dial, 1790, 86in (218.5cm) high.
£7,000–8,000
$10,200–11,600 ⊞ PAO

An oak and mahogany cross-banded longcase clock, by Barton, Whitehaven, with painted dial, c1785, 85in (216cm) high.
£3,450–3,950
$5,000–5,700 ⊞ ALS

A mahogany 8-day longcase clock, by Abraham, Frome, c1830, 86in (218.5cm) high.
£6,750–7,250
$9,800–10,500 ⊞ ALS

An oak 8-day longcase clock, by Barlow, Ashton, with Halifax moon, c1770, 84in (213cm) high.
£6,750–7,250
$9,800–10,500 ⊞ ALS

A walnut marquetry 8-day longcase clock, with brass and silvered dial signed Jno. Bennett, Plymouth, 82in (208.5cm) high.
£13,850–15,500
$20,100–22,500 ⚒ Bea

An oak 8-day longcase clock, by Batt, Petersfield, with lunar arch and strike/silent, c1770, 81½in (207cm) high.
£7,250–7,850
$10,500–11,400 ⊞ ALS

A flame mahogany longcase clock, by Wm. Beavington, Stourbridge, with rocking ship automaton, c1800.
£7,250–7,850
$10,500–11,400 ⊞ ALS

A Scottish mahogany domestic regulator longcase clock, by James Bell, Edinburgh, with 13in (33cm) silvered brass dial showing seconds and Roman chapters, c1840.
£6,000–7,000
$8,700–10,200 ⊞ PAO

An oak 8-day longcase clock, by Thomas Bodle, Reigate, with brass dial, silvered brass chapter ring, seconds and date, c1760, 86in (218.5cm) high.
£7,000–8,000
$10,200–11,600 ⊞ PAO

An oak 8-day longcase clock, by William Bothamley, Kirton, striking the hours on a bell, c1765, 74½in (189cm) high.
£6,500–7,500
$9,400–10,800 ⊞ PAO

A mahogany veneered 8-day longcase clock, by Braund, Dartford, 12in (30.5cm) high.
£7,000–8,000
$10,200–11,600
⊞ PAO

A mahogany 8-day longcase clock, by Edward Jones, Bristol, c1830, 86in (218.5cm) high.
£6,750–7,250
$9,800–10,500 ⊞ ALS

An oak and mahogany cross-banded 8-day longcase clock, by William Kemp, Lewes, the 5 pillar movement with latched centre pillar, c1770, 85in (216cm) high.
£7,000–8,000
$10,200–11,600 ⊞ PAO

A mahogany 8-day longcase clock, by Thomas Ogden, Ripponden, with date aperture, 18thC, 84in (213cm) high.
£7,350–8,150
$10,650–11,800 🔨 MAT

An 8-day longcase clock, by Thomas Kefford, Royston, green lacquered chinoiserie decoration, c1750, 84in (213cm) high.
£9,000–10,000
$13,000–14,500 ⊞ PAO

An oak 8-day longcase clock, by Thomas Rayment, Stamford, with brass dial and silvered chapter ring, c1770, 78½in (199cm) high.
£7,000–8,000
$10,200–11,600 ⊞ PAO

A mahogany-veneered 8-day longcase clock, with ebony line inlay, by William Latch, Newport, c1830, 87in (221cm) high.
£6,000–7,000
$8,700–10,200 ⊞ PAO

A mahogany regulator style 8-day longcase clock, by Laurence, Southampton, with glazed trunk door, c1850, 81in (205.5cm) high.
£7,000–8,000
$10,200–11,600 ⊞ PAO

A Scottish mahogany longcase clock, the 13in (33cm) dial signed J. Paterson, with 8-day movement, c1810, 85½in (217cm) high.
£6,500–7,350
$9,400–10,650 🔨 S(S)

A walnut marquetry 8-day longcase clock, by Francis Reynolds, Kensington, late 17thC, 85½in (217cm) high.
£13,050–16,300
$18,900–23,600 🔨 S(S)

An oak 8-day longcase clock, by William Mayhew, Woodbridge, 5 pillar movement striking the hours on a bell, with silvered chapter ring and brass spandrels, c1775, 78in (198cm) high.
£7,000–8,000
$10,200–11,600 ⊞ PAO

A mahogany 8-day longcase clock, by Morse, Stratton, c1830, 82in (208cm) high.
£5,250–5,750
$7,600–8,350 ⊞ ALS

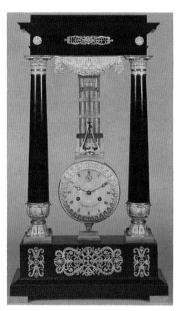

A Charles X ormolu and ebony portico mantel clock, the cast dial signed Delaunoy Elève de Breguet, 26in (66cm) high.
£14,900–18,600 $21,600–27,000 ⚒ C

A Regency gilt-bronze automaton mantel clock, signed Hy. Borrell, London, 19in (48.5cm) high.
£14,900–18,600 $21,600–27,000 ⚒ P

An Oriental gold, enamel and gem-set monstrance clock, with wood base and glazed cover, early 19thC, 11½in (29cm) high.
£13,000–14,900 $18,800–21,600 ⚒ CAG

A Meissen mantel clock, by George Fritzsche, restoration and firing cracks, c1727.
£29,750–33,500 $43,100–48,000 ⚒ C

An Empire ormolu mantel clock, c1800, with later ebonized base and glass dome, 12½in (32cm) high.
£11,150–13,000 $16,150–18,850 ⚒ C

◄ **A Louis XV ormolu-mounted *tôle* and porcelain mantel clock,** signed Musson à Paris, 14in (35.5cm) high.
£7,450–9,300 $10,800–13,500 ⚒ C

An Samson Imari ormolu-mounted clock garniture, with candelabra, with giltwood plinths, clock 21in (53.5cm) high.
£7,450–9,300 $10,800–13,500 ⚒ C

A walnut 8-day longcase clock, by William Underwood, London, 18thC, 100in (254cm) high.
£20,000–25,000
$29,000–36,000 ⊞ PAO

A William & Mary month-going walnut and marquetry longcase clock, by Daniel Quare, London, on later block feet, restored, 87in (221cm) high.
£16,300–17,950
$23,600–26,000 ⚒ C

A mahogany and shell inlaid 8-day longcase clock, by Thristle, Stogursey, c1790, 80in (203cm) high.
£6,950–7,450
$10,100–10,800 ⊞ ALS

A mahogany 8-day longcase clock, by Shepherd & Potter, Wotton, the 12in (30.5cm) dial with moonphase to arch, 19thC, 84in (213cm) high.
£7,350–8,150
$10,650–11,800 ⚒ Bri

A George II walnut long-case clock, by Benjamin Gray and Justin Vulliamy, London, c1750, 82in (208cm) high.
£13,050–16,300
$18,900–23,600 ⚒ S(NY)

A pale mahogany 8-day longcase clock, by Suggate, Halesworth, c1810, 85in (216cm) high.
£6,950–7,450
$10,100–10,800 ⊞ ALS

A mahogany 8-day longcase clock, by E. Siedle, Merthyr, mid-19thC, 89in (226cm) high.
£6,750–7,250
$9,800–10,500 ⊞ ALS

A Dutch mahogany and marquetry longcase clock, by Phy. Mensenbour, Groningen, c1780, 100in (254cm) high.
£6,200–7,200
$9,000–10,500 ⚒ C

A Cuban mahogany 8-day longcase clock, by Sutton, Stafford, c1785, 89½in (227cm) high.
£8,250–9,000
$11,500–13,000 ⊞ ALS

An oak 8-day longcase clock, lunar arch, high water at Bristol Key (sic), c1765, 82in (208cm) high.
£7,250–7,850
$10,500–11,400 ⊞ ALS

A mahogany longcase clock, by S. Wilkes, Birmingham, c1830, 93in (236cm) high.
£3,650–4,500
$5,300–6,500 ⚒ S(S)

A George III-style mahogany bracket clock, the 4 pillar single wire fusee movement with anchor escapement, 20thC, 14in (36cm) high.
£950–1,350
$1,380–1,950 ↗ CSK

A George III ebonized striking bracket clock, the dial signed Robt. Best, London, 16in (40.5cm) high.
£11,600–15,500
$16,800–22,500 ↗ C

A mid-Victorian painted mahogany striking bracket clock, signed D. Bagshaw, 28 Poland St, Oxford Street, 26in (66cm) high.
£1,750–2,800
$2,500–4,000 ↗ CSK

An 8-day mahogany bracket clock, by Benjamin Ward, London, the brass dial with chapter ring and spandrels, strike/silent to the arch, brass handle, feet and mounts, c1770, 20in (51cm) high.
£11,000–12,000
$16,000–17,400 ⊞ PAO

An 8-day mahogany bracket clock, by John Saunders, London, striking and repeating the hours on a bell, the backplate engraved with maker's name, c1810, 16in (40.5cm) high.
£6,000–7,000 $8,700–10,200 ⊞ PAO

A George II ebonized bracket clock, brass chapter ring signed Jon. Crampton, Dublin, 396, damaged, 16½in (42cm) high.
£5,800–7,700
$8,400–11,000 ↗ CSK

An Italian tortoiseshell quarter striking bracket clock, the dial signed Giovanni Hisla, Napoli, the top with a figure of Chronos, early 18thC, 26in (66cm) high.
£18,350–20,250
$26,600–29,000 ↗ C

A Louis XVI tortoiseshell boulle striking bracket clock, signed Roi à Paris, the top with later cherub, restored, 32in (81cm) high.
£7,700–9,650
$11,000–14,000 ↗ C

A Louis XV tortoiseshell boulle month-going bracket clock, the enamel dial signed Julien Le Roy, de la Société des Arts, 21in (53.5cm) high.
£7,700–8,700
$11,000–12,600 ↗ C

A Victorian inlaid mahogany musical bracket clock, 19thC, 25½in (65cm) high.
£5,800–6,750
$8,400–9,800 S(NY)

An 8-day bracket clock, by E. Thorpe, Stockwell, c1820.
£6,000–7,000
$8,700–10,200 PAO

A Victorian walnut bracket clock.
£7,700–8,700
$11,000–12,600 C

A Regency mahogany 8-day bracket clock, by Edward Lee, c1810, 15½in (39cm) high.
£6,000–7,000
$8,700–10,200 PAO

A Regency ebonized 8-day bracket clock, by Perigal, London, 11in (28cm) high.
£8,000–9,000
$11,600–13,000 PAO

A Victorian 8-day *grande sonnerie* **bracket clock,** 27½in (70cm) high.
£5,300–6,750
$7,700–9,800 AH

A George II walnut time-piece, signed Thomas Faldo, Shefford, 17in (43cm) high.
£6,750–7,700
$9,800–11,000 S(NY)

A Charles II bracket clock, by William Cattell, 12in (30.5cm) high.
£19,300–23,200
$28,000–33,500 C

A George III bronze-mounted mahogany musical bracket clock, by Adam Travers, London, restored, 25½in (65cm) high.
£12,550–14,500
$18,200–21,000 S(NY)

A Louis XV boulle bracket clock, dial and movement signed Panier à Paris, c1730, 40in (102cm) high.
£5,300–8,700
$7,700–12,600 S

A Regency 8-day rosewood brass-inlaid bracket clock, by William Turner, the 5 pillar movement striking the hours on a bell.
£4,000–5,000
$5,800–7,200 PAO

◄ **A Regency mahogany 8-day bracket clock,** by James Wilson, striking the hours on a bell, c1810.
£6,000–7,000
$8,700–10,200 PAO

A William & Mary ormolu-mounted ebony *grande sonnerie* table clock, the dial signed Thomas Tompion Londini Fecit, the backplate engraved and punch-numbered '217', 27in (68cm) high.
£558,000–650,000
$810,000–940,000 🔨 **C**

A George III ormolu-mounted quarter chiming bracket clock, the dial signed Recordon, Spencer & Perkins, London, 28½in (72.5cm) high.
£16,750–18,600
$24,300–27,000 🔨 **C**

A Regency brass-inlaid mahogany striking bracket clock, signed Dulin, Cornhill, London, with detailed and figured mahogany case, c1820, 18½in (47cm) high.
£6,000–7,500
$8,700–10,700 ⊞ **DRA**

◀ **A Regency ormolu-mounted marble Weeks' Museum mantel clock,** the case on gadrooned toupie feet, the 4 pillar chain fusee movement with deadbeat escapement, on velvet lined ebonized wood base and with glass dome, 12in (30.5cm) high.
£15,800–16,750
$22,900–24,300 🔨 **C**

A Victorian ebonized quarter chiming table clock, surmounted by a cupola with 8 gilded-brass mouldings, female figures on all 4 corners, the dial with a silver plaque inscribed Elkington, Regent St, London, 36in (91.5cm) high.
£12,000–15,000
$17,400–21,750 ⊞ **DRA**

A walnut quarter repeating table clock, signed Joseph Knibb, London, the backplate signed and engraved with tulips and scrolling leaves, the domed case veneered with richly figured wood, with brass carrying handle, c1685, 12in (30.5cm) high.
£83,700–102,300
$121,000–148,300 🔨 **S**

◀ **A George III mahogany musical and automaton table clock,** the dial signed Daye Barker, London, the inverted bell top surmounted by pineapple finials, 34in (87cm) high.
£24,200–26,050
$35,100–37,800 🔨 **C**

A mahogany table clock, by Francis Perigal, London, c1800, 18in (46cm).
£10,230–12,100
$14,800–17,550 S

An ebony-veneered table clock, by Joseph Knibb, c1680, 13in (33cm) high.
£37,200–46,500 $54,000–67,400 S

An ebony-veneered table clock, by Jonathan Lowndes, c1690.
£14,900–18,600
$21,600–27,000 S

An ebony-veneered basket-top table clock, by Johannes Fromanteel, c1690, 13in (33cm) high.
£14,900–18,600 $21,600–27,000 S

A mahogany musical table clock, by Eardley Norton, c1780, 29in (73.5cm) high.
£18,600–26,050
$27,000–37,800 S

A walnut table clock, by Edward Bird, c1685, 21½in (54.5cm) high.
£37,200–46,500
$53,950–67,400 S

An ebony-veneered quarter repeating table clock, by Henry Jones, c1690, 12in (30.5cm) high.
£18,600–27,900 $27,000–40,000 S

An ebonized quarter repeating table clock, the dial signed Ja. Boyce, London, c1700.
£11,150–13,000
$16,150–18,000 S

A silver-mounted quarter repeating walnut table clock, with brass dial, c1690.
£18,600–22,300
$27,000–32,300 S

An Arabesque marquetry table clock, by George Etherington, c1695.
£26,000–33,500
$37,800–48,600 S

An ebonized brass-bound chiming table clock, c1785.
£13,000–14,900
$18,500–21,600 S

A Régence ormolu-mounted boulle bracket clock, signed Mynuel à Paris.
£7,700–9,650
$11,150–14,000 ⚒ C

A Louis XIV ormolu-mounted tortoiseshell boulle bracket clock, 39in (99cm) high.
£7,700–9,650
$11,000–14,000 ⚒ C

A repeating carriage clock, by James McCabe, London, c1860, 8½in (21.5cm) high.
£12,250–15,300
$17,800–22,200 ⚒ S

A gilt-brass-mounted ebonized musical and chiming bracket clock, by Higgs & Evans, London, c1780, 26in (66cm) high.
£20,250–24,100
$29,350–35,000 ⚒ S

A mahogany 6 bell pull quarter repeat bracket clock, with original verge escapement, London, c1760.
£10,000–12,500
$14,500–18,000 ⊞ CLC

A Regency mahogany bracket clock, with brass stringing.
£4,800–6,150 $6,950–8,900 ⊞ CLC

A Regency bracket clock.
£5,500–6,500
$8,000–9,400 ⊞ CLC

A bronze and cut-glass-mounted japanned musical bracket clock, by George Prior, London, c1770, 32in (81cm) high.
£28,950–34,750
$42,000–50,400 ⚒ S(NY)

A Louis XV ormolu-mounted brass-inlaid rosewood and tortoiseshell boulle marquetry bracket clock, by François Clement, 18thC.
£4,650–5,600
$6,750–8,100 ⚒ C

A Napoleon III boulle bracket clock, Paris, 1850, with bracket.
£7,450–8,400
$10,800–12,200 ⚒ S

▶ **A French carriage clock,** with enamel chapter ring, in an ornamental brass case, 5½in (14cm) high.
£6,750–7,700
$9,800–11,000 ⚒ PCh

An ebony-veneered 8-day striking bracket clock, by John Bushman, London, with 6¼in (16cm) silvered chapter ring, restored, c1695.
£19,300–23,150
$28,000–33,600 ⚒ S(NY)

A striking bracket clock, signed J. Lowndes, London, c1685.
£19,300–23,150
$28,000–33,600 ⚲ Bon

A Charles II bracket clock, signed Cha. Gretton, London, 12in (30.5cm) high.
£34,750–42,450 $50,400–61,550 ⚲ C

A Charles II ebonized striking bracket clock, the dial signed J. Gerrard, London, strike/silent lever above XII, restored, 15in (38cm) high.
£17,350–23,150
$25,150–33,600 ⚲ C

A William III kingwood quarter repeating bracket clock, the 6 pillar movement signed James Tudman, Londini Fecit, 15in (38cm) high.
£15,400–19,300
$22,300–28,000 ⚲ S

A George II mahogany striking bracket clock, by Delander, 16in (40.5cm) high.
£23,150–27,000 $33,600–39,000 ⚲ C

A Charles II ebony-veneered bracket clock, signed Joseph Knibb, Londini Fecit, c1670, 14in (35.5cm) high.
£77,200–96,500 $112,000–140,000 ⚲ S

An ebony-veneered bracket clock, by John Barnett, London, 17thC, 15in (38cm) high.
£17,350–21,200
$25,150–30,750 ⚲ CSK

A George I ebony *grande sonnerie* bracket clock, by Dan Delander, altered.
£165,000–183,350
$240,000–265,850 ⚲ C

A Queen Anne striking bracket clock, signed Jos. Windmills.
£23,150–42,450
$33,600–61,550 ⚲ C

A George III ebonized striking bracket clock, signed, 17in (43cm) high.
£6,750–8,700
$9,800–12,600 ⚒ C

A bracket clock, signed Dorrell, London, with fusee movement, early 19thC.
£5,500–6,500
$8,000–9,400 ⊞ CLC

◀ **A Regency mahogany bracket clock,** the dial signed Wasbrough Hale & Co., Bristol, c1835.
£1,950–2,900
$2,800–4,200
⚒ SWO

▶ **An Edwardian oak mantel clock,** the 3 train movement with Westminster chimes on 8 bells and gong, 25in (64cm) high.
£1,950–2,900
$2,800–4,200 ⚒ SWO

A George III mahogany striking bracket clock, 19½in (49.5cm) high.
£12,550–14,500
$18,200–21,000 ⚒ C

A George III scarlet japanned musical bracket clock, signed Wm. Kipling, London, 25in (63.5cm) high.
£54,050–61,750 $78,400–89,500 ⚒ C

A Charles II bracket clock, signed Joseph Knibb, London, restored, 15in (38.5cm) high.
£28,950–38,600
$42,000–56,000 ⚒ C

A Charles II ebony bracket clock, signed Joseph Knibb, London, escapement rebuilt, 11½in (29cm) high.
£38,600–48,250
$56,000–70,000 ⚒ C

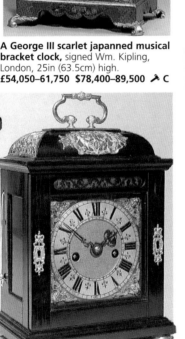

▶ **A Charles II ebonized striking bracket clock,** signed Joseph Knibb, London, restored, 13in (33cm) high.
£42,450–54,050
$61,550–78,400 ⚒ C

A George III tortoiseshell musical bracket clock, by Markwick Markham, London, 13in (33cm) high.
£38,600–48,250
$56,000–70,000 ⚒ C

A George II bracket clock.
£27,000–30,900
$39,000–44,800 ✒ C

A late George III mahogany and ebony quarter chiming and Dutch hour striking calendar equation bracket clock.
£15,450–19,300
$22,400–28,000 🔨 C

A Louis XIV cartel clock, 17½in (44.5cm) high.
£9,650–15,450
$14,000–22,400 ✒ C

A French gilt-metal mantel clock, the case surmounted by 2 lions, late 19thC, 20in (51cm) high.
£1,550–1,950
$2,250–2,800 ✒ SWO

A Neuchatel musical calendar bracket clock.
£23,150–27,000
$33,550–39,000 ✒ C

A Dutch ebony-veneered striking bracket clock, 15½in (39.5cm) high.
£11,600–15,450
$16,800–22,400 ✒ C

▶ **A Louis XV bracket clock,** signed Gudin à Paris.
£5,800–8,800
$8,400–12,750 ✒ CNY

A Louis XV bracket clock.
£11,600–15,450
$16,800–22,400 ✒ C

◀ **l. A longcase clock.**
£30,000–40,000
$43,500–58,000 ⊞ CLC
r. A Charles II longcase clock.
£21,250–27,000
$30,800–39,000 ✒ C

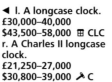

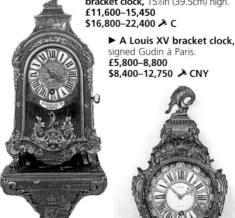

A Régence bracket clock.
£19,300–28,950
$28,000–42,000 ✒ C

◀ **A Louis XV bracket clock**
£9,650–13,500
$14,000–19,600 ✒ C

A William & Mary silver-mounted ebonized striking bracket clock, the later dial inscribed Francis Robinson, London, with pierced blued hands and 5 ringed pillar twin fusee movement, 15½in (39cm) high.
£12,550–14,500
$18,200–21,000 ⚹ C

A George III mahogany striking bracket clock, the dial signed Judah Jacobs, London, strike/silent ring in the arch, 5 pillar twin fusee movement with verge escapement and strike on a bell, engraved backplate, 18in (46cm) high.
£11,600–13,500
$16,800–19,600 ⚹ C

An ebony and ebonized striking bracket clock, the dial signed Dan Delander, London, the movement with bob escapement, engraved backplate, on a moulded plinth, 16½in (42cm) high.
£8,700–11,600
$12,600–16,800 ⚹ C

A George III mahogany automaton table clock, dial with calendar aperture signed John Darke, Barnstaple, strike/silent lever, 5 pillar fusee movement, 21in (53cm) high.
£8,700–11,600
$12,600–16,800 ⚹ S

◄ **A Regency brass-mounted ebonized striking bracket clock,** glazed white painted enamelled dial signed Grant, Fleet St, London, with a ripple-moulded brass-mounted base and lions' mask carrying handles, signed backplate, 19in (48cm) high.
£6,750–8,700
$9,800–12,600 ⚹ C

A George III ebonized striking bracket clock, the dial signed Mich L. Roth, London, strike/silent ring in the arch, 5 pillar twin chain fusee movement, 16in (41cm) high.
£5,800–7,700
$8,400–11,150 ⚹ C

A George III mahogany chiming table clock, the dial signed John Abchurch, London, 5 pillar fusee movement with verge escapement, 23½in (60cm) high.
£16,400–18,550
$23,800–27,000 ⚹ S

▶ **A Louis XV brass-inlaid and brown tortoiseshell boulle bracket clock,** with ormolu dial engraved with foliate arabesques and central cockerel, Roman blue and white enamel dial and further Arabic numeral dial to the outside, the movement stamped to the reverse 'De Lorme A Paris', the backboard inlaid with scrolling foliage surmounted by a figure of Minerva, 64in (163cm) high.
£16,400–19,300
$23,800–28,000 ⚹ C

A George II ebony-veneered table clock, the 7in (17.5cm) dial signed Fra. Mayhew, Parham, 6 pillar 2 train bell striking fusee movement, 18½in (47cm) high.
£4,800–6,300
$6,950–9,100 ⚹ S

A Charles II ebony striking bracket clock, backplate signed J. Knibb, London, Fecit, 11in (28cm) high.
£46,300–57,900 $67,100–84,000 ⚒ C

A Régence boulle bracket clock, signed Boucheret à Paris, restored, 35in (89cm) high.
£5,800–7,800
$8,400–11,300 ⚒ C

A Charles II ebony striking bracket clock, signed Joseph Knibb, London, restored, 12in (30.5cm) high.
£48,250–57,900
$70,000–84,000 ⚒ C

A Victorian mahogany chiming 8-day bracket clock, 22½in (57cm) high.
£4,850–6,300
$7,000–9,100 ⚒ CSK

A stained horn *grande sonnerie* bracket clock, probably Swiss, mid-18thC, 37½in (95cm) high.
£14,500–16,400
$21,000–23,800 ⚒ CSK

An ormolu musical automaton bracket clock, 'nonsense' signature, 22in (56cm) high.
£67,550–77,200
$98,000–112,000 ⚒ C

▶ A green and gilt lacquer longcase clock, with 12in (30.5cm) dial, signed Willm Pridham, London, inscribed 'The Royal George', the 4 pillar movement with anchor escapement, mid-19thC, 86in (218.5cm) high.
£4,900–5,700
$7,100–8,250 ⚒ Bea

A George III mahogany 8-day longcase clock, signed James Pond, London, 79in (200.5cm) high.
£12,250–13,850
$17,750–20,000 ⚒ Bea

A walnut and marquetry longcase clock, with 10in (25.5cm) dial, signed Joseph Windmills, the 8-day 6 pillar movement with anchor escapement, 75in (190.5cm) high.
£29,350–32,600
$42,550–47,250 ⚒ Bea

▶ A mahogany longcase clock, the silvered dial signed Robert Fairey, London, 108in (274cm) high.
£27,700–32,600
$40,000–47,250 ⚒ Bon

An ebony-veneered bracket clock, by Daniel Quare, London, early 18thC, 17in (43cm) high.
£42,450–46,300 $61,550–67,100 ⚒ P

A Restauration equation regulator, by Lepaute, restored, 83in (211cm) high.
£24,000–30,000 $34,800–43,500 ⚒ C

The Longstreet Family Federal inlaid mahogany longcase clock, dial signed Aaron Lane, Elizabethtown, New Jersey, c1790, 94in (239cm) high.
£45,650–52,150
$66,200–75,600 ⚒ CNY

▶ **A Louis XV ormolu-mounted *corne verte* bracket clock,** the glazed dial and backplate signed Pierre Leroy à Paris, bracket stamped St. Germain Jme, 37in (94cm) high.
£15,450–19,300
$22,400–28,000 ⚒ C

A Louis XV boulle marquetry *religieuse*, early 18thC, 22in (56cm) high.
£11,400–14,650 $16,500–21,250 ⚒ CNY

A Louis XV ormolu bracket clock, attributed to Charles Cressent, signed Viger.
£13,500–17,350
$19,600–25,000 ⚒ C

A mid-Georgian scarlet japanned quarter striking musical automaton bracket clock, in the style of Giles Grendey, 37in (94cm) high.
£115,800–135,000
$168,000–195,900 ⚒ C

A Louis XV boulle marquetry bracket clock, late 18thC, 52in (132cm) high.
£13,500–15,450
$19,600–22,400 ⚒ CNY

Mantel Clocks & Garnitures

The vast majority of mantel clocks were made in France and appealed to the French taste for ornament and embellishment. Unlike bracket clocks, which are normally larger and wooden-cased, the mantel clock is typically made of metal or marble, heavily applied with brass or ormolu decoration. In some cases, the clock itself seems almost an afterthought, taking second place to the expertise and imagination of the sculptor or metal worker. Allegorical figures, cupids, birds or animals support or sit astride delicate clocks framed by garlands of flowers or scrolls. Whereas British clocks chiefly relied only on the clockmaker and cabinetmaker, in France a whole team of craftsmen could be involved, such as gilders, founders, engravers, enamellers and so on, each contributing different skills to the design. So much attention being lavished on one clock means that most French clocks are very well finished and beautifully made.

In the 18th century French clocks, made mainly in Paris, were at their most ornamented, with a profusion of rococo scrolls, flowers and shells. Porcelain panels were introduced, held in place by ormolu mounts. Towards the end of the century the rococo excesses were curbed by neo-classical tastes: classical or Egyptian forms were introduced with marble and cast bronze being favourite materials. A particularly elegant French clock of this period is in the form of a lyre, incorporating marble, onyx or porcelain with bronze and decorated with flowers. When a clock with a particularly complex movement was required it usually took the form of a tall clock, often on a pedestal. Tall clocks are among the most interesting from a horologist's point of view, as the movements are usually by important makers and they have interesting escapements and other complicated features.

Early French mantel clocks are fairly rare today, with the majority produced between 1800 and 1900. Dials of this period were made of porcelain or enamel, usually convex, covered by a hinged circular glass bezel. One-piece porcelain dials are most common, but some dials are two-piece, for example with an enamelled centre and a gilt chapter ring. Hands were often elaborate; earlier ones were made of brass, later ones of steel. Backs may be glazed or metal, and either hinged or lift-out.

Garnitures were made in sets of three or sometimes five, consisting of the clock as centrepiece, flanked by candelabra or matching side urns. Most garnitures date from the mid- to late 19th century. It is quite important to ascertain whether the side ornaments being sold with the clock are part of the original set and have not been added later to enhance the price.

Mantel clocks were not always signed, but about three-quarters of those made in the 19th century were signed with the maker's name. If the signature is there, it is normally in the form of a circular stamp on the back of the movement, with the retailer's name appearing on the dial.

If a name was applied after the dial was enamelled, however, it could have been wiped off in cleaning.

Oliver Saunders from Bonhams feels that the demand for good decorative pieces makes this category of clock one of the strongest. The more elaborate, and those with enamelled or ceramic panels, will fetch high prices. James Stratton at Phillips reports a strong market in the middle range as well; in a recent sale an attractive 19th-century mantel clock with a case surmounted by heraldic lions fetched £1,500 ($2,150), exceeding its estimate of £700–£900 ($1,000–1,300), despite the enamel dial being slightly chipped.

Roderick Mee, a specialist in French mantel clocks of the 19th century, is confident that they offer good value for money. Prices rise from £700 ($1,000) to £2,500 ($3,600) for one in good bronze with porcelain panels, and 18th-century clocks fetch even higher prices. He acknowledges that some French foundries were better than others, but would never buy on the name alone, reiterating that it is quality and condition that ultimately determine the price.

One of the factors contributing to quality and affecting the price of mantel clocks is the type of metal used for the cases or mounts. Preferably the casting should be bronze, not spelter which is lighter and less durable. Bronze cases are usually in very good condition, as the bronze is not susceptable to wear or deterioration. Any clock made before the mid-1830s has an attractive dark thick mercury gilding. This was introduced in the 17th century or earlier and produced a beautiful finish but, unfortunately, also nasty side effects for the workers; some even died of 'mercury madness' caused by the vapours. Understandably it was banned, so clocks after this date have a thinner electro-gilding which wears off more quickly. If the clock is re-gilded correctly it can be made to look original; this is acceptable as long as it is carried out professionally.

French mantel clocks are not often faked. Modern reproductions exist but can be spotted, if they are trying to be passed off as genuine, by the quality of the casting and the way the movements are made. According to Roderick Mee, the easiest way of identifying a reproduction is to look underneath and check the nuts and screws; old ones will be hand-cut and not symmetrical. Signs of corrosion and general wear will also indicate an old clock. For the untrained eye spotting a new movement is more difficult so do seek an expert's opinion if in any doubt about authenticity. Similarly, it is advisable to have your clock overhauled professionally rather than attempting it yourself. A reputable specialist dealer's stock should be presented in fully over-hauled and mechanically guaranteed condition.

A French ormolu and white marble mantel clock, the enamel dial signed for Aubert & Klaftenberger, Genève, c1850, 12½in (32cm) high.
£2,200–3,150
$3,200–4,550 ⚒ P

A French Empire ormolu mantel clock, signed Alibert à Paris, with later glazed bezel, the later twin train movement striking on a bell, depicting Minerva urging on the horses of Diomedes, slight damage, c1815, 17½in (44cm) high.
£7,450–8,350
$10,800–12,100 ⚒ P

A French white marble and ormolu-mounted mantel clock, signed F. Barbedienne à Paris, with enamel dial, 19thC, 16½in (42cm) high.
£2,200–3,700
$3,200–5,500 ⚒ P

◄ **A Louis XV ormolu-mounted kingwood mantel clock,** the enamel dial signed Baret à Brevanne, later movement, re-veneered, c1880, 17½in (44.5cm) high.
£1,500–2,200
$2,000–3,200 ⚒ C

An ormolu-mounted mantel clock, with white enamel dial, the 8-day movement by Baird of London, the case surmounted by a model of Cupid and a chariot drawn by 2 doves, early 19thC, 16in (40.5cm) high, with glass dome and on satinwood plinth.
£2,600–3,350
$3,800–4,850 ⚒ RBB

A Regency mantel clock, by Bedward & Collier, with 2 train movement, c1815, 16in (40.5cm) high.
£1,000–1,400 $1,500–2,000 ⊞ SH

A French walnut mantel clock, with silvered brass dial, inscribed 'Examd by Barraud and Lunds, 44 Cornhill, London, No. 4274', c1860, 10½in (27cm) high.
£1,200–1,400
$1,750–2,000 ⊞ DRA

A Regency walnut mantel clock, the chipped 4½in (11cm) enamel dial and backplate signed Barraud, London, the movement with arched plates, chain fusees and anchor escapement, 12in (30.5cm) high.
£2,800–3,700
$4,000–5,350 ⚒ S

A gilt-bronze nautical mantel timepiece, the French movement with cylinder escapement, and E. Bertaux label, 1890, 15½in (39cm) high.
£1,850–2,800
$2,700–4,000 ⚒ S(C)

An ormolu mantel clock, the 5in (12.5cm) enamel dial signed Bunon A Paris, drum case signed Viel, c1775, 15in (38cm) high.
£10,250–13,000
$14,850–18,850 ⚒ S

A satinwood-veneered mantel timepiece, inscribed Birch, Fenchurch St, London, with engraved silver dial, backplate and 8-day fusee movement, bevelled glass panels, ogee frieze to plinth base, c1821, 8½in (21cm) high.
£2,800–4,650
$4,000–6,750 ⚒ WW

A mantel clock, the dial signed Bourdin à Paris, 17in (43cm) high.
£2,600–3,350
$3,800–4,850 ⚒ C

A French porcelain-mounted ormolu mantel clock, signed Bourdin à Paris, with porcelain dial, the bell striking movement with Brocot escapement and outside countwheel, the sides and front inset with porcelain panels, c1850, 12in (30.5cm) high.
£2,800–4,100
$4,000–6,000 ⚒ S

A French mahogany portico clock, the gilt dial with engine-turned centre, signed Bernard et fils, Bordeaux, the 8-day movement with outside countwheel striking on a bell, with decorative pendulum, on ebonized base with glass dome, c1830, 18½in (47cm) high.
£950–1,700
$1,380–2,450 ⚒ CSK

An Austrian ormolu *grande sonnerie* mantel clock, the 4in (10cm) silvered dial with central calendar, signed Brändl in Wien, 3 train movement with silk suspension and striking on 2 bells, drum case surmounted by an eagle and raised on bird feet, on a later white onyx plinth, c1815, 10in (25cm) high.
£2,400–3,150
$3,500–4,550 ⚒ S

A Victorian rosewood four-glass mantel clock, signed Brockbank and Atkins, London, No. 2291, the twin chain and fusee movement with anchor escapement striking on a gong, 11½in (29cm) high.
£4,650–6,500
$6,750–9,400 ⚒ CSK

◄ **A French ormolu mantel clock,** by Martin Baskell, the movement with Brocot escapement, perpetual calendar and moonphase, c1850, 17in (43cm) high.
£5,600–7,450
$8,100–10,800 ⊞ BS

▶ **A French gilt mantel clock,** with 3in (7.5cm) painted dial, signed Achille Brocot, bell striking movement, the case with pink porcelain panels and lions' masks, with dome and plinths, c1850, 14½in (37cm) high,
£1,500–2,250
$2,150–3,250 ⚒ S(S)

A French faïence-mounted gilt-brass mantel clock, with gong striking Achille Brocot movement and dial decorated against a cream ground, the gilt case flanked by faïence columns, c1880, 15½in (39cm) high.
£2,250–3,350
$3,250–4,850 ✗ S

▶ **An Austrian *grande sonnerie* repeating and alarm boulle mantel clock,** with silvered foliate engraved dial signed Chatourel à Paris, 4 train gong striking movement with fusee and train for the gong, standing barrels for the strike and alarm, verge and balance escapement, c1812, 9½in (24cm) high.
£3,160–3,700
$4,600–5,350 ✗ S(S)

A satinwood mantel timepiece, with 4in (10cm) silvered dial signed Bunyan & Gardner, Manchester, the single train fusee movement with anchor escapement, c1820, 9½in (24cm) high.
£2,800–3,700
$4,000–5,350 ✗ Bon

A brass-inlaid ebonized mantel timepiece, with silvered dial inscribed Jas Brown, London, with screw adjusting locking pendulum, in case, c1825, 9½in (24cm) high.
£1,500–1,850
$2,150–2,700 ✗ GSP

A mahogany and brass-inlaid mantel clock, the painted dial signed Condliff, Liverpool, the twin fusee movement striking on a bell, with anchor escapement, c1820, 14in (35.5cm) high.
£4,650–5,950
$6,750–8,600 ✗ P

A mahogany and brass-inlaid mantel clock, signed Catchpool, Bishopsgate St, London, with 6in (15cm) cream dial, twin fusee movement, with pull repeat, the backplate with engraved border, c1820, 16½in (42cm) high.
£2,050–2,250
$3,000–3,500 ✗ S(S)

A Louis XV ormolu-mounted boulle bracket clock, the movement signed G. I. Champion à Paris, the case surmounted by a figure of Father Time, 43in (109cm) high.
£3,700–5,600
$5,350–8,100 ✗ C

A French mantel clock, by F. C. Paris, silk suspension, the 8-day movement with outside count strike on a bell, c1840.
£500–1,000
$720–1,500 ▦ SO

A French ormolu and silvered mantel clock, stamped Cléret No. 4058, the 2 train movement with silk suspension and floral bezel, c1815, 20in (51cm) high.
£1,850–2,800
$2,700–4,000 🔨 Bon

▶ A Directoire ormolu and bronze mantel clock, signed Cronier Aíné, rue St. Honoré Mo. 165 à Paris, the enamel dial with Roman numerals, twin going barrel movement with anchor escapement, silk suspended pendulum, and countwheel strike on a bell, c1797, 14in (35.5cm) high.
£3,700–4,650
$5,350–6,750 🔨 CSK

◀ A Sèvres-mounted ormolu mantel clock, the bell striking J. B. Delettrez movement with Brocot escapement signed for Thomas Agnew & Sons, the porcelain dial painted at the centre with a putto within tooled gilt and rose pink borders, c1870, 19½in (49.5cm) high.
£3,700–5,600
$5,350–8,100 🔨 S

A gilt brass perpetual calendar mantel clock, signed Cotonie, Paris, the 3in (7.5cm) enamelled dial with subsidiary dials for day, date and month, with silk suspension and Japy Frères movement, the associated case with leaf engraved and pierced mask, c1860, 8½in (21cm) high.
£1,850–2,800
$2,700–4,000 🔨 S(S)

◀ A French brass and silvered mantel clock, inscribed Cattaneo & Co, Paris, with porcelain dial, the 8-day movement striking on a gong, c1860, 15in (38cm) high.
£1,300–2,050
$1,900–3,000 🔨 CSK

▶ A rosewood and brass-inlaid mantel timepiece, signed Carpenter, London, with silvered dial, the fusee movement with shaped plates and anchor escapement, c1840, 9½in (24cm) high.
£2,800–3,700
$4,000–5,500 🔨 P

◀ A mantel clock, signed Dawson of Heddington, with single train chain fusee movement, c1820, 10in (25cm) high.
£1,800–2,000
$2,600–2,900 ⊞ DRA

◄ **A Meissen clock and stand,** signed Chabrier, London, with enamel dial, the movement within rococo gilt metal surround, blue crossed swords mark on each piece, minor damage, restored, c1750, 13in (33cm) high.
£4,850–5,600
$7,000–8,100 ⚒ C

A French porcelain and ormolu mantel clock, stamped Denière à Paris, with 2 train movement, c1850, 14in (36cm) high.
£2,800–3,700
$4,000–5,350 ⚒ Bon

A French bronze and Sienna marble mantel clock, signed Duval à Paris, with engine-turned silvered dial, the 8-day movement with silk suspension, outside countwheel, striking on a bell, c1830, 24in (61cm) high.
£1,650–2,250
$2,400–3,250 ⚒ CSK

A French Third Empire bronze mantel clock, inscribed J. B. Delettrez, 62 Rue Charlot, Paris, with enamel dial, the 8-day movement striking on a bell, with a Roman emperor standing by a plinth, c1870, 21in (53cm) high.
£1,300–1,650
$1,900–2,400 ⚒ WW

► **An ormolu-mounted white and red marble mantel clock,** signed Drouot à Paris, with enamel dial, c1790, 15in (38cm) wide.
£4,650–6,500
$6,750–9,400 ⚒ C

A French ormolu and marble mantel clock, signed S. Devaulx, Palais Royal, with enamel dial, the case with bands of green marble, with mask feet, c1835, 23in (59cm) high.
£2,800–4,650
$4,000–6,750 ⚒ Bon

A burr walnut mantel clock, signed F. Dent, 61 Strand, 1466, with enamel dial, the single chain fusee movement with anchor escapement and pendulum, c1840, 10in (25cm) high.
£3,350–4,450
$4,850–6,450 ⚒ CSK

A French ormolu mantel clock, signed Cachard, successor to Ch. Le Roy, signed at the base Dubuisson, with enamel dial, outside countwheel and bell striking, c1795, 22in (56cm) high.
£4,650–6,500
$6,750–9,400 ⚒ S

A walnut mantel clock, signed Dent, 61 Strand, London, 1711, with chain fusees and anchor escapement, minute hand missing, c1850, 10in (25cm) high.
£5,200–7,450
$7,550–10,800 ⚒ S

A **Dutch mahogany and marquetry mantel clock,** with enamel dial, the movement stamped Dales, Westbourne, the case inlaid with floral cornucopia with turned columns and plinth base, cresting missing.
£1,300–1,850
$1,900–2,700 🔨 C

A **French Empire mahogany mantel clock,** the white enamel dial signed Devillaine, the large drum-shaped movement with outside countwheel striking on a bell, c1805, 12in (30.5cm) high.
£2,250–3,700
$3,250–5,350 🔨 CSK

A **French mantel clock,** signed Dupont of Paris, and numbered 600, the 2 train movement with silk suspension and countwheel strike on a bell, the case rosewood veneered and decorated with floral inlay and boxwood stringing, c1840, 9½in (24cm) high.
£1,350–1,600
$1,900–2,300 ⊞ DRA

A **Second Empire ormolu and bronze mantel clock,** signed Michelez Elève de Breguet, with chased dial, c1870, 19in (48cm) high.
£1,650–2,800
$2,400–4,000 🔨 C

Mantel Clocks

Mantel clocks were made in France in large numbers from 1780 to 1880, in a wide range of highly decorative cases with figural decoration. Those of the 1830s to 1850s are usually a little more subtle and of better quality. As with the garnitures of that period, the movements are of a fairly standard type and not therefore of great importance. Mantel clocks are abundant and widely available, being second in popularity to the carriage clock, but quality and condition do vary. Most European countries have produced them in large numbers since the mid-19th century.

A **mantel clock,** by Elkington, c1880, 11in (28cm) high.
£1,500–2,250 $2,150–3,250 🔨 Bon

A **George III gilt-metal mantel clock,** by Ellicott, with chain fusee movement and lever escapement, 12in (30.5cm) high.
£3,700–5,600
$5,500–8,100 🔨 S

A **French perpetual calendar polished bronze four-glass mantel clock,** signed Frennele Bté. S. G. Du, the 4¼in (11cm) enamel dial with central month hand, and subsidiary dials for date and day of the week, the bell striking movement with Brocot escapement, c1875, 14in (35cm) high.
£3,700–5,600
$5,500–8,100 🔨 S

◀ **A rosewood mantel timepiece,** the silvered dial signed Frodsham, Gracechurch Street, London, the fusee movement with anchor escapement, c1830, 9in (23cm) high.
£2,000–3,000
$3,000–4,400 🔨 P

An ebonized mantel timepiece, signed Finer & Nowland, High Holborn, the chain fusee movement with shaped plates, turned pillars, and anchor escapement, 1825, 9in (23cm) high.
£2,800–3,700
$4,000–5,300 🔨 C

A fusee mantel clock, by Frodsham, c1850, 9½in (24cm) high.
£1,100–1,500
$1,600–2,150 ⊞ RFA

A walnut four-glass mantel clock, signed Chas. Frodsham, Clockmaker to the Queen, No. 2057, the silvered dial with engraved spandrels, the fusee movement with anchor escapement, 1830, 12in (30.5cm) high.
£4,100–5,200
$6,000–7,500 🔨 P

A walnut mantel clock, signed Charles Frodsham, Clockmaker to H. M. The King and Queen, 115 New Bond Street, No. 2111, with engraved silvered dial, the movement with anchor escapement, pendulum and key, 19thC, 10in (25cm) high.
£1,850–2,800
$2,700–4,000 🔨 RID

An ebonized mantel clock, the silvered 3in (7.5cm) dial with foliate engraving and signed Frodsham, Gracechurch Street, London, the fusee movement also signed, anchor escapement, c1840, 8in (20cm) high.
£1,650–2,800
$2,400–4,000 🔨 S(S)

A French bronze and ormolu-mounted clock, signed Gallé à Paris, the movement with silk suspension and countwheel strike, early 19thC, 27½in (70cm) high.
£2,250–3,000
$3,250–4,400 🔨 P

A gilt-metal and marble mantel clock, by R. Ganthony, Cheapside, London, with enamel dial, single train movement, decorated with scroll and swag frieze, on spool feet, c1820, 8½in (21.5cm) high.
£1,300–2,200
$1,900–3,200 🔨 P(EA)

A French ormolu and porcelain-mounted mantel clock, signed Chas. Frodsham, Paris, with enamel dial, c1850, 14in (36cm) high.
£3,000–4,450
$4,400–6,450 🔨 P

A Sèvres pattern mantel clock, the movement by Gasnier à Paris, Quai Voltaire, 17, c1875, 16in (40.5cm) high.
£2,800–3,700
$4,000–5,300 🔨 C

An ebonized mantel clock, signed Frodsham, Gracechurch Street, London, the 3in (7.5cm) silvered dial with foliate engraving, the fusee movement with anchor escapement, c1840, 8in (20cm) high.
£1,650–2,800
$2,400–4,000 S(S)

▶ **A George III mahogany balloon clock,** the painted dial signed Chas. Goodall, London, the twin fusee movement with shaped plates and anchor escapement, signed on backplate, the case with swept spire and cone finial, 19in (48.5cm) high.
£2,800–3,700
$4,000–5,300  P

◀ **A French oak mantel clock,** signed Goldsmiths Co, 112 Regent St, the enamel dial with Roman numerals, the movement striking on a gong, with broken-arch pediment, c1895, 14in (36cm) high.
£350–550
$500–800 Bon

A Regency burr walnut, brass and ebony-inlaid mantel timepiece, the silvered dial signed Grimalde & Johnson, Strand, London, the fusee movement with signed backplate and anchor escapement, damaged, c1835, 12in (30.5cm) high.
£2,800–3,700
$4,000–5,300 P

A French tortoiseshell and cut-brass-inlaid mantel clock, the gilt dial with enamel numerals, signed Gaudron A Paris, the movement with anchor escapement and square plates, 18thC, 20in (51cm) high.
£7,450–9,300
$10,800–13,500 ⚒ P

◀ **A French marble mantel clock,** the 4in (10cm) enamelled dial signed Guydamour à Paris, with bell striking movement, c1800, 16in (40.5cm) high.
£2,800–4,650
$4,000–6,750 ⚒ S

A Louis XV-style mantel clock, the gilt dial signed Gorohé Paris, the 8-day movement No. 541, c1820, 22½in (57cm) high.
£2,400–3,350
$3,500–4,850 ⚒ Bea

A regulator mantel clock, signed Howell & Co, c1880, 15½in (39.5cm) high.
£2,250–3,350
$3,250–4,850 ⊞ JMW

A Regency black slate and gilt-bronze mantel timepiece, the fusee movement signed Grimalde & Johnson, 431 Strand, London, 11in (28cm) high.
£1,850–2,800
$2,700–4,000 ⚒ P

A William IV rosewood mantel clock, the 5in (12.5cm) painted dial signed Huggins, London, the fusee and chain movement with anchor esapement, c1830, 13in (33cm) high.
£1,500–2,250
$2,150–3,250 ⚒ S

A gilt-bronze mantel clock, with 3¼in (8.5cm) engine-turned dial, the slender vertically aligned fusee movement signed Thomas Hawley, Strand, London, the suspension with horizontal adjustment, the waisted case with foliate scrolls, c1830, 14in (35.5cm) high.
£2,250–3,150
$3,250–4,550 ⚒ S(S)

A mantel clock, the painted dial marked Howell James & Co, London, with 8-day striking movement and porcelain case, c1860, 12in (30.5cm) high.
£3,150–3,700
$4,550–5,350 ⚒ DSH

A French gilt-spelter and porcelain-mounted mantel clock, with porcelain dial, 8-day movement striking on a bell, bearing the maker's stamp Japy et fils, with pendulum, giltwood base, on cast gilt feet, c1860, 14½in (37cm) high.
£1,100–1,500
$1,600–2,100 ⚒ CSK

A bronze and gilt-bronze mantel timepiece, the enamel dial signed Louis Habram à Montbrison, the similarly signed verge watch movement numbered 377, watch replaced, late 18thC, 4in (10cm) high.
£2,250–3,350
$3,250–4,850 ⚒ S

A French *champlevé* enamel and gilt-metal lyre-shaped mantel clock, with Japy Frères movement striking on a bell, c1890, 13in (33cm) high.
£1,300–2,000
$1,900–3,000 ⚒ Bea

A gilt-bronze and mantel clock, signed Japy Frères, the movement with silk suspension and outside countwheel, c1840, 23½in (59.5cm) high.
£2,800–4,650
$4,000–6,750 ⚒ S

A French bronze and gilt-bronze mantel clock, with enamelled annular chapter ring with blue Roman numerals and regulator square above XII, with 8-day movement by Japy Frères, c1850, 22in (56cm) high.
£3,150–4,650
$4,550–6,750 ⚒ Bea

A French mantel clock, with 8-day movement stamped Japy & Frères, the enamelled dial Howell James & Co, c1850, 11in (28cm) high.
£3,350–4,650
$4,850–6,750 ⚒ DSH

A French mantel clock, the 2 train movement striking on a bell, stamped Japy Frères Médaille d'Honneur, initialled F & PF and numbered 111, with porcelain panels, c1850, 12in (30.5cm) high.
£3,000–3,250
$4,400–4,700 ⊞ DRA

French gilt-brass mantel clock, with Japy bell striking movement, o. 1125, c1870, 16in (41cm) high.
2,800–3,700
4,000–5,300 ⚒ S

A Victorian black marble clock, with Japy Frères striking movement and female mask designs to the sides, c1845.
£350–550
$500–800 ⚒ GAK

▶ **A French gilt-bronze-mounted red boulle mantel clock,** with 24 piece cartouche dial, Japy Frères bell striking movement, No. 3644, the case veneered with red shell inlaid with brass, c1870, 18in (46cm) high.
£1,850–2,800
$2,700–4,000 ⚒ S

A *champlevé* **enamel-mounted four-glass mantel clock,** the enamel dial painted with garlands of flowers and signed for Tiffany & Co, the Japy Frères gong striking movement with mercury pendulum, c1890, 11in (28cm) high.
£3,700–4,650
$5,350–6,750 ➶ S

A French gilt-brass mantel clock, with Japy Frères bell striking movement, No. 7857, the ogee arched case inset at the front and sides with faïence polychrome panels, on a plinth with elephant head feet, c1880, 15in (38cm) high.
£1,100–1,500
$1,600–2,100 ➶ S

A French green onyx and *champlevé* **enamel four-glass mantel clock,** the gilt dial with enamel surround and centre, the gong striking movement stamped Japy Frères, with Brocot suspension, c1905, 13½in (34cm) high.
£1,500–2,400
$2,150–3,500 ➶ S(S)

A French ormolu, bronze and marble mantel clock, the white enamel dial inscribed Lacour A Aubigny, the twin train movement with countwheel strike, c1840, 18in (46cm) high.
£1,100–2,200
$1,600–3,200 ➶ CSK

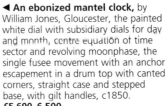

A French four-glass mantel clock, the enamel dial signed Tiffany & Co, the Japy Frères gong striking movement with Brocot escapement and miniature set pendulum bob, the case with glazed cushion form cresting and moulded base, 1900, 10½in (27cm) high.
£2,200–3,350
$3,200–4,850 ➶ S

An ormolu mantel clock, by Japy Frères, Paris, the white enamel dial with black Roman numerals, inscribed Muirhead à Paris, the 8-day movement with outside countwheel striking on a bell, the case surmounted with figures, c1840, 21in (53cm) high.
£1,500–1,850
$2,100–2,700 ➶ Bea

◀ **An ebonized mantel clock,** by William Jones, Gloucester, the painted white dial with subsidiary dials for day and month, centre equation of time sector and revolving moonphase, the single fusee movement with an anchor escapement in a drum top with canted corners, straight case and stepped base, with gilt handles, c1850.
£5,600–6,500
$8,100–9,400 ➶ Bon

A French four-glass mantel clock, the movement inscribed Klaftenberg Paris, 19thC, 11in (28cm) high.
£1,850–2,800
$2,700–4,000 ➶ P

A silvered and gilt-bronze Gothic Revival mantel clock, signed Le Plastriers, Paris, with gilt pierced dial, the movement with silk suspension, striking on a gong in the mahogany plinth base, the ornate case surmounted by a bell tower, with pierced and gilt pendulum, c1835, 26in (66cm) high.
£950–1,500
$1,380–2,150 ➶ S(S)

◀ **A French ormolu and porcelain mantel clock,** inscribed Le Roy à Paris, the bell striking movement with outside countwheel, 19thC, 16in (40cm) high.
£2,200–3,350
$3,200–4,850 ⊞ PWC

A French gilt-bronze and black marble mantel clock, signed Laguesse & Farrett A Paris, the bell striking movement with outside countwheel and silk suspension, c1835, 15½in (39.5cm) high.
£1,300–1,650
$1,900–2,400 ➶ S(S)

◀ **A French ormolu mantel clock,** by Le Roy & Fils, Paris, the dial with green patinated frame, c1835, 10in (25.5cm) high.
£1,500–2,200
$2,150–3,200 ➶ WHB

A French four-glass *régulateur de table*, signed Le Roy et fils Pals Royal Grie, Montpensier 13–15 Paris, with enamel dial, twin going barrel movement striking on a bell, with 3 rod gridiron pendulum, 22in (56cm) high.
£3,700–5,600
$5,300–8,100 ➶ C

A Charles X ormolu and porcelain clock, signed Le Roy, Paris 1102, with silvered face and foliate bezel, c1840, 16in (41cm) high.
£1,500–2,200
$2,100–3,200 ➶ C

▶ **A French rosewood mantel clock,** by Lainé of Paris, with 8-day striking movement, 1840, 10in (25.5cm) high.
£1,100–1,650
$1,600–2,400 ⊞ BD

An Empire bronze and ormolu mantel clock, the twin train movement with bell strike, the white enamel dial with Roman and Arabic chapter ring, inscribed Le Sieur à Paris, with engine-turned bezel, c1825, 14in (35.5cm) high.
£2,800–3,350
$4,000–4,850 ✗ CSK

A French ebony and enamel clock, by Lainé A Paris, c1850, 14in (35.5cm) high.
£700–800
$1,000–1,200 ⊞ SBA

A French mahogany portico clock, the 5in (12.5cm) dial signed Le Roy Hr Du Roi A Paris, with centre seconds, the movement with pinwheel escapement, knife-edge suspension, gridiron pendulum, outside countwheel cut for the quarters and striking on 2 bells, the 4 pillar case with engine-turned ormolu capitals, c1810, 21½in (54.5cm) high.
£4,650–5,600
$6,750–8,100 ✗ S

A Meissen mantel clock, the enamel dial signed Le Roy & Cie, blue crossed sword and impressed 28, the case moulded with pink-edged shell scrolls and foliage, surmounted by Venus with cupid attendant, some repairs, c1750, 16½in (42cm) high.
£3,700–5,600
$5,300–8,100 ✗ C

A Directoire mahogany four-glass mantel clock, the 5½in (14cm) enamel dial with central calendar ring and signed Pierre Le Roy à Paris, the silk suspension movement with anchor escapement, outside countwheel and bell striking, the brass-bound glazed case with bun feet, c1795, 16½in (42cm) high.
£3,350–3,700
$4,850–5,500 ✗ S

A French gilt-brass and porcelain panel mantel clock, the 4½in (11.5cm) dial painted with a garland and signed Le Roy à Paris, the movement with silk suspension and with stamped backplate, c1845, 18½in (47cm) high.
£3,350–4,650
$4,850–6,750 ✗ S

▶ **An Empire mahogany striking portico clock,** stamped Le Roy à Paris on the backplate, with silvered Roman chapter disc, blued moon hands, twin going barrel movement with anchor escapement and countwheel strike on bell, the case with rectangular plinth applied with foliate ormolu mounts, c1825, 20in (50.5cm) high.
£1,500–1,850
$2,100–2,700 ✗ C

A French gilt-brass mantel clock, the enamel dial inscribed Breveté, Le Roy & Fils, Paris, 19thC, 21in (53.5cm) high.
£5,100–7,000
$7,400–10,200 ✗ P

An English ormolu mantel timepiece, signed James Leslie, Strand, London, the chain and fusee movement with verge escapement, No. 81, c1800, 12in (30.5cm) high.
£3,000–4,650
$4,400–6,700 ⚒ CSK

A Georgian ebonized balloon clock, the restored enamel dial signed Leroux, Charing Cross, the fusee movement with shaped plates and anchor escapement, 1765, 21in (53.5cm) high.
£8,400–11,150 $12,200–16,000 ⚒ P

A French brass and copper industrial architectural mantel clock, the dial inscribed Marsh, Paris, 19thC, 16in (41cm) high.
£4,650–6,500 $6,750–9,400 ⚒ P

A mantel clock, with brass and bevelled glass case, the 8-day movement by Marti et Cie, striking to bell, the enamel dial with exposed deadbeat escapement having a compensating mercury pendulum, c1870, 13½in (34.5cm) high.
£2,250–3,000
$3,250–4,400 ⚒ DA

A French World Time mantel clock, main chapter ring with I–XII twice in Roman numerals, outer Arabic minutes, the movement stamped Marti et Cie, Paris, and Breveté of Dutot, SBDG, striking on a bell, in a four-glass case with glazed panel to top, c1890, 14in (35.5cm) high.
£2,750–3,500
$4,000–5,000 ⊞ DRA
Within the chapter ring is a rotating centre displaying the time at some 70 places throughout the world.

A gilt, bronze and marble mantel clock, the enamel dial signed J. B. Marchand A Paris, bell striking movement, the gilt case with the seated figure of a woman in classical dress and a young scholar with a book, the white marble plinth profusely decorated with gilt-bronze mounts, c1850, 24in (61cm) high.
£3,700–4,650
$5,350–6,750 ⚒ S

▶ **A boulle and red tortoiseshell mantel clock,** by Marti, with repoussé brass dial, the movement striking the hours and half-hours on a gong, stamped, c1880, 13½in (34.5cm) high.
£1,500–1,800
$2,150–2,600 ⊞ DRA

◀ **A French bronze patinated-brass mantel clock,** the gilt-brass dial with blue on white enamel Roman numeral panels, pendulum missing, c1890, 23in (58.5cm) high.
£1,100–1,700
$1,600–2,400 ⚒ P(S)

A French Art Nouveau four-glass and brass mantel clock, by S. Marti, the movement with Brocot type suspension, gong striking, mercurial pendulum, trade stamped, c1880, 15½in (40cm) high.
£750–950
$1,100–1,300 ⚒ L

A Napoleon III oval four-glass perpetual calendar mantel clock, the bell striking Marti movement No. 6635 with Brocot escapement and mercury pendulum, the two-piece enamel dial centred by a colourful calendar indicating date, day of the week and month, an aperture above showing moonphases, in a gilt-brass moulded oval case, c1880, 15in (38cm) high.
£5,600–7,500
$8,100–10,800 ⚒ S

A Louis XV-style mantel clock, with white enamelled dial signed Meunier à Paris, with 8-day spring-driven striking movement, 19thC, 22½in (57cm) high.
£2,250–3,350
$3,250–4,850 ⊞ TKN

A French ormolu mantel clock, the 4½in (11.5cm) enamel dial decorated with garlands of flowers, bell striking S. Marti movement No. 154 with Brocot escapement, c1890, 21in (53.5cm) high.
£2,800–3,700
$4,000–5,300 ⚒ S

A French ormolu and bronze striking mantel clock, with white enamel Roman chapter ring, blued moon hands, pierced gilt centre, twin going barrel movement with Brocot escapement and foliate cast pendulum, strike on bell on backplate, stamp for Samuel Marti, c1900, 19½in (50cm) high.
£3,700–4,650
$5,350–6,750 ⚒ C

A French ebony-veneered table clock, the 7in (18cm) gilt chapter ring set on a black velvet surround with flower spandrels, signed Balthazar Marinot A Paris, a hinged pendulum aperture cover below, the similarly signed movement with tandem drive from a single spring barrel, verge escapement with altered cycloidal cheeks, outside numbered countwheel and well-pierced steel striking gates, distressed, c1670, 14in (35.5cm) high.
£4,650–5,600
$6,750–8,100 ⚒ S

A French gilt mantel clock, by S. Marti et Cie, with countwheel striking on a bell, c1880.
£550–950
$800–1,300 ⊞ IAT

▶ **A Meissen clock case,** moulded with foliage heightened in pink and turquoise, with 3 putti emblematic of Winter, Spring and Autumn, chips to flowers, blue Meissen mark, the movement by Lenzkirch, c1890, 20½in (52cm) high.
£1,700–2,250
$2,400–3,250 ⚒ C

A French ormolu and porcelain mantel clock, signed Martin & Co, c1850, 13½in (34.5cm) high.
£1,500–2,800
$2,500–3,500 ⚒ Bon

A French tortoiseshell-veneered mantel clock, with 4½in (11.5cm) white enamel dial, the movement stamped S. Marti, c1870, 13½in (34cm) high.
£2,250–3,350
$3,250–4,850 ⚒ GSP

A French boulle and tortoiseshell clock, by Morgan, Paris, 8-day duration, c1860, 13½in (34.5cm) high.
£1,500–1,700 $2,000–2,500 ⊞ SO

A French bronze and marble mantel clock, the 3½in (8.5cm) dial with serpent hands, bell striking movement No 4921, with jewelled lever platform escapement, signed Ed. Minart, c1875, 20in (51cm) high.
£3,700–5,600
$5,300–8,100 ⚒ S

◄ **A gilt-metal-cased mantel clock,** by T. Moss, Ludgate Street, the gilt dial with black Roman numerals and engine-turned decoration to centre, strike and silent movement, supported on gilt-metal Ionic scroll, the white marble base with applied gilt-metal decoration, c1815.
£2,250–2,800
$3,250–4,000 ⚒ LANG

◄ **A French red boulle mantel clock,** with 5½in (14cm) 13-piece enamel cartouche dial, square plated gong striking movement No. 42013 with Brocot escapement, sunburst pendulum stamp of A. D. Mougin, c1885, 23½in (60cm) high.
£2,250–3,350
$3,250–4,850 ⚒ S

▶ **A French ormolu and porcelain mantel clock,** the decorated dial signed for Miller & Co, Bristol, c1870, 17in (43cm) high.
£1,850–3,250
$2,700–4,700 ⚒ P

◄ **An ebonized and brass-inlaid mantel timepiece,** inscribed on the backplate D. & W. Morrice, 86 Cornhill, c1820, 7½in (19cm) high.
£2,800–4,650
$4,000–6,750 ⚒ P

A mahogany and brass-inlaid table clock, with 8in (20.5cm) painted dial, strike/silent above XII, 5 pillar bell striking fusee movement signed James McCabe, Royal Exchange, London, c1810, 19in (48.5cm) high.
£1,850–2,800
$2,700–4,000 🔨 S

A French four-glass brass mantel clock, the movement with Brocot type escapement, mercury pendulum, bell striking, stamped H. P. & Co, c1870, 14in (35cm) high.
£2,250–2,800
$3,250–4,000 🔨 L

A French Empire mantel clock, by BP & F, No. 4618, with 4½in (11.5cm) dial, 8-day striking movement, bird's-eye maple veneered case with 4 gilt-mounted columns, c1840, 22½in (57cm) high.
£1,300–1,700
$1,900–2,500 ⊞ GA(W)

A French ormolu mantel clock, the 5in (12.5cm) white enamelled dial signed Perrache à Paris, the drum movement with signed backplate, silk suspension and outside countwheel, bell striking, c1770, 16½in (42cm) high.
£3,700–4,650
$5,350–6,750 🔨 S(S)

Transporting a clock

The spring from which the pendulum is suspended is fragile and may break when the clock is moved. Spring-driven clocks with a short pendulum, such as most 19th-century French clocks, should be held upright when carried. When transporting a bracket clock, take out the pendulum, if it is detachable, or pack the back with tissue paper. When transporting a longcase clock, remove the weights and pendulum. The hood should be taken off, and the dial and movement packed separately.

▶ **A gilt-metal mantel timepiece,** the movement signed Payne, 163 New Bond Street, with anchor escapement, c1840, 12½in (32cm) high.
£2,800–3,350
$4,000–4,850 🔨 C

A French striking mantel clock, by Jacob Petit, Paris, with enamel dial, c1860, 15½in (39.5cm) high.
£2,250–3,350
$3,250–4,850 🔨 McC

A gilt-bronze mantel clock, by Payne, 163 New Bond Street, the twin fusee movement with anchor escapement, c1830, 13½in (34.5cm) high.
£2,800–3,350 $4,000–4,850 🔨 P

A French mantel clock, by Jacob Petit, Paris, porcelain with blue ground, the movement by Hri. Marc à Paris, c1835, 13in (34cm) high, with ebonized wood stand and glass dome.
£1,850–2,250
$2,700–3,200 🔨 C

A Louis XVI ormolu and marble portico mantel clock, the enamel dial signed Piolaine A Paris, c1795.
£2,800–3,700 $4,000–5,000 ⚒ C

A gilt-metal mantel clock, in the form of a Gothic tower, by Raingo, Paris, with outside countwheel, c1830, 28in (71cm) high.
£1,300–2,250 $1,900–3,250 ⚒ AGr

▶ **A mahogany and chequer-strung mantel clock,** the 7in (18cm) silvered dial inscribed Willm. Ray, Sudbury, twin train fusee movement with anchor escapement, c1790, 20in (51cm) high.
£2,800–3,700 $4,000–5,350 ⚒ C

A French mantel clock, the gilded dial set into a multicoloured panel of *champlevé* enamels, the 8-day movement striking the hours and half-hours and signed R. & C, London & Paris, No. 569, c1890, 9½in (24cm) high.
£1,500–1,800 $2,100–2,600 ▦ DRA

A French mantel clock, by Jacob Petit, with engraved silvered metal dial, the striking movement inscribed Dupont à Paris 2371, the case decorated in gilt, blue and white with a trellis pattern, with brass pineapple finial and ormolu bezel, on a matching stand, c1840, 12in (30.5cm) high.
£1,500–2,250 $2,150–3,250 ⚒ MCA

A French gilt-bronze and porcelain mantel clock, with painted 3½in (9cm) dial, cast chapter ring with enamel cartouche numerals, the bell striking Japy movement signed Robin A Paris, with outside countwheel and Brocot suspension, c1860, 16in (40.5cm) high.
£3,000–3,700 $4,400–5,300 ⚒ S(S)

◀ **A French ormolu mantel clock,** with replaced 2in (5cm) silvered dial, the drum movement stamped Robert à Paris, with silk suspension, c1825, 11in (28cm) high.
£750–1,100 $1,100–1,600 ⚒ S(S)

A French ormolu and Sèvres-style porcelain mantel clock, the 8-day striking movement stamped Rollin à Paris, No. 436, c1850, 15in (38cm) high.
£1,850–3,350 $2,700–4,500 ▦ GC

A French porcelain mantel clock, the dial signed Felix Sandoz, London, with striking movement, c1790, 11in (30cm) high.
£3,700–5,600
$5,300–8,100 ⚒ C

A French ormolu mantel clock, by Stainville & Robin, Paris, c1860, 19in (48cm) high.
£750–1,700
$1,100–2,400 ⚒ WHB

A Louis XIV tortoiseshell and brass boulle mantel clock, the 4½in (11.5cm) enamel dial signed Sibelin A Paris, the movement now with anchor escapement and lacking striking train, backplate also signed, c1710, 16in (40.5cm) high.
£3,700–4,650
$5,350–6,750 ⚒ S(S)

A French gilt-bronze and green onyx mantel clock, the keyless movement with gilt dial signed Sorley, Paris, the 6in (15cm) diam. magnifying sphere between the outstretched wings of an eagle seated on a rocky base above a turned support with a square base, c1900, 18in (45.5cm) high.
£1,850–2,800
$2,700–4,000 ⚒ S(S)

A South German rococo table clock, with rocaille carved giltwood frame, the dial with pewter chapter ring, front swinging pendulum to verge escapement, above twin going barrel movement, with twin countwheel quarter strike on 2 vertically planted bells, 21in (53.5cm) high.
£3,700–5,600
$5,350–7,000 ⚒ C

A French ormolu mantel clock, the circular exposed dial with enamelled numerals inscribed Silvany à Paris, enclosing a brass 8-day movement inscribed Raingo Frères, Paris, with silk suspension, pendulum and strike on a single bell, case and movement No. 2393, c1870, 20in (51cm) high.
£1,850–3,350
$2,700–4,500 ⚒ DDM

◀ **A French mantel clock,** by M. Roy, Paris, with 8-day striking movement, the ormolu case mounted with 13 Sèvres porcelain panels, c1850, 20in (50.5cm) high, on giltwood plinth.
£5,600–6,500 $8,100–9,400 ⚒ DSH

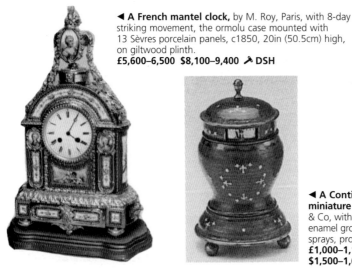

◀ **A Continental silver-gilt and enamel miniature urn clock,** the Swiss movement by Schild & Co, with revolving chapter ring, the guilloche blue enamel ground decorated with fleur-de-lys and floral sprays, probably Austrian, 3in (7.5cm) diam.
£1,000–1,100
$1,500–1,600 ⚒ Bea

◄ **A French gilt-bronze and porcelain mantel clock,** the 3¼in (8.5cm) dial signed Raingo Frèves, A Paris, the bell striking movement with outside countwheel and Brocot suspension, c1850, 21½in (54.5cm) high.
£2,250–3,000
$3,250–4,400 ✗ S(S)

► **A French silvered and ormolu mantel clock,** the movement with countwheel strike on a bell and silk suspension, signed Richond à Paris, c1840, 21in (53cm) high, glass dome.
£900–1,300
$1,300–1,900 ✗ CSK

A French ormolu and white metal clock, with white marble dial, raised numerals, 8-day movement with outside countwheel strike on a bell, signed Rollin à Paris, c1850, 14½in (37cm) high.
£1,850–2,800
$2,700–4,000 ✗ CSK

◄ **A French ormolu and marble perpetual calendar mantel clock,** with two-piece enamel dial signed W. C. Shaw, Paris, bell striking movement with Brocot escapement, a lever connected to the calendar, marble cracked, c1860, 19in (48cm) high.
£4,650–5,600
$6,750–8,100 ✗ S

A French ormolu and bronze mantel clock, the gilt dial with enamel numerals, the movement with silk suspension and countwheel strike, c1840, 22in (56cm) high.
£3,000–4,450
$4,400–6,450 ✗ P

► **A French Empire bronzed mantel clock of Centurion form,** the two-train movement signed Alexandre Roussel à Paris, No. 515, with silk suspension, on marble base, 28½in (71cm) high, with associated granite base inscribed 'Sevastapol, 1855'.
£3,700–5,600
$5,300–8,100 ✗ Bon

◄ **A Regency mahogany and brass-inlaid mantel timepiece,** the enamel dial signed Scott, Horlr to HRH The Duke of Kent, No. 674, the fusee movement with anchor escapement and signed shaped plates, c1820, 10in (25.5cm) high.
£2,800–3,350
$4,000–4,850 ✗ P

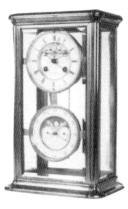

◀ **A gilt-brass four-glass striking mantel clock,** with perpetual calendar dial below the chapter ring with jewelled visible Brocot escapement in the recessed centre, signed Steward, Glasgow, with blued Breguet hands, the movement with twin going barrels striking on a bell on backplate, gorge type case, later plinth base, 17in (43cm) high.
£4,650–5,600
$6,750–8,100 ⚹ C
This clock is possibly a marriage or modern cased.

A late Recency rosewood mantel timepiece, with ball finial to stepped gadrooned top, the arched engraved silvered dial with Roman numerals and signed Thos. Cox Savory, 47 Cornhill, London, No. 762, blued steel Breguet hands, the 4-pillar single chain fusee movement with anchor escapement, c1830, 12in (30.5cm) high.
£2,600–3,150
$3,800–4,500 ⚹ C

A French mantel clock, the movement with countwheel strike on a bell, stamped Vincenti et Cie on the backplate, signed in full Thomas à Paris, c1840, 8½in (21.5cm) high.
£1,200–1,500
$1,750–2,100 ⊞ DRA

A German silvered table clock, with 3 chapter rings, the centre ring showing minutes and inner quarters, flanked by 12 and 24 hour rings, linear fly back hour sector below signed Joseph Laminit, with steel arrow head hand, front swinging pendulum to verge escapement, the movement with 4 ringed pillars and going barrel, c1715, later cover and stand, 13in (33cm) high.
£8,350–11,150
$12,100–16,150 ⚹ C

A Regency ormolu mantel timepiece, signed Tupman, London, the single train fusee movement with anchor escapement, c1820, 8in (20.5cm) high.
£3,350–4,650
$4,850–6,750 ⚹ Bon

A French ormolu and white marble lyre clock, the enamel dial marked Camus, Paris, 19thC, 22in (56cm) high.
£4,650–5,600
$6,750–8,100 ⚹ SK(B)

A French mantel clock, the striking movement by J. Valery, Paris, c1850.
£950–1,700
$1,380–2,400 ⊞ MN

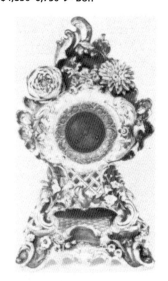

A French porcelain mantel clock, the movement signed Vanson à Paris, the case modelled in relief with flowerheads and sprays, c1850, 13in (33cm) high.
£950–1,700
$1,380–2,400 ⚹ C

A Regency ormolu mantel clock, the striking movement with backplate signed Tupman, Gt Russell St, Bloomsbury, 8in (20.5cm) high.
£2,800–3,700
$4,000–5,300 ⚹ C

A French mantel clock, the 8-day movement by Vincenti & Cie and striking on a bell, the ornate gilt bronze and ormolu case set with Sèvres-style porcelain plaques painted with portraits, cherubs and gilt foliage on a turquoise ground, c1880, 14½in (37cm) high.
£1,700–2,800
$2,450–4,000 🔨 Bea

A French ormolu and porcelain mantel clock, with enamel dial signed Vieyres & Repignon à Paris, c1860, 11in (28cm) high.
£2,050–3,350
$2,950–4,850 🔨 P

A French/English tortoiseshell and silver mantel clock, with enamel dial signed for J. C. Vickery, Regent St, London, 8-day movement with lever escapement, rectangular case with domed cresting and turned finial, the front inlaid with finely cut silver and with silver mouldings, feet and back, hallmarked 1913, shell cracked on cresting, 8½in (21.5cm) high.
£3,000–4,650
$4,400–6,750 🔨 S

A rosewood mantel clock, the twin fusee movement with lever platform escapement striking on a gong and signed on the backplate Viner, London, 19thC, 9in (23cm) high.
£9,300–11,150
$13,500–16,150 🔨 P

A William IV burr walnut mantel clock, with silvered-brass dial signed Vulliamy, London, single fusee 4 pillar movement with anchor escapement and pendulum with adjustable brass bob, c1835, 10½in (26.5cm) high.
£7,450–8,950
$10,800–13,000 🔨 P(M)

LOCATE THE SOURCE
The source of each illustration in Miller's can be found by checking the code letters below each caption with the Key to Illustrations, pages 6–7.

A bronze-mounted red marble mantel clock, with 3in (7.5cm) silvered dial signed Vulliamy, London, pierced heart hands, rubbed, engine-turned centre and ormolu serpent bezel, similarly signed fusee movement, No. 599, with circular plates, half-deadbeat escapement, rise-and-fall regulation and steel rod pendulum with similarly numbered bob, c1820, 11½in (29cm) high.
£2,800–3,700
$4,000–5,300 🔨 S

A black slate, bronze and gilt-metal-mounted mantel timepiece, the fusee movement with anchor escapement and rise and fall regulation, signed Vulliamy, London, No. 510, c1810, 12½in (32cm) high.
£7,450–9,300
$10,800–13,500 🔨 P

◄ **A Regency red marble and gilt-metal mantel timepiece,** by Vulliamy, London, No. 598, the fusee movement with half-deadbeat escapement, c1820, 12in (30.5cm) high.
£2,600–3,150
$3,800–4,500 🔨 C

A burr walnut mantel timepiece, signed John Walker, London, No. 3202, the fusee movement with anchor escapement, c1830, 9½in (24cm) high.
£2,250–3,350
$3,250–4,850 ⚲ P

A Regency marble mantel timepiece, with white enamel dial, the 8-day chain fusee movement signed Vulliamy, London, No. 462, c1810, 11½in (29cm) high.
£7,450–9,300 $10,800–13,500 ⚲ CSK

An oak mantel clock, edged in boxwood, by W. H. of Germany, 8-day duration, striking on ting-tang chimes, c1890, 13in (33cm) high.
£1,100–1,500
$1,600–2,100 ⊞ SBA

A Louis XV gilt-bronze mantel clock, the 5½in (14cm) enamel dial signed Ate. Wolff A Paris, with central calendar and pierced gilt hands, the bell striking movement with circular flat-bottomed plates, verge escapement, silk suspension and outside countwheel, the case re-gilded, c1770, 14½in (36.5cm) high.
£6,900–8,400
$10,000–12,200 ⚲ S

A pale rosewood chiming mantel clock, with 8in (20cm) silvered dial signed Widenham, London, the triple fusee movement quarter chiming on 8 bells and striking on one, with engraved and signed backplate, pull repeat, on brass bun feet, c1835, 18½in (47cm) high.
£4,650–6,500
$6,750–9,400 ⚲ S(S)

A rosewood mantel clock, the 3½in (9cm) silvered dial, with shaped top, signed Wright, London, the fusee movement with anchor escapement, c1840, 12½in (31.5cm) high.
£2,250–3,150
$3,250–4,550 ⚲ S(S)

A rosewood mantel clock, the dial signed Wm. Wilson, Southampton Street, Strand, the 5 pillared fusee movement with anchor escapement, c1840, 12in (30.5cm) high.
£3,350–4,650
$4,850–6,750 ⚲ P

A walnut mantel clock, with 7in (18cm) silvered dial signed John Walker, c1860, 17½in (44.5cm) high.
£2,800–3,700
$4,000–5,300 ⚲ S

A Charles X bronze and ormolu mantel clock, with seated figure of Cato with his helmet and sword amidst the ruins of Carthage, the stepped *griotte* marble base edged with foliage, on bun feet, c1820, 17½in (44.5cm) high.
£2,800–3,700
$4,000–5,300 ⚲ C

An inlaid mantel clock, with 8-day striking movement, c1840.
£700–900
$1,000–1,300 ⊞ MGM

A French mantel clock, in white marble ormolu-mounted case, late 19thC.
£2,250–2,800
$3,250–4,000 ⊞ MIL

A gilt-brass Gothic mantel clock, signed E. White, 20 Cockspur Street, London, with 3½in (9cm) white enamelled dial, the substantial twin fusee movement gong striking and with signed backplate, the case with onion dome, leafy scroll pierced frets and baluster finials, 17½in (44cm) high.
£2,800–3,700
$4,000–5,300 ⚒ S(S)

◀ **A French alabaster and gilt-metal mantel clock,** the movement winding through the face and striking on a single bell, numbered 5754, c1850.
£1,200–1,400
$1,700–2,000 ⚒ HSS

◀ **A Regency white marble and gilt-bronze mantel timepiece,** signed Viner, London, with gilt dial, the fusee movement with anchor escapement, c1810, 8in (20cm) high.
£2,800–3,700
$4,000–5,300 ⚒ P

◀ **A gilt porcelain panelled mantel clock,** with Brocot escapement, c1880, 15in (38cm) high.
£2,800–3,700
$4,000–5,300 ⚒ P

▶ **A Charles X ormolu striking mantel clock,** in a foliate drum case with glazed backplate, the stepped plinth with a relief panel of Cupid and Psyche after Gérôme, c1820, 19in (48cm) high.
£2,250–3,350
$3,250–4,800 ⚒ C

A French red marble perpetual calendar mantel clock and barometer, the movement with Brocot-type suspension, striking on a bell, 2 thermometers, both tubes defective, c1850, 18½in (47cm) high.
£5,600–7,450
$8,100–10,800 ⚒ L

An ornate metal elephant clock, the 8-day movement with outside countwheel, c1870, 21in (53cm) high.
£1,700–2,800
$2,450–4,000 ⚒ AGr

A Regency mahogany and brass-inlaid mantel timepiece, with enamel dial, the fusee movement with anchor escapement, c1820, 9½in (24cm) high.
£2,250–2,600
$3,250–3,800 ⚒ P

◄ **A French boulle mantel clock,** with embossed gilt dial and 2 train movement, c1850, 23in (58.5cm) high.
£2,800–4,650
$4,000–6,700 ⚒ Bon

A Louis XVI marble and ormolu mantel clock, the movement mounted between two Ionic pilasters, with countwheel strike, c1790, 28in (71cm) high.
£4,100–5,950
$6,000–8,600 ⚒ P

A French ormolu mantel timepiece, c1830, 9½in (24cm) high.
£1,850–2,800
$2,700–4,000 ⚒ P

A French green boulle mantel clock, with countwheel striking on a bell, c1850, 13in (33cm) high.
£1,500–2,000 $2,100–2,900 ⊞ IAT

An ormolu mantel timepiece, the calendar verge watch movement with Continental bridge cock and diamond endstone, c1790, 12in (30.5cm) high.
£2,250–3,350
$3,250–4,850 ⚒ Bon

A late Empire bronze ormolu and *griotte* **marble mantel clock,** c1810, 31in (79cm) high.
£4,650–5,600
$6,750–8,100 ⚒ C

A Paris porcelain clock, with Paris movement, the case decorated in gold on a turquoise ground, on a wood stand, with glass dome, c1850, 13in (33cm) high.
£1,500–2,250
$2,150–3,200 ⚒ **Bea**

◀ **A French red marble and bronze mantel clock,** with Louis XVI-style case, in the form of an urn surmounted by a pineapple finial, c1810, 33in (84cm) high.
£18,600–22,300
$27,000–32,300 ⚒ **P**

A terrestrial globe mantel time-piece, signed The Empire Clock, Patent 19460, the sphere rotating with a fixed 24-hour chapter ring, c1890, 11½in (29cm) high.
£2,250–2,800
$3,250–4,000 ⚒ **P**

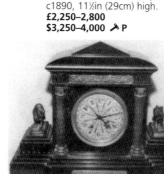

A French mantel clock, c1740, 39in (99cm) high.
£4,650–6,500 $6,750–9,400 ⊞ **EA**

A German walnut mantel clock, striking on a gong, c1880, 14in (35.5cm) high.
£350–500
$500–720 ⊞ **IAT**

A large Victorian black marble mantel clock, with 8-day striking movement, and brass commemorative plaque, c1890.
£650–950
$950–1,300 ⚒ **CBS**

A Sèvres pattern porcelain and ormolu-mounted mantel clock, enriched with gilt and enamel spiral-berried foliage, glass to dial cracked, c1880, 24½in (62cm) high.
£2,800–3,700
$4,000–5,300 ⚒ **C**

A French *champlevé* enamel mantel clock, c1890.
£2,250–2,600 $3,250–3,800 ⚒ **JD**

▶ **A French brass four-glass mantel clock,** c1870, 13in (33cm) high.
£1,250–1,600
$1,800–2,300 ⊞ **IAT**

▶ **A French onyx and gilt-metal mantel timepiece,** c1890, 13in (33cm) high.
£750–1,500
$1,100–2,150 ⚒ **HSS**

A French ormolu mantel clock, c1860, 16in (40.5cm) high.
£1,500–2,250
$2,150–3,250 ⚒ **CSK**

A French ivory mantel clock, with 2½in (6.5cm) enamel dial, movement No. 4153, platform cylinder escapement, outside countwheel striking on a bell, fluted half column case surmounted by a tazza, on scroll feet, 11in (28cm) high.
£5,950–6,900
$8,600–10,000 ⚒ S

◀ **A Meissen mantel clock,** with enamel dial and 8-day striking movement, the case enriched with gilding, with blue crossed swords mark, c1880, 16½in (42cm) high.
£2,250–2,800
$3,250–4,000 ⚒ C

▶ **A Dresden mantel clock,** encrusted with flowerheads and leaves, decorated in underglaze blue, black, flesh tones and gilt, crossed swords mark, damaged, 25in (63.5cm) high.
£1,700–2,250
$2,450–3,250 ⚒ HSS

An Edwardian mahogany mantel clock, c1900, 13in (33cm) high.
£1,100–1,500
$1,600–2,100 ⚒ TW

A French ormolu mantel clock, the movement striking on a bell, c1860, 21in (53.5cm) high.
£2,250–3,700
$3,250–5,300 ⚒ CSK

A French gilt mantel clock, with 8-day striking movement, embossed with cherubs, c1820.
£1,500–2,000 $2,150–2,900 ⊞ MGM

◀ **A French rosewood and marquetry-inlaid architectural-style mantel clock,** the 8-day striking movement with deadbeat escapement, No. 857, with glass dome, c1830, 25½in (65cm) high.
£1,100–1,850
$1,600–2,700 ⊞ GC

An ebony mantel clock, late 19thC.
£950–1,500
$1,380–2,100 ⊞ CER

A tortoiseshell and brass-inlaid mantel clock, the triple fusee movement with anchor escapement, striking the hours on a gong, with Louis XIV-style case, 19thC, 23in (58.5cm) high.
£6,500–8,350
$9,400–12,100 ⚒ P

An Edwardian mahogany mantel clock, with French lever escapement, 6in (15cm) high.
£100–120
$145–175 ⊞ IAT

A French ormolu mantel clock, with 2 train movement, c1820, 16½in (42cm) high.
£3,350–4,650
$4,850–6,750 ✗ Bon

An ormolu mantel clock, with jewelled Sèvres pattern porcelain dial, striking movement, 15in (38cm) high.
£3,350–4,650
$4,850–6,750 ✗ C

A French gilt-brass mounted mantel clock, the bell striking movement in a spherical case painted with zodiacal devices and supported on a winged eagle, on a white marble base, c1870, 13½in (34.5cm) high.
£1,100–1,700
$1,600–2,400 ✗ S(S)

A French ormolu and enamel panelled mantel clock, with striking gong, with musical trophy surmount, c1890, 10½in (26.5cm) high.
£1,850–2,800
$2,700–4,000 ✗ S(S)

A Meissen mantel clock, painted with gilt panels of birds perched amongst branches, slight damage and restoration, crossed swords mark in underglaze blue and incised numerals, c1880, 16in (40.5cm) high.
£3,150–4,100
$4,500–6,000 ✗ S

A Gothic-style brass mantel clock, with enamel dial, 8-day duration, c1840, 9½in (24cm) high.
£950–1,400
$1,300–2,000 ⊞ SBA

A mahogany and brass-inlaid mantel clock, the twin chain fusee movement with pendulum lock striking on a bell, c1825, 20in (51cm) high.
£2,800–3,700
$4,000–5,300 ✗ CSK

A Viennese architectural clock case, painted *en camaieu* rose in the manner of J. P. Dannhofer, the upper part with a portrait of Emperor Franz Stephan, c1730, 15in (38cm) high.
£3,700–5,600
$5,500–8,100 ✗ C

▶ **A mantel clock,** in a French porcelain case, painted with sprays of flowers in bright enamel colours and gold, c1850, 18in (42.5cm) high.
£650–750
$950–1,100 ✗ Bea

◀ **A mantel timepiece and barometer,** revolving via a power source in the base, c1880, 17in (43cm) high.
£1,500–2,250
$2,150–3,250 ✗ P

A French boulle clock,
with 8-day duration, c1835,
8in (20cm) high.
£900–1,200
$1,300–1,700 ⊞ SO

An oak balloon clock, with
8-day French movement, c1905,
10in (25.5cm) high.
£250–350
$360–500 ⊞ SO

For further examples of
Mantel Clocks please refer
to the Colour Reviews.

A Charles X gilt-bronze mantel clock,
with engine-turned gilt dial flanked by a
dog and a classical figure playing a flute,
surmounted by a two-handled urn, the
2 train spring-driven movement with
countwheel mechanism striking
on a bell, c1820, 17in (43cm) high.
£1,850–2,800
$2,700–4,000 ✦ P(M)

**A French rosewood and marquetry
mantel clock,** 8-day duration,
c1840, 13½in (34.5cm) high.
£1,200–1,500
$1,750–2,100 ⊞ SO

A French mantel clock, c1900, 5in (13cm) high.
£80–120
$115–175 ⊞ SO

A grey spelter mantel clock,
the French brass 8-day movement
striking on a single bell, with a
classical figure over a tapering
case with mask mounts, on a
stepped base and marble plinth,
c1890, 17in (43cm) high.
£400–550
$580–800 ✦ DDM

**A French gilt-brass mantel
clock,** the porcelain dial with
Roman numerals, the
movement striking the hours
and half-hours on a gong, with
giltwood stand and pendulum,
c1890, 17½in (44.5cm) high.
£1,100–1,700
$1,600–2,500 ✦ Bea

A French balloon clock, c1900,
10in (25.5cm) high.
£350–450 $500–650 ⊞ SO

A French gilt clock, c1860, 17in (43cm) high.
£2,800–3,700
$4,000–5,500 ⊞ SBA

A French gilt mantel clock,
8-day striking movement,
c1890, 15in (38cm) high.
£700–800
$1,000–1,200 ⊞ SO

A Meissen porcelain mantel clock,
slight damage, c1850, 21in (53cm) wide.
£1,850–2,800
$2,700–4,000 ⚒ HCH

A mantel clock in a Meissen case,
modelled as a putto reading from an
open book, cockerel's tail feathers
repaired, c1890, 11in (28cm) high.
£3,700–4,650
$5,350–6,750 ⚒ CSK

**A French four-glass mantel
clock,** c1890, 11in (28cm) high.
£1,100–1,300
$1,600–1,900 ⊞ SO

A French gilt mantel clock, with 3½in
(9cm) enamelled chapter ring, the drum
movement with silk suspension and
outside countwheel, the case in the form
of a stylized chariot on a fanciful cloud
base, c1820, 14½in (37cm) high.
£3,700–4,650
$5,350–6,750 ⚒ S

A French balloon clock,
inlaid with satinwood,
c1905, 10in (25.5cm) high.
£300–500
$450–750 ⊞ SO

▶ **A French ormolu and ebony
clock,** c1850, 26in (66cm) high.
£1,400–1,800
$2,000–2,600 ⊞ RFA
A similar clock is in the Royal
apartments in Windsor Castle.

**A French ormolu ebonized
and boulle mantel clock,** with
striking movement, c1870.
£1,850–2,600
$2,700–3,800 ⚒ GAK

**A French ormolu and white marble
mantel clock,** the enamel dial with pierced
gilt hands, c1850, 27½in (70cm) high.
£2,050–3,350
$3,000–4,850 ⚒ P

A French gilt-metal mantel timepiece, the 8-day
movement with Farcot escapement, with swinging
cherub pendulum, skeletonized case, white
enamelled chapter ring, c1875, 9½in (24cm) wide.
£1,500–1,850
$2,150–2,700 ⚒ CSK

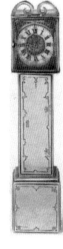

◄ **A silver mantel timepiece,** in the form of a miniature longcase clock, the lever movement with engraved gilt spandrels and silvered chapter ring, c1900, 5½in (14cm) high.
£750–1,100
$1,100–1,600 ⚒ P

A French white marble and ormolu-mounted mantel clock, c1850, 15in (38cm) high.
£1,850–2,600
$2,700–3,800 ⚒ GM

A Charles X mahogany and ormolu-mounted mantel clock, the silvered chapter ring with gilt foliate cast bezel and centre, pierced grille below, the 8-day movement striking on a bell, c1825, 16in (41cm) high.
£1,500–2,250
$2,150–3,250 ⚒ CSK

An Empire-style ormolu and bronze mantel clock, the frieze with Apollo in his chariot, the movement No. 8829 3 9, dated 1889, 15in (38cm) high.
£1,100–1,650
$1,600–2,400 ⚒ C

A French gilt mantel clock, with white enamel dial, with blue numerals and blued steel moon hands, the 8-day movement with countwheel strike on bell, pendulum and bell missing, c1860, 18in (45.5cm) high.
£950–1,650
$1,380–2,400 ⚒ CSK

A French ormolu mantel clock, with enamel dial, c1850, 21½in (55cm) high.
£1,300–2,050
$1,900–3,000 ⚒ P

A French ormolu and porcelain mantel clock, on giltwood base, c1860, 14in (35.5cm) high, on an ebonized base under a glass dome.
£3,000–3,700
$4,400–5,500 ⚒ P

► **A Louis XV style white marble and ormolu mounted lyre-shaped clock,** with white enamel and swagged dot dial and swinging paste-set bezel, the 8-day movement striking on a bell, c1890, 16½in (42cm) high.
£3,700–5,600
$5,350–8,100 ⚒ CSK

A Regency mahogany mantel clock, the white painted dial inscribed Yonge & Son, Strand, London, with twin fusee movement, striking on a bell, some damage and repairs, c1815, 18½in (47cm) high.
£3,350–4,650
$4,850–6,750 ⚒ CSK

A French ormolu and enamel mantel clock, the enamel dial with pierced gilt mask, the case with bowed front flanked by turned and decorated Corinthian columns, c1890, 12in (30.5cm) high.
£2,600–3,350
$3,800–4,850 ⚒ P

An Empire gilt-metal mantel clock, 1820, 21in (53cm) high.
£2,400–3,150
$3,500–4,500 ↗ LRG

A classical revival marble mantel clock, c1890, 22in (53cm) high.
£750–1,300
$1,100–1,900 ↗ SK(B)

A Berlin porcelain mantel clock, with enamel dial, the case painted with scenes of figures in 18thC dress, the handles modelled as cherubs' heads, surmounted by a draped urn and cover, standing on 4 scroll feet, enriched in colours and gilt, blue sceptre mark, c1880, 13½in (34.5cm) high.
£1,700–2,250
$2,500–3,250 ↗ CSK

A French Empire-style mantel clock, c1880, 14in (35.5cm) high.
£950–1,400
$1,380–2,000 ⊞ JeB

A French Louis XV-style mantel clock, the gilt dial with enamel numerals, 8-day striking movement in red tortoiseshell and brass boulle case with leafage scroll ormolu mounts, c1880, 17in (43cm) high.
£1,300–2,250
$1,900–3,250 ↗ RBB

A rosewood mantel timepiece, with 4in (10cm) silvered brass dial, backplate signed Brockbank & Atkins, No. 419, c1840, 10½in (27cm) high.
£2,500–3,000
$3,600–4,400 ⊞ DRA

◄ **An ormolu-mounted bluejohn urn clock,** with pineapple finial on a domed lid, swan-neck handles, revolving enamel dial, fluted socle square plinth, 19thC, 14½in (37cm) high.
£12,100–14,000
$17,500–20,200 ↗ AH

A cast-brass mantel clock,
8-day striking movement, on
claw feet, c1895.
£750–850
$1,100–1,250 ⊞ **MGM**

A French mantel clock, the
3¾in (9.5cm) dial with black
Roman numerals and blued steel
hands, the movement with
outside countwheel striking on
a bell, in rococo bronzed spelter
case, c1890, 27in (68.5cm) high.
£950–1,500
$1,380–2,100 ⚒ **L**

**A French gilt-spelter mantel
clock,** with white enamel Roman
dial, twin going barrel movement
with countwheel strike on a bell,
c1880, 12in (30.5cm) high.
£350–550
$500–800 ⚒ **CSK**

**A French tortoiseshell and
brass-inlaid mantel clock,**
with 8-day striking move-
ment, gilt-metal mounts to
case, c1870.
£2,500–3,000
$3,600–4,400 ⊞ **MGM**

**A Louis XVI ormolu and biscuit
porcelain mantel clock,** the glazed
enamel dial marked A Paris, c1790,
13½in (34.5cm) high.
£5,000–6,500
$7,250–9,400 ⚒ **C**

**A French gilt-brass and bronze-mounted
mantel clock,** the dial painted with garlands,
bell striking movement, the case flanked by a
reclining putto, on a white marble base, c1875,
10½in (26.5cm) high.
£1,500–2,250
$2,150–3,250 ⚒ **S**

A French rosewood mantel clock, c1840.
£1,500–2,250
$2,150–3,250 ⚒ **DaD**

**A French Empire ormolu and marble
mantel clock,** with a 3½in (9cm) dial, the
movement with outside countwheel
striking on a bell, in a gilt-brass case in
the form of a cloth-covered table, with a
figure of woman reading a book by the
light of an oil lamp, on an *antico verde*
marble base and turned feet, damaged,
c1805, 12½in (32cm) high.
£4,650–6,500
$6,750–9,400 ⚒ **L**

**An ebonized mantel
calendar timepiece,** the
engine-turned gilt dial with
Roman numerals and engraved
arch below, numbered from
centre with mechanical day
dial, simple fusee movement,
c1820, 7in (18cm) high.
£3,700–5,600
$5,350–8,000 ⚒ **GSP**

A French gilt, silvered and patinated bronze automaton mantel clock, the 3in (7.5cm) silvered dial with serpent bezel, bell striking movement with altered pendulum suspension, c1840, 17in (43cm) high.
£1,500–2,250
$2,150–3,250 ⚒ S

A French revolving chapter ring mantel clock, the altered movement with lever escapement, 2 enamel chapter rings in a globe flanked by Venus with a lyre and Cupid, the red marble plinth applied with ormolu mounts, c1880, 19½in (49.5cm) high.
£5,600–7,450
$8,100–10,800 ⚒ S

A French boulle mantel clock, with 5½in (14cm) cartouche dial and bell striking movement, c1850.
£1,300–2,050
$1,900–3,000 ⚒ S(S)

A French ormolu and Belgian black marble mantel clock, surmounted by a bronze group personifying Summer, c1845, 27in (68.5cm) high.
£1,500–2,250
$2,150–3,250 ⚒ CSK

A gilt-bronze and white marble mantel clock, with 2in (5cm) enamel dial, the fusee movement with anchor escapement, altered pendulum, the drum surmounted by an eagle, repaired, c1810, 16in (41cm) high.
£1,300–2,250
$1,900–3,250 ⚒ S(S)

A French white marble and ormolu mantel clock, with enamel convex dial, restored, c1895, 7in (18cm) high.
£750–1,100
$1,100–1,600 ⊞ HAW

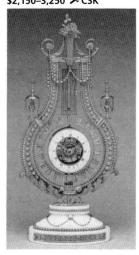

◄ **A Louis XVI gilt, bronze and white marble calendar lyre clock,** the annular enamel dial with central calendar and centre seconds, the bell striking movement with pinwheel escapement and large sunburst movement, gridiron rod and knife-edge suspension, the lyre crisply cast and chased with leaf, bead and guilloche decoration raised on an oval marble plinth, c1790, 22½in (57cm) high.
£14,900–16,750
$21,600–24,300 ⚒ S
This is a particularly fine example of a lyre clock.

A French mantel clock, with porcelain dial and columns, restored, c1890.
£750–1,100
$1,100–1,600 ⊞ HAW

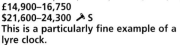

A French bronze and ormolu automaton windmill mantel clock, the 3½in (9cm) silvered dial with engine-turned centre and gilt bezel, bell striking silk suspension movement, the windmill case concealing a subsidiary mechanism for driving the sails, sails and some animals replaced, c1835, 23½in (60cm) high.
£2,250–2,800
$3,250–4,000 ⚒ S

A French gilt-brass mantel clock, with 3½in (9cm) enamel dial, the gong striking movement with Brocot suspension, the Louis XV-style waisted case cast with rococo scrolls, c1850, 20½in (52cm) high.
£1,500–2,250
$2,150–3,250 ⚒ S(S)

A French ormolu and silvered-bronze mantel clock, with bell striking Vincenti movement No. 194, contained in a silvered globe applied with Gothic Roman numerals and with serpent hands, the young Bacchus seated above, the leaf-cast plinth decorated with a fruiting vine, c1850, 14in (35.5cm) high.
£1,500–2,250
$2,150–3,250 ⚒ S

▶ **A French ormolu, bronze and marble mantel clock,** with 3½in (9cm) gilt dial, bell striking movement with pinwheel escapement and silk suspension, the fluted drum case carried on the head of a seated putto with pipes and a tambourine, on a Siena marble plinth with ormolu mounts, c1825, 18in (45.5cm) high.
£3,700–4,650
$5,350–6,750 ⚒ S

A French gilt-metal and white marble mantel clock, the white enamel dial with Roman numerals, the case set with a classical portrait plaque, a cherub to either side and surmounted by goats and a basket of flowers and fruits, late 19thC, 16in (40.5cm) high.
£1,500–2,250
$2,150–3,250 ⚒ Bea

A French marble and gilt-bronze mantel clock, with 4in (10cm) enamel dial, the bell striking movement with outside countwheel and silk suspension, sunburst pendulum, c1810, 19½in (49.5cm) high.
£1,850–2,800
$2,700–4,000 ⚒ S(S)

◀ **A black slate and decorative porcelain-cased mantel clock,** with decorative ormolu mounts, French striking movement, resting on paw supports, c1875, 20in (51cm) high.
£450–650
$650–950 ⚒ MSL

A French bronze mantel clock, with 4½in (11.5cm) dial, formerly silvered, with bell striking silk suspension movement, c1820, 18in (45.5cm) high.
£1,500–2,250
$2,100–3,250 ⚒ S

A Paris porcelain twin train mantel clock, the cartouche-shaped blue-ground case heightened in gilt, painted and modelled with vignettes of flowers, flanked by figures of seated children, the movement with countwheel strike, on a giltwood and gesso stand, c1840, 20in (51cm) high.
£1,850–2,800
$2,700–4,000 ✗ CSK

A French Empire gilt-bronze mantel clock, on marble base, damaged, c1810.
£4,650–6,500
$6,750–9,400 ✗ LRG

A French ormolu and silvered-bronze musical automaton mantel clock, with glass dome, c1840, 17in (43cm) high.
£1,850–2,800
$2,700–4,000 ✗ S

▶ A French gilt mantel clock, c1860, 16in (41cm) high, on giltwood plinth.
£850–1,000
$1,250–1,500 ✗ S(S)

A French ormolu mantel clock, late 19thC, 20in (51cm) high.
£500–900
$720–1,300 ⊞ AHL

A French ormolu mantel clock, c1835, 17in (43cm) high.
£1,000–1,200
$1,500–1,700 ⊞ AHL

A French gilt mantel clock, with drum cased bell striking movement, on scroll supports and shaped plinth, c1880, 15in (38cm) high.
£1,300–2,050
$1,900–2,950 ✗ S(S)

A French ormolu-mounted boulle mantel clock, with 7½in (19cm) cartouche dial, bell striking movement with outside countwheel, the case inlaid throughout with pierced brass decoration, inverted bracket top, surmounted by Minerva, c1870, 42in (107cm) high.
£4,650–6,500
$6,750–9,400 ✗ S

A French Empire mantel clock, with white enamel dial, the 8-day movement striking the hours and half-hours, c1810, 16in (41cm) high.
£2,800–4,100
$4,000–5,950 ✗ Bea

A French brass mantel clock, in late 18thC style, the dial forming the wheel, c1880, 20½in (52cm) high.
£2,800–3,700
$4,000–5,300 ✗ S(S)

A French ormolu mantel clock, with a 4in (10cm) chased dial and bell striking movement, c1825, 14in (35.5cm) high.
£1,500–2,250
$2,150–3,250 ➤ S(S)

A French ormolu mantel clock, surmounted by a figure of Molière seated at a table with manuscripts, c1840.
£1,650–2,800
$2,400–4,000 ➤ LRG

An Austrian carved walnut mantel clock, with a 4½in (11.5cm) cartouche dial, now with a French bell striking movement, the case carved with deer climbing on a rocky mound, c1890, 27in (68.5cm) high.
£1,100–1,500
$1,600–2,100 ➤ S(S)

A Louis XV style bronze elephant mantel clock, c1890.
£2,800–3,700
$4,000–5,300 ➤ P(S)

A French gilt ormolu portico clock, with engine-turned gilt dial, the Roman chapter surrounded by an acanthus leaf cast bezel, round bell striking 8-day movement, putti on a swing pendulum, four-column case with acanthus capitals on a stepped decorated base on 4 feet, c1810, 18in (46cm) high.
£1,500–1,850
$2,150–2,700 ➤ Bon

A small French mantel clock, the silvered dial with Roman numerals, drum case striking movement, gilded case, c1820, 5in (12.5cm) high.
£1,100–2,000
$1,600–3,000 ➤ GAK

▶ **A French/Austrian gilt-bronze-mounted cut-glass mantel clock,** the enamel dial with gilt engine-turned bezel, later French 8-day lever movement, the cylindrical cut-glass case surmounted by an eagle on a ball with gilt-bronze base, damaged, c1825, 15in (38cm) high.
£950–1,300
$1,380–1,900 ➤ S

◀ **A French gilt-brass year-going four-glass mantel timepiece,** the 4in (10cm) two-piece enamel dial with visible Brocot escapement, two-tier movement with high count train, massive spring barrel mounted on the backplate, glazed Ellicott gridiron pendulum, c1870, 14in (35.5cm) high.
£4,650–5,600
$6,750–8,100 ➤ S

A French gilt-brass mantel clock, with a 3½in (9cm) cartouche dial, bell striking, c1860, 17½in (44.5cm) high.
£1,200–1,400
$1,750–2,000 ⚒ S(S)

A French bronze and marble mantel clock, the gilt dial with central engraving, the bell striking movement with outside countwheel and silk suspension, the domed case flanked by figures of Cupid and Psyche, above a base with bronze mounts and feet, c1830, 22in (56cm) high.
£3,700–4,600
$5,350–6,750 ⚒ S(S)

A Louis XVI gilt-bronze mounted white marble mantel clock, the 5in (12.5cm) enamel dial signed A Paris, bell striking movement with circular flat-bottomed plates, later spring suspension and sun mask pendulum, c1790, 24in (61cm) high.
£3,700–5,600
$5,300–8,100 ⚒ S

A French ormolu and Meissen mantel clock, the drum-shaped case with enamel dial, supported within a floral bouquet of applied flowerheads, mounted with winged figures of children, the shaped platform pierced and chased with rocaille, c1890, 13½in (34.5cm) high.
£1,100–1,300
$1,600–1,900 ⚒ CSK

A gilt-metal striking mantel clock, with outside countwheel in the form of a Gothic arch, mid-19thC, 20½in (52cm) high.
£1,500–1,850
$2,150– 2,700 ⚒ AGr

A French brass and boulle mantel clock, with brass dial, the case mounted and surmounted with cherubs, drum case striking movement, c1850, 18in (45.5cm) high.
£1,500–2,250
$2,150–3,250 ⚒ GAK

A French inlaid black marble perpetual calendar mantel clock, with exposed Brocot escapement, calendar dial, in a shaped rectangular case, c1860, 18½in (47cm) high.
£1,850–2,800
$2,700–4,000 ⚒ S(S)

▶ **An Austrian bronze and gilt-bronze mantel clock,** with 3½in (9cm) enamel dial, circular movement with silk suspension, chalet case flanked by a ram and putto, c1840, 12in (30.5cm) high.
£750–1,100
$1,100–1,600 ⚒ S

A Continental parcel-gilt wooden mantel clock, with enamel dial, bell striking silk suspension movement with outside countwheel, bronze patinated wood figure to the side, c1770, 15in (38cm) high.
£3,700–4,650
$5,350–6,750 🔨 S

A French rouge and black marble perpetual calendar mantel clock, the 6in (15cm) white enamelled dial with exposed Brocot escapement, centre second hand, subsidiary calendar and barometer dials and with glazed pendulum aperture, the case mounted with Fahrenheit and Réaumur thermometers, with mercury pendulum, c1850, 18in (46cm) high.
£5,600–7,500
$8,100–10,800 🔨 S(S)

A sculptural bronze mantel clock, the gilt dial with black Roman numeral panels on white enamel, on Siena marble pedestal, c1850, 21in (53.5cm) high.
£950–1,650
$1,300–2,400 🔨 P(S)

◄ **A French vari-coloured marble and gilt mantel clock,** surmounted by a marble urn finial, the base with beading, on gilt turned feet, the white enamel dial with quarter-hour divisions, with timepiece movement, c1900, 8in (20cm) high.
£550–950
$800–1,300 🔨 CSK

A Louis Philippe lacquered brass case mantel clock, the dial with an engine-turned centre and enamel chapter ring, the 8-day movement striking on a bell, with gilt-bronze neo-classical style mounts, c1870.
£950–1,500
$1,380–2,150 🔨 WW

A French ormolu and bronze automaton mantel clock, with silvered engine-turned dial, silvered bell striking silk suspension movement, the automaton galleon driven by a separate key-wound movement, on a bronze plinth, c1835, 17in (43cm) high.
£4,650–5,600
$6,700–8,100 🔨 S

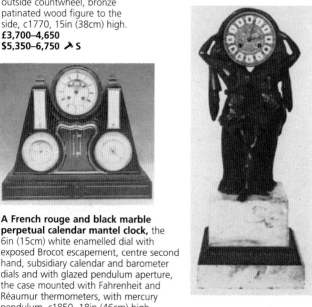

A French mantel clock, with bell striking movement, c1890, 12½in (32cm) high.
£1,100–1,650 $1,600–2,400 🔨 S(S)

◄ **A French Empire bronze and ormolu mantel clock,** with white enamel dial, 2 train movement with suspension, in an arched case with ormolu trophies and cherub appliqués, urn and butterfly finial, c1815, 12in (30.5cm) high, on ebonized base with bowfronted glazed dome, cracked.
£1,850–2,800
$2,700–4,000 🔨 Bon

A French brass mantel clock, with ivorine dial, the pendulum bob in the shape of a stewing pot with detachable cresset fender, on rouge marble base with bracket feet, the 8-day movement with outside countwheel strike on a gong, c1900, 17in (43cm) high.
£750–1,100
$1,100–1,600 ⚹ CSK

A French chinoiserie salon clock, inscribed 'Janvier à Paris', the 8-day movement striking on a bell, the ormolu drum case surmounted by a Chinaman beating a drum and suspended between tiered pagodas with milled galleries and spirals hung with bells and chains, sunburst pendulum, the shaped white marble base with ormolu balustrade and chains, on milled feet, late 18thC, 23½in (60cm) high.
£8,350–10,250
$12,100–14,500 ⚹ N

A French Empire ormolu and simulated malachite mantel clock, the 2 train movement with silk suspension, c1810, 12in (30.5cm) high.
£1,500–2,000
$2,100–2,900 ⚹ Bon

A French four-glass mantel clock, with enamel dial, the bell striking movement No. 2483, visible Brocot escapement and Ellicott pendulum, c1880, 10in (25.5cm) high.
£1,500–2,400
$2,150–3,500 ⚹ S

A French gilt-brass and porcelain mantel clock, the 2 train movement with white enamel annular chapter ring, decorated in gilt against a dark blue ground, c1900, 16in (41cm) high.
£3,700–4,450
$5,350–6,450 ⚹ Bon

An inlaid satinwood mantel clock, with 7in (18cm) cartouche dial and bell striking movement, the waisted case with ebonized and mahogany stringing, c1860.
£1,850–2,800
$2,700–4,000 ⚹ S

◄ **A gilt-bronze and marble calendar mantel clock,** with enamel dials, the bell striking silk suspension movement with a lever leading from the strike train to the calendar mechanism below indicating the date and the day of the week, the black marble case surmounted by an urn and profusely decorated with gilt and formerly patinated bronze mounts, c1850, 19½in (49.5cm) high.
£2,800–3,700
$4,000–5,300 ⚹ S

An ormolu and bronze mantel clock, c1820, 13in (33cm) high.
£1,650–2,600
$2,400–3,800 ⚹ C

Garnitures

► **A French garniture,** the clock by A. Quintrand, with 8-day striking movement, surmounted by Nymphe de Torrent, 19thC.
£400–750
$600–1,100 ⊞ **MGM**

◄ **A German garniture,** the clock movement by Le Roy, Paris, with a pair of two-branch candelabra modelled as musicians, adapted for electricity, some damage, late 19thC, clock 17in (43cm) high.
£1,500–3,000
$2,150–4,400 ⚒ **CEd**

A white marble and gilt-metal garniture, the clock by J. Marti & Cie, c1880, clock 23in (58.5cm) high.
£1,500–2,250
$2,150–3,250 ⚒ **AGr**

A French garniture, in the manner of Jacob Petit, with enamel dial and 8-day bell striking movement by Henri Marc, slight damage, 19thC, clock 17½in (44.5cm) high.
£2,250–3,000
$3,200–4,400 ⚒ **P(S)**

A French gilt-brass garniture, the clock signed Rollin à Paris, the 2 train movement with Brocot type suspension, outside locking plate, belling striking No. 1022, c1850, clock 21in (53cm) high.
£3,000–4,450
$4,400–6,500 ⚒ **L**

A Louis XV-style ormolu-mounted tortoiseshell clock garniture, retailed by R. & W. Sorley, Paris, c1880, clock 23in (58cm) high.
£3,000–4,450
$4,400–6,500 ⚒ **CEd**

► **A French clock garniture,** by Villamesens, Paris, the 8-day movement with outside countwheel striking on a bell, 19thC, clock 20in (51cm) high.
£1,500–2,250
$2,150–3,250 ⚒ **CSK**

A French gilt-brass clock garniture, c1880, 15in (38cm) high.
£1,500–3,000 $2,150–4,400 ⚒ **P**

◄ **A gilt-spelter garniture,** with printed Limoges panels, French 8-day 2 train movement, c1870, clock 16½in (42cm) high.
£1,050–1,800
$1,500–2,600 ⚒ **SWO**

A French gilt, ormolu and porcelain clock garniture, the 4in (10cm) painted porcelain dial with Roman numeral reserves, the decorated centre signed Hry. Marc, Paris, the bell striking movement stamped Japy Frères, c1880, clock 14½in (37cm) high, together with a pair of matching urns.
£3,600–4,200
$5,200–6,100 ⚱ Bon

A French marble and bronze clock garniture, the clock surmounted by a recumbent lion on a stepped marble platform, the dial with gilt-painted Roman numerals, flanked by Corinthian columns, 17in (43cm) high, and 2 side ornaments in the form of a pair of bronze Marley horses, after Coustou, rearing and being restrained by their grooms, 7in (18.5cm) high, on marble bases.
£1,200–1,800
$1,700–2,600 ⚱ S(Am)

A French black marble and bronzed clock garniture, the 5½in (14cm) enamel dial with Roman numerals, signed for Elkington & Co, the square gong movement in an arch-top case, c1880, clock 15in (38cm) wide, together with a pair of urn garnitures.
£1,350–1,800
$2,000–2,600 ⚱ Bon

A French ormolu-mounted white marble clock garniture, signed Le Roy & Fils, the 3½in (9cm) enamel dial decorated with garlands of flowers, bell striking movement with Brocot escapement, on an oval base, with a pair of four-light candelabra fitted for electricity, clock 14in (36cm) high.
£5,200–5,950
$7,500–8,600 ⚱ S

▶ **A French red boulle clock garniture,** with 4in (10cm) 12-piece enamel cartouche dial, bell striking Vincenti movement No. 1482 with sun mask pendulum, together with a pair of conforming three-light candelabra, c1870, clock 15in (38cm) high.
£2,250–2,700
$3,250–3,900 ⚱ S

A French brass and *champlevé* enamel clock garniture, with blue enamel dial, 8-day 2 train movement striking on a bell, signed Wartenberg, Paris, No. 18808, 19thC, clock 16½in (42cm) high, together with 2 ovoid pot-pourri with domed covers.
£2,100–2,400
$3,000–3,500 ⚱ DN

A French clock garniture, with silver and gilt-decorated dial, white enamel chapter ring, black Roman numerals, 8-day movement striking on a bell, 19thC, clock 9½in (24cm) high, together with a pair of similarly decorated urns.
£2,100–2,400
$3,000–3,500 ⚱ Gam

▶ **A French gilt-bronze marble clock garniture,** the 5in (13cm) dial with Arabic numerals and floral swags, signed Thiébault Frea, Paris, 32 Avenue de l'Opéra, bell striking move-ment signed Marti, set into a white marble case, c1880, clock 22½in (57cm) high, and a pair of matching six-light candelabra.
£4,200–4,750
$6,100–6,900 ⚱ Bon

▶ **A bronze night timepiece garniture,** in the style of Thomas Hope, the 4in (10cm) satin glass dial with engine-turned gilt centre, the fusee movement signed Vieyres & Repingon, 129 Regent Street, London, lever escapement and plain steel balance, bronze bezel supported by an owl, c1860, clock 15¼in (39cm) high, with a pair of conforming candlesticks.
£2,100–2,400
$3,000–3,500 ⚱ S

◄ **A French porcelain and ormolu-mounted clock garniture,** the enamel dial inscribed Le Roy & Fils, with circular movement, the bi-metallic pendulum designed for a paste ring to oscillate outside the dial, c1880, clock 19in (48.5cm) high, with a matching pair of four-branch candelabra.
£5,950–7,450
$8,600–10,800 🔨 P

A French white marble, bronze and ormolu clock garniture, the dial signed N. Crouille, Amiens, with 2 train movement, clock 12in (30.5cm) high, flanked by a pair of matching 2 light candelabra.
£3,750–4,850
$5,400–7,000 🔨 Bon

▶ **A French brass, enamel and porcelain-mounted clock garniture,** signed Lefranc, the dial within a bezel, c1880, clock 15in (38cm) high, with a matching pair of side urns, on giltwood bases.
£3,000–3,750
$4,400–5,400 🔨 P

A Sèvres-style porcelain ormolu-mounted clock garniture, with pink and white dial, stamped PH Mourey, c1870, clock 18in (46cm) high, with a pair of matching ormolu-covered two-handled urns.
£3,750–5,200
$5,400–7,500 🔨 CNY

A French gilt-metal garniture, with enamelled dial signed T. Simpson et Cie, Paris, with blue Roman numerals and regulator square above XII, the centre painted with military trophies, the 8-day movement by Japy Frères, striking on a bell, clock 12in (30.5cm) high, with accompanying candelabra, all on giltwood stands and under glass domes.
£2,250–3,000
$3,250–4,400 🔨 Bea

For further examples of Garnitures please refer to Colour Reviews.

A parcel gilt-bronze-mounted black marble clock garniture, the 8-day movement by Marti & Cie, the clock surmounted by a bronze model of the Warwick vase, c1860, 19in (48cm) high, the side pieces in the form of Medici vases.
£900–1,200
$1,300–1,700 🔨 Bea

A French 8-day clock garniture, the dial inscribed Maple & Co Ltd, Paris, some damage, clock 30in (76cm) high.
£5,200–7,450
$7,500–10,800 🔨 Bea

A French red tortoiseshell and ormolu garniture, in the style of Louis XV, the gilt embossed dial with blue Roman numerals on white enamel cartouches, signed on enamel cartouche Martino, Paris, c1090, the 8 day clock 24in (61cm) high, with matching side pieces of five-arm candelabra, on tortoiseshell bases.
£1,800–3,000
$2,600–4,400 🔨 CSK

A black and russet slate garniture, clock dial inscribed Myers, with seated bronze Egyptian figures representing night and day, surmounted by a bust of a pharoah, c1880, clock 17½in (44cm) high, together with twin obelisks.
£900–1,050
$1,300–1,500 🔨 P

A French gilt-metal garniture, the clock with 8-day striking movement by Japy Frères, retailed by A. Carlhian and Beaumetz à Paris, stamped P. H. Mourey, on a gilt-painted stand, 26in (66cm) high, and a pair of candelabra.
£2,250–2,700
$3,250–3,900 ⚒ AG

A pink marble and ormolu garniture, the clock with enamel dial inscribed Made in France for Jas Crighton & Co, Edinburgh, surmounted by an urn on a fluted column and canted plinth, the candlesticks with beaded festooned nozzles on fluted columns, c1870, 8½in (21.5cm) high.
£1,200–1,800
$1,750–2,600 ⚒ C

◀ **A French gilt-bronze and** *champlevé* **enamel garniture,** the clock with brass dial with foliate engraved centre, the bell striking movement stamped Leroy & Fils A Paris, N8038, Brocot suspension, 10½in (26.5cm) high, with a pair of matching cupids formerly with candle branches.
£3,000–4,450
$4,400–6,500 ⚒ S(S)

A French white marble and gilt-brass garniture, the four-glass clock striking on a gong, the bevelled glasses mounted with garlands and with vase surmount, c1800, clock 18½in (47cm) high.
£3,000–4,100
$4,400–6,000 ⚒ S(S)

A French onyx, ormolu and enamel garniture, the clock with gilt dial, signed for Sir John Bennett, the movement with decorated twin glass mercury pendulum, c1890, 12½in (32cm) high, with a pair of side ornaments.
£2,250–2,700
$3,250–3,900 ⚒ P

A French white marble and gilt-metal-mounted composite garniture, the clock with 8-day movement, outside countwheel striking on a gong, c1895, 16in (40.5cm) high.
£1,050–1,650
$1,500–2,400 ⚒ CSK

Garnitures

A *garniture de cheminée* is the French term applied to sets of vases used as chimney-piece decoration, usually in porcelain or delft, with a clock as the central piece. Sets consisted of three, five or seven covered vases and beakers, and were the height of fashion in France in the early 18th century. Garnitures of Chinese porcelain were especially popular. Later examples in Sèvres porcelain were mainly European in style. However, with the advent of the rococo style the symmetrical nature of garnitures was less popular. Single vases and beakers can be found today which once formed part of a garniture.

A French gilt-mounted green marble garniture, the clock with bell striking movement by Gustav Becker, the case applied with gilt caryatids, swags and trophies, c1900, 19in (48cm) high, and a pair of matching vases.
£2,250–2,700
$3,250–3,900 ⚒ S

A French gilt and patinated bronze elephant clock, by Japy Frères, with bell striking movement No. 5697, c1885, 16½in (42cm) high, and a pair of candlesticks.
£4,900–5,500
$7,100–8,000 ⚒ S

A Louis XVI ormolu and salmon marble garniture, the enamel clock dial with zodiac signs, 19thC, clock 22½in (57cm) high, and a pair of candelabra.
£8,200–9,700
$11,900–14,000 ➤ SK(B)

A gilt-metal-mounted cream and brown marble garniture, the movement No. 8608 striking on a bell, surmounted by an eagle, damaged, clock 20in (51cm) high.
£900–1,050
$1,300–1,500 ➤ HSS

A French ormolu and *champlevé* enamel garniture, with decorated dial, twin train movement striking on a bell, the clock case with all-over polychrome designs, 19thC, clock 21½in (54.5cm) high, and a pair of matching side ornaments.
£3,750–4,500
$5,400–6,500 ➤ P

A Second Empire ormolu and white marble garniture, the clock with an alabaster dial with gilt spade hands, the twin going barrel movement with anchor escapement and striking on a bell, clock 15½in (39.5cm) high, and 2 figures of classical ladies, all on foliate cast plinths.
£2,250–3,000
$3,250–4,400 ➤ C

An ormolu and porcelain garniture, the clock with later bell striking movement No. 2853–92, in a *bleu-royale* vase case, 20½in (52cm) high, and a pair of five-branch candelabra.
£1,050–1,650
$1,500–2,400 ➤ Bon

A French boulle garniture, the clock with a 5½in (14cm) cartouche dial, bell striking movement, in a waisted case with gilt-brass scroll mounts and putto finial, 17in (43cm) high, and a pair of four-light candelabra.
£1,800–2,700
$2,600–3,900 ➤ S(S)

▶ **A French gilt-metal and pink and grey striated marble garniture,** the clock movement striking on a bell, gilt-metal putto pendulum, c1900, clock 24in (61cm) high, and a pair of two-handled urns.
£1,200–2,100
$1,750–3,000 ➤ HSS

A French ormolu and enamel garniture, the clock dial and case enamelled with flowers in colours on a black ground, 8-day bell striking movement, 14in (36cm) high, and a pair of candelabra each in the form of a cherub supporting 3 candle sconces.
£1,500–2,250
$2,000–3,250 ➤ P(S)

A Sèvres pattern garniture, the clock dial set into a gilt-metal surround above a porcelain plaque, surmounted by a gilt-metal and porcelain vase held by 2 putti, c1900, 20½in (52cm) high, and 2 vases with turquoise ground porcelain bodies.
£1,500–2,250
$2,100–3,250 ➤ C

A French green onyx and *champlevé* enamel garniture, the clock with a 4in (10cm) enamelled dial, gong striking movement, mercury pendulum, c1900, 13in (33cm) high, and a pair of matching vases.
£1,150–1,850
$1,700–2,700 ⚖ S

A French decorated ormolu and Sèvres porcelain garniture, the clock with a white enamel dial, 8-day striking movement, 19thC, 17½in (44.5cm) high, with a pair of matching candelabra.
£3,750–4,500
$5,400–6,500 ⚖ DSH

A black marble garniture, the clock with 5in (12.5cm) dial, bell striking, 20½in (52cm) high, and a pair of matching tazzas.
£1,200–1,800
$1,750–2,600 ⚖ S

A French ormolu and bronze garniture, c1885, clock 17in (42.5cm) high, with a pair of matching side urns.
£3,000–4,450
$4,400–6,500 ⚖ P

A French white marble and gilt-metal garniture, the clock with white enamel dial, c1890, 15in (38cm) high, and a pair of matching candelabra.
£1,350–2,250
$2,000–3,250 ⚖ C(S)

A Charles X marble and bronze-mounted composite garniture, the clock surmounted by a group depicting the Oath of Horatio, with gilt dial, 8-day movement striking on a bell, silk suspension, 19in (48cm) high, and a pair of matching tazzas.
£2,700–3,300
$3,900–4,800 ⚖ CSK

A French gilt and porcelain garniture, the clock with a 4in (10cm) white enamelled dial and bell striking movement, 12½in (32cm) high, and a pair of matching four-light candelabra, with plinths.
£2,700–3,750
$3,900–5,400 ⚖ S

A French garniture, 19thC, with a pair of matching tazzas.
£2,700–3,300
$3,900–4,800 ⚖ HSS

◄ **A French garniture,** the clock with enamel dial and 8-day striking movement, surmounted by a swan and girl, on a marble base, and a pair of vases in the form of swans.
£550–700
$800–1,000 ⊞ MGM

◄ **A French ormolu garniture,** the clock with white enamelled dial, countwheel striking the hours and half-hours on a bell, c1890, 11in (28cm) high, and a pair of two-light candelabra.
£1,800–2,700
$2,600–3,900 ⚲ HAM

An ormolu and porcelain garniture, the clock with a blue porcelain dial with gilt decoration, Roman numerals in white cartouches with seed pearl decoration, the 8-day movement striking on a bell, 18in (45.5cm) high, and a pair of similarly decorated side pieces, the removable tops with painted scenes to the front and reverse, seed pearl decoration, on gilt bases, some damage.
£3,300–4,200
$4,800–6,000 ⚲ CSK

A French silver-plated brass garniture, the clock surmounted by a putto and floral decoration, 19thC, and a pair of candlesticks.
£3,000–4,500
$4,400–6,500 ⊞ PWC

▶ **A French veined marble garniture,** the clock with white enamel dial indistinctly signed, the 8-day movement with outside countwheel striking on a bell, c1900, 17in (43cm) high, with a pair of matching urns with gilt tops, all on square marble bases with gilt mounts and feet.
£1,500–2,250
$2,100–3,250 ⚲ CSK

A French ormolu garniture, the clock in the form of an owl, the dial with enamel numerals, 19thC, 19½in (49.5cm) high, and a pair of matching three-branch candelabra.
£3,750–5,200
$5,400–7,500 ⚲ P

A Louis XVI-style white marble garniture, the clock with gilt-bronze mounts and French drum movement, late 19thC, clock 14in (35.5cm) high.
£3,000–4,500
$4,400–6,500 ⚲ SWO

A pale rouge marble and ormolu three-piece garniture, c1810, clock 34in (85cm) high.
£17,900–23,850 $26,000–34,600 ⚲ AGr

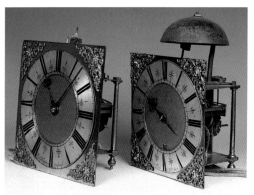

A Napoleon III Egyptian-style mantel clock, in *rosso antico* marble, *nero Belgio* and parcel-gilt bronze, signed Hry Marc, Paris, 18½in (47cm) high.
£1,000–1,200
$1,500–1,700 ✎ CSK

A Directoire mahogany mantel clock, the twin going barrel movement with later Brocot escapement, 20in (51cm) high.
£1,100–1,300
$1,600–1,900 ✎ CSK

A George IV mahogany mantel clock, with white painted Roman dial, twin wire fusee movement, striking on a bell, 18½in (47cm) high.
£5,600–6,500
$8,100–9,400 ✎ CSK

An Empire ormolu urn clock, signed Rodier à Paris, the twin going barrel movement with anchor escapement, 16in (40.5cm) high.
£2,800–3,700
$4,000–5,500 ✎ C

An Empire ormolu striking urn clock, by Le Roy, Paris, with twin going barrel movement, 15in (38cm) high.
£3,700–4,650
$5,300–6,750 ✎ C

A George III mahogany tavern clock, with a painted wooden dial, and single train movement.
£2,500–3,100
$3,600–4,500 ✎ SWO

A French carriage clock, the 8-day movement with quarter and hour striking on 2 gongs, the enamel dial with chapter ring and decoration, the English brass case with carrying handle, c1880.
£2,500–3,000
$3,600–4,400 ⊞ PAO

A Swiss *grande sonnerie pendule d'officier*, by Robert & Courvoisier, No. 8863, c1795, 8in (20cm) high.
£11,000–12,250
$16,000–17,750 ✎ C

A Louis XVI-style ormolu-mounted pink marble three-piece *garniture de cheminée*, the lyre form clock with Arabic chapters and glazed dial, with a pair of five-light candelabra, each with an urn form standard flanked by classical masks and floral garlands, late 19thC, clock 20in (51cm) high.
£7,450–8,200 $10,800–11,900 ✎ CNY

A French Louis XVI-style ormolu and bronze cartel clock, the enamelled dial with Roman and Arabic numerals, signed Bagues Frères fabrts de Bronzes, Paris, 19thC, 32in (81cm) high.
£3,850–4,600
$5,600–6,700 ⚒ C

A French late Louis XVI-style marble and bronze band clock, the movement contained in a vase and cover, supported by 2 cherub terms, on marble plinth, c1870, 22in (56cm) high.
£5,950–7,450
$8,600–10,800 ⚒ S

A brass repeater carriage clock, by Elkington & Co, mid-19thC, 6½in (16.5cm) high.
£1,700–2,000
$2,450–2,900 ⚒ LT

A Directoire long duration quarter striking equation skeleton clock, the Y-form plates signed Bouchet, Horloger du Roy Paris, gilt arrowhead pointer, 18in (46cm) high.
£31,200–36,000
$35,250–52,500 ⚒ C

A French Empire ormolu and bronze *pendule au nègre,* with 3in (7.5cm) enamel dial, bell striking silk suspension movement, c1805, 11in (28cm) high.
£13,400–14,900
$19,400–21,600 ⚒ S

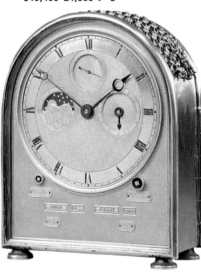

A mahogany dial clock, the painted dial signed Wm. Carter, Hampstead, outer zodiac indication above the automaton scene, c1770, movement and case late 19thC, 15in (38cm) diam.
£2,300–2,900
$3,350–4,200 ⚒ C

A copper lustreware clock, 8in (20cm) high.
£30–40
$45–60 ⚒ PCh

A south German gilt-metal quarter striking *Türmchenuhr,* transverse alarm train lacking, c1600, later verge escapement, 13in (33cm) high.
£15,650–22,350
$22,700–32,400 ⚒ C

◀ **A silver-cased astronomical, calendar and alarm carriage timepiece,** the silver dial signed Breguet, with calendar indicating day, date, month and year, the going barrel movement numbered on the gilt backplate 'B. No. 1624', 1928, 6in (15cm) high.
£64,050–73,200
$92,900–106,000 ⚒ C

A French Empire ormolu mantel clock, with 3¼in (8.5cm) enamel dial, bell striking silk suspension movement, with Cupid and a maiden viewing him through a zograscope, c1810, 14in (36cm) high.
£3,700–4,650
$5,300–6,750 ⚒ S

A French ormolu-mounted 'jewelled' porcelain mantel clock, with bell striking movement by S. Marti, No. 2365, with Brocot escapement, c1880, 20in (51cm) high.
£5,600–6,500
$8,100–9,400 ⚒ S

A French porcelain-mounted ormolu singing bird automaton mantel clock, the enamel dial with visible Brocot escapement, stamped 'H & F Paris', c1875, 26½in (67cm) high.
£20,450–24,200
$29,650–35,100 ⚒ S

A French bronze, ormolu and red marble mantel clock, the bell striking movement signed Hemon A Paris, in a bronze and ormolu star-studded globe with an equatorial ring cast with the signs of the zodiac and supported by an eagle, the figure of Zeus to the side holding aloft a bolt of lightning, the marble plinth applied with chased ormolu mounts, c1815, 28in (71cm) high.
£18,600–20,450
$27,000–29,650 ⚒ S

An Empire ormolu-mounted bronze and white marble mantel clock, the glazed enamelled dial with Arabic numerals signed Revel, surmounted by a winged cupid caressing Venus, on a stiff-leaf moulded stepped plinth and red *griotte* marble base, the movement numbered '135490', 31in (79cm) high.
£8,350–11,150
$12,100–16,000 ⚒ C

A French ormolu mantel clock, 3¼in (8.5cm) enamel dial, bell striking movement with silk suspension, the case in the form of a centurion's plumed helmet, with a seated figure of Cupid, c1805, 13½in (34cm) high.
£5,600–7,450
$8,100–10,800 ⚒ S

A French ormolu musical mantel clock, the 3¼in (8.5cm) enamel dial signed Comminge, Palais Royal No. 62 A Paris, bell striking silk suspension movement releasing the music every hour, with a young woman and a winged putto, c1810, 21in (53cm) high.
£8,400–9,300
$12,200–13,500 ⚒ S

A French gilt and patinated bronze mantel clock, the enamel dial signed Manière à Paris, bell striking movement with silk suspension, the case surmounted by Cupid playing with a butterfly, c1815, 15in (38cm) high.
£3,700–4,650
$5,350–6,750 ⚒ S

A mahogany 8-day fusee drop dial wall clock, the 8in (20cm) painted dial signed McCabe, c1820.
£3,000–3,500 $4,400–5,000 ⊞ PAO

A mahogany table clock, with verge escapement, by John Hanckles, London, c1765, 15in (38cm) high.
£11,000–12,000 $16,000–17,400 ⊞ PAO

A Limoges porcelain-mounted silvered table clock, with bell striking movement by Japy Frères, stamped Dufaud, Paris, c1885, 27in (69cm) high.
£6,350–7,500 $9,200–10,500 ⚒ S

A table clock, by Hunter & Son, c1795.
£2,900–3,450 $4,200–5,000 ⚒ S

An ebonized table clock, signed Geo. Philp., Strigel, c1780.
£3,450–4,050 $5,000–6,000 ⚒ S

◄ **A brass-bound ebonized table clock,** the painted dial signed Perigal, London, c1810, 17in (44cm) high.
£1,750–2,300 $2,500–3,350 ⚒ S

A gilt-bronze clock, by Hemmel à Paris, partly mid-18thC.
£2,300–3,500 $3,350–5,000 ⚒ S

A lantern clock, by Kingsnorth of Tenterden, 18thC.
£2,400–3,000 $3,500–4,400 ⊞ SHO

A French porcelain and gilt white metal-mounted clock garniture, late 19thC.
£3,000–4,500 $4,400–6,500 ⚒ Sim

A mahogany table clock, signed Frodsham, London, c1840, 14in (36cm) high.
£2,600–3,200 $3,800–4,600 ⚒ S

A walnut quarter repeating table clock, by Joseph Windmills, London, c1720, 18½in (47cm) high.
£13,800–17,250 $20,000–25,000 ⚒ S

A French Empire gilt portico clock.
£1,700–1,850 $2,450–2,700
A French rococo ormolu mantel clock, 19thC.
£1,100–1,300 $1,600–1,900
A French gilt-spelter mantel clock, 19thC, 23in (59cm) high.
£550–650 $800–950 ⚒ SWO

A Directoire ormolu mantel clock, enamel dial signed Laurent A Paris, c1795, 14in (36cm) high.
£3,700–4,650
$5,350–6,750 ⚖ S

A mantel clock, late 19thC, 14in (35.5cm) high.
£1,300–1,400
$1,900–2,000 ⚖ PCh

A Regency mantel timepiece, signed Vulliamy, No. 466.
£9,300–11,150
$13,500–16,150 ⚖ C

A French perpetual calendar mantel clock, 14in (36cm) high.
£6,500–8,400
$9,400–12,200 ⚖ C

A carved wood and parcel-gilt mantel clock, signed Callerström, Stockholm, c1810.
£4,650–6,500 $6,750–9,400 ⚖ S

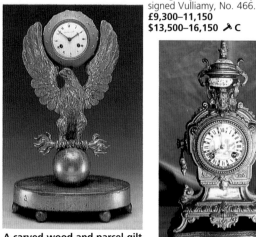

A French gilt-brass mantel clock, with porcelain dial and urn surmount, c1880.
£650–700 $950–1,000 ⚖ JH

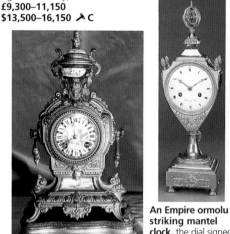

An Empire ormolu striking mantel clock, the dial signed Simon à Paris, 17in (43cm) high.
£4,650–5,600
$6,750–8,100 ⚖ C

A bronze, gilt-bronze and marble mantel timepiece, with enamel dial, 4 pillar fusee drum movement, backplate signed Vulliamy, London, 298, c1797, 17½in (44cm) high.
£16,750–22,300
$24,300–32,300 ⚖ S

◄ **A satinwood-veneered mantel timepiece,** with glass panelled sides, top and back, on brass bun feet, the silvered dial signed Parkinson and Frodsham, Change Alley, London, early 19thC, 8in (20cm) high.
£2,250–3,350
$3,250–4,850 ⚖ DN

An Edwardian inlaid mahogany mantel clock, with 8-day striking movement, by Clerke, Royal Exchange, London, 15in (38cm) high.
£1,500–2,250
$2,100–3,250 ⚖ MSW

An Empire ormolu mantel clock, the 4¾in (12cm) enamel dial signed Jean Perin à Paris, c1810, 19½in (49.5cm) high.
£6,500–7,450
$9,400–10,800 🔨 S

A Louis XVI ormolu mantel clock, the dial inscribed Petitdant à Paris, late 18thC, 14½in (36.5cm) high.
£19,550–22,300
$28,350–32,300 🔨 S(NY)

A Louis XVI ormolu and white marble Directoire mantel clock, the 4¾in (12cm) enamel dial signed Coteau, c1795, 15in (38cm) high.
£6,500–7,450
$9,400–10,800 🔨 S

A Regency ormolu-mounted *griotte* marble striking mantel clock, by Benjamin Vulliamy, 12in (30.5cm) high.
£13,000–14,900
$18,850–21,600 🔨 C

A Revolutionary ormolu and marble mantel clock, the 4in (10cm) enamel dial signed Duval à Paris, c1795, 17in (43cm) high.
£13,000–14,900
$18,850–21,600 🔨 S

A Second Republic mantel clock, with Japy Frères bell striking movement and Brocot escapement, c1850, 29in (73cm) high.
£6,500–7,450
$9,400–10,800 🔨 S

A Louis XVI ormolu and marble mantel clock, the enamel dial inscribed Lepaute, H. du Roi, late 18thC, 23in (58cm) high.
£17,700–18,600
$25,650–27,000 🔨 S(NY)

A French bow-sided porcelain-mounted ormolu mantel clock, the movement with maker's stamp of J. B. Delettrez, c1870.
£4,650–5,600
$6,750–8,000 🔨 S

▶ **A Louis XVI ormolu-mounted marble clock,** the dial signed Le Pareur, c1790, 22in (55cm) high.
£4,650–5,600
$6,750–8,000 🔨 S

A mantel clock, c1840.
£1,850–2,800
$2,700–4,000 ✗ S

A mantel clock, by Japy & Fils.
£2,250–2,800
$3,250–4,000 ✗ GAK

**A Louis Philippe
ormolu mantel clock,**
signed D. F. Dubois, à
Paris, 17in (43cm) high.
£3,700–5,600
$5,350–8,000 ✗ C

An Empire ormolu mantel clock,
by Lesieur, 18½in (47cm) wide.
£10,250–12,100 $14,850–17,500 ✗ C

◄ **An Empire ormolu and
mahogany mantel
timepiece,** the fusee
movement signed Barwise,
London on the backplate,
23in (58.5cm) high.
£13,950–16,750
$20,200–24,300 ✗ C

A mantel clock, 19thC.
£11,150–14,900
$16,150–21,600 ✗ C

An Empire clock, 15in (38cm) wide.
£5,600–7,450 $8,100–10,800 ✗ C

**An Austrian ormolu and
bronze troubadour mantel
clock,** the pinnacle with a
bell above a pointed arch, the
quarter striking movement
with 2 gongs, mid-19thC,
19½in (49cm) high.
£1,650–2,250
$2,400–3,250 ✗ C

**A Louis XVIII ormolu and bronze mantel
clock,** signed, 30in (76cm) high.
£15,800–18,600 $22,900–26,000 ✗ C

A Louis XVI mantel clock, 19in (48cm) wide.
£22,300–26,050 $32,300–37,000 ✗ C

**A George III ormolu, jasper ware and biscuit-
porcelain mounted mantel clock,** by Benjamin
Vulliamy, c1799, 13½in (34cm) wide.
£22,300–27,900 $32,300–40,500 ✗ S(NY)

**A French 'singing bird' mantel
clock,** c1880, 16in (41cm) high.
£16,750–20,450
$24,300–29,000 ✗ S

An ormolu mantel clock,
c1870, 16½in (42cm) high.
£3,350–4,100
$4,850–6,000 ✗ S

A Louis XVI ormolu and white marble clock, the dial signed, regilded.
£5,600–9,300 $8,100–13,500 ⚒ C

▶ **A Louis XVI ormolu-mounted porcelain mantel clock,** 19thC, 17½in (44.5cm) high.
£74,400–83,700
$107,900–121,300 ⚒ C

A French spelter figural clock, c1880, 22½in (57cm) high.
£450–600
$650–870 ⚒ JL

A Charles X ormolu and bronze mantel clock, 1827, 26½in (68cm) high.
£3,700–5,600
$5,350–8,100 ⚒ C

An ormolu-mounted and Chinese porcelain mantel clock, 19thC, later movement.
£6,500–8,400
$9,400–12,200 ⚒ C

An ormolu and marble mantel clock, restored, early 19thC, 18½in (47cm) high.
£2,200–2,800
$3,200–4,000 ⚒ C

A neo-classical urn clock, 19thC, 23in (59cm) high.
£18,600–22,300
$26,950–32,300 ⚒ C

A Louis XVI design ormolu and bronze table clock, 30in (76cm) high.
£6,500–7,450
$9,400–10,800 ⚒ C

A Louis XVI ormolu urn clock, the pedestal inset with marble, 16in (41cm) high.
£37,200–46,500
$54,000–67,400 ⚒ C

◀ **A French ormolu and bronze matched clock garniture,** mid-19thC, clock 16in (41cm) high.
£10,200–12,100
$14,800–17,500 ⚒ C

A Regency mantel clock, signed
Vulliamy, 9½in (24cm) high.
£7,450–9,300 $10,800–13,500 ⚒ C

**A Napoleon III ormolu and bronze mantel
clock,** the movement within a blue enamelled
globe, 23in (58.5cm) high.
**£3,700–4,650
$5,350–6,750** ⚒ C

**A Louis Philippe portico
mantel clock,** signed Hry Marc
à Paris, 17in 43cm) high.
£3,700–4,650 $5,350–6,750 ⚒ C

A Louis XVI calendar clock, signed
Bouchet à Paris.
**£13,950–14,900
$20,200–21,600** ⚒ CNY

**An Empire ormolu-mounted burr
elm portico clock,** dial and backplate
signed, 18in (46cm) high.
£7,450–9,300 $10,800–13,500 ⚒ C

◄ **A George II giltwood cartel clock,**
later movement, cover and eagle,
34½in (88cm) high.
£3,700–4,650 $5,350–6,750 ⚒ C

A French 'swinging clock', the dial
signed Breguet et Fils, 22½in (57cm) high.
**£12,000–14,000
$17,400–20,300** ⊞ DRA

An orrery clock, in a glazed ormolu
case, c1770, 95in (241cm) high overall.
**£600,000+
$870,000+** ⚒ C

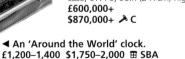

◄ **An 'Around the World' clock.**
£1,200–1,400 $1,750–2,000 ⊞ SBA

An automaton clock, in a giltwood
case, with a magician, 33in (84cm) high.
**£11,150–13,000
$16,150–18,800** ⚒ CSK

A George III ormolu clock, by Matthew Boulton.
£2,950–3,700
$4,250–5,300 ⚒ C

A German mantel clock, 18thC, 11½in (29cm) high.
£1,500–2,250
$2,100–3,250 ⚒ C

A Louis Philippe ormolu and silver-plated garniture, clock 20in (51cm) high.
£4,450–5,200
$6,450–7,500 ⚒ C

A Regency bronze, ormolu and marble mantel clock, signed Vulliamy, London, No. 389, 10in (25.5cm) high.
£7,450–9,700
$10,800–14,000 ⚒ C

An ormolu mantel clock, signed Bausse, Rue de Richlieu, No. 47, c1810, 20½in (52cm) high.
£2,950–4,450
$4,250–6,450 ⚒ C

A Louis XVI ormolu and patinated bronze lyre clock, 27½in (70cm) high.
£22,350–23,850
$32,400–34,600 ⚒ C

A ormolu-mounted and marble lyre clock, the enamel dial signed Bréant à Paris, c1780, 21½in (54cm) high.
£8,950–10,450
$12,950–15,000 ⚒ C

A *grande sonnerie* carriage clock, 7in (18cm) high.
£7,500–9,000
$10,800–13,000 ⊞ DRA

A Louis XVI ormolu clock, the dial signed Furet, H'Ger du Roy, later parts, 12in (30.5cm) high.
£5,200–6,700
$7,550–9,700 ⚒ CNY

A Viennese silver gilt-mounted enamel and wood clock and jewel casket, c1870.
£8,950–10,450
$12,950–15,150 ⚒ CNY

A Directoire ormolu-mounted biscuit porcelain mantel clock, signed Gavelle L'Ainé à Paris, 15½in (39.5cm) high.
£1,800–2,250 $2,600–3,200 ⚒ C

◀ **A Regency bronzed and gilt-metal musical automaton clock,** by J. H. Borrell, London, restored, 25in (63.5cm) high.
£11,200–12,650
$16,250–18,350 ⚒ C

▶ **A Directoire ormolu-mounted French biscuit porcelain mantel clock,** 24½in (62cm) high.
£4,450–7,450
$6,450–10,800 ⚒ C

An Empire ormolu and bronze mantel clock, signed Coeur Père à Paris, lacking pendulum, 14in (35.5cm) high.
£9,300–11,150
$13,500–16,150 ⚒ C

A George III ormolu, Derby biscuit porcelain and white marble mantel clock, the movement by Vulliamy, London, with later enamelled dial, the porcelain damaged and restored, 31½in (80cm) wide.
£65,100–74,400
$94,400–107,900 ⚖ C

A George III bronze and ormolu Titus clock, by Matthew Boulton, with later glazed enamel dial, the later movement signed Arnold & Dent, London, 15in (38cm) high.
£46,500–55,800
$67,400–80,900 ⚖ C

An ormolu-mounted brass inlaid ebony mantel clock, the glazed brass dial signed I. Thuret à Paris, c1800, 22½in (57cm) high.
£18,600–22,300
$26,950–32,300 ⚖ C

A Directoire bronze and ormolu mantel clock, the dial signed à Paris, 17in (43cm) high.
£37,200–46,500
$53,950–67,400 ⚖ C

A Louis XVI ormolu urn clock, in the manner of Lepaute, 19in (48cm) high.
£14,900–18,600
$21,600–26,000 ⚖ C

A Louis XIV ebony and boulle mantel clock, the movement signed Thuret à Paris, 29in (74cm) high.
£24,200–27,900
$35,000–40,500 ⚖ C

A Louis XVI ormolu mantel clock, with glazed enamel dial and striking movement, 20in (51cm) high.
£14,900–18,600
$21,600–26,000 ⚖ C

A Federal mahogany longcase clock, by Reuben Tower, Hingham, c1816.
£93,000–102,300
$134,050–148,300 ⚖ CNY

▶ **An Empire ormolu and patinated bronze mantel clock,** the dial signed Ledure, Bronzier, à Paris, damaged, early 19thC, 29½in (75cm) high.
£7,450–9,300
$10,800–13,500 ⚖ CNY

A Louis XV ormolu mantel clock, the dial and movement signed Etienne Le Noir à Paris, 13½in (34.5cm) high.
£8,400–10,250
$12,200–14,500 ➴ C

A mantel clock, signed A. Duchesne, Lejeune à Paris, 18thC, 39in (99cm) high.
£9,300–11,150
$13,500–16,100 ➴ P

An Empire mantel clock, with circular enamel dial, in an urn-shaped case, 18in (46cm) high.
£7,450–9,300
$10,800–13,500 ➴ C

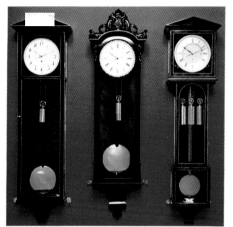

l. A Viennese regulator, by Lehrner, Pesten, in a walnut-veneered case, c1825. **£7,000–10,000 $10,200–14,500**
c. A late Biedermeier period Viennese regulator, by Mösslinger, Vienna. **£4,000–5,000 $5,800–7,200**
r. A lantern-style Viennese regulator, in a mahogany case, c1825. **£25,000–30,000 $36,200–43,500** ⊞ GeC

A French Directoire skeleton clock, by Laurent à Paris, c1790.
£24,000–30,000
$34,800–43,500 ➴ CAG

An 8-day carriage clock, signed James Gowland, London, the movement with lever escapement, in gilt brass case, 7in (18cm) high, with morocco travelling case.
£11,500–13,800
$16,700–20,000 ➴ Bea

A grande sonnerie Viennese regulator, by S. Glink, Pesten, Budapest, in a burr elm case, c1850.
£6,500–7,500 $9,400–10,800 ⊞ GeC

A Victorian bracket clock, the movement chiming on 8 bells with a gong, 30in (76cm) high.
£4,800–5,400 $6,950–7,800 ➴ WW

▶ **A Federal gilt and églomisé girandole clock,** by Lemuel Curtis, Concord, Massachusetts, base glass replaced, c1816, 46in (117cm) high.
£9,300–11,600
$13,500–16,800 ➴ CNY

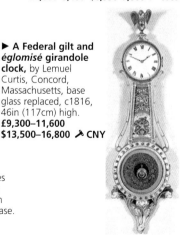

A French ormolu-mounted porcelain clock set, the clock with striking movement, 18in (45.5cm) high, the candelabra each with 4 foliate candle nozzles, 17in (43cm) high.
£5,950–7,450
$8,600–10,800 ⚒ C

A Louis XVI ormolu and terracotta mantel clock, the enamel dial with Roman numerals and days of the week, signed Sotiau A Paris, the case with figures of Minerva and attendants, 18in (45.5cm) wide.
£4,450–5,950
$6,450–8,600 ⚒ C

An ebony-veneered bracket clock, by Clarke & Dunster, London, with 8-day movement, Dutch strike and alarm, repaired, c1735, 17in (43cm) high.
£11,600–13,500 $16,800–19,600 ⚒ CSK

A Louis XVI Sèvres vase *solaire* **clock,** cover restored, 18½in (47cm) high.
£14,900–17,900
$21,600–25,000 ⚒ C

An Empire ormolu-mounted marble mantel clock, the enamel dial signed à Paris, the movement with outside countwheel strike, 21in (53.5cm) high.
£7,450–8,950
$10,800–13,000 ⚒ C

An Empire bronze, ormolu and marble mantel clock, after a design by Thomas Hope, 21½in (54.5cm) high.
£8,950–10,450
$12,950–15,150 ⚒ C

A Louis XVI ormolu and alabaster rotunda clock, signed Festeau à Paris, 16½in (42cm) high, with later glass dome.
£8,950–10,450
$12,950–15,150 ⚒ C

A George III mahogany bracket clock, the 2-train movement with verge escapement, strike/silent regulation in the arch, recessed plaque with maker's name William Garrett, London, c1785, 20in (51cm) high.
£11,000–12,500
$16,000–18,100 ⊞ DRA

RODERICK ANTIQUES
CLOCKS

A porcelain carriage clock, 8in (20.5cm) high.
£5,350–6,900
$7,750–10,000 ⚘ **CNY**

A porcelain carriage clock, signed Drocourt, No. 8849, 6½in (16.5cm) high.
£7,650–9,200
$11,100–13,300 ⚘ **CNY**

A porcelain carriage clock, with alarm, 7½in (19cm) high.
£6,100–7,650
$8,850–11,100 ⚘ **CNY**

A Sicilian coral mantel clock, early 19thC, 21in (54cm) high.
£3,700–4,650 $5,350–6,750 ⚘ **C**

An Empire ormolu and bronze mantel clock, enamel dial signed L. J. Laquesse et Fils à Paris, 16in (40.5cm) high.
£3,700–5,200 $5,350–7,500 ⚘ **C**

A Louis XVI urn clock, the dial with enamel numerals, the case signed Courieult à Paris, 16½in (42cm) high.
£14,900–17,900
$21,600–25,000 ⚘ **C**

A Louis XV cartel clock, 42½in (108cm) high
£10,350–11,500 $15,000–16,700 ⚘ **C**

A George III satinwood mantel clock, signed Weeks.
£10,250–12,100
$14,850–17,500 ⚘ **C**

A skeleton clock, with calendar, signed Julien Beliard, late 18thC.
£24,000–30,000
$34,800–43,500 ⚘ **CNY**

A mahogany mantel clock, the dial signed Breguet, early 19thC, 11in (28cm) high.
£18,600–22,300
$26,950–32,300 ⚘ **P**

Carriage Clocks

Compact, elegant and easy to transport, the carriage or 'travelling' clock has proved the most collectable of antique clocks. The large number on the market today is the legacy of an industry that began in France in the 19th century, originating from the complicated mechanisms made by Abraham-Louis Breguet. Later in the century clockmaker Paul Garnier (1801–69), using his own escapement and simplifying the design, made it possible for these clocks to be produced more cheaply, and by the 1850s large-scale production had begun. Movements were made in various provincial towns and sent to Paris to be finished and cased. From these Parisian workshops the clocks were then sold on to retailers. The majority of these clocks are unsigned by the makers, and it is often the retailer's name that appears on the dial.

The range of cases varied widely, although there were certain standard case shapes, of which the obis, corniche and gorge were the most common. The obis was made in large numbers and is the most basic and plain, made of thinly pressed metal and consequently lighter. The corniche case, made from the 1870s, is similar to the obis but of better quality: the case is more substantial and slightly more elaborate, while the gorge is the most expensive standard carriage-clock case and houses movements of high quality. Lacquered or gilt-brass cases in these traditional styles remained popular throughout the century, but in the last quarter of the 19th century more elaborate carriage clocks appeared with champlevé enamel or porcelain panelling. Usually both dial and side panels are decorated, and sometimes the back and top as well.

The great majority of French carriage clocks were exported, particularly to England. Dealer Andrew Forster warns that even if an English name appears on the dial this would probably be the name of the retailer rather than the manufacturer as the clock would almost certainly have been made in France. England did have its own carriage clock makers, but they produced far fewer clocks for a more select market. Their clocks tended to be larger, heavier and more expensive, and made use of a fusee and chain. English travelling cases were usually of wood, not leather, as with the French clocks. English examples also incline towards restraint, with plainer, more solid-looking cases.

Although English carriage clocks were produced in relatively small numbers, they were generally by the best London makers: McCabe, Frodsham, Dent, Vulliamy, Barwise, Smith and Jump were the top names, and their clocks fetch the highest prices. Oliver Saunders of Bonhams confirms this, saying that the top prices remain with English carriage clocks because of their substantial quality. As far as French carriage clocks are concerned, vast quantities were never signed, so those that were marked by known makers are valued highly. Prominent French names are Jacot, Drocourt and Margaine. Oliver Saunders points out that it is not only by signature that experts identify makers; there are other clues: for instance the way the arrows are engraved, or the style of the dial.

Apart from the case style, another factor affecting price will be the complexity of the movement. The least expensive clock is a timepiece – that is, a clock that does not strike. Prices then go up according to the degree of sophistication of the striking and repeating work. Striking on a bell pre-dates that of a gong, with a changeover period occurring in the mid-19th century. Size also makes a difference: miniature carriage clocks made in sizes ranging from 3¼in (8.5cm) to 4¼in (11cm) high with the handle raised are very popular and command high prices. Also known as mignonettes, or 'little darlings', they were produced mainly during the late 19th century, and their decoration could be as elaborate as that found on standard sized carriage clocks. These miniatures were usually timepieces only, as their small size made it impractical to fit a standard striking movement of 8-day duration. A particularly small silver-plated miniature carriage timepiece, only 2⅛in (5.5cm) high, made in France c1910, inscribed with the English retailer's name, was sold at Christie's South Kensington recently together with its red travelling case for £713 ($1,030), over twice its estimate of £200–300 ($290–440).

The average simple carriage timepiece in good condition, with glass intact and uncracked dial, will fetch between £200–400 ($290–580) and could cost a further £250 ($360) to have it overhauled and re-gilded. A striking version would be in the £400–700 ($580–1,000) range, with the price rising for more elaborate cases, and would cost at least £100 ($145) more to overhaul. A signature will increase the price, as will a complicated movement or porcelain or enamel panelled examples, a small number of which were produced in the last quarter of the 19th century. At a recent Sotheby's sale, the French repeating carriage clocks dating from the 1890s fetched in the region of £630–750 ($910–1,100). In the same sale, an unusual Japanese-style repeating carriage clock made in Paris, with blue and white enamel dial and elaborate decoration, fetched £3,105 ($4,500), and a fine porcelain panelled carriage clock with an engraved case would fetch appreciably more.

Experts agree that identifying reproductions of carriage clocks is a matter of experience and comparison, but the inexperienced buyer can check for a maker's stamp, often found on the backplate, study the dial (reproductions do not normally have enamelled dials), and look at the quality of the case, as new ones tend to be more thickly lacquered.

The production of carriage clocks decreased with the outbreak of World War I, and by 1939 very few were being made. Today, however, production has picked up, and there are now probably more being made than in the past 50 years, both in France and in England.

An engraved carriage clock, with enamelled dial, striking and repeating on a gong, signed Aubert & Co, 2 Regent Street, London, No. 3428, c1875, 6in (15cm) high.
£3,500–4,000
$5,000–5,800 ⊞ DRA

A lacquered brass calendar carriage timepiece, the movement with modern lever platform to the going section, stamped B in a circle, and B^te S.G.D.G. Déposé, late 19thC, 6½in (16.5cm) high.
£600–900
$870–1,300 ⚒ C

A repeating carriage clock, with white enamelled dial and subsidiary alarm dial, the gong striking movement stamped B in a circle, c1875, 6in (15cm) high.
£1,400–1,550
$2,000–2,200 ⚒ S(S)

A French engraved brass carriage clock, the lever movement striking on a gong, with alarm and push repeat, bearing the trademark B in a circle, 19thC, 7½in (19cm) high.
£2,750–3,350
$4,000–4,850 ⚒ P

A gilt-brass carriage clock, with 2½in (6.5cm) white enamelled dial, signed Barwise, London, c1840, 5in (13cm) high.
£1,850–2,300
$2,700–3,300 ⚒ S(S)

A Victorian decorated miniature carriage clock, maker's mark J. B. London, 1890, 3½in (9cm) high.
£600–750
$870–1,100 ⚒ Bea

An 8-day gilt carriage timepiece, with Roman numerals and gilt hands, with platform escapement, backplate signed Bell and Sons, 131 Mount Street, Berkeley Square No. 14477, c1850.
£2,150–2,750
$3,100–4,000 ⚒ CSK

A satinwood carriage clock, by Barwise, London, with chain fusee movement, c1830, 9in (23cm) high.
£6,000–8,000
$8,700–11,600 ⊞ SO

A French gilt bamboo chinoiserie carriage clock, inscribed John Bennett, Paris, late 19thC, 8in (20.5cm) high.
£3,850–5,350
$5,600–7,700 ⚒ DWB

An enamel-mounted carriage timepiece, the movement No. 921, with cylinder escapement, the top dated 1898, 2in (5cm) high, with leather travelling case from J. W. Benson, London.
£3,050–4,500
$4,400–6,500 ⚒ Bon

A silver and lilac enamel miniature carriage timepiece, the lever escapement backplate stamped JTC, 2in (5cm) high.
£1,200–1,850
$1,750–2,700 ⚒ Bon

An engraved carriage clock, in the manner of Thomas Cole, signed Hunt & Roskell, 156 New Bond St, London, No. 10044, the silvered dial with Roman chapter, the fusee movement with maintaining power, plain steel balance and lever escapement, c1840, 4½in (11cm) high.
£3,050–3,850
$4,400–5,600 ⚒ Bon

A George V silver-mounted tortoise-shell carriage clock, by W. Comyns, London 1910, 4½in (11cm) high.
£1,550–2,300
$2,250–3,300 ⚒ Bea

A silver and tortoiseshell carriage clock, by William Comyns, London 1909, 4½in (11cm) high, in original fitted case.
£1,850–2,300
$2,700–3,300 ⚒ HOD

A French alarm carriage clock, with subsidiary alarm dial, striking the hours and half-hours on a single bell, with repeat mechanism, c1880, 7in (18cm) high, in leather covered carrying case.
£1,400–1,700
$2,000–2,500 ⚒ HSS

A French 8-day brass alarm carriage clock, signed by Dent 61 Strand, London, the striking movement with 2 hammers on a single gong, 19thC, 7in (18cm) high, with leather travelling case and brass key.
£900–1,200
$1,300–1,700 ⚒ DDM

An 8-day repeating gilt carriage clock, by Drocourt, with ivory chapter ring, the movement with silvered lever platform escapement striking on a gong, c1890, 6½in (16.5cm) high, with original red leather numbered case.
£1,550–2,300
$2,250–3,300 ⚒ CSK

An ebonized carriage clock, signed Dent, London 477, the twin fusee movement with lever platform escapement, striking on a gong, with strike/silent lever, 19thC, 9½in (24cm) high.
£18,350–22,950
$26,650–33,250 ⚒ P

◄ **A silver *grande sonnerie* carriage clock,** the dial signed Dent, 1893, 4½in (11cm) high.
£6,100–6,900
$8,800–10,000 ⚒ S

► **A lacquered-brass striking alarm carriage clock,** with uncut compensated balance to lever platform, stamp of Drocourt, c1870, 6in (15cm) high.
£1,200–1,400
$1,700–2,000 ⚒ C

A repeating carriage clock, the enamel dial signed Dent, 33 Cockspur St, London, with chain fusee movement, maintaining power, the lever escapement with gilt platform and free-sprung compensation balance and gong striking, backplate signed M. F. Dent, c1863, 8in (20.5cm) high.
£21,500–27,550
$31,200–39,000 ⚒ S

A gilt-metal alarm carriage clock, with uncut compensated balance to silvered lever platform, stamp of Drocourt, late 19thC, 7in (18cm) high, with travelling case.
£1,200–1,400
$1,750–2,000 ⚒ C

A gilt-brass carriage clock, signed by retailer, J. W. Benson, 25 Old Bond St, London, the white enamel dial with blued spade hands, bi-metallic balance to silvered lever platform strike/repeat on gong, the backplate with stamp for Drocourt, c1870, 6in (15cm) high.
£750–1,100
$1,100–1,600 ⚒ C

Carriage Clocks

Carriage clocks originated in France from the *pendule de voyage*, literally 'travel clock', made by Abraham-Louis Breguet (1747–1823). Paul Garnier (1801–69) then introduced a simple basic design, making it possible to produce these clocks more cheaply. Many carriage clocks were exported to England at the time of manufacture.

A French 8-day repeating alarm carriage clock, the dial signed Dent, Strand, London, with lever escapement striking the hours and half-hours on a gong, c1860, 6½in (16.5cm) high.
£3,500–4,000
$5,000–5,800 ⊞ PAO

A French gilt-brass carriage clock, signed by Dent, 33 Cockspur Street, London, the white enamel Roman chapter disc with pierced blued hands, with stamp for Drocourt, c1875, 5½in (14cm) high, with original brown leather case.
£2,300–3,050
$3,300–4,400 ⚒ C

A gilt-brass carriage clock, with 2½in (6cm) enamel dial, signed F. Dent, Chronometer Maker to the Queen, 1442, the signed fusee movement with maintaining power, under-slung ratchet-tooth lever escapement with compensation balance and helical spring, free-sprung, with safety ratchet winder, c1850, 6in (15cm) high.
£9,200–18,250
$13,350–26,500 ⚒ S

◀ An 8-day repeating carriage clock, the white enamel dial signed Chas. Frodsham, Clockmaker to the Queen, 84 Strand, London, No. 187, the chapter ring with Roman numerals and alarm dial below, the lever movement striking the hour and half-hour on a bell, 19thC, 6in (15cm) high.
£2,150–2,600
$3,100–3,800 ✗ Bea

A French quarter striking and repeating gilt-brass corniche carriage clock, signed Cles. Frodsham, Paris, the 3in (7.5cm) white enamelled annular chapter ring with blued steel moon hands, the movement with bi-metallic compensated balance wheel, lever escapement and blued steel spring, striking on 2 bells, c1880, 10in (25.5cm) high.
£2,600–3,050
$3,800–4,400 ✗ L

A French brass carriage clock, with enamel dial, the lever movement striking on a gong, with alarm and push repeat and bearing the Drocourt trademark, No. 44663, c1880, 6½in (16.5cm) high, with a travelling case.
£850–900
$1,250–1,300 ✗ P

A carriage timepiece, the fusee movement with lever platform escapement and compensated balance, with maintaining power, signed on the backplate Clarke, London, 19thC, 5½in (14cm) high, with leather travelling case.
£2,300–3,050
$3,350–4,400 ✗ P

▶ A reproduction engraved silver striking carriage clock, the white dial with blued spade hands, signed Charles Frodsham, London, No. 0012 on base, uncut balance to lever platform, strike/repeat on a bell, c1870, 6½in (16.5cm) high.
£850–1,050
$1,250–1,500 ✗ C

◀ A French gilt-brass carriage clock, with enamel dial, lever movement striking on a gong, Drocourt trademark, 19thC, 7in (18cm) high.
£1,400–1,550
$2,000–2,250 ✗ P

◄ **A French 8-day carriage clock,** made for James Grohe of London, the brass mask dial surround engraved and silvered, with round enamel signed chapter ring, the movement striking the hours and half-hours on a bell, c1865, 6in (15cm) high, including handle.
£4,000–4,500
$5,800–6,500 ⊞ **PAO**

A French repeating carriage clock, retailed by A. E. Halfhide, Wimbledon, 19thC, 7in (18cm) high.
£1,450–1,700 $2,100–2,500 ⚹ **BS**

A French gilt-brass miniature carriage clock, by Henri Jacot, No. 12730, with white enamel dial, the movement stamped, lever platform escapement, c1900, 3in (7.5cm) high.
£1,050–1,200
$1,500–1,700 ⚹ **S(S)**

A French striking and repeating carriage clock, by Henri Jacot, Paris, with lever escapement, c1880, 7½in (19cm) high, with travelling case.
£1,550–2,000
$2,250–2,900 ⚹ **THG**

A gilt-brass striking carriage clock, by Henri Jacot, with uncut bi-metallic balance to silvered lever platform, strike/repeat on gong, c1875, 5½in (14cm) high.
£1,550–2,150
$2,250–3,100 ⚹ **C**

A French carriage clock, with white enamel dial, 8-day movement with lever platform escapement striking on a gong, backplate marked LF, Paris, c1880, 6in (15cm) high.
£750–1,000
$1,100–1,500 ⚹ **CSK**

A French carriage clock, with white enamel dial marked Hall & Co, repeating the hours on a bell, the alarm movement stamped B within a circle, c1875, 6in (15cm) high, with travelling case.
£1,550–2,300
$2,250–3,300 ⚹ **McC**

A French carriage clock, the repeating movement stamped Henri Jacot, No. 14694, c1875.
£1,550–2,100
$2,250–3,100 ⚹ **Bon**

A gilt-metal porcelain-mounted carriage clock, by Japy Frères, with lever platform, striking on a bell, c1870, 9½in (24cm) high.
£5,350–6,100
$7,750–8,800 ⚒ C

◀ **A repeating carriage clock,** the movement stamped E. G. L., in a Corinthian column case, c1875, 6in (15cm) high.
£900–1,050
$1,300–1,500 ⚒ Bon

A brass *grande sonnerie* carriage clock, with white enamelled dial and backplate signed C. J. Klaftenberger, subsidiary alarm dial, gorge case with bevelled glass, c1874, 5½in (14cm) high, in leather travelling case.
£4,600–5,350
$6,650–7,750 ⚒ S(S)

▶ **A gilt-brass striking carriage clock,** with white enamel dial, blued spade hands, stamped Jacot, corniche case, c1880, 5½in (14cm) high.
£900–1,150
$1,300–1,650 ⚒ C

◀ **A French gilt-brass miniature carriage timepiece,** with enamel dial, lever movement, 19thC, 4in (10cm) high, with leather travelling case.
£1,400–1,850
$2,000–2,700 ⚒ P

▶ **A gilt-brass one-piece striking carriage clock,** the dial marked Brevet d'Invention SGDG, blued Breguet hands, backplate stamped Japy Frères, with compensated three-arm balance to lever platform, c1870, 5½in (14cm) high.
£1,400–1,850
$2,000–2,700 ⚒ C

◀ **A French gilt-brass alarm carriage clock,** the cylinder movement striking on a bell, by Ingold à Paris, made for the Turkish market, 19thC, 7in (18cm) high.
£550–600
$800–900 ⚒ P

A gilt-brass carriage clock, the white enamelled dial with moon disc hands, the bell striking movement stamped Japy Frères, c1875, 5in (13cm) high.
£1,000–1,150
$1,500–2,000 ⚒ S(S)

A French brass carriage clock, signed Jules, Paris, 827, the movement striking on a bell, c1850, 6½in (16.5cm) high.
£1,000–1,100
$1,500–1,600 ⚒ P

A giant French striking and repeating gilded carriage clock, signed Le Roy et Cie à Paris, No. 23063, c1875, 9in (23cm) high, with leather travelling case.
£6,000–6,500
$8,700–9,400 ⊞ DRA

An 8-day repeating carriage clock, with white enamel dial with subsidiary alarm pointer, the lever movement striking on a gong, the backplate No. 10360, inscribed Le Roy & Fils, 13 & 15 Palais Royal, c1875, 6in (15cm) high.
£1,550–2,300
$2,250–3,300 ⚒ WW

A gilt-metal quarter striking carriage clock, signed enamel dial, No. 3995, Le Roy & Fils, Hgers du Roi Paris, with gilt balance to lever platform, c1850, 6in (15cm) high.
£1,850–2,300
$2,700–3,300 ⚒ C

A French 8-day engraved carriage clock, by Lucien, Paris, with lever escapement, hourly and half-hourly strike on a bell, c1840, 5in (13cm) high.
£1,450–1,850
$2,100–2,700 ⊞ SBA

A *petite sonnerie* carriage clock, with white enamel dial, inscribed Lund & Blockley, No. 4095, repeat button and silent/strike lever on the base, c1890, 6in (15cm) high.
£3,050–3,850
$4,400–5,600 ⚒ GSP

▶ **A corniche alarm gilt-brass carriage clock,** with white enamel dial signed Le Roy & Fils 57 New Bond Street, Made in France Palais-Royal Paris, with blued spade hands, subsidiary alarm ring, with cut bi-metallic balance to silvered lever platform strike/repeat on gong, c1880, 5½in (14cm) high, with leather travelling case.
£750–1,100
$1,100–1,600 ⚒ C

◀ **A gilt-metal striking carriage clock,** with bridge to lever balance, outside countwheel strike on bell, stamped Lucien, Paris, on backplate, 19thC, 6in (15cm) high.
£1,850–2,300
$2,700–3,300 ⚒ C

A French 8-day repeating carriage clock, by François-Arsene Margaine, No. 12658, the movement with lever escapement and compensated balance wheel, late 19thC, 8in (20.5cm) high.
£900–1,200
$1,300–1,700 ⚖ Bea

An 8-day *grande sonnerie* brass carriage clock, by Louis Mallet, with silvered dial, the movement striking on 2 bells, pull-wound alarm and a pull-repeat cord, early 19thC, 8in (20.5cm) high.
£4,600–5,350
$6,650–7,750 ⚖ AH

A French 8-day carriage clock, with white enamel dial, signed Miroy Frères Btes, Paris and R. d'Angouleme du Temple 10, No. 2724, the lever movement with strike and repeat on a bell, with full sweep seconds hand, mid-19thC, 8in (20.5cm) high.
£1,500–1,850
$2,170–2,700 ⚖ DN

A silvered-brass oval miniature carriage clock, with silvered lever platform, stamp of A. Margaine, c1880, 3in (7.5cm) high.
£900–1,200
$1,300–1,700 ⚖ C

A French gilt-brass carriage clock, the lever movement with compensated balance, striking on a bell, with countwheel strike, stamped Mottu à Paris, c1860, 6½in (16.5cm) high.
£1,000–1,100
$1,500–1,600 ⚖ P

A gilt-brass carriage clock, with mother-of-pearl dial, the earlier watch movement signed Tho Mudge and Wm Dutton, London, c1840, 4½in (11.5cm) high.
£1,100–1,200
$1,600–1,700 ⚖ S(S)

A French engraved corniche brass carriage clock, with enamel dial signed for Mackay, Cunningham & Co, Edinburgh, the movement with lever platform escapement with push repeat striking on a gong, the backplate No. 9697, c1880, 9in (23cm) high.
£1,550–2,300
$2,250–3,300 ⚖ P

◀ **An 8-day repeating carriage clock,** with white enamelled dial signed Müller/Twickenham, the movement with compensated balance wheel and lever escapement, late 19thC, 8in (20.5cm) high, with carrying case and key.
£600–750
$870–1,100 ⚖ Bea

A gilt-brass repeating carriage clock, the dial signed Rowell, Oxford, with engraved gilt mask, subsidiary day, date and alarm dials and gong striking movement, in a modern gorge case.
£450–600
$650–900 ⚒ S

An ormolu *pendule d'officier,* the fusee movement with lever escapement, alarm and pull quarter repeating, signed Robert & Courvoisier, early 19thC, 8½in (21.5cm) high.
£4,600–5,350
$6,650–7,750 ⚒ P

A French striking carriage clock, signed Soldano, c1870, 5½in (14cm) high.
£1,850–2,300
$2,700–3,300 ⊞ SO

◄ **A French** *anglaise* **gilt-brass carriage clock,** with enamel dial, within an engraved gilt mask, the lever movement striking on a gong, with push repeat and bearing the Richard trademark, damaged, 19thC, 7½in (19cm) high.
£900–1,100
$1,300–1,600 ⚒ P

► **A gilt-brass striking carriage clock,** the white enamel dial with blued Breguet hands, with uncut bi-metallic balance to silvered platform level escapement, strike/repeat on gong, c1875, 5½in (14cm) high.
£1,100–1,200
$1,600–1,700 ⚒ C

A German 8-day miniature alarm carriage clock, with lever escapement, c1890, 2½in (6.5cm) high.
£600–700
$900–1,000 ⊞ SBA

An engraved oval alarm carriage clock, the enamel dial signed Tiffany & Co, New York, c1900, 6in (15cm) high.
£1,000–1,150
$1,500–1,650 ⚒ Bon

A corniche *grande sonnerie* **striking gilt-brass carriage clock,** the white enamel dial signed Smith & Sons, with Roman numerals and blued spade hands, with later platform lever escapement, strike/repeat on 2 gongs, 3 position selection lever to base, c1900, 6in (15cm) high.
£1,550–1,900
$2,250–2,700 ⚒ C

An engraved gilt-brass *grande sonnerie* **alarm carriage clock,** with white enamel dial, the silvered lever platform stamped No. 308 by J. Soldano, movement with strike/repeat on 2 gongs, c1875, 6½in (16.5cm) high.
£3,800–5,350
$5,500–7,750 ⚒ C

A silver-cased minute-repeating carriage clock, the white enamel dial inscribed E. White, 32 Haymarket, London, c1900, 3½in (9cm) high.
£5,350–6,900
$7,750–10,000 ⚒ CSK

An Austrian carriage clock, with date, month, days and full *grande sonnerie* strike alarm/strike/silent, c1870, 7in (18cm) high.
£2,300–2,750
$3,350–4,000 ⊞ SO

A French carriage clock, with repeater chiming movement, pierced brass and blue enamel dial, in glass and brass case with loop handle and bracket feet, c1890, 7in (18cm) high.
£1,200–1,850
$1,750–2,700 ⚒ AH

A gilt-brass month-going carriage timepiece, the ivorine dial with subsidiary seconds at XII, bevelled surround, composite, late 19thC, 5in (23cm) high.
£750–900 $1,100–1,300 ⚒ C

A gilt-brass striking carriage clock, with white enamel dial, blued spade hands, subsidiary alarm ring, uncut bi-metallic balance to lever platform, strike/repeat and alarm on gong, c1900, 6in (15cm) high.
£900–1,200
$1,300–1,700 ⚒ C

An architectural carriage clock, the enamel dial above an alarm to an 8-day striking repeat alarm movement, c1880, 8½in (21.5cm) high, in original leather case.
£2,300–2,750
$3,350–4,000 ⚒ B

A miniature brass-cased carriage time-piece, with white enamel dial, 8-day movement, lever platform escapement, dial cracked, c1880, 3in (7.5cm) high.
£300–400
$440–600 ⚒ CSK

◄ **A repeating carriage clock,** with white enamel dial, the 8-day movement with silvered lever platform escapement striking on a gong, c1880, 5½in (14cm) high.
£600–700
$870–1,000 ⚒ CSK

► **A gilt-metal bamboo carriage clock,** the cloisonné enamel dial with birds and bees among flowers on a blue ground, with strike/repeat and alarm on gong, c1900, 7in (18cm) high.
£2,300–3,050
$3,350–4,400 ⚒ C

A Continental striking carriage clock, the white enamel Roman dial with blued moon hands and subsidiary alarm ring below, the movement with simple balance to the cylinder platform, strike/repeat/alarm on bell housed in the base, the rack and snail strike-work planted on the backplate, case possibly composite, c1845, 7½in (19cm) high.
£900–1,200
$1,300–1,700 ⚡ C

A striking and repeating carriage clock, with silvered case, gilded atlantes to the corners, solid ebony moulds and base, c1890, 6½in (16.5cm) high.
£7,000–8,000
$10,200–11,600 ⊞ DRA

An English carriage timepiece, the 8-day movement with single fusee and under-platform lever escapement, the engine-turned gilt-brass case with columns at the corners and scroll handle, c1850, 5in (12.5cm) high.
£2,000–2,600
$2,900–3,800 ⚡ DN

A French brass carriage clock, with white enamel dial, the bell-striking movement signed Moser A Paris, 1824, with outside countwheel and replaced platform escapement, in a plain case with front and rear doors, c1850, 4in (10cm) high.
£1,000–1,150
$1,500–1,650 ⚡ S(S)

A French repeating carriage clock, with 2½in (6.5cm) dial, silvered annular chapter ring with Roman numerals, in a blue mask decorated with scrolling foliage, the movement with bi-metallic compensated balance wheel with lever escapement, striking and repeating the hours on a gong, in a gilt-brass case, c1880, 6in (15cm) high.
£1,100–1,400
$1,600–2,000 ⚡ L

A carriage clock, with 1¼in (3cm) white enamel dial, Roman numerals and parcel gilt blued steel hands, the movement with compensated balance wheel and lever escapement, c1880, 3in (7.5cm) high, with winding key and travelling case.
£550–700
$800–1,000 ⚡ L

For further examples of Carriage Clocks please refer to Colour Reviews.

◀ **A French brass *grande sonnerie* carriage clock,** with later trefoil hands and alarm ring, plain gorge case with engine-turned gilt mask for the top viewing glass, c1875, 6in (15cm) high.
£2,300–2,750
$3,350–4,000 ⚡ C

An ivory and marquetry panelled timepiece carriage clock, signed with monogram FD, Bte, with platform escapement, late 19thC, 5in (13cm) high.
£1,200–1,400
$1,750–2,000 ⚒ C

A French gilt-brass alarm carriage clock, the movement with compensated balance wheel and lever escapement mounted on the backplate, striking and repeating on a bell, c1875, 5½in (14cm) high.
£1,150–1,200
$1,650–1,700 ⚒ L

A gilt-metal striking carriage clock, the white enamel chapter disc with blued hands, strike/ repeat on gong, later lever platform, c1900, 7in (18cm) high.
£900–1,100
$1,300–1,600 ⚒ C

A French carriage clock, with fluted columns, yellow dial with Arabic numerals, gilt and silvered mask of flowers and leaves, single train movement, restored, c1870, 7in (18cm) high.
£1,000–1,200
$1,500–1,700 ⊞ HAW

A French repeating brass-cased carriage clock, the 2in (5cm) annular chapter ring with Arabic numerals in pierced gilt mask, the movement with compensated balance wheel and lever escapement striking and repeating the hours on a gong, c1900, 6½in (16.5cm) high.
£1,150–1,200
$1,650–1,700 ⚒ L

A French brass-cased carriage clock, the 8-day lever movement striking the hours on a gong with repeat and alarm, requires restoration, late 19thC, 7½in (19cm) high.
£600–800
$870–1,100 ⚒ DN

◄ **A French gilt-brass miniature carriage time-piece,** the gilt dial with pierced centre, movement with lever platform escapement, the case cast with caryatids and foliate scrolls, c1900, 3½in (8.5cm) high.
£1,850–2,150
$2,700–3,100 ⚒ S(S)

► **A French brass quarter repeating carriage clock,** the white enamel dial with subsidiary alarm dial, the movement chiming on 2 gongs, lever platform escapement, in a corniche case, c1880, 5½in (14cm) high.
£900–1,200
$1,300–1,700 ⚒ S(S)

A French porcelain-mounted gilt-brass *grande sonnerie* **carriage clock,** the front with painted dial and landscape, 3 inset Sèvres panels painted to represent the seasons, the movement with ratchet tooth lever escapement and striking on 2 gongs, strike control lever in the base, c1870, 6in (15cm) high, with leather-covered travelling case.
£16,050–18,350
$23,250–26,600 🔨 S

A French gilt-brass repeating carriage clock, with white enamel dial, gong striking movement, lever platform escapement, Brocot No. 330, c1870, 6½in (16cm) high.
£1,400–1,850
$2,000–2,700 🔨 S(S)

A gilt-brass *grande sonnerie* **striking carriage clock,** the white enamel dial with blued steel spade hands, bi-metallic balance to silvered lever platform, strike/repeat/alarm on 2 gongs and with 3 position selection lever at base, *anglaise*-style case with engraved dedication, 6½in (16.5cm) high, with brown leather travelling case.
£1,850–2,300
$2,700–3,300 🔨 C

Carriage Clock cases

Although the cases of English carriage clocks are plainer than those of French carriage clocks, they are often much larger and more solid in appearance. There are many decorative variations to the basic design. From c1860 the most elaborately engraved cases feature *champlevé* enamel or porcelain panels in the sides and back of the case. Few were made but a number were produced for the Chinese market, and the best are signed on the back of the panel. Engraved cases with decorative panels are among the most desirable of all carriage clocks.

A French gilt-brass repeating carriage clock, with cream enamel chapter ring, leaf scroll-engraved mask, gong striking movement, the case with upper and lower pierced friezes, fluted columns and bail handle, c1900, 6in (15cm) high, and leather travelling case.
£1,200–1,800
$1,750–2,600 🔨 S(S)

A silver-cased carriage clock, with plain white enamel dial, platform lever escapement, the case die-struck with masks and leafy scrolls, on knurled bun feet, London 1891, 4½in (11cm) high.
£900–1,200
$1,300–1,700 🔨 S(S)

◄ **A French gilt-brass carriage clock,** with white enamelled dial and bell striking movement, in a one-piece case with bevelled glass and moulded pillars, c1850, 5in (13cm) high.
£900–1,200
$1,300–1,700 🔨 S(S)

A French carriage clock with barometer, the 4in (10cm) annular dial with visible lever escapement and paste-set bezel, gong striking movement No. 13850, c1900, 9in (23cm) high, with leather-covered travelling case.
£1,850–2,600
$2,700–3,800 ✗ S

A grande sonnerie calendar and alarm carriage clock, by Drocourt, with white enamel dial, the 8-day movement with silvered platform lever escapement striking on 2 bells with a change lever in the base, c1875, 5½in (14cm) high, with leather carrying case.
£3,050–4,600
$4,400–6,600 ✗ CSK

A silver-plated carriage clock, with single train movement, c1860, 6in (15cm) high.
£700–850
$1,000–1,250 ✗ Bon

▶ **A French brass grande sonnerie carriage clock,** with enamel dial, the lever movement chiming on 2 gongs, with push repeat, No. 24861, c1880, 7in (18cm) high.
£2,300–3,050
$3,300–4,400 ✗ P

A Continental silver miniature carriage timepiece, with enamel dial, the case decorated with repoussé flowers, marked London 1895, 4in (10cm) high.
£1,100–1,200
$1,600–2,000 ✗ P

A French brass 8-day striking carriage clock, with repeat, c1880, 7in (18cm) high, in a case.
£1,100–1,200
$1,600–2,000 ✗ DN

A brass miniature carriage timepiece, with white enamel dial, oval case with scroll handle, c1885, 3in (7.5cm) high.
£1,000–1,200
$1,500–2,000 ✗ C

A French gilt-brass carriage clock, with enamel dials, the movement with replaced lever platform, No. 3532, c1880, 7½in (19cm) high, with leather travelling case.
£1,200–1,550
$1,750–2,250 ✗ P

◄ **A calendar carriage timepiece,** the movement with cylinder platform, late 19thC, 5in (12.5cm) high.
£600–700
$870–1,000 ⚒ Bon

► **An Austrian gilt-metal carriage clock,** the lever movement with *grande sonnerie* striking on 2 gongs, with alarm, calendar and push repeat, 19thC, 6in (15cm) high.
£850–1,150
$1,250–1,650 ⚒ P

A miniature carriage timpiece, with white enamel dial, engraved mask, Roman numerals, 8-day movement with lever escapement, c1875, 3in (7.5cm) high.
£1,200–1,850
$1,750–2,700 ⚒ CSK

A gilt-brass-cased carriage timepiece, the movement with lever escapement, mid-19thC, 5in (12.5cm) high.
£900–1,100 $1,300–1,600 ⚒ Bea

A French gilt-brass alarm carriage clock, the lever movement with *grande sonnerie* striking on 2 bells, 19thC, 7in (18cm) high.
£3,000–4,600 $4,400–6,600 ⚒ P

A *champlevé* enamelled-brass carriage clock, the dial with seconds hand, alarm dial below, cut compensated balance to lever platform, handle damaged, 7in (18cm) high, with travelling case.
£4,300–4,900
$6,200–7,100 ⚒ C

A French gilt-brass carriage clock, the lever movement striking on a gong, 7in (18cm) high.
£3,050–4,600 $4,400–6,600 ⚒ P

A gilt carriage timepiece, with subsidiary alarm dial, 8-day movement with gilt lever platform escapement and bi-metallic balance, c1900, 3in (7.5cm) high, with red leather travelling case.
£400–550
$580–800 ⚒ CSK

► **A gilt-metal striking carriage clock,** with uncut compensated balance to silvered lever platform, c1880, 7in (18cm) high.
£2,150–2,750
$3,100–4,000 ⚒ C

A porcelain-mounted carriage clock, with lever platform, the repeating movement No. 2492, c1880, 6in (15cm) high.
£4,600–6,100 $6,650–8,850 ⚒ Bon

A carriage clock, with white enamel dial, repeating movement with lever platform, in a moulded gorge case, c1875, 6in (15cm) high.
£1,300–1,700
$1,900–2,500 ✗ Bon

A gilt-brass repeating carriage clock, with 3in (7.5cm) white enamelled dial, gong striking movement and push button repeat, the case with spiral-fluted columns and ripple-moulded upper and lower friezes, c1880, 6½in (17cm) high.
£1,850–2,750
$2,700–4,000 ✗ S(S)

A gilt-brass miniature carriage clock, the gilt dial with silvered scroll-engraved mask and cast scroll handle, c1850, 3½in (9cm) high, with leather travelling case.
£1,500–2,300 $2,170–3,300 ✗ S(S)

◄ **A carriage clock,** the repeating movement No. 2403, lever platform, c1875, 7in (18cm) high.
£850–1,150
$1,250–1,650 ✗ Bon

A brass-cased carriage clock, with repeater movement, c1900, 8in (20cm) high.
£900–1,100
$1,300–1,600 ✗ AH

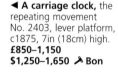

A carriage clock, with white enamel dial, the front sections set with red enamel beads, 6½in (16.5cm) high.
£450–600
$650–900 ✗ Bon

◄ **A five-minute and hour repeating carriage clock,** with enamel dial, the gong striking GL movement No. 2271 with ratchet tooth lever escapement and patent twin button repeat mechanism, in a numbered corniche case, c1880, 6in (15cm) high, with later leather travelling case.
£1,850–2,750
$2,700–4,000 ✗ S

A gilt-brass and bronze carriage clock, the silvered dial with moon hands, the movement with lever escapement visible through a panel in the top, slow/fast lever in the top, the base with spring clip and recess for the numbered key, both No. 1069, c1840, 5½in (14cm) high, with velvet-lined glazed rosewood travelling case.
£1,150–1,850
$1,650–2,700 ✗ Bon

A French gilt-brass carriage clock, with enamel dial, the lever movement striking on a gong with push repeat, in a bamboo-style case, c1890, 7½in (19cm) high.
£900–1,050
$1,300–1,500 ⚒ P

A repeating carriage clock, the enamel dial with chime/silent dial below, Westminster chimes on 4 bells and a gong, 3 train movement with lever escapement, c1880, 7in (18cm) high, with travelling case.
£4,600–6,100
$6,650–8,800 ⚒ S

A French carriage clock, the case in the form of a house, the dial with gilt mask, ivorine chapter ring with gilt and silvered centre field, 8-day movement striking on a gong, c1900, 9in (23cm) high.
£1,000–1,150
$1,500–1,650 ⚒ CSK

A gilt-brass enamel-mounted carriage clock, the movement with lever escapement, compensated balance, gong striking and repeating at will, late 19thC, 8in (20cm) high, with travelling case.
£2,300–2,750
$3,350–4,000 ⚒ L

A French *grande sonnerie* repeating carriage clock, the numerals on the white enamel dial replaced with the names Margaret and Kate, day, date and alarm subsidiary dials, backplate stamped W.T. & Co, 19thC, 6in (15cm) high, with red morocco travelling case.
£3,050–3,850
$4,400–5,600 ⊞ BS

A French miniature carriage clock, the single train movement with cylinder escapement, 19thC, 3½in (9cm) high, with travelling case.
£1,000–1,200
$1,500–1,700 ⊞ TKN

A French brass carriage time-piece, late 19thC, 5in (13cm) high.
£270–330 $390–500 ⚒ CEd

A gilt-metal engraved striking carriage clock, with uncut compensated balance to gilt lever platform, c1875, 5in (13cm) high.
£1,800–2,300 $2,600–3,300 ⚒ C

A *champlevé* enamel striking carriage clock, with bi-metallic balance to lever platform, c1890, 6½in (16.5cm) high.
£3,050–3,800 $4,400–5,500 ⚒ C

A French gilt-brass carriage clock, the movement with replaced lever platform, push repeat, alarm and calendar, striking on a bell, 19thC, 6in (15cm) high.
£850–1,000
$1,250–1,500 ⚒ P

An Austrian *grande sonnerie* carriage clock, with enamel dial, alarm, the repeating 4 train 30-hour gong striking movement with double wheel duplex escapement, in a floral engraved case with Gothic style frets and feet, c1840, 7½in (19cm) high.
£1,050–1,400
$1,500–2,000 ⚒ S

A gilt-brass and enamel carriage clock, with 2in (5cm) white enamel dial, striking on a gong, c1880, 6in (15cm) high.
£2,300–3,000 $3,350–4,400 ⚒ S(S)

► **A French *grande sonnerie* calendar carriage clock,** the enamel dial with subsidiary chapters for date and alarm, the movement No. 2414 striking on 2 bells, later lever escapement, in a gorge case with lever in the base with *Gde. Sonnerie/Silence/Pte. Sonnerie*, c1875, 6in (15cm) high.
£3,050–4,600
$4,400–6,600 ⚒ S

◄ **A brass-cased carriage clock,** with cream enamel annular chapter ring against a pierced foliate mask, the movement with lever escapement, c1900, 5½in (14cm) high.
£1,050–1,400
$1,500–2,000 ⚒ Bon

A brass repeating carriage clock, with white enamel dial and striking movement, in a corniche case, c1880, 6½in (16.5cm) high, with morocco-covered travelling case.
£550–600 $800–1,000 ⚒ HCH

► **A brass repeating carriage clock,** the painted pale blue dial with leafy scroll-pierced mask and side panels, bevelled glass, c1880, 5½in (14cm) high.
£1,400–1,850
$2,000–2,700 ⚒ S

A French decorative carriage clock, c1900, 5in (13cm) high.
£450–600 $650–900 ⊞ SO

A brass-cased carriage clock, with polychrome *champlevé* enamel panels, French 8-day striking movement, No. 2441, c1880, 7in (18cm) high.
£2,750–3,800
$4,000–5,500 ⊞ GC

A silver-cased carriage clock, with round enamel dial, French lever movement, swing handle and bun feet, Chester 1906, 4½in (11cm) high.
£1,050–1,450
$1,500–2,100 ⚒ DN

A miniature carriage clock, with 8-day movement, in a *cloisonné* decorated serpentine case, c1900, 3in (8cm) high.
£900–1,200 $1,300–1,700 ⊞ SO

A French gilt-brass repeating alarm carriage clock, with enamel chapter ring and alarm dial within a floral fretwork panel, striking the hours and half-hours, c1900, 6½in (16.5cm) high.
£1,550–1,850
$2,250–2,700 ⚒ GSP

A French brass carriage clock, with 8-day movement, c1880, 7in (18cm) high.
£1,000–1,400
$1,500–2,000 ⚒ DN

◄ **A French gilt-brass carriage clock,** with enamel chapter ring, lever movement striking on a gong, push repeat, c1900, 7½in (19cm) high.
£900–1,100
$1,300–1,600 ⚒ P

A French engraved carriage clock, with white enamel dial, 8-day movement with lever escapement, c1880, 6in (15cm) high.
£2,300–3,050
$3,350–4,400 ⚒ Bea

A French brass carriage clock, set with porcelain plaques and signed LS, with 8-day striking and repeating lever movement, 7½in (19cm) high.
£4,600–6,100
$6,650–8,800 ⚒ DN

► **A French brass carriage clock,** the lever movement striking on a gong, c1885, 7in (18cm) high.
£900–1,200
$1,300–1,700 ⚒ P

A miniature brass carriage clock, c1870, 3in (8cm) high.
£650–750 $950–1,100 ⊞ RFA

A French brass *grande sonnerie* and alarm carriage clock, the dials with white chapter on a black and pink enamel ground, platform lever escapement striking on 2 gongs mounted on the backplate, late 19thC, 7½in (19cm) high.
£3,050–4,600
$4,400–6,600 ⚒ P(M)

▶ **A *petite sonnerie* alarm carriage clock,** with white enamel dial, subsidiary alarm dial beneath, No. 7272, with lever platform, the repeating movement quarter striking on 2 gongs, in a moulded case with bands of beading, c1885, 5½in (14cm) high.
£1,400–1,700
$2,000–2,500 ⚒ Bon

A brass carriage clock, with cream chapter ring and alarm, c1890, 5in (13cm) high.
£700–850 $1,000–1,200 ⚒ S(S)

A *petite sonnerie* alarm carriage clock, with cream enamel dial, movement No. 7851, quarter striking and repeating on 2 gongs, lever escapement, strike/silent lever in the base, c1890, 6in (15cm) high, with travelling case.
£1,550–2,150
$2,250–3,100 ⚒ Bon

A brass repeating alarm carriage clock, c1880, 6in (15cm) high.
£700–750
$1,000–1,100 ⚒ GSP

A French repeating carriage alarm clock, with enamel dials set within a gilt surround, gong striking movement with lever escapement, the glazed case composed of gilt-brass simulated bamboo, c1875, 8½in (21cm) high.
£1,100–1,400 $1,600–2,000 ⚒ S

A brass carriage clock, c1880, 5in (13cm) high.
£1,000–1,200 $1,500–2,000 ⊞ SBA

A gilt-brass striking carriage clock, with white enamel dial, blued Breguet hands, uncut bi-metallic balance to silvered lever platform, strike/repeat on gong, c1875, 5½in (14cm) high.
£1,200–1,500 $1,750–2,200 ⚒ C

Wall Clocks

A wall clock is by definition any weight- or spring-driven clock made to hang on a wall, hence this category embraces a variety of styles. The first hooded wall clocks date from the time of celebrated maker Edward East (the last quarter of the 17th century) and are the earliest known 8-day clocks made with a wooden case. This style, similar to a longcase but without a trunk, was used by eminent makers throughout the 18th century. However, they are harder to find than the popular round-dial wall clocks that were designed in large numbers for domestic use and public buildings (see Tavern or Act of Parliament clocks, page 220).

Most English round-dial wall clocks are simple timepieces with good fusee movements. The earliest examples had silvered dials with moulded mahogany surrounds. As the 19th century progressed the convex painted dials became more fashionable, and eventually the flat dial with plain mahogany or oak surround became the most popular design. Towards the 1870s these clocks were copied by American and German manufacturers in large numbers. German makers such as Winterhalder and Hofmeier included them in their range, some with fusee movements, but most German makers omitted the fusee. Similarly the American manufacturers thought they could undercut the English by fitting their clocks with machine-made movements and retailing them more cheaply.

Trunk-dial wall clocks, sometimes referred to as drop-dial clocks, had the addition of a trunk or box under the dial to accommodate a longer pendulum and began to appear from c1785. The early mahogany bases sloped back to a sharp point at the wall (known as a chisel foot). Gradually the cases became more decorative, with the addition of inlay or features such as shaped 'ears' on either side.

Very different from the restrained style of British wall clocks are the French cartel clocks which originated c1750. Movements are usually fairly plain, but the cases tended towards high rococo ornamentation, and this style was repeated and copied through the years. Michael Turner of Sotheby's points to the degree of 'prettiness' as being the main factor in determining the price. Three top-quality cartel clocks from the Vitale Collection sold at Christie's New York achieved $20,700 (£13,000), $19,500 (£12,000) and $25,300 (£15,800) respectively.

Prices of wall clocks vary according to category. Recently Sotheby's sold a mahogany hooded wall clock of c1775 by John Ellicott, which was an attractive piece but with a reconstructed bracket. According to Michael Turner it could have fetched as much as £12,000 ($17,400) had it been wholly original. Trunk-dial prices are also dependent on quality and age and can be between £550 ($800) and £3000 ($4,400), similarly round-dial wall clocks can fetch between £350 ($500) and £1,500 ($2,150).

◄ **A George III mahogany striking wall clock,** the 13in (33cm) painted dial signed T. Banks, Preston, the false plate signed Finnemore, the teardrop case outlined with ebony and boxwood stringing, c1800, 52in (132cm) high.
£1,600–2,100
$2,300–3,000 ⚒ S

▶ **A black and gilt japanned chinoiserie decorated 'teardrop' tavern timepiece,** by J. Bartholomew, Sherborne, with weight-driven movement, c1750, 57in (145cm) high.
£3,500–4,050
$5,000–5,800 ⚒ S(S)

A Victorian mahogany gallery clock, the white dial inscribed John Bennett, 65 and 64 Cheapside, with fusee movement striking on a single gong, 36in (92cm) high, on a scroll carved wall-mounted fixed bracket.
£850–1,100
$1,250–1,600 ⚒ DDM

◄ **A heavy brass ship's bulkhead clock,** Kelvin Bottomley & Baird Ltd, Glasgow, with lever escapement, c1920, 10in (25.5cm) diam.
£700–800
$1,000–1,200 ⊞ IAT

▶ **A George III mahogany dial timepiece,** signed Г. Berguer of London, with 12in (30.5cm) silvered dial, 8-day movement, the case with turned front bezel, c1800, 15in (38cm) diam.
£1,150–1,750
$1,650–2,500 ⚒ CAG

◄ **A Victorian ebonized combination wall clock and barometer,** the moulded case with panelled front displaying an aneroid barometer, the silvered dial signed Cary, 181 Strand, London, 601, with steel hand and brass recorder, the clock with 4 pillar single chain fusee movement with cut bi-metallic balance to lever platform, mercurial thermometer in the centre with silvered scale, frame 24in (61cm) wide.
£1,400–2,100
$2,000–3,000 ⚒ C

A carved walnut Gothic-style dial timepiece, the painted dial signed J. Brunner, Birmingham, with fusee movement, c1875.
£950–1,400
$1,380–2,000 ⊞ SBA

A Swedish giltwood clock, the painted dial signed Carl Bergstein, the striking 8-day movement with silkwork suspension, c1800, 30in (76cm) high.
£1,500–2,000 $2,170–2,900 ⊞ SO

A black and gilt japanned tavern wall timepiece, signed Jn. Clarkson, London, c1785.
£3,500–4,500
$5,000–6,500 ⊞ EHL

A mahogany dial timepiece, the 12in (30.5cm) painted dial signed Cohen, Hastings, heavy moulded cast brass bezel, c1830, 14½in (37cm) diam.
£1,100–1,200
$1,600–2,000 ⊞ DRA

A mahogany gallery timepiece, the painted dial signed Brown, 104 Praed St, Paddington, with fusee movement, c1885, 14½in (37cm) diam.
£1,200–1,400
$1,750–2,000 ⊞ DRA

A brass-inlaid mahogany trunk-dial clock, signed De la Salle, London, double fusee movement, c1840, 21in (53cm) diam.
£1,500–2,000 $2,170–2,900 ⊞ SO

◄ **A rosewood dial timepiece with alarm,** the engraved silvered dial signed De la Salle & Christie, Cannon St, London, with centre sweep minute hand, hour and alarm hands, fusee movement, c1820, 12½in (32cm) diam.
£3,000–3,500
$4,400–5,000 ⊞ DRA

A brass-inlaid mahogany trunk-dial clock, signed De la Salle, London, with double fusee movement, c1840, 21in (53cm) high.
£1,000–1,500
$1,500–2,200 ⊞ SO

A black japanned tavern timepiece, the dial signed Thomas Fenton, London, the 5 pillar movement with anchor escapement, c1775.
£1,950–2,300
$2,800–3,300 🔨 L

A mahogany dial timepiece, the painted dial signed Ellicott, Royal Exchange, London, with rise and fall regulation, fusee movement, c1820, 23in (58.5cm) high.
£800–1,050
$1,150–1,500 🔨 C

A verge wall timepiece with alarm, with silvered chapter ring, signed in arch Geo Graham, London, the movement with knife-edge verge escapement, the alarm with separate pulley operating on bell in top plate, restored, c1740, 5in (13cm) wide.
£4,650–5,200
$6,750–7,500 🔨 C

A mahogany trunk-dial timepiece, the engraved brass dial signed Mattw. & Thos. Dutton, London, fusee movement with anchor escapement, late 18thC, 26½in (67.5cm) high.
£3,500–4,650
$5,000–6,750 🔨 P

An oak calendar wall timepiece, the cream painted dial with black Roman numerals, signed Fredjohns Ltd, Jewellers, Wimbledon, the case with turned columns and dentil cornice, on a matching bracket with hand set perpetual calendar, c1875, 62in (157.5cm) high.
£1,400–2,100
$2,000–3,000 🔨 Bea

A George III black lacquer Act of Parliament clock, the painted dial signed Pet. Bargeau, London, with later weight-driven movement with deadbeat escapement, 60½in (153.5cm) high.
£2,300–2,900
$3,350–4,200 🔨 CNY

◄ **A late George III mahogany dial timepiece,** the engraved silvered dial signed John Good, London, with fusee movement verge escapement, 15½in (39.5cm) high.
£1,750–2,300
$2,550–3,500 🔨 C

Hints to dating wall clocks

Dials

Square	to c1755	George II or later
Broken arch	c1720 to c1805	Georgian
Painted/round	from c1740	George II or later
Silvered	from c1760	George III or later

Case finish

Ebony veneer	c1690 to William & Mary	
Marquetry	c1680 to 1695	Carolean to William & Mary
Mahogany	from c1740	George II
Oak	all periods	

A mahogany dial timepiece, the painted convex dial signed Fontana, High Wycombe, c1830.
£750–900 $1,100–1,300 ⊞ SBA

A French bronze lobster wall clock, the 3in (7.5cm) annular enamel dial with gilt centre, bell striking movement by Japy Frères, No. 105, with cylinder escapement, dial cracked, c1890, 29in (73.5cm) high.
£2,300–3,500
$3,350–5,000 ⚒ S

▶ **A brass-inlaid mahogany trunk-dial timepiece,** the 14in (35.5cm) painted dial signed Haley, London, with fusee movement, c1840.
£1,200–1,500 $1,750–2,200 ⊞ SO

A Georgian dial clock, the 8in (20cm) engraved silvered dial with mock pendulum aperture and pierced hands, signed Thomas Harvey, London, 4 pillar single gut fusee movement with knife-edge verge escapement and short bob pendulum, in later mahogany case.
£2,300–3,500
$3,350–5,000 ⚒ C

◀ **A French *tôle peinte* wall clock,** the 5in (12.5cm) enamel dial signed Guillaume à Paris, bell striking silk suspension movement, octagonal stepped case with scalloped upper section, the whole painted with flowers on a simulated wood ground, c1810, 15in (38cm) high.
£900–1,400
$1,300–2,000 ⚒ S

▶ **A German rosewood and brass-inlaid wall clock,** retailed in Exeter by S. F. Hettish, c1850, 27in (68.5cm) high.
£800–900
$1,150–1,300 ⊞ RFA

◀ **A mahogany 'Norwich' wall clock,** the 14in (35.5cm) dial signed John Gudgeon, Bury, with cast brass-moulded concave bezel incorporating the lock, weight-driven movement with large great wheel and anchor escapement, c1810, 49in (124.5cm) high.
£2,100–2,900
$3,000–4,200 ⚒ S

◀ **A rosewood dial clock,** inlaid with mother-of-pearl, with twin fusee striking movement, c1850.
£1,500–1,800
$2,170–2,600 ⊞ GIB

A French gaming wall clock, the chequerboard dial with counter numeral plaques, playing card spandrels and billiard motifs, square Japy Frères gong striking movement with Brocot escapement, the moulded case with chess piece finials, c1890, 24in (61cm) square.
£1,750–2,300
$2,550–3,300 ⚒ S

A mahogany striking wall clock, the dial inscribed T. Joyce, Whitchurch, with 5 pillar fusee movement, c1840, 39in (99cm) high.
£900–1,400 $1,300–2,000 ⚒ P

A walnut trunk-dial timepiece, the dial signed J. Maple & Co, London, c1870.
£500–750 $720–1,100 ⚒ JH

A mahogany dial timepiece, the silvered dial signed Robt. Mawley, with fusee movement re-converted to verge escapement, c1770, 13½in (34.5cm) diam.
£1,400–2,100 $2,000–3,000 ⚒ C

A French tôle peinte wall clock, 19thC, 18in (45.5cm) diam.
£900–1,050 $1,300–1,500 ⚒ P

A mahogany wall timepiece, the dial signed Joseph Newman, London, with fusee movement, engraved tapered backplate and verge escapement, c1780, 18in (45.5cm) diam.
£1,150–1,750
$1,650–2,500 ⚒ P

A mahogany timepiece, the painted dial signed J. R. Parker, Walsingham, the weight-driven movement with tapered plates, 5 wheel train and anchor escapement, c1830, 53½in (136cm) high.
£1,750–2,300
$2,550–3,300 ⚒ S

◄ **A dial clock,** the 14in (35.5cm) dial signed John Neve, Hingham, with verge escapement in tapering plates, 16½in (42cm) diam.
£1,850–2,300
$2,700–3,300 ⚒ Bon

A British Railways mahogany dial clock, with fusee movement.
£400–500 $600–900 ⊞ IAT

A black and gilt japanned Act of Parliament clock, the oak trunk signed Perinot, Paddington, with painted dial 2 train bell striking movement, c1775, 44in (112cm) high.
£15,000–18,000
$21,700–26,000 ⊞ DRA
Striking Act of Parliament clocks are unusual and therefore more expensive.

An oak chiming wall clock, signed W. Potts & Sons, Leeds, with blued spade hands, the 5 pillar triple chain fusee movement with anchor escapement chiming on 8 bells, c1880, 35in (90cm) high.
£2,300–2,900
$3,300–4,200 ✎ C

A Dutch Zaandam wall clock, the brass-posted frame movement with Tuscan angle columns, striking on 2 bells above the velvet covered dial, signed Cornelis van Rossen on chapter ring, 36in (91.5cm) high.
£3,500–4,650
$5,000–6,750 ✎ C

A brass-inlaid and carved mahogany trunk-dial timepiece, the painted dial signed Pyott, Lewes, with fusee movement, c1840, 20in (51cm) high.
£1,000–1,700
$1,500–2,500 ⊞ RFA

A mahogany dial timepiece, by Rhodes & Son, Bradford, with fusee movement, c1860, 15in (38cm) diam.
£400–500
$600–900 ⊞ BL

A Victorian oak trunk-dial time-piece, with white painted dial inscribed G.W.R., the single fusee movement with anchor escapement, 27½in (70cm) high.
£600–800 $870–1,200 ✎ CSK

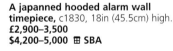

A japanned hooded alarm wall timepiece, c1830, 18in (45.5cm) high.
£2,900–3,500
$4,200–5,000 ⊞ SBA

Dial clocks

The basic round-dial clock was introduced in the 1770, its forerunner being the later versions of the tavern clock. Cases were plain and almost invariably of solid mahogany. From c1785 trunk-dial clocks were made, probably for the study or library of large houses, and were often finely figured, inlaid and strung with brass. All are spring-driven, and typically have a fusee movement.

◄ **A mahogany wall clock,** the 14in (35.5cm) painted dial signed T. R. Russell, Liverpool, with double fusee half-hour striking movement, with integral bracket, restored, c1875.
£1,800–2,200
$2,600–3,200 ⊞ HAW

A Victorian mahogany trunk-dial timepiece, the painted dial signed Pratt, Norwich, with fusee movement, the case carved with grape and vine leaf decoration, c1840.
£600–800
$870–1,200 ✎ GAK

Tavern or Act of Parliament Clocks

Tavern or Act of Parliament clocks were made for taverns and coaching inns throughout England from c1740 to 1800. Their main purpose was to provide accurate local time and, in particular, to regulate the arrival and departure of stage coaches, which kept to very reliable schedules.

The term Act of Parliament clock arose from the Act which was passed in 1797 putting a tax on all clocks and watches. This was 2s 6d (22p) for a silver watch, 10s (50p) for a gold watch, and 5s (25p) for each clock. The result of this tax was that people stopped buying clocks and watches and concealed those they already had, thus producing an increased need for public clocks. This is exactly what tavern clocks had been made for in the first instance and is why they also acquired the name Act of Parliament clocks.

Because of the dramatic fall in the sale of clocks and watches, many makers faced bankruptcy. King George III was petitioned and within a year of its introduction the Act was repealed.

The diameter of the dials of these clocks was usually between 20in and 30in (51cm and 76cm), and their overall length was from 53in to 72in (134.5cm to 183cm). They were not usually protected by any glazing. The cases were painted with black lacquer and decorated with ornamental scenes, but sometimes were just left black or enlivened with gilt lines. The use of black was mainly traditional, but was also more practical in the smoke-laden atmosphere of an inn than a finely polished mahogany case. It was only towards the end of the 18th century that mahogany-cased clocks started to appear, frequently with glazed doors to the dial. The majority of tavern clocks had round-dials, but other shapes such as octagonal and shield shapes were also used.

A solid mahogany wall clock, the 14in (35.5cm) painted wood dial signed Walter Rowland, Berwick, with moulded mahogany bezel, weight-driven movement with inverted Y-shaped plates, anchor escapement and double pulley arrangement, the narrow trunk with shaped top to the door and *bombé* plinth, with sliding front panel, c1800, 47in (119.5cm) high.
£2,300–3,500
$3,350–5,000 ⚒ S

► **An oak Gothic-style wall clock,** the 10in (25.5cm) painted dial signed Short & Mason, Hatton Garden, London, with single fusee movement, spire pediment with applied carved cresting, Gothic-style foil and carved foliage, decorated and carved front panel and base, c1875, 29in (73.5cm) high.
£700–1,400
$1,000–2,000 ⚒ Bon

A mahogany trunk-dial wall clock, the 8¼in (21cm) painted wood dial signed J. Thwaites, London, with cast brass bezel, fusee movement, ogee shouldered footed plates and anchor escapement, the case with moulded wood dial surround and under curved trunk incorporating a door, c1820, 14in (35.5cm) high.
£1,400–2,100
$2,000–3,000 ⚒ S

◄ **A Georgian mahogany wall clock,** the dial inscribed Simpson, Yarmouth, the weight-driven 8-day movement with anchor escapement and tapered plates, c1810, 43in (109cm) high.
£1,600–2,100
$2,300–3,000 ⚒ P

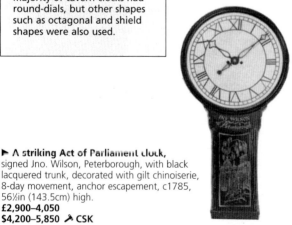

► **A striking Act of Parliament clock,** signed Jno. Wilson, Peterborough, with black lacquered trunk, decorated with gilt chinoiserie, 8-day movement, anchor escapement, c1785, 56½in (143.5cm) high.
£2,900–4,050
$4,200–5,850 ⚒ CSK

► **A mahogany wall clock,** with 14in (35.5cm) painted dial, the false plate stamped Wilkes & Son, 8-day bell striking movement, c1825, 61in (155cm) high.
£1,600–2,100
$2,300–3,000 ⚒ S(S)

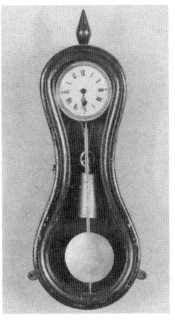

An Austrian giltwood picture frame *grande sonnerie* wall clock, with 3 train movement striking on 2 bells, sunburst pendulum, c1835, 21in (53.5cm) high.
£900–1,400
$1,300–2,000 ⚒ HSS

A green and gilt japanned tavern timepiece, with 29in (73.5cm) white painted dial, pierced blued spade hands, the 4 pillar movement with tapered plates and anchor escapement, c1780, 58½in (148.5cm) high.
£2,300–3,000
$3,350–4,400 ⚒ C

An Austrian miniature wall clock, with 2½in (6.5cm) enamel dial, weight-driven movement, in a waisted simulated rosewood case, glazed door, weights replaced, 14in (35.5cm) high.
£1,400–2,000
$2,000–3,000 ⚒ S

▶ **A brass-inlaid mahogany timepiece,** with convex octagonal painted dial, single fusee movement, c1830.
£900–1,400
$1,300–2,000 ⊞ SBA

For further examples of Wall Clocks please refer to the Colour Reviews.

◄ **A mahogany wall clock,** the dial signed Cater, with 2 train weight-driven movement, rack striking on a bell, c1830, 48in (122cm) high.
£1,800–2,500
$2,600–3,600 ⊞ IAT

► **A Dutch oak Staartklok,** with painted dial, striking on 2 bells, weight-driven movement, c1850, 48in (122cm) high.
£1,400–2,100
$2,000–3,000 ⚒ CSK

An Austrian *petite sonnerie* **musical giltwood picture frame wall clock,** with annular enamel dial and gilt engine-turned centre, the 3 train gong striking movement with silk suspension, a distressed musical movement with 8½in (21.5cm) pinned cylinder mounted above, the case with egg-and-dart moulded border, c1840, 20in (51cm) square.
£800–1,050
$1,150–1,500 ⚒ S

A brass ship's bulkhead timepiece, early 20thC, 9in (23cm) diam.
£600–700
$870–1,000 ⊞ RFA

Ship's Clocks

Produced in England from c1860 until WWII, ship's clocks were made in a round brass case to be screwed on to a bulkhead. Dials are usually silvered brass or enamelled metal, although some later examples are painted metal. Almost all are timepieces only, and those which strike the hours are rare. Early examples with a fusee movement are rare and the most collectable today, whereas later pieces, with a going barrel, are less sought after. All have a seconds dial, most have blued steel hands though some are brass, and the majority have a signature on the dial.

A brass-inlaid mahogany trunk-dial timepiece, the painted dial with Roman numerals, fusee movement with shaped plates, c1835, 25in (63.5cm) high.
£2,200–2,400
$3,200–3,500 ⊞ DRA

A mahogany trunk-dial railway timepiece, the painted dial signed London 801SE, with fusee movement, c1875, 20in (51cm) high.
£750–900
$1,100–1,300 ⊞ RFA

► **A Dutch Frieseland** *Stoelklok,* the painted dial with moonphase, the movement with spiral angle posts, cast lead mounts to the colourful case, late 18thC, 31½in (80cm) high.
£1,600–2,100
$2,300–3,000 ⚒ C(Am)

A mahogany trunk-dial wall timepiece, with painted dial, fusee movement, c1880, 20in (51cm) diam.
£750–900 $1,100–1,300 ⊞ RFA

A German walnut trunk-dial wall clock, striking on a gong, c1900, 24in (61cm) high.
£300–350 $440–500 ⊞ IAT

A brass-inlaid mahogany trunk-dial timepiece, with 12in (30.5cm) dial, fusee movement, c1830, 25in (63.5cm) high.
£900–1,400
$1,300–2,000 ⚒ CAG

An adapted George III brass-mounted mahogany wall clock, the 14in (35.5cm) dial signed Mattw. & Willm. Dutton, with anchor escapement and rack strike to fusee movement, 38in (96.5cm) high.
£1,750–2,300
$2,500–3,300 ⚒ C

◀ **A brass-inlaid octagonal mahogany dial clock,** with convex painted dial, double fusee movement striking on a bell, c1830, dial 10in (25.5cm) diam.
£900–1,400
$1,300–2,000 ⊞ P(Re)

▶ **A brass-inlaid mahogany and rose-wood crossbanded trunk-dial timepiece,** the silvered dial signed George Muston, Small Street, Bristol, c1840, 25½in (65cm) high.
£2,400–2,800
$3,500–4,000 ⚒ DRA

▶ **A mahogany trunk-dial wall clock,** by Birkle Bros, London, with fusee movement, c1870, 19in (48.5cm) high.
£700–750
$1,000–1,100 ⊞ IAT

◀ **An early Victorian papier mâché wall clock,** with glazed enamel dial, the case painted with flowers and highlighted with mother-of-pearl, 30in (76cm) high.
£700–900
$1,000–1,300 ⚒ C

Cartel Clocks

◀ **A George III carved gilt-wood cartel clock,** the dial with false pendulum aperture signed William Glover, London, fusee movement with verge escapement, c1765, 31in (78.5cm) high.
£1,750–2,300
$2,500–3,350 ⚒ C

▶ **A French ormolu cartel clock,** the 6½in (16.5cm) enamel dial signed F. Barbedienne à Paris, with bell striking movement and Brocot escapement, the case with berried leaves and trellis fretwork, later painted decoration, c1870, 28in (71cm) high.
£1,150–1,600
$1,650–2,300 ⚒ S

A French ormolu cartel clock, the enamel dial signed Bryson & Sons, Paris, with blue Roman chapters and black Arabic 5 minute divisions, pierced gilt hands, twin train movement with bell strike, above a pierced trellis grille and female mask, late 19thC, 20in (51cm) high.
£1,300–1,750
$1,900–2,500 ⚒ C

A French gilt-brass cartel clock, with enamel dial, Japy Frères bell striking movement, c1890, 20in (51cm) high.
£800–1,200
$1,150–1,700 ⊞ SO

A French gilt-bronze cartel clock, by Mynuel, Paris, mid-19thC.
£1,400–2,100
$2,000–3,000 ⚒ DA

A Louis XVI ormolu cartel clock, the enamel dial signed Hans à Paris, movement with pull quarter repeat, incomplete 18in (45.5cm) high.
£1,150–1,750
$1,650–2,500 ⚒ P

Cartel Clocks

The word 'cartel' probably originates from the Italian *cartella*, or wall bracket. Introduced in the 18th century in France, cartel clocks are decorative, gilt, spring-driven, usually with verge escapements. The few English cartel clocks that were made from 1730 to 1770 are highly collectable, especially if the case is in good condition.

A Louis XV-style ormolu cartel clock, 38in (96.5cm) high.
£950–1,050
$1,380–1,500 ⚒ Bon

▶ **A French Louis XV-style cartel clock,** the 2 train movement with countwheel strike on a bell, some damage to chapters, late 19thC, 30in (76cm) high.
£950–1,400
$1,300–2,000 ⚒ HSS

A French Louis XV ormolu cartel clock, with enamel dial, bell striking movement with Brocot escapement, the rococo case cast with scrollwork, c1875, 24in (61cm) high.
£2,300–3,500
$3,350–5,000 ⚒ S

◀ **A Louis XV gilt bronze cartel clock,** the case stamped St Germain, the dial signed Jean Fol à Paris, mid-18thC, 24½in (62cm) high.
£11,000–13,900
$16,000–20,000 🔨 S

▶ **A French Louis XVI-style ormolu cartel clock,** the enamel dial signed Guibal, Paris, c1890, 26in (66cm) high.
£950–1,400
$1,380–2,000 🔨 C

A French ormolu rococo cartel timepiece, the enamel dial signed Joannes Biesta, Paris, c1765, 32in (81.5cm) high.
£6,400–8,100
$9,300–12,000 🔨 C

A French Louis XV ormolu cartel clock, signed on the movement Jean Fol à Paris, the enamel dial with asymmetric winding holes, the rococo case signed St Germain, c1765, 22in (56cm) high.
£11,600–17,400
$16,800–25,500 🔨 S

A French Louis XVI-style cartel clock, the enamel dial signed T. Martin, Paris, c1890, 27in (68.5cm) high.
£1,150–1,750
$1,650–2,500 🔨 C

A French Louis XV ormolu cartel clock, the dial and bell striking movement signed Ferdinand Berthoud à Paris, c1765, 24½in (62cm) high.
£13,900–20,900
$20,150–30,500 🔨 S
Berthoud was one of the most important makers of this period.

A Louis XV gilt-bronze cartel clock, the dial and movement signed Etienne Lenoir à Paris, mid-18thC, 14½in (37cm) high.
£5,200–7,500
$7,550–11,000 🔨 S

A French Louis XV-style ormolu striking cartel clock, the dial signed De Hemant, Paris, c1875.
£1,400–2,100
$2,000–3,000 🔨 C

A French ormolu cartel clock, the enamel dial signed Leroy à Paris, the striking rack planted on the backplate, the shaped case cast with upturned foliage, c1775, 20in (51cm) high.
£2,300–3,500
$3,500–5,000 🔨 C

Skeleton Clocks

The skeleton clock is one of the most interesting from a horological point of view as nothing is hidden away: the mechanism becomes its most important feature. Skeleton clocks were spring-driven table clocks with the plates cut away in loops and scrolls so that the wheels in the train and the workings of the escapement could be clearly visible. Their origins were in France, where manufacture began in the last half of the 18th century, but by 1850 the English were producing many more skeleton clocks than the French. Perhaps due to the 19th-century interest in science, these clocks particularly appealed to the Victorians, and they were featured at the Great Exhibition of 1851 in London.

To protect the movement from dust, skeleton clocks were covered with an oval glass dome. According to dealer M. D. Tooke, herein lies the main problem with owning a skeleton clock: although necessary, these covers are highly vulnerable and over the years can easily get damaged. If the original dome is missing the value of a clock could be reduced by as much as £1,000 ($1,500). Replacement domes are obtainable, but can cost as much as £400 ($580). Dealer Gaby Gunst points out that while it is possible to find old domes, the problem is to get one that will fit the base. She insists, however, that old glass will always look much better than a modern replacement.

Skeleton clocks vary in quality. Assess the quality of the plates of the frame and avoid the clock if they are very thin or not well finished. Check how many spokes there are in the wheels – the better quality ones have five and six spokes whereas those with four spoke wheels are probably apprentice pieces. Look at the quality of the dial – the best dials are of silvered brass with black numerals – and then at the complexities of the movement, for instance how often it strikes and whether it chimes. Good-quality clocks sometimes have musical boxes in the bases.

Smith & Son, J. Moore & Son and other Clerkenwell makers provided a large number of skeleton clocks. Of those made outside London some of the best quality clocks were by James Condliff of Liverpool: he signed his name on an engraved silver plate screwed to the front. However, these seldom come on the market and reach very high prices. Many skeleton clocks are not signed at all or only with the retailer's name, not the maker's.

From c1855 a popular type of skeleton clock was that modelled on famous buildings. Popular subjects include York Minster, Lichfield and St Paul's cathedrals, and Edinburgh's Scott Memorial. A York Minster example of c1860, with glass dome cracked but complete, was sold at Sotheby's for £1,600 ($2,300). According to Sotheby's expert, Michael Turner, if it had been a chiming example it could have fetched around £7,500 ($10,875).

A skeleton clock, the engraved and silvered chapter ring with chamfered edges, signed William Bishop, Bond St, London, with chain fusee, dome and matched base, c1845, 7½in (19cm) high.
£2,500–3,500
$3,600–5,000 ⊞ DRA

◄ **A French calendar skeleton clock,** signed on the dial and backplate Bright, Paris, No. 4672, the movement with external countwheel striking on a bell above the calendar work with its hand settings, on replacement brass strung rosewood base, with dome, mid-19thC, 9in (24cm) high.
£3,000–3,400
$4,400–4,900 ⊞ DRA

► **A brass skeleton clock,** by W. F. Evans and Sons, Soho Clock Factory, Handsworth, depicting Westminster Abbey, 3 train movement striking on a gong and 8 bells, with mercury pendulum, 24in (61cm) high, with oval dome.
£9,000–10,800
$13,000–15,000 ⚒ AGr

A brass skeleton clock, with passing strike, with silvered chapter ring, the movement with going barrel, large great wheel, half deadbeat escapement and passing strike on a gong in the base, the scrollwork frame supported on a base with applied plaque signed James Condliff, Liverpool c1850, 15in (38cm) high.
£6,000–7,200
$8,700–10,500 ⚒ S

A brass skeleton timepiece, the 4in (10cm) silvered chapter ring with Roman numerals, the single fusee movement and half deadbeat escapement with a polished scroll-shaped frame, 11¼in (28.5cm) high, c1845, on an oval mahogany base with glass dome.
£1,100–1,300
$1,600–1,900 ⚒ **Bon**

A Victorian brass skeleton timepiece, with lyre-shaped frame and Roman chapter ring, moon hands, single chain fusee movement with anchor escapement, 9in (23cm) high, on ebonized base and later glass frame.
£850–1,000
$1,250–1,500 ⚒ **CSK**

A brass skeleton timepiece, with pierced chapter ring, the fusee movement with pierced spired plates, passing strike and anchor escapement, on 4 turned supports, late 19thC, 16½in (42cm) high, on marble base with ebonized stand and glass dome.
£700–850
$1,000–1,500 ⚒ **P**

A skeleton timepiece, attributed to William Evans, with 4¼in (10cm) pierced silvered chapter ring, fusee and chain movement with 6 spoke wheels and anchor escapement, the frame in the form of the Scott Memorial monument, with the seated figure of Sir Walter Scott and his dog below, c1865, 19in (48cm) high, on white marble plinth, velvet-covered ebonized base and cracked glass dome.
£1,300–1,700
$1,900–2,500 ⚒ **S**

A Victorian brass skeleton clock, signed J. T. Barry, Cardiff, the pierced dial with Roman numerals to ivy leaves, with bell and gong striking twin fusee movement, c1870, 24½in (62cm) high, on a mahogany base.
£1,800–2,400
$2,600–3,500 ⚒ **Bri**

▶ **A French ormolu and white marble skeleton clock,** the pierced re-enamelled annular dial with Roman and Arabic chapters, restored, part 18thC, 10½in (27cm) high, on white marble plinth with glazed case.
£1,100–1,300
$1,600–1,900 ⚒ **C**

A brass skeleton timepiece, the pierced and engraved chapter ring with Roman numerals and fleur-de-lys hands, the 5 pillar single train fusee movement with anchor escapement, in scrolling brass frame, 12½in (32cm) high, with plinth and glass dome.
£1,100–1,300
$1,600–1,900 ⚒ **DN**

A Victorian brass skeleton clock, with pierced dial, 5 spoke train wheels, passing strike on a bell, fusee movement between lyre-shaped open plates, 16¾in (42.5cm) high, on white marble base with replaced glass dome.
£900–1,300
$1,300–1,900 ⚒ **B**

A **skeleton clock,** the dial signed John Carr, Swaffham, the fusee movement with anchor escapement, 9½in (24cm) high.
£950–1,100 $1,380–1,600 ⚒ S

A Victorian brass-frame skeleton timepiece, by Dwerrihouse, Ogston and Bell, the subsidiary seconds dial with star pierced centre, single fusee and chain movement, on mahogany base, no dome, 13½in (34cm) high.
£3,000–3,600
$4,400–5,200 ⚒ GSP

A **skeleton clock,** based on Westminster Abbey, attributed to Evans of Handsworth, chiming the quarters on 8 bells, on replacement macassar ebony base, c1865, 27in (68.5cm) high.
£16,800–12,000
$24,300–17,400 PC

A **brass skeleton clock,** the dial inscribed Hry Marc à Paris, the movement with outside countwheel and bell strike, c1860, 18in (45.5cm) high.
£500–600
$700–900 ⚒ S(S)

A lyre design skeleton clock, by Read of Ipswich, 19thC, 11½in (29cm) high.
£1,450–1,900
$2,100–3,000 ⊞ RFA

An early Victorian month-going skeleton clock, attributed to Parker and Pace, Bury St Edmunds, with 8½in (21.5cm) silvered chapter ring, twin fusee movement driving the intermediate pinion, 4 wheel train with deadbeat escapement and cylindrical bob pendulum, the backplate of solid arched form, the frontplate consisting of interlocking scrolls, marble base with glass dome, c1850, 11½in (29cm) high.
£3,600–4,200
$5,200–6,100 ⚒ S

A **brass skeleton clock,** inscribed George Orpwood, 1838, Improved Lever, single train fusee movement and lever escapement, 19thC, 9½in (24cm) high.
£1,450–1,800
$2,100–2,600 ⚒ DN

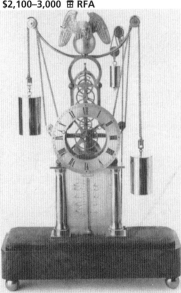

◀ **A French Empire weight-driven skeleton clock,** stamped on the rafter frame Augte. Moirau et Roland Degrège, No 33, the bullet-shaped weight driving the maintaining power, suspension chains of square section running over a series of pulleys, the movement supported on 2 brass columns inset with a silvered thermometer, on a walnut veneered base, 23in (58.5cm) high.
£3,600–4,800
$5,200–7,000 ⚒ Bon

A month-going skeleton clock, the 4½in (11.5cm) silvered and engraved dial signed E. Saxby, Maker, Lambeth, London, with subsidiary seconds and calendar dials, the fusee and chain movement with 6 wheel train, half deadbeat escapement and 5 spoke wheels, the frame with ball and spire finials, 2 lacking, raised on wood plinth with glass dome, 9½in (24cm) high.
£2,050–2,400
$2,950–3,500 ⚒ S

A skeleton clock, attributed to Smiths of Clerkenwell, based on the Brighton Pavilion, the chain fusee movement wheelwork with 5 crossings, half-hour strike on a bell mounted vertically between the plates with a halbard for the hammer, hours struck on a three-rod gridiron pendulum gong, the base with a silver plaque inscribed 'Presented to the Revd. Andrew Pope MA by his Parishioners and Friends on leaving Cusop, July 30th 1873', 18½in (47cm) high.
£10,000–12,000
$14,500–17,400 ⊞ DRA

◀ **A brass skeleton clock,** by Alfred Smith of Huddersfield, depicing York Minster, with 8in (20cm) silvered chapter ring, 6 spoke wheels, twin fusee movement, rack and snail strike on a gong and bell pull repeat, stamped on base, on an ebonized plinth, c1860, 21in (53.5cm) high.
£2,400–3,000
$3,500–4,400 ⚒ S(S)

A scroll frame skeleton timepiece, with silvered brass chapter ring, signed Robert Stewart of Glasgow, 6 graduated plate pillars and 6 spoke wheelwork to the chain fusee movement, on original brass-inlaid mahogany base, glass replaced, mid-19thC, 11in (28cm) high.
£2,000–2,500
$2,900–3,600 ⊞ DRA

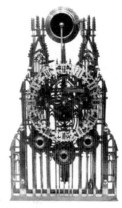

A brass skeleton clock, by W. F. Evans, Birmingham, depicting York Minster, with pierced silvered chapter ring, fusee movement striking on a gong and Westminster chimes on 8 bells at the quarters, on white marble plinth, glass dome, late 19thC, 21½in (54.5cm) high.
£6,000–7,200
$8,700–10,500 ⚒ HSS

A scroll-frame brass skeleton clock, the 5½in (14cm) silvered chapter ring inscribed J. D. Taylor, Liverpool, 2 train fusee movement with bell striking and pull repeat, 5 spoke wheels, 19thC, 13in (33cm) high, on a wood base and ebonized stand, glass dome.
£1,200–1,800
$1,750–2,600 ⚒ P(S)

A brass skeleton timepiece, with silvered chapter ring, fusee movement with 6 spoked wheels and anchor escapement, on 4 turned supports, later ebonized base, glass dome, 18thC, 15in (38cm) high.
£700–950
$1,000–1,500 ⚒ P

A brass skeleton clock, by J. Smith & Sons, London, depicting Lichfield Cathedral, 19thC, 17½in (44.5cm) high.
£1,200–1,800
$1,750–2,600 ⚒ P

A small Gothic-design skeleton clock, with fusee movement, c1840.
£1,650–2,000
$2,400–2,900 ⚒ JD

A skeleton clock, with 6¼in (16cm) silvered chapter ring, fusee and chain movement, 6 spoke wheels and anchor escapement, the 5 pillar, well pierced scroll frame with top mounted bell, on white marble plinth, original glass dome, c1860, 20in (51cm) high.
£1,800–2,400
$2,600–3,500 ⚒ S

A French skeleton alarm clock, the 2in (5cm) enamel annular chapter ring with central alarm disc, 8-day going barrel movement No. 4203, anchor escapement and silk suspension, in a scissor-shaped frame on a bow-ended brass base, ebonized plinth concealing the pull/wind alarm mechanism, glass dome, c1850, clock 9in (23cm) high.
£850–950
$1,250–1,500 ⚒ S

◄ **A skeleton clock,** depicting Lichfield Cathedral, with 5in (12.5cm) pierced chapter ring, 2 train fusee and chain repeating movement, with deadbeat escapement, half-hour strike on a bell and hour gong, the frame on a stepped brass plinth and rosewood base applied with carved leaves, spires reduced, c1850, 17in (43cm) high.
£2,400–3,600
$3,350–5,200 ⚒ S

A Victorian chiming skeleton clock, with 9in (23cm) pierced silvered chapter ring, 3 train fusee and chain movement with anchor escapement and chiming on 8 bells with a further hour bell, pull chords for repeat and strike/silent, elaborate leaf-cast frame with 7 substantial ring turned pillars, white marble plinth, glazed brass cover, 25in (63.5cm) high.
£12,000–14,400
$17,400–20,900 ⚒ S

A Victorian balance wheel skeleton clock, with 4½in (11.5cm) chapter ring, fusee movement with 6 spoke wheels, pierced barrel covers, maintaining power and deadbeat escapement with vertical balance and lever, scroll frame on a stepped rosewood plinth, c1850, later glass cover, 12½in (32cm) high.
£3,600–4,200
$5,200–6,100 ⚒ S

A Walter Scott Memorial skeleton clock, with brass inlaid rosewood base, c1851, 20in (51cm) high.
£2,400–3,000 $3,500–4,400 ⊞ SBA

► **A skeleton clock,** with plain engraved and silvered brass chapter ring, on rosewood base, 14in (35.5cm) high.
£2,000–2,500
$2,900–3,600 ⊞ DRA

A brass skeleton clock, by S. Smith & Sons, Clerkenwell, depicting a simple version of Westminster Abbey, with silvered and pierced 6in (15cm) chapter ring, single fusee movement with passing strike, anchor escapement, Gothic frame with later oak base, 17½in (44.5cm) high.
£850–1,000
$1,250–1,500 ⚒ S(S)

A Victorian brass skeleton clock, by W. F. Evans, Birmingham, depicting Westminster Abbey, with triple chain fusees, anchor escapement, mercury pendulum, inscribed and dated 1881, 25in (63.5cm) high.
£9,600–12,000
$13,900–17,400 ⚒ C

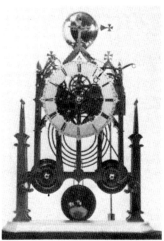

A skeleton clock, the movement with chain fusees, anchor escapement, striking the hours on a gong and the half-hours on a bell, with glass dome, 19in (48cm) high.
£1,450–1,700
$2,100–2,500 ⚒ S

◄ **A brass skeleton timepiece,** with strike and chain drive, glass dome, 15in (38cm) high, and an orrery clock, limited edition No. 259, with glass dome.
£950–1,450 each
$1,380–2,100 each ⚒ Wor

A brass skeleton clock, by Smith & Son, Clerkenwell, of delicate ivy leaf open design, with passing strike on a bell, 17½in (44.5cm) high.
£1,450–2,000
$2,100–2,900 ⚒ HSS

A pierced brass repeating skeleton clock, by W. F. Evans, Birmingham, depicting York Minster, the movement having chain fusee, anchor escapement, striking hourly on a gong, half-hourly on a central bell, c1854, 21½in (54.5cm) high.
£2,400–3,000
$3,500–4,400 ⚒ AGr

A scroll-frame skeleton clock, with engraved and silvered brass chapter ring, with twin fusee movement, striking on a bell mounted on top, on brass-inlaid rosewood base, glass dome, 19thC, 17in (43cm) high.
£3,000–3,500
$4,400–5,000 ⊞ DRA

▶ **A brass skeleton clock,** the twin chain and fusee movement with anchor escapement striking on a bell above, with wood rod pendulum, on oval wooden stand, glass dome, 19½in (49.5cm) high.
£1,450–1,900
$2,100–2,750 ⚒ CSK

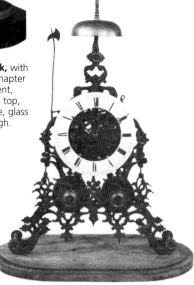

English Regulators

The development of the regulator arose from the need for an extremely accurate standard timekeeper by which other clocks could be set. Produced in England and in France from the mid-18th to around the end of the 19th century, the regulator was used in observatories, large country houses, clock work-shops and important retailers. They were wall-hung or floor-standing, their cases protecting the movement, weight and long pendulum.

The early English floor-standing or longcase regulator closely resembles a longcase clock, although plainer in style, as the regulator was used to fulfil a practical rather than decorative role. The case was usually mahogany, with an architectural top and a solid, veneered trunk door. Those made after c1820 often have a glazed door and a rounded top. The backs of those with glazed doors were often veneered, as they were visible through the glass. Dials were made of engraved and silvered brass with separate indications for seconds, minutes and hours. Longcase regulators are usually signed on the dial and sometimes on the backplate. Wall-hanging examples were produced from the mid-19th century in smaller numbers than the floor-standing type. Cases were usually mahogany veneered, although a few are in walnut. They were made chiefly by London firms, notably Edward Dent, Charles Frodsham and Vulliamy.

Refinements to the movements included maintaining power, a system of springs which ensured the clock kept going during winding. A longcase regulator by George Graham of 1722 was sold at Christie's in 1996 as part of the Bute Collection and fetched £61,000 ($88,500), over twice its estimate. Today it could fetch £80,000–100,000 ($116,000–145,000). A similar regulator in a more attractive case by Dutton, Graham's successor, climbed to £73,000 ($105,800) at Sotheby's, but again would fetch far more today. These are exceptional prices achieved only by the top makers who worked before 1770. Other names in this category are Tompion, Shelton, Ellicott, Arnold and Cumming. During the late 18th and early 19th centuries a considerable number of regulators were produced with simpler movements contained in good quality mahogany cases. A good mid-19th century regulator would now fetch around £10,000 ($14,500) and a Georgian one double this.

Regulators were generally weight-driven and of 8-day duration. Occasionally month-going clocks are seen, which can fetch as much as 20 per cent more. Dealer Gerard Campbell maintains that because of their relatively recent history, regulators are usually in good condition and have not been altered. However, it is not uncommon to see a regulator with a changed name. Regulators which stood in clock shops quite frequently had their dial rewritten when the ownership of the shop changed.

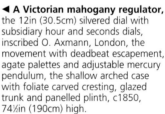

◄ **A Victorian mahogany regulator,** the 12in (30.5cm) silvered dial with subsidiary hour and seconds dials, inscribed O. Axmann, London, the movement with deadbeat escapement, agate palettes and adjustable mercury pendulum, the shallow arched case with foliate carved cresting, glazed trunk and panelled plinth, c1850, 74½in (190cm) high.
£11,000–13,800
$16,000–20,000 ⚘ S(S)

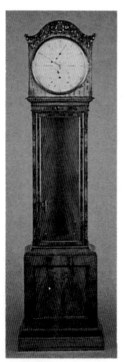

A mahogany regulator, by Arnold & Dent, The Strand, London, 19thC, 76in (193cm) high.
£13,800–16,600
$20,000–24,100 ⚘ McC

▶ **A teak wall regulator,** by T. Cooke & Sons of London and York, the silvered brass dial with 24-hour ring, the pendulum of Buckneys form, 19thC, 54in (137cm) high.
£10,000–12,000
$14,500–17,400 ⊞ DRA

A Victorian mahogany longcase regulator, by S. Bloomfield & Co, London, the 12½in (32cm) silvered dial inscribed with maker's name, the 8-day movement with deadbeat escapement and maintaining power, 72in (183cm) high.
£4,850–5,500
$7,000–8,000 ⚘ HSS

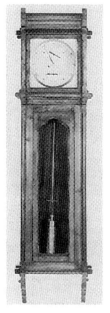

A walnut wall regulator, by Chapman, Oxford, the 10in (25.5cm) silvered dial with engraved Arabic numerals, subsidiary seconds and 24-hour dial, sweep minute hand, the 5 pillar, spring-driven, angle force movement with deadbeat escapement and steel/mercury compensated pendulum, the case with giltwood dial around the pediment, side pegged and wedged joints, glazed trunk door with Gothic detail, c1860, 62in (157.5cm) high.
£2,750–4,150
$4,000–6,000 ⚘ Bon

A Victorian mahogany longcase regulator, with brass glazed bezel to 12in (30.5cm) dial signed P. G. Dodd & Son, Cornhill, London, dust cover to movement of high count with Harrison's maintaining power, jewelled deadbeat escapement and cranked roller crutch, 75in (190.5cm) high.
£4,150–5,500
$6,000–8,000 ⚘ C

A rosewood striking longcase regulator, the engraved silvered brass dial signed French, Royal Exchange, London, the 5 pillar movement with Graham deadbeat escapement, Harrison's maintaining power, 75in (190.5cm) high.
£11,000–12,000
$16,000–17,400 ⊞ DRA
Santiago James Moore French worked at the Royal Exchange in Sweetings Alley and was a member of the Clockmaker's Company from 1810 to 1840.

An ebonized table regulator, by Robert Gibson, the 6in (15cm) painted dial with centre seconds, the hours and minutes dials contained within the seconds ring, the weight-driven movement signed, with 4 fixing brackets, half deadbeat escapement, maintaining power and 6 spoke wheels, the steel rod pendulum with roller suspension, the flat lead weight with integral pulley and suspended from the gut line carried on a pair of rollers above the movement and travelling down the back of the case, the arched case with a brass framed pendulum aperture, c1820, 15in (38cm) high.
£4,150–5,500
$6,000–8,000 ⚘ S

Miller's is a price GUIDE not a price LIST

▶ **A mahogany longcase chiming regulator,** the 13in (33cm) enamel dial signed C. & T. Hammond, Manchester, the movement with deadbeat escapement, rack striking on a gong and chiming on 8 overhead bells, 4 spoke work, with 3 brass-cased weights, mid-19thC, 82½in (209.5cm) high.
£2,050–2,750
$3,000–4,000 ⚘ S(C)

◀ **A Victorian mahogany wall regulator,** the 12in (30.5cm) painted dial signed Jas. Gowland, London Wall, with concentric minute ring, subsidiary seconds and hour dial, movement with tapering pillars, high count train, Harrison's maintaining power, short ebony rod pendulum, in a well-figured case with concave base, 44in (112cm) high.
£2,750–3,450
$4,000–5,000 ⚘ Bon

A Regency mahogany regulator, the 12in (30.5cm) silvered dial signed Hamley, London, the 6 pillared movement with deadbeat escapement and maintaining power, 75in (190.5cm) high.
£6,200–8,300
$9,000–12,000 ⚘ P

► **A zebra-veneer table regulator,** with silvered-brass dial, signed Geo. McLean, Glasgow, the movement with lost beat detented escapement mounted externally to the backplate, mid-19thC, 18½in (47cm) high.
£8,000–9,000
$11,600–13,000
⊞ **DRA**

An oak longcase regulator, by Moore of Leeds, the dial signed, with 4 legged gravity escapement mounted externally to the backplate, with 5 spoke wheelwork and side winding.
£10,000–11,000
$14,500–16,000 ⊞ **DRA**

A mahogany longcase regulator, the 8-day movement with steel cased weight, mercury compensated pendulum and deadbeat escapement by Harper, Wolverhampton, 19thC, 83in (211cm) high.
£1,400–1,500
$2,000–2,500 ⚒ **DWB**

◄ **A Caledonian mahogany railway signal box wall regulator clock,** the white enamelled dial signed, Roman numerals, blued hour and minute hands, the 4 pillared movement with deadbeat escapement, Harrison's maintaining power, wood rod pendulum, 62in (157.5cm) high.
£2,350–2,750
$3,400–4,000 ⚒ **CSK**

A Georgian mahogany cased regulator, by Thomas Morgan, Edinburgh.
£2,750–4,150
$4,000–6,000 ⚒ **Mit**

◄ **A George III astronomical longcase regulator,** by Richard Roe of Midhurst, with silvered-brass break-arch dial, with aperture showing annual zodiacal calendars, the 2 minute hands showing mean and solar time.
£11,000–12,000
$16,000–17,400 ⊞ **DRA**

A Regency mahogany and crossbanded regulator, by Benjamin Russell, Norwich, the silvered dial with second subsidiary supporting a timepiece movement, the trunk enclosed by a full length door.
£4,150–5,250
$6,000–7,600 ⚒ **P(EA)**

A mahogany regulator longcase clock, c1840.
£2,750–3,450
$4,000–5,000 ⊞ **HOD**

◄ **A rosewood striking longcase regulator,** the dial signed W.C. Shaw, Glasgow, the going train with deadbeat escapement, 83in (211cm) high.
£4,150–5,500
$6,000–8,000 ⚒ **Bon**

► **A Regency mahogany regulator,** by Thurdite & Reed, finished in ebony, 5 pillar movement, jewelled pallets, c1810.
£11,000–12,500
$16,000–18,000 ⊞ **BF**

A longcase regulator, by George Tight, London and Reading, with 8-day 5 pillar movement, deadbeat escapement and maintaining power, the 12in (30.5cm) silvered-brass dial showing seconds, date and strike/silent, c1815, 82½in (209.5cm) high.
£12,000–14,000
$17,400–20,300 ⊞ PAO

◀ **A month-going domestic regulator,** with annual calendar and passing quarter strike, the lower dial signed John Woodwiss, Birmingham, 1862, 88½in (225cm) high.
£8,300–11,050
$12,000–16,000 ⚷ S

A longcase regulator, the silvered dial signed Smith & Sons, strike/ silent and full chime/ Westminster, the 3 train movement with deadbeat escapement, 86in (218.5cm) high.
£8,300–11,050
$12,000–16,000 ⚷ Bon

A George III mahogany regulator, the silvered dial inscribed Luke Wooton, 8-day movement and deadbeat escapement, 74in (188cm) high.
£6,900–8,300
$10,000–12,000 ⚷ DWB

A mahogany regulator, the 11in (28cm) silvered dial with subsidiary seconds, 8-day movement with deadbeat escapement, the case with carved pediment, glazed trunk door and panel base, c1830, 82in (208cm) high.
£5,500–6,900
$8,000–10,000 ⚷ S(S)

An early Victorian mahogany domestic regulator, the silvered dial with Roman numerals and seconds ring, the 4 pillar movement with deadbeat escapement and maintaining power, pendulum and weight missing, 70in (178cm) high.
£2,350–3,050
$3,400–4,400 ⚷ C

A Georgian mahogany regulator, c1820.
£2,500–3,050
$3,600–4,400 ⚷ Mit

▶ **A late Victorian mahogany regulator,** by George Wilson of Edinburgh, the silvered dial with subsidiary hours and seconds dials, the case carved with foliate scrolls and acanthus, fitted with a glazed door enclosing a mercury-filled pendulum, the panelled base on a plinth, 82½in (209.5cm) high.
£5,500–6,900
$8,000–10,000 ⚷ C(S)

A mahogany and ebonized wall regulator, the 7in (18cm) silvered dial with subsidiary seconds and hour dials, scroll-pierced mask in a plain arched case with scroll shoulders, 39in (99cm) high.
£1,050–1,100
$1,500–1,600 ⚷ S(S)

Vienna Regulators

The finest Viennese wall and longcase clocks were produced from c1800 to c1845. After that date the classic and restrained style of the Viennese case tended to be fussy and overdecorated, with additional carvings and pillars, and ornate pierced hands replacing the earlier simple elegance. From the 1870s imitations of Viennese regulators were produced in German clock factories. These vary in quality; for example those made by the Lenzkirch factory in the Black Forest area are considered of good quality, while many others were not finished to the same high standard. It is quite common for a German factory-made wall regulator to be referred to as a Vienna wall regulator. The true Viennese clocks have a one-piece enamel, silvered brass or milk-glass dial, and the numerals will be very finely written.

The earliest form of Viennese regulator was called a *Laterndluhr* because of its likeness to a glazed lantern. It is architectural in style, with 'roof-top', square hood, narrow middle section for the pendulum rod and square lower portion for the pendulum bob. All surfaces are glazed, usually with nine pieces of glass (known as a nine-light clock), and the cases are generally veneered in mahogany, but occasionally walnut, cherry or ash, and are delicately strung with maple. Some very beautiful clocks were produced.

The *Laterndluhr* was expensive to make and a simplified form called the *Dachluhr* (roof-top clock) was produced in about 1820, with a six-light case. These early clocks were usually timepieces only, running for eight or 30 days, and rarely for one year. The striking clocks were nearly always *grande sonnerie*. Vienna regulators were almost invariably weight-driven and to begin with had one-piece enamel or silvered dials with engine-turned and gilded rings.

Some of the *Laterndluhr* regulators have a number of subsidiary dials, commonly showing the date. Any clock with three subsidiary dials is desirable. They were produced in small numbers c1805–45 and are rare today. Most clocks with 'complications' are signed on the dial. Some of the best makers included Joseph Jessner, Philipp Fertbauer, Maranzeller and Schönberger.

According to specialist dealer Gerard Campbell, prices range from £25,000–£35,000 ($36,200–50,700) for a well proportioned, month-going Viennese *Laterndluhr*-style regulator, with scarcity, quality and elegance contributing to price, to £8,000–9,000 ($11,600–13,000) for an 8-day *Dachluhr*. Decorative *grande sonnerie* clocks of the period 1840–70 would be priced in the region of £6,500–10,000 ($9,500–14,500). These prices would be proportionally less at auction.

A rosewood-veneered and boxwood-strung Vienna regulator, with 8-day duration, deadbeat escapement and maintaining power, single weight, c1860, 42in (106.5cm) high.
£3,700–4,400
$5,350–6,400 ⊞ SBA

▶ **A walnut Vienna wall regulator,** by Gustav Becker, with rack striking and double weight, c1890.
£700–950
$1,000–1,300 ⊞ IAT

◀ **A walnut Vienna wall regulator,** by Gustav Becker, with 2 weights, c1890, 48in (122cm) high.
£700–800
$1,000–1,200 ⊞ IAT

An ash-veneered *grande sonnerie* Vienna regulator, by Glink, the two-piece dial with piecrust bezel, c1850, 45in (114.5cm) high.
£8,000–12,000
$11,600–17,400 ⊞ GeC

A late Biedermeier period rosewood Vienna regulator, stamped Crot Berlin 302, with weight-driven movement and deadbeat escapement, 39½in (100.5cm) high.
£1,100–1,650
$1,600–2,400 ⚒ C

A month-going mahogany Vienna regulator, the 8in (20cm) two-piece enamel dial signed Adolf Hradetzkn in Brünn, with flower and scroll-cast bezel, movement with wide tapering plates, deadbeat escapement, micrometer adjustment to the crutch, ebonized wood rod pendulum with brass bob, c1850, 49in (124.5cm) high.
£5,500–6,900
$8,000–10,000 ⚒ S

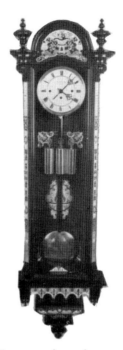

A rosewood *grande sonnerie* Vienna regulator, signed Alous Gruner in Wien, with strike/silent and repeat, 3 weights, c1860, 53in (134.5cm) high.
£9,000–10,000
$13,000–14,500 ⊞ DRA

A Vienna regulator, signed Lehrner Kaschan, with glass enclosed movement and Huygens winding method, compensated pendulum with knife-edge suspension, c1830, 60in (152.5cm) high.
£20,000–25,000
$29,000–36,000 ⊞ GeC

An Austrian walnut-veneered *petite sonnerie* wall regulator, the 6½in (16.5cm) two-piece enamel dial signed A. Schlesinger in Wien, with Roman numerals, the triple-train weight-driven movement with deadbeat escapement, wooden rod pendulum and striking on 2 gongs, the case with swallow break-arch pediment and turned finial, c1875, 46in (117cm) high.
£1,650–2,350
$2,400–3,400 ⚒ Bon

A walnut striking Vienna regulator, the 7in (18cm) enamel dial signed M. Schonberger, Vienna, with 2 train weight-driven movement, 54in (137cm) high.
£1,650–2,100
$2,400–3,000 ⚒ Bon

A Vienna wall regulator, the enamel dial signed W. Schonberger, Vienna, the twin-train weight-driven movement with deadbeat escapement, 19thC, 56in (142cm) high.
£850–1,100
$1,250–1,600 ⚒ P

► **A mahogany Vienna wall regulator,** with engraved and silvered-brass dial, signed Wendelin Naban in Melnik, with strike/silent and repeat, 66in (167.5cm) high.
£18,000–20,000
$26,000–29,000 ⊞ DRA

A walnut Vienna regulator, signed H. Samuel, Manchester, c1890, 48in (122cm) high.
£700–950
$1,000–1,500 ⊞ JMW

A walnut and ebonized Vienna regulator, the white enamel dial with Roman chapters, twin-train movement and gong strike, break-arch pediment 19thC, 48in (122cm) high.
£1,400–1,650
$2,000–2,400 ⚹ CSK

A mahogany month-going Vienna regulator, the 'rooftop' six-light case with lift-off lower door, steel pendulum, c1835, 43in (109cm) high.
£7,000–10,000
$10,200–14,500 ⊞ GeC

A walnut and ebony Vienna wall regulator, with 8-day movement, centre seconds sweep, Harrison's gridiron pendulum maintaining power, 19thC.
£6,200–8,300
$9,000–12,000 ⊞ SBA

A mahogany-veneered year-going Vienna floor-standing regulator, with brass-encased movement and end stops, seconds-beating gridiron pendulum, the case wtih maple stringing, c1825, 72in (183cm) high.
£50,000–70,000
$72,500–100,000 ⊞ GeC

▶ **A walnut Vienna regulator,** with double weight, 44in (112cm) high.
£2,100–2,750
$3,000–4,000 ⊞ SBA

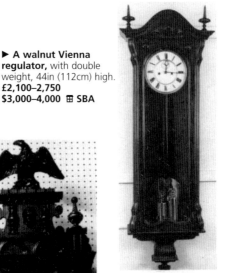

A simulated rosewood Vienna regulator, with enamelled dial, c1860, 40½in (103cm) high.
£2,750–3,250
$4,000–4,700 ⊞ DRA
The centre sweep seconds hand and time-only weight-driven movement are rare for a Vienna regulator of this size.

A Vienna regulator, with carved case, 40in (101.5cm) high.
£350–500
$500–800 ⚹ PCh

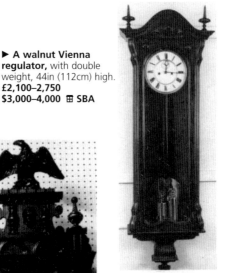

A walnut Vienna regulator, with white dial and 8-day 2 weight striking movement, bobbin-turned finial, ring-turned decoration to the case, late 19thC, 47½in (120.5cm) high.
£550–850
$800–1,250 ⚹ DDM

◀ **A walnut musical Vienna regulator,** spring-driven, c1860, 19in (48.5cm) high.
£600–750
$870–1,100 ⊞ SBA

A walnut miniature Vienna regulator, with 8-day spring-driven movement, c1880, 18in (45.5cm) high.
£2,100–2,750
$3,000–4,000 ⊞ SBA

A mahogany Vienna regulator, with 7in (18cm) enamel dial, engine-turned bezel, movement with square plates, c1830, 43in (109cm) high.
£4,150–4,850
$6,000–7,000 ⚒ S

A small ebonized Vienna regulator, with gold inlay, spring-driven, late 19thC.
£600–700
$870–1,000 ⊞ SBA

A walnut and ebony Vienna regulator, the door edged with barley twists, c1870, 41in (104cm) high.
£2,100–2,750
$3,000–4,000 ⊞ SBA

▶ **A mahogany Vienna regulator,** with 7in (18cm) milk-glass dial, cast and chased bezel, the movement with square plates, deadbeat escapement, micrometer adjustment to the crutch, ebonized wood rod pendulum with brass bob, case lacking cresting, 37½in (95.5cm) high.
£1,800–2,100
$2,600–3,000 ⚒ S

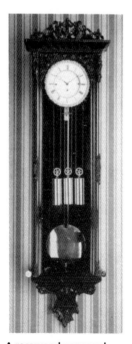

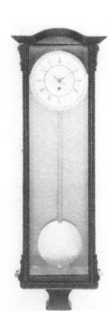

A rosewood-veneered *grande sonnerie* **striking Vienna regulator,** the two-piece enamel dial with piecrust bezel, with maple stringing and carved decoration, c1850, 47in (119.5cm) high.
£8,000–12,000
$11,600–17,400 ⊞ GeC

A rosewood *grande sonnerie* **Vienna regulator,** the 8in (20cm) one-piece enamelled dial with blue Roman numerals and gilt decoration between, piecrust bezel, 8-day movement striking on 2 gongs and with repeat and strike/silent regulation, the pendulum just less than seconds-beating, c1845, 50in (127cm) high.
£12,000–14,000
$17,400–20,300 ⊞ DRA

◀ **A mahogany Vienna regulator,** the 7in (18cm) two-piece enamel dial indistinctly signed, the movement with square arched top plates, deadbeat escapement, ebonized wood rod pendulum with brass bob, dial cracked, c1845, 37in (94cm) high.
£1,100–1,400
$1,600–2,000 ⚒ S(S)

◄ **A rosewood Vienna *grande sonnerie* wall clock,** the 6in (15cm) two-piece enamel dial with Roman numerals, signed I. E. Gohing in Wien, the weight-driven movement with arched plates, deadbeat escapement, beat adjustment quarter striking on 2 gongs, c1870, 48in (122cm) high.
£4,850–6,200
$7,000–9,000 ⚒ Bon

► **A stained beech miniature Vienna wall timepiece,** c1880, 30in (76cm) high.
£2,000–2,750
$3,000–4,000 ⚒ S

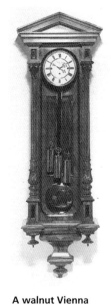

A walnut Vienna *grande sonnerie* wall clock, by Gustav Becker, the 6in (15cm) silvered chapter ring with Roman numerals and engraved gilt centre, deadbeat escapement, beat adjustment and quarter striking on 2 gongs, c1880.
£1,650–2,000
$2,400–3,000 ⚒ Bon

► **A pale oak wall regulator,** the silvered dial signed Georg Ledel, Wien, with weight-driven movement, c1910, 25in (63.5cm) high.
£2,000–2,750
$3,000–4,000 ⚒ S

A walnut Vienna *grande sonnerie* wall clock, the two-piece enamel dial signed Rudolf Keller, c1885, 53in (134.5cm) high.
£2,500–3,450
$3,600–5,000 ⚒ S

◄ **An Austrian mahogany Vienna wall timepiece,** with one-piece enamel dial, c1835, 37in (94cm) high.
£4,150–5,500
$6,000–8,000 ⚒ S

A walnut Vienna *grande sonnerie* wall clock, with two-piece enamel dial, c1885, 52in (132cm) high.
£2,500–3,450
$3,600–5,000 ⚒ S

An Austrian walnut year-going wall timepiece, with silvered dial, in a six-light case, c1840, 68in (172cm) high.
£24,150–27,600
$35,000–40,000 ⚒ S

► **An Austrian mahogany month-going Vienna wall timepiece,** with silvered chapter ring and engine-turned gilt centre, signed Carl Suchy in Prag, in a nine-light *Laterndluhr* case, c1835, 45in (114.5cm) high.
£24,850–30,350
$36,000–44,000 ⚒ S

◄ **An Austrian mahogany Vienna wall timepiece,** with milk-glass dial and six-light case with architectural pediment, c1830, 34in (86.5cm) high.
£7,600–9,000
$11,000–13,000 ⚒ S

A satinwood carriage clock, with enamel dial signed Hy. Marc A Paris, bell striking movement No. 18562, with ratchet tooth lever escapement, c1850.
£1,200–1,550
$1,750–2,250 ⚒ S

A red boulle carriage clock, with enamel dial signed Hy. Marc A Paris, bell striking movement No. 18839, with lever escapement, c1850, 6in (15cm) high.
£2,500–2,850
$3,600–4,100 ⚒ S

A gilt-brass and enamel striking carriage clock, stamped E. M. & Co, 6½in (16.5cm) high.
£5,350–6,500
$7,750–9,400 ⚒ C

A gilt-brass porcelain-mounted striking carriage clock, signed Howell James & Co, 5½in (14cm) high.
£3,800–5,350
$5,500–7,700 ⚒ C

A French repeating carriage clock, with 8-day heavy plate movement, the brass masked dial plate engraved and inset with enamel chapter ring, separate alarm dial, original carrying case and winding key, c1875.
£4,000–5,000 $5,800–7,200 ⊞ PAO

A gilt-brass striking and musical carriage clock, for the Chinese market, stamped Japy Frères, 7½in (19cm) high.
£3,800–4,600
$5,500–6,600 ⚒ C

A gilt-brass carriage clock, with automaton singing bird, stamped Japy Frères, 11½in (20cm) high.
£15,350–18,350
$22,250–26,600 ⚒ C

A Victorian gilt-brass carriage chronometer, signed E. White, 20 Cockspur Street, London, No. 1449, 9½in (23.5cm) high.
£12,250–15,300
$17,750–22,200 ⚒ C

A brass carriage clock, complete with a leather-covered case, early 20thC, 5in (13cm) high.
£300–400
$400–600 ⚒ PCh

A gilt-brass _grande sonnerie_ striking calendar carriage clock, with stamp for Drocourt, signed by Tiffany & Co, New York, with leather case, 8½in (21.5cm) high.
£18,350–22,950
$26,600–33,250 ⚒ C

A French brass striking carriage clock, c1890, 5½in (14cm) high.
£1,400–1,700 $2,000–2,500 ✣ GAK

A Louis XV bracket clock, dial signed Glaesner à Lyon, 37in (94cm) high.
£6,100–9,200 $8,850–13,500 ✣ S

A William IV carriage timepiece, by Howell & James, c1835, 4in (10cm) high.
£9,950–11,500 $14,400–16,700 ✣ S

A German walnut bracket clock, by Lenzkirch, with quarter strike on 2 gongs, c1880, 10in (25.5cm) high.
£1,000–1,200 $1,500–1,750 ⊞ SO

A gilt-brass striking carriage clock, by Japy Frères, c1870.
£15,300–18,350 $22,200–26,600 ✣ C

A miniature 8-day carriage timepiece, c1885, restored, 3in (7.5cm) high.
£5,350–6,500 $7,750–9,400 ✣ CSK

◀ **A French repeating and alarm carriage clock,** the gong striking movement stamped Pons. Médaille d'Or, 1827, with lever escapement, c1865, 6in (15cm) high.
£2,300–2,700 $3,350–3,900 ✣ S

◀ **A repeating carriage clock,** the enamel dial signed for Dent, the bell striking movement No. 301, with lever platform escapement, in gorge case, c1870, 5in (12.5cm) high.
£3,050–3,800 $4,400–5,500 ✣ S

A Louis XV boulle bracket clock, the dial and movement signed Bertrand à Paris, surmounted by a trumpeting angel, c1730, 35in (89cm) high.
£9,650–11,600 $14,000–16,800 ✣ S

A French enamel-mounted repeating carriage clock, stamped E. M. & Co, later lever escapement, c1900.
£2,300–3,050 $3,350–4,400 ✣ S

A brass alarm carriage clock, by Henri Jacot.
£1,400–1,800 $2,000–2,600 ✣ CSK

A porcelain-mounted repeating carriage clock, c1870, 6in (15cm) high.
£5,200–6,100 $7,500–8,850 ✣ S

A Louis XV/XVI Transitional gilt-bronze wall clock and barometer, the clock dial signed Hana à Paris, in guilloche cast cases mounted with leaves and husks and surmounted by vases, barometer movement replaced.
£33,650–38,300 $48,800–55,500 ✗ S

A Louis XVI gilt-bronze clock, signed Frédéric Duval à Paris, c1775, 14in (35.5cm) high.
£24,000–26,000
$34,800–37,700 ✗ S

An enamelled clock, the domed top with a peacock and fish finial, the white enamel dial signed Child & Child, London, S.W., and sunflower mark, French movement No. 4639, damage to enamels, 4½in (11cm) high.
£5,600–7,450
$8,100–10,800 ✗ P

An 8-day mahogany clock, by Forestville Manufacturing Co, Connecticut, c1847, 24½in (62.5cm) high.
£20,000–21,000
$29,000–30,500 ✗ CNY

An ormolu-mounted japanned table clock, by Weeks, London, c1800, 76in (193cm) high.
£5,200–6,700
$7,550–9,700 ✗ S

A gilt-bronze mounted white marble and *nero Belgio* portico clock, signed Faisant à Paris, on a plinth inset with foliate cast frieze below a stiff-leaf gallery on *toupie* feet, mid-19thC, 20½in (52cm) high.
£3,700–5,600
$5,300–8,100 ✗ CSK

A George IV gilt-bronze-mounted and brass-inlaid ebony pedestal clock, the movement signed George Wilkins, London, 76in (193cm) high.
£12,500–15,000
$18,000–21,500 ✗ C

A Viennese mahogany *grande sonnerie* table clock, dial signed Johan Sachs, late 18thC, 16in (40.5cm) high.
£4,650–5,600
$6,750–8,100 ✗ C

A Louis XIV boulle clock, surmounted with a figure of Time, the movement signed Jacques Cogniet à Paris, c1700, 46½in (118cm) high.
£25,000–29,000
$36,250–42,000 ✗ S

A skeleton clock, by Smiths, London, in the form of the central dome of the Royal Pavilion, Brighton, with twin fusee and chain movement, c1860, 23in (60cm) high.
£7,200–8,400
$10,500–12,200 ⚹ S(NY)

A George III mahogany clock, the painted dial signed Massey, Strand, London, with brass bezel, 4 pillar single gut fusee movement, 14in (36cm) diam.
£1,300–1,600
$1,900–2,300 ⚹ C

A Victorian mother-of-pearl inlaid ebony and rosewood wall clock, by James McCabe, London, No. 2438.
£1,150–1,400
$1,500–2,000 ⚹ C

A mahogany 8-day striking table clock, by Barwise, London, brass- and ebony-inlaid, c1795, 21in (53.5cm) high.
£6,000–7,000
$8,700–10,200 ⊞ PAO

A Viennese ebonized and parcel-gilt *grande sonnerie* musical table clock, signed Weillbourg, 23in (59cm) high.
£4,100–5,000
$6,000–7,250 ⚹ C

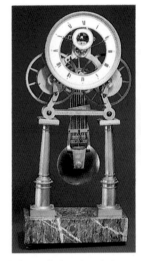

A 6-month duration skeleton clock, by Lepaute de Belle Fontaine, Paris, 22in (56cm) high.
£7,800–8,400
$11,300–12,200 ⚹ S(NY)

A Louis XV-style parcel-gilt-bronze table clock, resting on the back of a bull, on a naturalistic base, late 19thC, 23in (59cm) high.
£3,700–4,650
$5,250–6,700 ⚹ CSK

A French ormolu, bronze and patinated wall clock, the case in the form of billowing clouds, with putti around the dial, c1900, 28in (71cm) high.
£5,200–5,800
$7,500–8,400 ⚹ S(NY)

A Louis Philippe ormolu musical automaton striking table clock, the twin going barrel movement with anchor escapement, 29½in (75cm) high over glass dome.
£8,200–9,700
$11,900–14,000 ⚹ C

A Black Forest fruitwood cuckoo clock, white enamel dial with Roman numerals and pierced hands, the case with arched top and moulded base, late 19thC, 15½in (39.5cm) high.
£600–750
$870–1,100 ✠ CSK

An early George II alarm clock, the foliate engraved gilt dial signed Danl. Catlin, Godmanchester, c1730, 7in (17.5cm) high.
£2,050–2,600
$3,000–3,800 ✠ C

A Black Forest automaton clock, surmounted by a painted wood figure of a knife grinder at a treadle wheel, c1875, 23in (58.5cm) high.
£9,150–11,000 ✠ S
$13,250–16,000

A world time *petite sonnerie* and alarm carriage clock, by Le Roy & Fils, Paris, c1870, 5½in (14cm) high, with original signed travelling case.
£23,000–30,600
$33,300–44,500 ✠ S

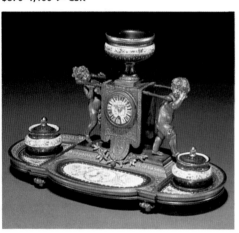

A Napoleon III gilt-bronze and porcelain encrier clock, the case modelled as a rug draped over rods supported on the shoulders of 2 *amorini*, with urn surmount, the shaped base with floral painted pots, the tray with a portrait of a lady held in a garland by cherubs, on stiff-leaf cast *toupie* feet, 14½in (37cm) wide.
£1,400–1,900
$2,000–2,750 ✠ CSK

A French bronze wall clock, designed by Hector Guimard, the white face with Arabic numerals, mounted on the sides with penwork plant forms, 18in (46cm) high, suspended by chains.
£2,100–2,850
$3,000–4,100 ✠ P

A Black Forest fruitwood cuckoo clock, with painted white enamel dial, inlaid with enamel and boulle scrolls, late 19thC, 19in (48cm) high.
£1,800–2,550
$2,600–3,700 ✠ CSK

A silver timepiece, with platform lever escapement, signed Asprey, 166 Bond Street, London, 1905, 3in (8cm) high.
£1,500–1,850
$2,170–2,700 ✠ CSK

A French ormolu-mounted marble lyre mantel clock garniture, the 5½in (14cm) enamel chapter ring signed Le Roux A Paris, the case decorated with garlands of flowers, on an oval base, 18thC, 22in (56cm) high, with a pair of paste-set candelabra.
£7,700–8,900
$11,100–13,000 ✠ S

An ormolu-mounted ebonized **musical clock,** the 7in (18cm) dial signed George Prior, c1780.
£22,500–27,500 $32,600–40,000 ⚒ S

A night clock, early 20thC, 10in (25.5cm) high.
£300–350
$440–600 ⊞ BWA

A French inlaid striking balloon clock, c1900.
£1,500–2,000
$2,170–2,900 ⊞ CLC

An ebonized brass-bound chiming table clock, by William Webster, c1765.
£11,000–12,000
$16,000–17,400 ⚒ S

A Gothic-style oak quarter chiming clock, by William Roskell, c1880.
£1,200–1,500
$1,750–2,250 ⊞ BWA

An American ship's striking clock, by the Goldsmiths & Silversmiths Co, in a heavy brass case, 9in (23cm) wide.
£300–350
$400–500 ⚒ PCh

A Victorian brass skeleton clock, inscribed Widenham, London.
£1,450–1,700
$2,100–2,500 ⚒ SWO

A Louis XVI ormolu-mounted porcelain musical automaton clock, the dial signed Ardiot.
£22,000–23,000
$32,000–33,500 ⚒ C

An American inlaid rosewood 8-day wall clock, late 19thC.
£675–725
$950–1,000 ⊞ ALS

A japanned clock, with wood dial, by John Longhurst, Kingston, c1780.
£5,800–9,850
$8,400–14,500 ⚒ JH

A black and gilt japanned tavern clock, by John Wright of Dorking, c1790.
£8,100–9,850
$11,750–14,500 ⚒ S

An iron chamber clock, south German/Swiss, dated 1693.
£13,000–13,800
$18,150–20,000 ⚒ S

A Charles X ormolu clock, signed Le Roy, 17½in (44cm) high.
£3,700–5,200 $5,350–7,500 🔨 C

A French ormolu mantel clock with calendar, c1850, 17½in (44cm) high.
£4,650–6,500 $6,750–9,500 🔨 S

A Sèvres ormolu clock, 21½in (54cm). £7,500–9,000
$10,500–13,000 🔨 S

Two Viennese regulators, l. c1810.
£35,000–50,000 $50,750–72,500
r. c1835. £7,500–8,000
$10,875–11,600 ⊞ GeC

A wall clock, by Vulliamy, 19thC, 23½in (60cm) high.
£1,400–1,750
$2,000–2,500 🔨 PCh

A wall clock, by T. Amoore, Worthing, mid-19thC.
£450–500
$650–750 🔨 PCh

A German brass-mounted mantel clock, late 18thC.
£15,800–17,700
$22,900–25,600 🔨 C

A Regency mahogany drop-dial wall clock, with brass inlay.
£950–1,400 $1,380–2,000 🔨 GAK

Two Viennese regulators, l. c1825.
£12,000–15,000 $17,400–21,750 r. c1830.
£35,000–45,000 $50,750–65,250 ⊞ Gec

A Louis XVI ormolu mantel clock, signed Peignat A Paris.
£7,450–8,350 $10,800–12,100 🔨 C

A Louis XV ormolu and tôle mantel clock, signed Thibault A Paris, adapted, 8in (20cm) high.
£7,450–8,350 $10,800–12,100 🔨 C

A German mahogany brass-mounted obelisk mantel clock, late 18thC, 29in (73.5cm) high.
£31,600–37,200 $45,800–54,000 🔨 C

An Austrian rosewood regulator, c1850.
£8,300–9,650
$12,000–14,000 ↗ S(NY)

A Louis XIV ormolu-mounted brass-inlaid tortoiseshell and ebony mantel clock, 20in (50cm) high.
£7,300–10,200 $10,600–14,800 ↗ C

A wall regulator, with Riefler deadbeat escapement, c1905.
£36,000–38,600
$52,200–56,000 ↗ S

A gilt-bronze mantel clock, 11in (28cm) high.
£650–850
$950–1,250 ↗ E

A Louis XV Meissen mantel clock, c1750.
£7,900–8,800
$11,500–12,750 ↗ C

A mahogany month-going wall regulator, by Charles Frodsham, late 19thC.
£27,600–34,500
$40,000–50,000 ↗ S

A German mahogany wall clock, by Gustaf Becker.
£450–600 $650–870 ↗ JH

A mahogany regulator, with jewelled deadbeat escapement, c1860, 71in (180cm) high.
£16,000–18,000
$23,200–26,000 ⊞ CLC

▶ **A mahogany weight-driven table regulator,** by Benjamin Martin, c1775, 25in (64cm) high.
£25,500–26,900
$37,000–39,000 ↗ S

A French bow-sided porcelain-mounted mantel clock, c1870, 20in (51cm) high.
£3,700–4,650
$5,350–6,750 ↗ S

A Regency month-going mahogany longcase regulator, signed Barwise, St Martin's Lane, London, early 19thC, 76½in (194.5cm) high.
£10,300–12,400
$14,950–18,000 🔨 C

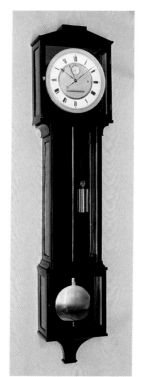

A month-going regulator, by Pfeiffer, with subsidiary seconds dial, and fully perpetual calendar hands, c1810, 45in (114cm) high.
£35,000–40,000
$50,750–58,000 ⊞ GeC

A George III mahogany regulator longcase clock, by Jas. Bullock, London, with silvered dial, and subsidiary seconds dial, 69in (175cm) high.
£19,300–22,000
$28,000–32,000 🔨 Bea

A Viennese year-going floor-standing mahogany seconds beating regulator, by Binder, c1825, 76in (193cm) high.
£50,000–70,000
$72,500–101,500 ⊞ GeC

A Viennese roof-top 8-day regulator, with an enamel dial, in a mahogany case with maple stringing, c1825, 37in (94cm) high.
£6,500–8,500
$9,400–12,300 ⊞ GeC

A Viennese month-going lantern-style regulator, by Glückstein, with Huygens method of winding, c1810, 45in (114cm) high.
£30,000–40,000
$43,500–58,000 ⊞ GeC

An 8-day precision regulator, with compensated pendulum, and Huygens method of winding, c1830.
£30,000–40,000
$43,500–58,000 ⊞ GeC

A Viennese month-going regulator, the enamel dial signed Joseph Jessner, c1830, 41in (104cm) high.
£7,000–10,000
$10,200–14,500 ⊞ GeC

An Austrian walnut, kingwood, ebonized and parcel-gilt regulator, c1780, 79in (200.5cm) high.
£15,000–16,500
$21,750–24,000 🔨 C

A Georgian mahogany regulator clock, with silvered dial and minute dial, 75in (190cm) high.
£17,250–19,300
$25,000–28,000 ⚒ BWe

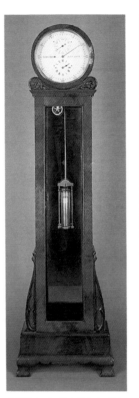

A Regency mahogany month-going longcase regulator, signed Margetts, London, 74½in (189cm) high.
£48,300–52,450
$70,000–76,000 ⚒ C

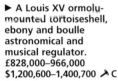

A Regency regulator, dial signed Webster, London, No. 6096, 77in (196cm) high.
£9,650–11,000
$14,000–16,000 ⚒ C

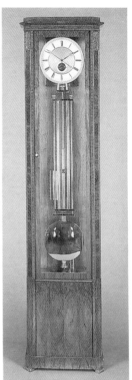

An Austrian walnut year-going longcase regulator, signed V. Bittner in Komotau No. 5, 1856, 76in (193cm) high.
£30,000–35,000
$43,500–50,750 ⚒ C

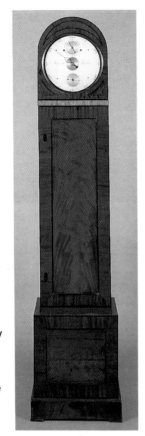

A Victorian ormolu-mounted walnut month-going wall regulator, signed Chas. Frodsham, No. 1702, 62in (157cm).
£62,100–75,900
$90,000–110,050 ⚒ C

▶ **A Louis XV ormolu-mounted tortoiseshell, ebony and boulle astronomical and musical regulator.**
£828,000–966,000
$1,200,600–1,400,700 ⚒ C

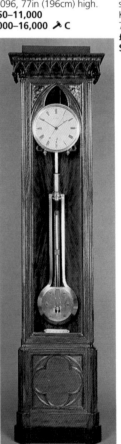

A Louis Philippe mahogany 6-month-going longcase regulator, signed Ame. Jacob, 85in (216cm) high.
£55,200–69,000
$80,000–100,000 ⚒ C

A Regency mahogany longcase regulator, the dial signed Matthews, Leighton, with 6 pillar movement, 75½in (192cm) high.
£10,350–13,100
$15,000–19,000 ⚒ C

A Viennese regulator, the dial signed Brandl in Wien, month-going precision movement, in a lantern-style mahogany-veneered case with ebonized stringing, c1810, 54in (137cm) high.
£30,000–35,000
$43,500–50,750 ⊞ GeC

A Viennese _grande sonnerie_ striking regulator, two-piece enamel dial, in a rosewood case, with applied decorations and stringing, c1845, 48in (122cm) high.
£6,500–8,500
$9,400–12,300 ⊞ GeC

A Viennese rooftop-style regulator, the enamel dial with engine-turned bezel, in a mahogany-veneered case with maple stringing, c1830, 35in (89cm) high.
£7,000–10,000
$10,200–14,500 ⊞ GeC

A Viennese regulator, in a burr walnut-veneered lantern-style case with marquetry inlay, precision month-going movement, c1825, 46in (117cm) high.
£30,000–35,000
$43,500–50,750 ⊞ GeC

A dome-topped mahogany shop regulator, by S. Bloomfield & Co, London, with deadbeat escapement, c1860, 71½in (181.5cm) high.
£8,000–9,000
$11,600–13,000 ⊞ **PAO**

A mahogany month-going wall regulator, signed Gebhard Bosch Lübeck, the bob as a terrestrial globe, 1877, 54in (137cm) high.
£13,800–16,500
$20,000–24,000 ⚒ **C**

A French week-duration four-glass regulator, signed Tiffany & Co, c1890, 15in (38cm) high.
£1,250–2,000
$1,800–2,900 ⊞ **PAO**

A Viennese lantern-style regulator, by Phillip Happacher, the mahogany case with maple stringing, *grande sonnerie* striking with engraved dial centre, c1825, 44in (111.5cm) high.
£25,000–30,000
$36,250–43,500 ⊞ **GeC**

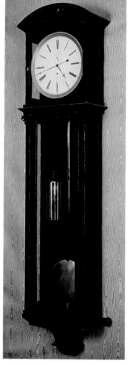

A Viennese year-going wall regulator, with precision movement, in mahogany case, c1835, 60in (152cm) high.
£40,000–50,000
$58,000–72,500 ⊞ **GeC**

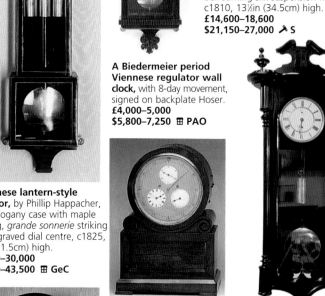

A Biedermeier period Viennese regulator wall clock, with 8-day movement, signed on backplate Hoser.
£4,000–5,000
$5,800–7,250 ⊞ **PAO**

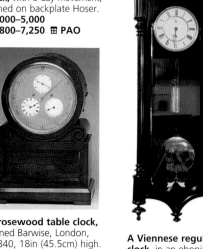

A rosewood table clock, signed Barwise, London, c1840, 18in (45.5cm) high.
£5,800–6,700
$8,400–9,700 ⚒ **S**

A lantern style Viennese regulator, c1810, 30in (76cm) high.
£24,000–26,000
$34,800–37,700 ⊞ **GeC**

A French Empire ormolu and bronze *pendule au nègre,* with enamel dial, bell striking silk suspension movement, c1810, 13⅖in (34.5cm) high.
£14,600–18,600
$21,150–27,000 ⚒ **S**

A Viennese regulator clock, in an ebonized case, 19thC, 40in (101.5cm) high.
£550–700
$800–1,000 ⚒ **PCh**

A spherical striking skeleton clock, the meridian ring signed Barraud, Cornhill, London, 19thC, 12in (30.5cm) high.
£10,200–11,400
$14,800–16,500 ⚒ **C**

A Georgian mahogany stick barometer, by W. & J. Jones, 40in (101.5cm) high.
£6,200–6,700
$9,000–9,700 ✗ CSK

A mahogany stick barometer, signed Zerboni & Co, c1825.
£2,750–3,000
$4,000–4,400
⊞ PAO

A mahogany stick barometer, by George Adams, London, c1785.
£3,000–3,500
$4,400–5,000
✗ W&W

A mahogany wheel barometer, by A. Alberti, Sheffield, c1825, dial 8in (20cm) diam.
£1,700–2,000
$2,500–2,900 ⊞ PAO

A mahogany wheel barometer, signed Vittory & Merone, Manchester, c1785.
£4,500–5,000
$6,500–7,250 ✗ W&W

An inlaid mahogany round-top wheel barometer, by James Gatty, London, c1780.
£3,200–3,700
$4,650–5,350 ✗ W&W

An aneroid barometer and thermometer, by John Good & Sons Ltd, Hull, 11in (28cm) diam.
£60–75 $90–110 ⊞ BEL

◄ **An oak stick barometer,** by Negretti & Zambra, London, c1870.
£1,000–1,100
$1,500–1,600 ⊞ PAO

A Dutch ebonized barometer, signed Geb Lurafco te, late 18thC.
£4,000–4,600
$5,800–6,500 ✗ C

A brass-inlaid mahogany and rosewood wheel barometer, by Dollond, London.
£4,500–5,500
$6,500–8,000 ⊞ PAO

► **A sympiesometer,** by A. Adie, Edinburgh, No. 372, c1822.
£3,000–3,500
$4,400–5,000 ✗ W&W

A rosewood-cased wheel barometer, with hygrometer, thermometer, mirror and spirit level, c1840.
£1,750–2,000
$2,500–3,000 ⊞ PAO

A leftward-pointing mahogany Masonic 'signpost' barometer, by Giobbio, Trowbridge, c1800.
£7,000–8,000
$10,200–11,600 ✗ W&W

A mahogany round-top wheel barometer, with wooden bezel, by Domenico Gatty, London, c1780.
£3,500–4,600
$5,000–6,500 ⚒ **W&W**

A mahogany stick barometer, by Dollond, London, c1835.
£4,000–5,000
$5,800–7,250 ⚒ **W&W**

A mahogany wheel barometer, by Matthew Woller, Birmingham, c1800, dial 10in (25.5cm) diam.
£1,600–2,000
$2,300–2,900 ⚒ **W&W**

A mahogany stick barometer, with waisted door, by Francis Pelegrino, London, c1800.
£2,200–2,800
$3,200–4,000 ⚒ **W&W**

A rosewood and brass-inlaid wheel barometer, by Francis Amadio, London, c1830.
£2,400–2,800
$3,500–4,000 ⚒ **W&W**

A satinwood wheel barometer, by Gabalio, London, dial 12in (30.5cm) diam, and pagoda top, c1810.
£4,200–4,500
$6,100–6,500 ⚒ **W&W**

A flame-mahogany 'two-dial' wheel barometer, by King, Bristol, c1830.
£1,000–1,300
$1,500–1,900 ⚒ **W&W**

A mahogany-inlaid wheel barometer, with Masonic symbols, by Peter Caminada, Taunton, c1820.
£1,000–1,200
$1,500–1,750 ⚒ **W&W**

A flame-mahogany wheel barometer, by John Braham, Bristol, dial 6in (15cm) diam, c1830.
£1,600–2,000
$2,300–2,900 ⚒ **W&W**

A flame-mahogany scroll-top wheel barometer, by Cox, Devonport, c1860.
£600–800
$850–1,150 ⚒ **W&W**

A Queen Anne walnut barometer, marked Invented & Made by Danl. Quare London, No. 24 on side plate, 39in (99cm) high.
£75,000–85,000
$108,000–123,000 ⚒ C

A rosewood stick barometer, by Dobell, Hastings, the ivory aslant scales with weather notations, c1840.
£2,000–3,000
$2,900–4,400 ⊞ PAO

A mahogany bowfront stick barometer, by John Ewen, Aberdeen, c1810.
£7,000–8,000
$10,200–11,600 ⊞ PAO

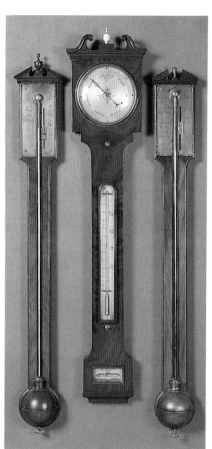

l. A George III mahogany stick barometer, by Watkins, Charing Cross, with brass vernier scale, 39½in (100cm) high.
£2,200–3,000 $3,200–4,400
c. A George III mahogany wheel barometer, by P. Aggio, Colchester, with swan-neck pediment, 39½in (100cm) high.
£5,700–7,000 $8,250–10,200
r. A George III mahogany stick barometer, by Troughton, London, 38in (96.5cm) high.
£2,200–3,000 $3,200–4,400 ⚒ C

A Sheraton mahogany and boxwood-inlaid wheel barometer, by G. Martinoia, York, with silvered-brass scale, dial 8in (20cm) diam.
£1,300–1,600
$1,900–2,300 ⊞ PAO

A George III mahogany and chequer-strung barometer, with central fluted Corinthian column, signed Jno. Russell, Falkirk, beneath the vernier scale, c1745, 43½in (110cm) high.
£35,000–45,000
$50,000–65,000 ⚒ C

A rosewood-veneered wheel barometer, inlaid with pewter leaves and a bird, by B. Pedroncini, Southampton, with silvered brass scale, c1840.
£1,400–1,600
$2,000–2,300 ⊞ PAO

A rosewood-veneered wheel barometer, by Carughi, London, with silvered brass scale, swan-neck top and brass finial, c1840.
£1,750–2,250
$2,500–3,250 ⊞ PAO

An 8-day skeleton clock, with passing strike on the hour, mid-19thC, 16in (40.5cm) high.
£1,300–1,500
$1,900–2,100 ⊞ **GUN**

A 'Western Union' time and calendar regulator, by Ingraham, c1910, 36in (91.5cm) high.
£350–450
$500–650 ⚒ **RSch**

A walnut 'Index' perpetual calendar clock, c1880, 33in (84cm) high.
£850–950
$1,250–1,500 ⚒ **RSch**

A walnut 8-day wall clock, by Jerome & Co, with striking movement, c1870, 30in (76cm) high.
£500–550
$720–800 ⊞ **GUN**

A longcase clock, by J. Winslow, Massachusetts, with *églomisé* dial, c1820, 48in (122cm) high.
£4,700–5,300
$6,800–7,700 ⚒ **S(NY)**

l. A mahogany banjo timepiece, with painted dial, c1840, 33in (84cm) high.
£850–950 $1,250–1,380
c. A giltwood and *verre églomisé* banjo timepiece, c1820, 39½in (100cm) high.
£2,200–2,750 $3,200–4,000
r. A mahogany and *églomisé* banjo timepiece, by D. Williams, c1830, 35in (89cm) high.
£2,200–2,750 $3,200–4,000 ⚒ **S(NY)**

An oak and walnut longcase regulator clock, by Seth Thomas Clock Co, c1900, 100in (254cm) high.
£5,500–6,000
$8,000–8,750 ⚒ **S(NY)**

A mahogany 8-day regulator wall clock, by Ansonia Co, c1860, 32in (81.5cm) high.
£500–550
$720–800 ⊞ **GUN**

A Victorian walnut and elm crossbanded No. 8 regulator, by Ansonia, c1870, 124in (315cm) high.
£18,700–22,000
$27,100–32,000 ⚒ **RSch**

A mahogany and veneered pine shelf clock, by Elmer O. Stennes, Weymouth, Mass., with special short drop movement, kidney dial, c1873, 39in (99cm) high.
£2,200–2,750
$3,200–4,000 ⚒ **RSch**

An 8-day striking four-glass mantel clock, by Ansonia Co, with crystal glass pillars, enamel dial, restored, c1890, 17in (43cm) high.
£1,600–1,750
$2,300–2,500 ⊞ **GUN**

American Clocks

The earliest examples of American clocks were modelled closely on European products, as immigrant clockmakers from Britain and northern Europe brought their skills to the United States. In the mid- to late 18th century longcase clocks (known as tallcase clocks in America) by makers such as English-born Thomas Harland from Connecticut echoed the proportions and materials of the English longcase style. Demand for a cheaper and smaller type of clock led to the American shelf or bracket clock, which differs greatly in appearance from its British counterpart: the forms are more varied, the 'steeple' shape being a popular type, and the cases more decorative, with panels depicting patterns, birds, flowers or landscape scenes. They were first produced in the United States in the early 1800s, but most date from the 1840s, following the introduction of spring-driven movements.

During the 18th century, central Connecticut attracted a number of skilled clockmakers, and the Cheney family from East Hartford were prominent among them. The distinguished American clockmakers Eli Terry and Benjamin Willard were both apprenticed under the Cheneys. At that time nearly all clocks were handmade, making each one unique, resulting in little interchangeablility of parts. Eli Terry began experimenting with mass-produced wooden movements as early as 1807, and soon realized that this would lead to lower costs, along with increased volume and profit. In order to produce a large quantity of these clocks Terry built a factory where many of the parts could be made to be assembled subsequently. This laid the foundation for today's mass-production methods. Terry's first 'pillar and scroll' shelf clock was produced in 1814. By 1845, the Connecticut clock industry was turning out one million shelf clocks a year, many of which were exported to Europe.

In the late 1820s and through the 1830s, inventors scrambled to produce a low-cost metal movement that would improve accuracy and durability. Chauncey Jerome, who at one time had made cases for Terry, had the idea of replacing the wooden movement with a cheaper brass one. Jerome's brother created a simple movement, and rectangular cases were designed with an ogive moulding at the front. The 'OG' one-day weight clock, as it was known, was introduced in 1837, later selling for only one US dollar. These durable clocks can still be found all over the world, with the maker's name usually on a label on the inside of the case.

In the 1850s, Connecticut manufacturers developed inexpensive and reliable spring movements, eliminating the clumsy weights previously used in most clocks. This led to the rapid growth of all the prominent firms in the state, namely the Seth Thomas Clock Co, Forestville Manufacturing (later Welch), Jerome Manufacturing Co (later the New Haven Clock Co), Waterbury Clock Co, E. & A. Ingraham, W. L. Gilbert & Co, and the Ansonia Clock Company.

A useful aid in identifying items are the old manufacturers' catalogues, many of which have been recently reprinted. These also give the collector a picture of every model in a series.

Simon Willard, Benjamin's brother, invented his 'Improved Timepiece' in the early 1800s, giving the details of his design to the US Patent office in 1802. This design, known as the banjo clock, became not only very popular with most of the prominent Connecticut manufacturers but also the best-selling model of E. Howard & Co, Boston. Handmade examples are still being made today by Foster Campos of Pembroke, MA, and factories in Korea and China have recently copied the design as well. Another popular form was the octagon drop timepiece, commonly called a school clock in America, an adaptation of the English drop-dial and dating from c1830. There are also Asian reproductions of these clocks on the market, both short- and long-drop, but specialist auctioneer Bob Schmitt does not see this as a problem as they are sold as reproductions rather than fakes and can provide a low-cost alternative to the original. They can be identified by the colour and quality of the wood, which is often imitation mahogany, and details such as the use of new screws.

Bob Schmitt points to the continued popularity of the banjo, shelf and school clocks today, as any sale catalogue which includes American clocks will confirm, but he advises buyers not to overlook the myriad of other case styles and materials on offer. As with European examples, American clock cases may be found in porcelain, china, carved wood, iron, brass and spelter. Regardless of the material chosen, basic architectural styles have always predominated, sometimes with cast figural adornments. According to Bob Schmitt, the demand is strong for American clocks of all types, from inexpensive items such as black mantel clocks, to the early and rare clocks which are steadily rising in price, owing to increased interest and relative scarcity. Factors contributing to the top-quality clocks are date, especially pre-1820, craftsmanship and condition, and the presence of a signature. An early 19th-century banjo or tall clock will fetch thousands of dollars, while late 19th-century factory-made clocks can be bought for a few hundred dollars. At the top end of the market, the maker's name can make a considerable difference in prices realized; for example, a standard early 19th-century banjo clock may fetch $2,175 (£1,500), while a banjo clock dated c1827 recently sold at R.O. Schmitt's spring auction for $12,500 (£8,750). Why the difference in price? The latter was signed on the movement by Jacob Merrill, Plymouth, NH.

Longcase Clocks

A carved and figured walnut longcase clock, signed John Brooker, Germantown, with phases of the moon and calendar, c1790, 98in (249cm) high.
£8,250–11,000
$12,000–16,000 ⚒ S(NY)

◀ A longcase clock, signed James C. Cole, Rochester, the 8-day movement with typical New Hampshire cut-outs to the plates, c1820, 89in (226cm) high.
£3,000–4,000
$4,400–5,800 ⚒ RSch

▶ An inlaid and figured walnut longcase clock, signed Jacob Fry, Woodstock, the white painted dial with phases of the moon, subsidiary seconds and date, painted below with terrestrial globes, c1800, 96in (244cm) high.
£13,200–15,400
$19,100–22,300 ⚒ S(NY)

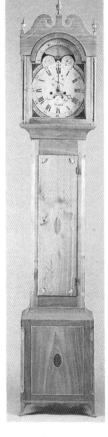

◀ A cherrywood longcase clock, by Asa Hopkins, Litchfield, Connecticut, with 30-hour wooden pull-up weight-driven movement, refinished, c1820, 92in (234cm) high.
£1,650–2,750
$2,400–4,000 ⚒ SK(B)

◀ A figured mahogany longcase clock, by John Davis, New Holland, Pennsylvania, c1795, 96in (244cm) high.
£7,900–8,800
$11,500–12,750 ⚒ S(NY)

◀ A carved and figured walnut longcase clock, by Thomas Crow, Wilmington, Delaware, with calendar, date and seconds registers, the hood with swan-neck crest surmounted by urn and flame finials, c1780, 100in (254cm) high.
£10,450–12,000
$15,150–17,400 ⚒ S(NY)

▶ A longcase clock, Style No. 214, by Herschede Clock Co, Cincinnati, the gilded mask dial with rolling moon, with 5 tube, 3 weight movement, c1935, 78in (198cm) high.
£950–1,200
$1,300–1,750 ⚒ RSch

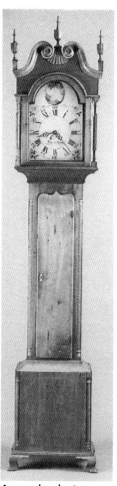

A carved walnut longcase clock, by Fry & Davis, Woodstock, the dial with calendar register, some restoration, c1800, 94in (239cm) high.
£16,500–18,700
$24,000–27,100 ⚒ S(NY)

◀ **A mahogany longcase clock,** Style No. 217 by Herschede Clock Co, Cincinnati, the gilded mask dial with rolling moon, with 5 tube, 3 weight movement, c1935, 80in (203cm) high.
£1,100–1,650
$1,600–2,400 ⚒ RSch

▶ **A 'Louis XVI' longcase clock,** Style No. 276 by Herschede Clock Co, Cincinnati, the brass dial with gilded overlay, with 9 tube, 3 weight chiming movement, and a choice of 3 tunes, c1925, 78in (198cm) high.
£1,900–2,000
$2,750–2,900 ⚒ RSch

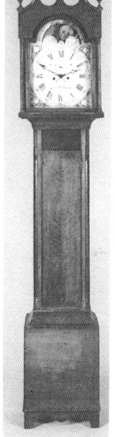

◀ **A cherrywood longcase clock,** signed A. & W. Thomas, Tennessee, the white painted dial with subsidiary seconds and date aperture, c1800, 98in (249cm) high.
£5,500–7,700
$8,000–11,150 ⚒ CNY

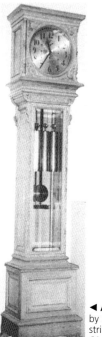

◀ **A stained maple longcase clock,** signed Noah Ranlat, Gilmanton, New Hampshire, the enamelled dial with Arabic and Roman numerals, seconds and calendar registers, gold-painted spandrels, the case with pierced fretwork crest, quarter columns, restored, c1820, 87in (221cm) high.
£2,000–2,750
$2,900–4,000 ⚒ S(NY)

◀ **An oak and elm No. 21 longcase clock,** by Seth Thomas, with Westminster quarter striking movement, c1900, 84in (213cm) high.
£1,900–3,000
$2,750–4,400 ⚒ RSch

▶ **An inlaid mahogany longcase clock,** south-eastern America, restored, c1790, 104½in (265cm) high.
£7,100–8,250
$10,500–12,000 ⚒ SK

◀ **A carved walnut longcase clock,** by William Reinhardt, Reading, Pennsylvania, with phases of the moon, seconds and calendar mechanisms, dial restored, c1800, 104in (264cm) high.
£5,300–6,050
$7,700–8,750 ⚒ S(NY)

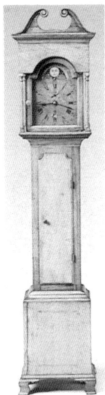

◀ **An inlaid mahogany longcase clock,** by Aaron Willard, Boston, Massachusetts, with polychrome painted rocking ship movement, the inlaid door flanked by brass stop-fluted quarter columns, c1805, 105in (267cm) high.
£24,200–27,500
$35,100–39,500 ⚒ S(NY)

▶ **A pine longcase clock,** by Riley Whiting, Winchester, CT, painted red and with simulated stringing in gold and black, c1830, 83in (211cm) high.
£6,800–7,700
$9,500–11,150 ⚒ SK(B)

An inlaid mahogany miniature longcase clock, the case probably Pennsylvania, the dial inscribed Christopher Weaver, restored, c1795, 31½in (80cm) high.
£52,800–55,000
$76,500–79,750 ⚒ S(NY)
This longcase clock is a very rare example.

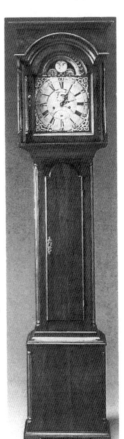

▶ **A walnut longcase clock,** the dial signed David Ritten House, Norriton, Pennsylvania, with phases of the moon, calendar and seconds mechanisms, feet reduced, c1780, 87in (221cm) high.
£5,700–6,600
$8,250–9,500 ⚒ S(NY)

◀ **A longcase clock,** by Riley Whiting, Winchester, Connecticut, with floral polychrome gilt dial, 30-hour wooden weight-driven movement, c1830, 85in (216cm) high.
£1,700–2,400
$2,450–3,500 ⚒ SK

▶ **An inlaid mahogany longcase clock,** attributed to Aaron or Simon Willard, Roxbury, Massachusetts, the crossbanded door flanked by reeded quarter columns with brass Corinthian capitals, c1800, 98in (249cm) high.
£7,900–8,800
$11,500–12,750 ⚒ S(NY)

Wall Clocks

A gallery clock, by Atkins Clock Co, with 30-day fusee movement, restored, c1860, 27in (68cm) high.
£1,100–1,300
$1,600–1,900 ➢ RSch

A rosewood and gilt wagon spring clock, by Atkins Clock Co, Bristol, CT, the dial inscribed 'Presented by D. Arnold, May 1857', with 30-day movement, c1860, dial repainted 1985, 27in (68cm) high.
£1,500–1,750
$2,170–2,500 ➢ RSch

A mirror timepiece, by Abiel Chandler, Concord, New Hampshire, with inscribed white painted iron dial, 8-day weight-driven brass movement, in ebonized and gold-painted split baluster case, with red, silver, green and gold stencilled tablet, c1830, 30in (76cm) high.
£8,800–9,600
$12,750–14,000 ➢ SK

A mirror timepiece, by James Collins, Goffstown, New Hampshire, with painted inscribed iron dial, 8-day weight-driven movement, the glass tablet with silver, green, red, gold and black foliate stencilled design, c1830, 30in (76cm) high.
£1,650–2,200
$2,400–3,200 ➢ SK

A mahogany wall timepiece, by Differential Power Clock Co, Chicago, with silvered dial and year-going movement, c1910, 39in (99cm) high.
£900–1,300
$1,300–1,900 ➢ S(NY)

A mahogany wall clock, by Differential Power Clock Co, Chicago, with year-going movement, c1920, 41in (104cm) high.
£950–1,100
$1,380–1,600 ➢ RSch

A mahogany wall clock, by New Haven, with 8-day striking movement, c1870, 32in (81.5cm) high.
£600–660
$850–1,000 ⊞ GUN

A rosewood wall clock, by E. Fitch, New York and London, with 8-day striking movement, c1900, 28in (71cm) high.
£600–650
$870–950 ⊞ GUN

A mahogany 'Saturn' wall clock, by New Haven, with weight-driven movement, restored, c1910, 34in (86.5cm) high.
£650–800
$950–1,150 ➢ RSch

◄ **An oak 'Queen Anne' wall clock,** by Seth Thomas, with original dial and 8-day movement, c1880, 36in (91.5cm) high.
£350–500
$500–700 ➢ RSch

Banjo Clocks

A Federal mahogany, giltwood and *églomisé* banjo clock, by William Cummins, Roxbury, Massachusetts, with inscribed white painted dial, polychrome throat panel flanked by pierced side arms, the box door panel depicting a public building in polychrome, c1820, 34in (86cm) high.
£3,300–4,950
$4,800–7,150 ⚹ S(NY)

► A 'Brookfield' banjo clock, by Seth Thomas, the 8-day movement striking the hours and half-hours on 2 straight rods, minor damage, c1970, 28in (71cm) high.
£150–200
$220–300 ⚹ RSch

◄ A brass and *églomisé*-mounted mahogany banjo clock, signed Phipps, New England, the white enamelled dial decorated with Roman numerals, with eagle finial, the throat panel with a giltwood and rope-twisted border and *églomisé* centre panel, c1800, 33in (83.5cm) high.
£2,200–2,750
$3,200–4,000 ⚹ S(NY)

◄ A mahogany No. 4 banjo clock, by E. Howard & Co, hands from an earlier clock, incorrect weight and refinished case, c1890, 32in (81cm) high.
£1,100–1,500
$1,600–2,170 ⚹ RSch

► A 'Treasure Island' banjo clock, by Ingraham, the movement now attached to case back, the case decorated with scenes of islands, c1930, 38in (96cm) high.
£300–400
$440–600 ⚹ RSch

► A mahogany banjo clock, by New Haven, 8-day lever movement, flaking to tablet, c1925, 17in (43cm) high.
£65–85
$95–125 ⚹ RSch

► A mahogany and *églomisé* banjo clock, by Stephen Smith, Massachusetts, the inscribed white painted dial surmounted by a cast metal eagle finial, with decorated throat panel, brass side arms flanking the box door painted with a scene, damaged, c1825, 33in (84cm) high.
£2,000–2,750
$2,900–4,000 ⚹ S(NY)

A 'Neptune' banjo clock, by Ingraham, with 8-day lever movement, eagle finial above the dial, decorated with landscape scene at the base, c1930, 23in (58cm) high.
£45–65
$65–95 ⚹ RSch

► A 'Whitney' banjo clock, with 8-day striking movement, minor crazing to marine tablet, c1910, 31in (79cm) high.
£250–350
$360–500 ⚹ RSch

◄ **A lever banjo clock,** by New Haven, movement in working order, replaced eagle and scene card, c1930, 18in (46cm) high.
£80–120
$115–175 ➶ RSch

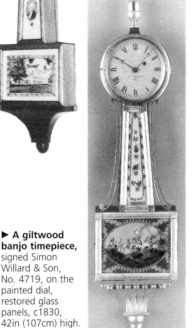

◄ **A mahogany banjo clock,** by Waltham, decorated with Washington and Mt Vernon tablets, c1920, 19in (48cm) high.
£130–160
$190–230 ➶ RSch

► **A mahogany and _églomisé_ banjo clock,** by Aaron Willard, Boston, with white painted inscribed dial, surmounted by a gilt metal eagle finial, floral-painted throat panel flanked by brass side arms, the door painted with a lady holding flowers, restored, c1825 with later pendant, 42in (107cm) high.
£1,000–1,100
$1,500–1,600 ➶ S(NY)

► **A giltwood banjo timepiece,** signed Simon Willard & Son, No. 4719, on the painted dial, restored glass panels, c1830, 42in (107cm) high.
£1,100–1,650
$1,600–2,400 ➶ S

A 'Willard' banjo clock, by Waltham, decorated with Liberty Bell and Independence Hall tablets, ball and bracket base, c1920, 41in (104cm) high.
£1,400–1,750
$2,000–2,500 ➶ RSch

Calendar Clocks

An American calendar wall timepiece, the painted dial signed Calendar Clock Co, Curtisville, Connecticut, Patented Sept. 19 1854, giltwood and gesso case, c1860, 36in (91.5cm) diam.
£2,000–2,400
$2,900–3,500 ⚒ S(NY)

A mahogany-veneered Patent Galusha Maranville calendar clock, by Wm. L. Gilbert, case refinished, c1865, 24in (61cm) high.
£500–600
$720–870 ⚒ RSch

A double-dial parlour calendar clock, by E. Ingraham & Co, Lewis Patent, some damage, c1865, 22in (56cm) high.
£900–1,050
$1,300–1,500 ⚒ RSch

An American calendar wall timepiece, signed Gale's Patent, with painted dial and moulded wood case, c1880, 37in (96cm) diam.
£2,750–3,300
$4,000–4,800 ⚒ S(NY)

A 'Dew Drop' time and calendar clock, by Ingraham, c1910, 24in (61cm) high.
£250–275
$360–400 ⚒ RSch

An 'Eclipse Calendar' clock, by E. Ingraham & Co, with rosewood sides, repapered dial, c1880, 29in (74cm) high.
£600–750
$870–1,100 ⚒ RSch

A 30-day oak double-dial calendar clock, by New Haven, c1900, 49in (124cm) high.
£900–1,100
$1,300–1,600 ⚒ RSch

A 'Peanut' rosewood perpetual calendar timepiece, by Seth Thomas, with painted dials and spring-driven movement, c1870, 24in (61cm) high.
£1,500–2,000
$2,170–2,900 ⚒ S

A rosewood perpetual calendar timepiece, with painted dials, weight-driven movement, c1870, 40in (101cm) high.
£1,650–2,200
$2,400–3,200 ⚒ S

An 8-day walnut double-dial calendar shelf clock, 'No 5 Round Top', by Ithaca, c1880, 19in (48cm) high.
£350–400
$500–600 ⚒ RSch

Regulators

A walnut regulator 'A', by Ansonia, with 8-day striking movement, c1890, 32in (81cm) high.
£300–400
$440–600 RSch

A walnut regulator 'A', by Ansonia, in working order, case damaged, dial badly stained, c1890, 32in (81cm) high.
£170–220
$250–350 RSch

An oak regulator No. 70, by E. Howard & Co, Boston, the pendulum with damascene pattern, tablet replaced, c1900, 31in (79cm) high.
£1,000–1,200
$1,500–1,750 RSch

A 'Vienna'-style regulator, by New Haven, c1900, 47in (119cm) high.
£550–750
$800–1,100 RSch

◀ **A rosewood No. 1 regulator,** by Seth Thomas, with dial by Martha Smallwood, with nickel weight, c1878, 34in (86cm) high.
£600–750
$800–1,100 RSch

An oak regulator No. 34, by Waltham Clock Co, Serial No. 3507, the original dial inscribed Nelson H. Brown, Boston, c1920, 33in (84cm) high.
£1,000–1,200
$1,500–1,750 RSch

A cherrywood regulator No. 6, by Self Winding Clock Co, New York, battery operated, c1890, 50in (127cm) high.
£650–900
$950–1,300 RSch

LOCATE THE SOURCE
The source of each illustration in Miller's can be found by checking the code letters below each caption with the Key to Illustrations, pages 6–7.

◀ **An oak No. 2 store regulator,** by Sessions, with an old piece of cut and etched glass as a floral tablet, c1910, 38in (96cm) high.
£250–350
$360–500 RSch

An oak regulator No. 5, by Sessions, with weight driven movement, c1910, 50in (127cm) high.
£450–550
$650–800 RSch

◀ **A rosewood regulator,** by Seth Thomas, with painted dial, c1880, 42in (107cm) high.
£800–1,000
$1,150–1,500 S

Shelf Clocks

An 8-day rosewood-veneered shelf clock, by Ansonia, with original dial, slight damage, c1860, 19in (48cm) high.
£350–450
$500–650 ✦ **RSch**

A 30-hour steeple alarm clock, by Ansonia, c1860, 15in (38cm) high.
£110–170
$160–250
✦ **RSch**

A 30-hour steeple clock, by Ansonia, with painted dial, c1870, 20in (51cm) high.
£90–130
$130–190 ✦ **RSch**

An 'Arcadian' rosewood 8-day shelf clock, by Ansonia, c1890, 18in (46cm) high.
£220–280
$320–410 ✦ **RSch**

A 'Vassar' bronze figural shelf clock, by Ansonia, with porcelain dial, slight damage, c1885, 11in (28cm) high.
£250–300 $360–440 ✦ **RSch**

A 'Burton' oak gingerbread shelf clock, by Ansonia, some wear, c1900, 22in (56cm) high.
£90–130 $130–190 ✦ **RSch**

A 'Target' green china shelf clock, by Ansonia, with paper dial, slight damage, c1890, 9½in (24cm) high.
£150–200
$220–290 ✦ **RSch**

A cast-iron shelf clock, by Ansonia, originally with imitation marble finish, now painted brown, c1900, 10in (25.5cm) high.
£80–110
$115–160 ✦ **RSch**

A carved mahogany and _églomisé_ musical shelf clock, by John J. Parry, Philadelphia, the lower section of the door painted with musical sheets and horns, c1780, 32in (81.5cm) high.
£20,300–20,900
$29,400–30,300 ✦ **S(NY)**

A 'Calais' enamelled iron shelf clock, by Ansonia, c1900, 13in (33cm) high.
£110–130
$160–190 ✦ **RSch**

◄ **A 'Orleans' enamelled iron shelf clock,** by Ansonia, with brass dial, c1910, 12in (30.5cm) high.
£110–130
$160–190 ✦ **RSch**

► **A 'Munich' enamelled iron and gold shelf clock,** by Ansonia, c1910, 11in (28cm) high.
£110–130
$160–190 ✦ **RSch**

A Rhode Island pillar and scroll shelf clock, by George Baker, Providence, c1825, 31in (79cm) high.
£1,200–1,550
$1,750–2,250 RSch

A bevel front shelf clock, by Edw. M. Barnes, Bristol, Connecticut, with original tablet and wooden dial, c1840, 26in (66cm) high.
£240–290
$350–450 RSch

A miniature stencilled column and splat clock, by E. & G. W. Bartholomew, Bristol, Connecticut, with carved pineapple and claw feet, c1825, 29½in (75cm) high.
£1,300–2,000
$1,900–2,900 RSch

A rosewood steeple-on-steeple wagon-spring shelf clock, by Birge & Fuller, Bristol, Connecticut, with 5in (13cm) painted dial on chapter ring, 8-day striking brass movement, c1845, 27in (69cm) high.
£1,450–1,650
$2,100–2,400 S(NY)

A mahogany steeple-on-steeple wagon-spring shelf clock, by Birge & Fuller, Bristol, Connecticut, with 5in (13cm) painted dial on chapter ring, 8-day brass striking movement, 26in (66cm) high.
£1,650–2,000
$2,400–2,900 S(NY)

A 'Queen Anne' carriage clock, by Boston Clock Co, with hand-painted dial, 7 jewel escapement, slight damage, c1890, 6½in (16.5cm) high.
£250–300
$360–440 RSch

A 30-hour cottage shelf clock, by D. S. Crosby, New York, c1850, 12in (30.5cm) high.
£260–300
$380–440 RSch

An 8-day steeple clock, by Harris & Wilcox, New York, movement replaced, c1845, 22½in (57cm) high.
£220–280
$320–400 RSch

A Gothic-style 30-hour rosewood shelf clock, by Wm. L. Gilbert, with original dial, c1875, 16½in (42cm) high.
£110–160
$160–230 RSch

An 'Amphion' walnut parlour clock, by Wm. L. Gilbert, dial faded, c1880, 25in (63.5cm) high.
£450–550
$650–800 RSch

A 'Sportsman' figural shelf clock, by Wm. L. Gilbert, on a wooden imitation marble base, crack to dial, c1900, 15in (38cm) high.
£150–200
$225–290 RSch

An 8-day shelf clock, by Joseph Ives, Bristol, Connecticut, repainted dial, tablet replaced, c1845, 31in (79cm) high.
£420–500
$610–720 ⚒ RSch

An 8-day shelf alarm clock, by Joseph Ives, c1845, 31in (79cm) high.
£1,100–1,650
$1,600–2,400 ⚒ RSch

A 'Doric Mosaic' 30-hour striking shelf clock, by E. Ingraham & Co, c1875, 16in (40.5cm) high.
£280–330
$410–480 ⚒ RSch

A 30-hour steeple alarm clock, by Jerome & Co, c1870, incomplete, 14½in (37cm) high.
£90–130
$130–190 ⚒ RSch

A 'Dewey' oak ginger-bread clock, by Ingraham, slight damage, c1910, 23in (58.5cm) high.
£290–330
$420–480 ⚒ RSch

A 'Ducat' oak gingerbread clock, by E. Ingraham & Co, original condition, c1900, 24in (61cm) high.
£140–170
$200–250 ⚒ RSch

A 'La Lanza' mission oak shelf clock, dial repapered and hands replaced, c1920, 22in (56cm) high.
£80–110
$115–160 ⚒ RSch

▶ **A Federal bird's-eye maple-inlaid cherrywood shelf clock,** by Benjamin Morrill, New Hampshire, c1815, 42½in (108cm) high.
£17,050–18,150
$24,700–26,300 ⚒ S(NY)

A 30-hour shelf clock, by Jerome & Co, New Haven, alarm mechanism missing, c1870, 16in (40.5cm) high.
£70–80
$100–115 ⚒ RSch

A 'San Martin' oak mission-style kitchen clock, with cardboard dial, c1920, 20in (51cm) high.
£70–110
$100–160 ⚒ RSch

▶ **A cottage clock,** by Henry Sperry & Co, New York, some wear, c1850, 12in (30.5cm) high.
£240–290
$350–420 ⚒ RSch

A 'Shelf Referee' oak shelf clock, c1910, 35in (89cm) high.
£370–420
$540–610 ⚒ RSch

An Empire-style 4-column shelf clock, by Sperry & Shaw, New York, with paper dial, c1845, 26in (66cm) high.
£160–220
$230–320 ⚒ RSch

A walnut pillar and scroll shelf clock, by Eli Terry & Sons, Connecticut, c1825, 30½in (77.5cm) high.
£900–1,100
$1,300–1,600 ➤ RSch

A Federal mahogany pillar and scroll shelf clock, by Eli Terry & Sons, Connecticut, with white painted dial and *églomisé* panel, restored, c1835, 31½in (80cm) high.
£1,500–1,650
$2,170–2,400 ➤ S(NY)

An 8-day steeple shelf clock, by Terry & Andrews, with lyre movement, dial worn, c1850, 20in (51cm) high.
£330–400
$480–580 ➤ RSch

A weight-driven shelf clock, by S. B. Terry, repaired, c1845, 19in (48cm) high.
£1,450–1,800
$2,100–2,600 ➤ RSch

A 30-hour cottage alarm clock, by S. B. Terry & Co, Connecticut, c1855, 11in (28cm) high.
£190–250
$275–360 ➤ RSch

A 'Column' 8-day shelf clock, by Seth Thomas, with gilded columns, c1870, 16in (40.5cm) high.
£240–280 $350–410 ➤ RSch

A Federal brass-mounted and inlaid mahogany shelf clock, c1810, 32½in (82.5cm) high.
£3,000–3,500
$4,400–5,000 ➤ S(NY)

A 'Lincoln' walnut shelf clock, by Seth Thomas, c1890, 27½in (70cm) high.
£500–575
$720–830 ➤ RSch

A 15-day mahogany tambour shelf clock, by Seth Thomas, with porcelain dial, c1910, 8in (20.5cm) high.
£140–170
$200–250 ➤ RSch

A rosewood 'Empress' shelf clock, by Welch Spring & Co, the dial repapered, 16in (40.5cm) high.
£140–180
$200–260 ➤ RSch

A Federal laminated mahogany shelf clock, with white painted dial and *églomisé* panel, on a plinth base, c1835, 15in (38cm) high.
£850–1,100
$1,250–1,600 ➤ S(NY)

A tambour shelf clock, by Seth Thomas, with Westminster chimes, c1900, 12in (30.5cm) high.
£140–180
$200–260 ➤ RSch

▶ **A 'Daisy & Button' blue tambour shelf clock,** c1930, 6in (15cm) high.
£90–130
$130–190 ➤ RSch

Novelty Clocks

A chess timer clock, by Yale Clock Co, New Haven, with 2 Yale 'Gems', mounted on cast-iron tilt and start base, c1885, 6in (15cm) high.
£380–420
$550–600 ↗ RSch

A 'Frog Band' novelty clock, the clock inset in the base of the banjo, c1900, 11in (28cm) high.
£260–300
$380–440 ↗ RSch

A Topsey 'blinking eye' novelty shelf clock, movement and dial original, c1880, 17in (43cm) high.
£1,550–2,000
$2,250–2,900 ↗ RSch

A 30-hour oil lamp night-light clock, by Standard Novelty Co, New York, c1890, 6in (15cm) high.
£330–400
$480–580 ↗ RSch

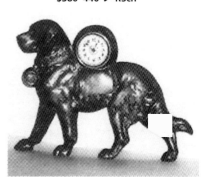

A bronze-plated cast-iron St Bernard novelty shelf clock, c1910, 9in (23cm) high.
£190–220
$275–350 ↗ RSch

Novelty Clocks

Novelty clocks are very varied, with many examples being produced as 'one-offs', and many are mechanical curiosities. Movements should be original and in good working order, as badly restored movements can reduce the value of a clock. The rarity value of novelty clocks makes them particularly popular with collectors.

◄ **A cast-bronze novelty shelf clock,** with exposed movement, c1890, 7in (18cm) high.
£110–130
$160–190 ↗ RSch

A Gem Damaskeene Razor advertising clock, by Gem Cutlery & Co, New York, c1930, 37in (94cm) high.
£1,300–1,650
$1,900–2,400 ↗ RSch

A 'Gambler' cabinet clock, the pressed poplar case with dice cup and poker chips, each side with a domino and Queen of Hearts playing card, c1920, 13½in (34cm) high.
£250–300
$360–440 ↗ RSch

An Ever Ready Safety Razor advertising clock, worn, c1930.
£260–300
$380–440 ↗ RSch

Electric Clocks

The focused study of electric clocks in the United Kingdom began when the specialist Electrical Group of the Antiquarian Horological Society was founded some 20 years ago. Increasing documentation and awareness of potential interest has resulted in steadily rising prices. Fifteen years ago examples of the Eureka clock could be bought for £20–30 ($30–45). Similarly Bulle clocks, first patented in England during 1922, realized only a few pounds. It is now common for Eureka clocks to reach and surpass the £1,000 ($1,500) mark, and Bulle examples to reach at least £100 ($145).

The Eureka is one of the most collectable electric clocks with many examples appearing regularly in the saleroom. Made by the Eureka Clock Company Limited between 1909 and 1914, the clock has many case styles, from those with a circular wooden base to house the battery and a glass dome to cover the movement, to those with the movement completely hidden away from view. Quality and style of case will affect the price; examples with fully visible movements generally fetch the highest prices and, according to Rita Shenton, a specialist in this field, are inevitably well above £1,000 ($1,500), whereas an example in a wooden case with the movement hidden will be worth less than half that figure.

Electric clocks tend to appeal more to people with an interest in the technical side of horology rather than the more decorative aspect of clocks, so it is important that the mechanism can be seen. Examples of high-quality Eureka clocks with clearly visible movements now sell at auction for between £1,000–1,500 ($1,500–2,150).

Alexander Bain (1811–77) is often referred to as the father of electrical horology. Bain took out a patent in 1841 and produced a number of clocks which occasionally appear on the open market but today tend to be museum pieces. Matthaus Hipp of Neuchâtel (1813–93) devised the Hipp Toggle (see page 274), a system used in a number of clocks from the late 19th century through to the 1970s, both here and on the Continent. Bain and Hipp pioneered the concept of using a master clock to drive a series of slave clocks, which could be sited around a town, factory or various other institutions. Master clocks have been under-appreciated in the past because of the noise some make, their great size, or possibly the utilitarian look of the majority of cases. In the UK, the most successful master clockmakers were the Synchronome Company, Gents of Leicester and Gillett & Johnston, examples of whose work are commonly found. Prices fall in the region of £200 ($290) to £900 ($1,300), depending, as with other electric clocks, on their date and the type of case. A few devotees are now turning their attention to the synchronous clocks which ran off the mains, dating from the 1930s. According to Rita Shenton, these are now available for a few pounds – who knows what price they will fetch in another ten years?

► **A battery-powered pendulum clock,** by Frank Holden, the 3½in (9cm) silvered chapter ring signed Apollo Patent, with visible hour wheel, the ratchet and pawl movement with 'free' pendulum oscillating over a permanent magnet with pivoted trailer contact, 1909, 11½in (29cm) high.
£1,650–2,200
$2,400–3,200 ✗ S

An oak electric mantel timepiece, the enamel dial signed The Brush Co Ltd, Loughborough, the case applied with pierced brass, on ball-and-paw feet, c1920, 19in (48cm) high.
£550–650
$800–950 ✗ P

◄ **A Bentleys Patent electric earth-driven mahogany longcase clock,** with 12in (30.5cm) annular silvered dial and seconds dial, the visible movement with shaped pierced plates, patent No. 19033/10, signed for John Dyson & Sons, Leeds, with a brass pendulum mounted with a coil oscillating over a fixed magnet, in a moulded glazed case with panelled plinth and optional mirror back, c1910, 84in (213.5cm) high.
£7,800–11,000
$11,300–16,000 ✗ S

► **A French electric mantel clock,** inscribed ATO, J. Bouyssou, Cahors, the movement with curved soft iron core pendulum oscillating between 2 coils, the electro-magnetic striking system mounted on the backplate, striking on a bell, c1920, 13½in (34cm) high.
£450–550
$700–800 ✗ CSK

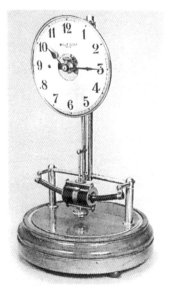

An electric mantel timepiece, the silvered dial signed Bulle Clock, France, the hollow solenoid pendulum bob arranged to pass over a fixed magnet, mounted above a mahogany base housing the battery, c1920, 15in (38cm) high, and a glass dome.
£500–800
$720–1,200 ⚹ DN

A mahogany electric table regulator, by Brillié Frères, with enamelled dial and sweep seconds hand, marble backboard, and fine threaded brass feet for accurate levelling, c1920, 19in (48.5cm) high.
£3,000–3,500
$4,400–5,000 ⊞ DHa

A massive gilt-brass electric table clock, the enamel cut-out dial signed Electrique Brillié, with sweep seconds hand, c1920, 22in (56cm) high.
£8,500–9,500
$12,300–13,800 ⊞ DHa

A Bulle electric clock, with cut crystal glass dome and ebony base, c1920, 13in (33cm) high.
£900–1,000
$1,300–1,500 ⊞ OFT

An electric mantel clock, by Favre-Bulle, in a glass and brass stylized trapezoid case, glass possibly Lalique, illuminated by 2 lamps to the interior, with conventional Bulle movement, c1925, 14in (35.5cm) high.
£3,500–4,500
$5,000–6,500 ⊞ DHa

A gilded brass four-glass electric table regulator, by Bardon of Clichy, Paris, the pendulum carrying a horseshoe magnet passing over a coil in the base of the case, switched in the manner of Brillié, c1925, 13in (33cm) high.
£2,500–2,750
$3,600–4,000 ⊞ DHa

▶ **An electro-magnetically controlled mantel clock,** signed on the rear plate C. Detouche, 228 rue St Martin, retailed by Peyrot of St Etienne, using an escapement mechanism devised by Robert Houdin, No. 6536, c1855, 16in (40.5cm) high, on an ebonized base.
£25,000–30,000
$36,250–43,500 ⊞ DHa

◀ **A Bulle electric clock,** the skeletonized silvered dial with retailer's signature for Jean Block, Lille, the arched mahogany case with swag inlay, c1935, 9¾in (25cm) high.
£200–300
$290–500 ⚹ S

A Eureka mantel timepiece, the enamel chapter ring with visible balance signed and numbered 5123, the mahogany crossbanded balloon-shaped case with inlaid shell medallion, c1912, 14in (35.5cm) high.
£600–900
$870–1,300 ⚒ P

A Eureka gilt four-glass mantel clock, the electro-magnetically maintained compensated balance visible below the dial, in a Madelaine-style case, c1909, 13½in (34.5cm) high.
£1,600–1,800
$2,300–2,600 ⊞ OFT

A Eureka mahogany wall clock, with short movement, London, c1909, 16in (40.5cm) diam.
£750–850 $1,100–1,250 ⊞ OFT

A Eureka four-glass mantel clock, with short movement, in a mahogany case, c1909, 11½in (29cm) high.
£900–1,100
$1,300–1,600 ⊞ OFT

◄ **A Eureka four-glass mantel clock,** with subsidiary seconds dial, c1909, 12in (30.5cm) high.
£1,450–1,600
$2,100–2,300 ⊞ OFT

An ATO regulator-style electric wall clock, by Leon Hatot, Paris, with subsidiary seconds dial, c1900.
£500–600
$720–870 ⊞ OFT

A gilt-brass and marble four-glass electric mantel clock, by Frank Holden, the pendulum carrying a fine coil alternately switched as it passes through the air gaps in horseshoe magnets, No. 14873, UK patent 1909, 12in (30.5cm) high.
£2,500–2,750
$3,600–4,000 ⊞ DHa

A gilt-brass and marble four-glass electric clock, by Frank Holden, No. 274373, with sweep seconds hand, electrically maintained balance visible below the dial, c1925, 10in (25.5cm) high.
£2,750–3,250
$4,000–4,700 ⊞ DHa

A gilt-brass electric clock, by Frank Holden, the dial marked Regina, on a mahogany base and with glass dome, c1908.
£1,800–2,000
$2,600–2,900 ⊞ OFT

▶ A synchronous electric automaton mantel timepiece, with glazed aperture revealing the automaton ship gently rolling against a constantly changing sky, in a pale green Bakelite case, the reverse signed Vitascope Ltd, c1940, 12½in (32cm) high.
£450–550
$690–800 🔨 S

An electric mystery timepiece, signed Jaeger-LeCoultre, chrome base concealing the 110 volt motor, c1940, 9in (23cm) high.
£1,800–2,000 $2,600–2,900 🔨 S

A gilded brass mantel clock, by Ch. Mildé & Fils, rue St Honoré, Paris, using an electro-magnetically powered movement with constant force, to the design of W. E. Newton and Ch. Mildé, No. 2339, UK patent 1870, 18in (45.5cm) high.
£20,000–25,000
$29,000–36,000 ⊞ DHa

▶ An electric mantel clock, by Matthaus Hipp of Neuchâtel, with silvered dial and gilt-brass supports for the movement, with Hipp Toggle visible below the dial, 1869, 19in (48cm) high.
£20,000–25,000
$29,000–36,000 ⊞ DHa

The Hipp Toggle

Dr Matthaus Hipp of Neuchâtel (1813–93) invented a 'toggle' or trailer attached to the pendulum of a clock, which passes over a notched block of steel until the swing falls below a pre-determined arc. The toggle is caught in the notch, depressing the block and closing the circuit, resulting in the pendulum being given a fresh impulse from the electro-magnet.

◀ A nickel-plated and mahogany electric clock, by Herbert Scott, with mirror back, c1910, 15in (38cm) high.
£2,000–2,500
$2,900–3,600 ⊞ OFT

Miscellaneous Clocks

A gilt-metal and wood strut timepiece, by Baudin Frères, Geneva, with cylinder escapement, gilt-metal signed cuvette, 19thC, 8in (20.5cm) high, in original velvet-lined tortoiseshell box.
£750–850
$1,100–1,250 ⚒ S

A gilt-metal strut timepiece, the dial inscribed Finnigans, c1900, 5in (13cm) high.
£1,000–1,250
$1,500–1,800 ⚒ P

A gilt-metal strut timepiece, by Thomas Cole, with silvered dial engraved with fruit and scrolls, retailers Tessier & Son, the case engraved and numbered 971, 19thC, 6in (15cm) high.
£1,900–2,250 $2,750–3,250 ⚒ GSP

Strut Clocks

The strut clock is a distinctive variation on the carriage clock, taking its name from the folding brass strut mounted on the backplate. When extended, the strut holds the clock upright at a slight angle. Many also have a swivelling foot mounted on the bottom of the case. They were probably designed to be used as travelling clocks and many still have their original leather travelling cases.

Strut clocks are all spring-driven, with a going barrel, rather than a fusee movement. Almost all are timepieces, although a few strike the hours. Many are of 30-hour duration, but those in larger and more expensive cases are usually of 8-day duration.

A gilt-brass strut timepiece, in the manner of Thomas Cole, 19thC, 8in (20.5cm) high.
£3,100–3,750
$4,500–5,400 ⚒ P

A gilt-brass strut timepiece, the 3 segments containing the movement, a thermometer, and a manual calendar, c1860, 6in (15cm) high.
£2,500–3,100
$3,600–4,500 ⚒ P

Black Forest Clocks

A Black Forest carved beech cuckoo clock, the 5in (12.5cm) chapter ring with carved bone hands, 8-day 2 train fusee movement, gong striking and sounding a cuckoo at the hour, the carved case applied with a fruiting vine and a bird, the backboard with label for Camerer Kuss & Co, c1865, 18in (45.5cm) high.
£1,900–2,500
$2,750–3,600 ⚒ S

A Black Forest marquetry cuckoo mantel clock, the 6in (15cm) dial with bone numerals and hands, the wooden plated fusee movement with outside countwheel, the case surmounted by a carved eagle above the cuckoo doors, with foliate carved decoration and geometric marquetry base, c1880, 26in (66cm) high.
£1,050–1,250
$1,500–1,800 ⚒ S(S)

A Black Forest walnut cuckoo and quail table clock, with 5½in (14cm) dial signed for Camerer Kuss & Co, with carved bone hands, 3 train fusee movement with wood plates and 3 bellows connected to the articulated wood birds, the chalet case profusely decorated with carved vine leaves, c1875, 23½in (59.5cm) high.
£1,500–2,100
$2,170–3,000 ⚒ S

Black Forest Clocks

Clock making began in the Black Forest region of Germany in the 17thC. The majority of Black Forest clocks were made to hang on a wall, for the simple reason that there were no chimneypieces in Germany. The clocks were rarely signed on the dial, unless by a retailer, but the maker's name sometimes appears on the back or on one of the side doors.

Nearly all Black Forest clocks are weight-driven and of 30-hour duration. From the late 18th century most were fitted with an anchor escapement, with a long pendulum, and usually have a painted wood shield dial.

Cuckoo clocks were made from c1850 until WWII and were designed with a gabled roof and back flap to allow access to the movement. Cuckoos were of painted wood, the finest having moveable wings and beaks. The twin bellows above the plates, which produce the 'cuckoo' sound, were originally made of chicken skin. As this can wear out easily, it has often been replaced, with no effect on the value of the clock.

A Black Forest carved beech musical cuckoo clock, with a 7in (18cm) dial, 3 train brass-plated weight-driven gong striking movement operating the cuckoo bellows and a 2 tune, 2¼in (6cm) cylinder mechanism playing every hour, a pair of doors above the dial opening to reveal the cuckoo and a seated musician, slight damage, c1890, 34½in (87.5cm) high.
£1,900–2,500
$2,750–3,600 ⚒ S

A Black Forest carved wall clock, the brass movement striking the hours on a gong, discharging an organ playing on 9 brass pipes, and a four-air musical box, 19thC, 83in (211cm) high.
£9,400–11,250
$13,600–16,300 ⚒ P

LOCATE THE SOURCE
The source of each illustration in Miller's can be found by checking the code letters below each caption with the Key to Illustrations, pages 6–7.

A Black Forest cuckoo clock, the 5½in (14cm) dial with carved bone hands, 2 train weight-driven brass-plated movement skeletonized in the form of a lyre, the leaf-carved chalet case surmounted by a stag's head, c1890, 27½in (70cm) high.
£950–1,200
$1,400–2,000 ⚒ S

A Black Forest cuckoo clock, the case of typical form with a cuckoo for the quarters and a trumpeter below for the hours, the movement stamped GHS, with anchor escapement, 19thC, 27in (68.5cm) high.
£1,900–2,250
$1,400–3,250 ⚒ P

◀ A Black Forest stained beech cuckoo wall clock, with a 6¾in (17cm) dial, 3 train brass-plated weight-driven movement stamped DRP No 219355, striking the quarters on 4 rod gongs with a further gong and cuckoo for the hour, the leaf-carved chalet case with stag's head cresting, a pair of nesting birds below and a door opening to reveal the cuckoo, c1900, 33½in (85cm) high.
£1,100–1,500
$1,600–2,500 ⚒ S

A Black Forest trumpeter clock, the 5½in (14cm) dial with bone hands, the 2 train wooden posted movement operating the trumpeter every hour, the bellows and 3 trumpets mounted above the movement, the Gothic case with fretted side doors and carved base, a door below the dial opening to reveal the bugle player, c1890, 25in (63.5cm) high.
£1,900–2,500
$1,400–3,600 ⚒ S(S)

A Black Forest cuckoo clock, the weight-driven movement with 2 bellows and striking on a gong, the cresting in the form of a stag's head with crossed sporting guns, late 19thC, 51in (130.5cm) high.
£1,600–2,000
$2,300–2,900 ⚒ **Bea**

A Black Forest rosewood cuckoo clock, the white enamel dial with gold-painted Roman numerals, wood frame movement with twin bellows and strike on gong to back door, the gabled case with carved fleur-de-lys cornice, with a painted scene of a youth smoking a pipe at a window, 19thC, 13½in (34.5cm) high.
£800–900
$1,100–1,300 ⚒ **CSK**

A Black Forest walnut cuckoo clock, the off-white painted Arabic dial with pierced steel hands, retailer's label on back for Camerer Kuss & Co, wood frame and brass wheelwork movement with twin bellows and strike on gong to the back door, the case with gabled, tiled roof and chimney, mirrored windows, 19thC, 21in (53.5cm) high.
£1,050–1,500
$1,500–2,200 ⚒ **CSK**

▶ **A Black Forest carved walnut musical cuckoo clock,** the dial with ebonized chapter ring and white enamel Roman numerals, turned centre and pierced bone hands, the metal frame movement with twin bellows to one side, 3in (7.5cm) pin barrel musical movement to the other, 19thC, 47½in (120.5cm) high.
£2,500–3,500
$3,600–5,000 ⚒ **CSK**

A Black Forest carved walnut cuckoo clock, the dial with ebonized chapter ring applied with bone Arabic numerals, turned centre and carved bone hands, the brass frame movement with bellows to each side and strike on gong to the back door, carved oak leaf pendulum, the case flanked by carved hanging models of a hare and a pheasant, the bezel formed as a hunting horn, 19thC, 55½in (141cm) high.
£1,250–1,900
$1,800–3,000 ⚒ **CSK**

A Black Forest carved beech cuckoo mantel clock, the 6½in (16.5cm) chapter with applied Roman numerals and decorated centre, the twin fusee wood posted movement sounding on a single cuckoo and gong coil, the cuckoo's doors missing, c1840, 23¾in (60.5cm) high.
£900–1,000
$1,300–2,000 ⚒ **Bon**

◀ **A Black Forest carved beech cuckoo mantel clock,** the 5½in (14cm) chapter with applied Roman numerals, the wooden posted twin fusee movement sounding on a cuckoo and wire gong at the hour, c1840, 17¾in (45cm) high.
£650–800
$950–1,100 ⚒ **Bon**

Desk & Table Clocks

A French table clock, with 8-day duration, c1890, 5½in (14cm) high.
£200–300 $290–440 ⊞ SO

A Germanic striking table clock, the gilt movement signed Kriedel, London, with foliate pierced and chased footed lock, chain fusee movement, resting barrel for the bell in the hinged base, pull wind alarm from central disc in silver *champlevé* arcaded dial, blued steel hour hand and later minute hand, c1700, dial 4in (10cm) diam.
£5,000–6,250 $7,250–9,000 🔨 CSK

A French equestrian clock, with 8-day striking silk suspension movement, mounted with bronze anthemion and leaf decorated corners, a floral border and scrolled bronze feet, mid-19thC, 23in (58.5cm) high.
£2,500–3,100 $3,600–4,500 🔨 B

A brass alarm clock, with stainless steel surround, c1900, 4in (10cm) diam.
£300–400 $440–580 ⊞ SBA

A Napoleon III parcel-gilt bronze souvenir Eiffel Tower clock, the backplate with stamp for Japy Frères, No. 10005, the going barrel movement with anchor escapement, crutch piece, bell and hammer missing, 43½in (110.5cm) high.
£2,100–2,500 $3,000–3,600 🔨 C

An inlaid mahogany miniature longcase clock, with 2in (5cm) dial, with replaced platform escapement, the case with inlaid paterae, c1900, 12in (30.5cm) high.
£550–750 $800–1,100 🔨 S(S)

◄ **A brass carriage or desk clock,** by Howell & Jones, c1875, 7in (18cm) high.
£850–950 $1,250–1,400 ⊞ RFA
This clock was given by Benjamin Disraeli to his private secretary, Sir Charles Wilson, who later became the President of the Grand Trunk Railway of Canada.

► **A French industrial automaton boiler clock,** with 2½in (6.5cm) silvered dial, 8-day movement No. 2230, with platform cylinder escapement, inset with an aneroid barometer and applied with a thermometer, separate mechanism causing the governor to revolve above, on a black marble plinth, c1880, 14in (35.5cm) high.
£1,250–1,900 $1,800–2,700 🔨 S

Automaton, Novelty & Mystery Clocks

A French automaton clock in the form of the stern of a ship, the 2 train movement striking on a gong bearing the stamp of S. Marti et Cie, and Medaille d'Or GLT Brt. SGDG Paris, c1880, 11½in (29cm) high.
£6,000–7,000
$8,700–10,200 ⊞ DRA

A Swiss automaton mantel clock, with enamel dial for bridge cock verge movement, with going barrel and 2 bellows, 19thC, 9in (23cm) high.
£3,300–3,700
$4,800–5,500 ⚒ C

A French novelty alarm timepiece, the spelter case in the form of a bearded old man with an articulated arm, inset with a pink enamel dial, on a stepped platform, striker plate missing, c1870, 10in (25.5cm) high.
£800–1,000
$1,150–1,500 ⚒ CSK

A walnut automaton organ clock, the doors below opening to reveal 2 military trumpeters, playing on 8 pipes every hour, the 3 train movement striking on a gong, anchor escapement, 19thC, 30½in (77.5cm) high.
£2,400–2,900
$3,500–4,200 ⚒ P

A French ship's quarterdeck automaton mantel clock, with gong striking Guilmet movement No. 2195, connected to the rocking helmsman above, case set with a compass and a mariner on the lower deck with a coil of rope, helmsman replaced, c1889, 12in (30.5cm) high.
£4,600–6,400
$6,650–9,300 ⚒ S

A French bronzed spelter mystery clock, the revolving movement contained in a black painted sphere applied with Roman numerals, suspended from 3 chains hanging from an elaborate suspension held by a cast figure of a girl, the upper pinion extended to engage with a fixed rod causing the movement to revolve, arm cracked, c1880, 27½in (70cm) high.
£6,400–7,300
$9,300–10,600 ⚒ S

A Continental spelter mystery timepiece, the movement forming the upper part of the pendulum, supported by a cast figure of a kangaroo, 19thC, 12½in (32cm) high.
£900–1,100
$1,300–1,600 ⚒ P

A French automaton windmill timepiece, with 2 thermometers and aneroid barometer in a naturalistic gun metal case, with revolving sails, 19thC, 17in (43cm) high.
£2,300–2,750
$3,350–4,000 ⚒ GSP

A French falling-ball gravity clock, with 7in (18cm) dial, the movement with Brocot escapement, the driving power produced by a supply of steel balls fed on to a large paddlewheel by an endless chain, driven by a concealed spring barrel movement, the gilt-brass frame with a thermometer and an aneroid barometer, c1890, with a later ebonized base and cracked glass dome, 22½in (57cm) high.
£15,500–18,300
22,500–26,500 🪝 S

A German stained beech talking table clock, the 4½in (11.5cm) Arabic chapter ring set on a gilt surround stamped DRP, signed Henry Rüttimann, Watchmaker, Lucerne, Switzerland, the 8-day movement by Gustav Becker, No. 2225739, with pin pallet escapement attached to the large talking mechanism, film record broken, c1915, 16in (40.5cm) high.
£2,550–3,650
$3,700–5,300 🪝 S

An Austrian giltwood musical wall clock, with 6½in (16.5cm) enamel dial, 8-day spring barrel movement with circular plates, anchor escapement, silk suspension, sunburst pendulum and gong striking, a hand-operated 2 tune musical mechanism below, with 2in (5cm) pinned cylinder plucking a comb, comprising 18 separate screwed sections, in a giltwood picture frame case with egg-and-dart moulded border surmounted by a carved eagle, c1830, 19½in (49.5cm) high.
£2,200–3,100
$3,200–4,500 🪝 S

Automaton, Mystery & Novelty Clocks

The variety of novelty clocks is almost endless. Their appeal is mainly derived from their working features rather than the clock mechanism. All clocks should be in good mechanical condition – automaton figures are most vulnerable to damage.

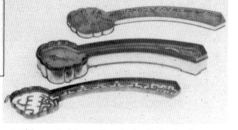

A Chinese Paktong fire clock, the body of copper, the interior with a brass incense tray, 19thC, 11½in (29cm) wide.
£900–1,100 $1,300–1,600 🪝 C
The shape of this type of fire clock derives from the sacred fungus, *ling-chih,* one of the Taoist emblems of longevity. It has been suggested that these clocks were used in Taoist and Buddhist temples to measure intervals between the striking of the prayer wheel.

An organ clock, attributed to George Ryke, London, the brass dial set in a cartouche flanked by Diana and Mercury, 2 subsidiary dials above for tune selection and lock/unlock for music, the timepiece fusee movement with verge escapement and a separate fusee organ movement driving a pinned wood barrel operating 15 valves and 44 pipes with 3 stops playing a choice of 9 tunes, c1750, 20in (51cm) high.
£50,000–60,000
$72,500–87,000 ⊞ PAO

A French gilt-brass mantel clock, the movement with countwheel strike section on a bell, 17in (43cm) high.
£800–1,100
$1,150–1,600 🪝 CSK

A brass Congreve rolling ball clock, the skeletonized movement with dials for the hours, minutes and seconds, the base signed for Dent, London, 19in (48.5cm) wide.
£3,650–4,600
$5,300–6,700 🪝 P

◄ **A gravity clock,** by Kee Less Clock Co, with 30-hour duration, c1900, 10½in (26.5cm) high.
£400–500
$580–720 ⊞ **SO**

► **A Victorian nightlight clock,** with glass shade, on alabaster and brass pillar, 9½in (24cm) high.
400–500
$580–720 ⚒ **McC**

A brass-cased novelty clock, the case in the form of a ship's bridge telegraph, engraved with the lever positions, on a pedestal base and wood plinth, replacement movement by Westclox, c1900, 11½in (29cm) high.
£550–750
$800–1,100 ⚒ **S(S)**

A silver digital flick clock, the hours and minutes indicated by rotating cards, the 8-day movement with platform lever escapement, the case with hammered finish, hallmarked Birmingham 1905, 7in (18cm) high.
£1,100–1,700
$1,600–2,500 ⚒ **S(S)**

A Georgian gilt-metal timepiece, the verge movement with engraved tapered plate signed Thomas Greenstreet fecit, the signed 24-hour dial with movable centre disc engraved with 24 cities around the world, held aloft by Father Time, 7½in (19cm) high.
£2,200–2,800
$3,200–4,000 ⚒ **P**

A French musical picture clock, the 8-day gong striking movement by Raingo Frères, with anchor escapement, releasing the independent musical movement on the hour, playing a tune on a pinned cylinder and a 71-tyne comb, c1840, 23 x 28in (58.5 x 71cm).
£4,600–5,500
$6,600–8,000 ⚒ **S**

A silver digital flick clock, the 8-day movement with platform lever escapement, hallmarked Birmingham 1905, 7in (18cm) high.
£3,650–5,050
$5,300–7,300 ⚒ **S(S)**

◄ **A *tôle peinte* Schwartzwald clockmaker figure,** naturalistically painted, carrying a timepiece in front, and a dummy one containing the key on his back, on a simulated maple base, late 19thC, 15in (38cm) high.
£3,650–5,500
$5,300–8,000 ⚒ **C(Am)**

► **A French ormolu and bronze globe clock,** depicting The Three Graces, with enamelled dial supported on a concave-sided Carrara marble base, c1880, 29in (73.5cm) high, on a composition and marble stand, 35½in (90cm) high.
£6,400–7,300
$9,300–10,600 ⚒ **C**

Decorative Arts

A Lalique clock, the Swiss 8-day movement set in a milky blue panel with naked female figures, in an onyx and malachite frame, marked Lalique in capitals, 5in (12.5cm) wide.
£1,900–2,500
$2,700–3,600 ➶ GSP

A Foley Intarsio earthenware timepiece, designed by Frederick Rhead, inscribed 'Carpe Diem, Dies and Nox', printed marks, 3160, Rd. No. 349574, c1900, 11in (28cm) high.
£1,500–1,750 $2,200–2,500 ➶ P

A Burmantofts Egyptianesque timepiece, showing yellow through a rich blood-red glaze, impresssed Burmantofts Faïence, No. F1434, c1880, 13½in (34.5cm) high.
£300–450
$440–650 ➶ P

A Lalique frosted glass clock, 'Sirènes', moulded with floating water nymphs, moulded mark R. Lalique, 11in (28cm) high.
£3,100–3,750 $4,500–5,400 ➶ Bon

A Lalique opalescent glass clock, 'Deux Colombes', the glass face surmounted by a pair of doves perched on flowering prunus branches, moulded mark R. Lalique, France, 9in (23cm) high.
£2,750–3,100
$4,000–4,500 ➶ Bon

A Lalique clear and frosted clock-luminaire, 'Deux Figurines', the bronze base enclosing the lighting fitment, wheelcut R. Lalique, France, 15in (38cm) high.
£5,000–6,900 $7,250–10,000 ➶ Bon

A Lalique opalescent glass clock, 'Inseparables', moulded mark R. Lalique, engraved France No. 760, 4½in (11.5cm) high.
£2,500–3,100 $3,600–4,500 ➶ Bon

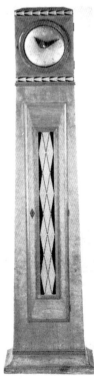

A Lalique frosted glass clock, moulded mark R. Lalique, 6in (15cm) high.
£1,600–2,000
$2,300–2,900 ➶ Bon

A Liberty & Co pewter timepiece, designed by Archibald Knox, with copper coloured numerals and red enamelled berry forms against shaded blue and green enamelling, stamped on the base English Pewter 0609, Made in England, and Rd. 468016, 8in (20.5cm) high.
£2,500–3,100
$3,600–4,500 ➶ P

An Arts and Crafts brass clock, with chased Celtic motifs on the face, pendulum and weights, with simple Black Forest movement, c1900, 15in (38cm) high.
£250–400
$360–580 ⊞ STW

◄ **A Secessionist walnut longcase clock,** inlaid with ebony and ivory, the movement by Gustav Becker, 77½in (197cm) high.
£1,200–1,500
$1,750–2,200 ➶ P

A Liberty & Co silver-cased mantel clock, early 20thC.
£2,500–3,100 $3,600–4,500 ✗ SWO

A Liberty & Co pewter and enamel clock, marked with Tudric and impressed number, c1900.
£1,250–1,600
$1,800–2,300 ⊞ ASA

A Liberty & Co pewter clock, with enamelled copper dial and black enamel Roman numerals, flanked by shaped columns, stamped marks Tudric, English Pewter, Liberty & Co, 0761, 8½in (21.5cm) high.
£1,250–1,900
$1,800–3,000 ✗ C

A Liberty & Co hammered pewter clock, decorated with stylized tree and foliate panels, the copper clock face with turquoise enamel centre and black enamel Roman numerals, stamped 01154, English Pewter, 7in (18cm) high.
£1,000–1,500
$1,500–2,200 ✗ C

A Liberty & Co pewter and enamelled clock, embossed with a stylized leafy tree, the blue/green enamelled clock face with Roman numerals, the door on the reverse with a pierced tree, stamped marks, Made in England, Tudric, c1900, 13in (33cm) high.
£3,100–3,750
$4,500–5,400 ✗ S(C)

A Liberty & Co pewter timepiece, the design influenced by C. F. A. Voysey, impressed Tudric 0101, 13½in (34.5cm) high.
£2,500–3,750 $3,600–5,400 ✗ P

A silver clock, inscribed on the bezel St Moritz 1900, hallmarked, c1891, 5in (12.5cm) high.
£600–650 $870–1,000 ⊞ RFA

A Tiffany & Co clock, the face set in a thin section of lapis lazuli, mounted in a gold coloured and enamelled bezel, the face signed Tiffany & Co, etched to the base VAN 19539, 4½in (11.5cm) high.
£950–1,250
$1,400–1,800 ✗ P

A Gouda earthenware clock case, c1923, 16½in (42cm) high.
£400–500
$600–900 ✗ PCh

A walnut hooded wall clock,
by Christopher Gould, London,
c1685, 11½in (29.5cm) high.
£6,250–8,750
$9,000–12,700 ⚒ S

A German silvered repoussé metal
telleruhr, by Johann Georg Mayr,
Munich, c1675, 16½in (42cm) high.
£6,900–8,750
$10,000–12,700 ⚒ S

**A South German repoussé gilt-
metal *telleruhr,*** by Marcus Bohm,
c1710, 13½in (34.5cm) high.
£5,600–7,500 $8,100–11,000 ⚒ S

**A South German repoussé
silvered brass *telleruhr,***
c1730, 16in (40.5cm) high.
£1,900–2,500
$2,750–3,600 ⚒ S

A Friesian *stoelklok,*
early 18thC,
26in (66cm) high.
£1,250–1,900
$1,800–3,000 ⚒ S

A Friesian *stoelklok,*
with Dutch striking
movement, c1790,
30in (76cm) high.
£1,750–2,250
$2,500–3,250 ⚒ S

A Dutch oak *staartklok,* c1850,
41in (104cm) high.
£1,000–1,500 $1,500–2,200 ⚒ S

**A French provincial *Comtoise* or
Morbier wall clock,** the enamel
dial signed Jn Pre Fleury à Gap, the
weight-driven movement with
verge escapement and double hour
striking, c1820, 15in (38cm) high.
£500–750
$720–1,100 ⚒ S

**A French provincial *Comtoise* or
Morbier wall clock,** the enamel dial
signed Ferrier à Cousance, the 3 train,
weight-driven movement with verge
escapement, quarter striking on 4 bells,
c1820, 17¾in (45cm) high.
£2,500–3,750
$3,600–5,400 ⚒ S

**An Austrian painted and giltwood
wall clock,** with enamel dial, quarter
striking, c1820, 30in (76cm) high.
£2,500–3,750
$3,600–5,400 ⚒ S

A Maltese wall timepiece, with colourful wooden dial and case, with alarm, 30-hour weight-driven movement, early 19thC, 35in (89cm) high.
£3,750–4,400
$5,400–6,400 ➤ S

An Austrian simulated rosewood calendar wall timepiece, c1870, 45in (114.5cm) high.
£2,500–3,750
$3,600–5,400 ➤ S

An Austrian quarter striking automaton picture clock, oil on metal, c1830, 32 x 37in (81.5 x 94cm).
£6,900–8,750
$10,000–12,700 ➤ S

A French picture clock, by Giteau, Paris, oil on canvas, with separate two-tune musical mechanism, 25 x 31in (63.5 x 78.5cm).
£2,500–3,100
$3,600–4,500 ➤ S

A German walnut digital dial wall timepiece, c1900, 38in (96.5cm) high.
£1,500–2,250
$2,200–3,300 ➤ S

◄ **A French brass and bronze wall clock,** with enamel dial, surmounted by a bell, c1890, 36in (91.5cm) high.
£1,900–2,500
$2,750–3,600 ➤ S

A French picture timepiece, the 1¼in (3cm) enamel dial with Roman numerals, square gong striking movement, mid-19thC, 10 x 9in (25.5 x 23cm).
£1,000–1,100
$1,500–1,600 ➤ Bon

A Viennese *verre églomisé* picture clock, the chapter ring with black Roman chapters painted on gilt cartouche with conjoining acorn decoration, the white-painted hands revolving behind the glass chapter ring, 4 pillar going barrel movement with anchor escapement and strike on gong, the glazed frame painted with oak leaves and acorns on a white ground, c1850, 37 x 32¾in (94 x 83cm).
£2,500–3,100
$3,600–4,500 ➤ C

A French mother-of-pearl wall clock, c1860, 40in (101.5cm) high.
£1,500–2,250
$2,200–3,300 ➤ S

► **A Swiss plate-glass mystery wall timepiece,** c1920, 24in (61cm) high.
£3,100–3,700
$4,500–5,400 ➤ S

Barometers

Antique barometers have a duel fascination 'for a collector': not only are they accurate scientific instruments that can foretell the changing weather patterns when read correctly, but they are also a record of the changing styles in English furniture and are elegant items in themselves.

From their invention in the late 17th century to about 1770, barometers were made in very limited numbers, mainly for clients who could afford such a luxury and who commissioned the few makers to supply an instrument that would be as accurate as possible and simple in design. Consequently, the vast majority of barometers up to 1770 are stick barometers, where the column of mercury to register the reading and changes in pressure was mounted in a simple case with an engraved or even paper scale.

The very first barometers were made by famous English clockmakers such as Daniel Quare, and in recent years such rare items have reached unprecedented prices of between £50,000 ($72,500) and £80,000 ($116,000). The main problem with this type of instrument is that copies were made at different periods, even in the 1950s, so it is vital that advice from a good specialist should be taken if such barometers become available on the market.

The early 18th century was a period when oak furniture was still in vogue, but oddly enough it is difficult to find good and original early oak stick barometers that will fit in with an oak collection. Some were made with an oak carcass and veneered in walnut, and today would be valued at £10,000–£15,000 ($14,500–21,500) if the colour and patina is of sufficient quality.

It is virtually impossible to offer an oak collector a good wheel barometer that fits in with oak furniture. The earliest wheel barometers cover a period from 1770 to 1800. After 1800 they became more mass-produced, so the difference in prices, even in a short period of 30 years, is considerable. Good early inlaid mahogany wheel barometers are reaching higher prices of £2,000–£3,500 ($2,900–5,000), and are leaving the slightly later examples far behind and a little stagnant at about £1,000 ($1,500) or just under. This is purely an example of supply and demand.

The finest wheel barometers will continue to out-grow their later examples, as they were made by the finest craftsmen who employed the best engravers and cabinetmakers. The collector of fine English furniture has a vast selection from which to choose a barometer to complement any setting. Some of the best examples and instruments with fine inlays were made in Scotland. Barometers by Knie and Adie of Edinburgh do come on the market, but undoubtedly the finest maker was John Russell of Falkirk, Clockmaker to the Prince of Wales. Russell wheel barometers have recently reached prices in excess of £75,000 ($108,000). Stick barometers by this eminent maker also command premium prices of upwards of £20,000 ($29,000).

During the first part of the 19th century, English furniture was at its peak, both in quality and quantity. Easier distribution enabled country towns and market towns to receive deliveries from London manufacturers, and this is noticeable in barometers, as there was a considerable expansion in the availability of instruments from retailers throughout the country. Businesses sprang up in places such as Whitby, Chester and even Penzance. Barometers and clocks were hardly a luxury item by this time. Every village and small town was somewhat isolated, without today's comforts, and therefore a clock that kept good time and a barometer that gave a good indication of the weather were an essential part of most households.

Most of the normally priced barometers costing £500–£850 ($750–1,200) today are examples of instruments made during the period from 1830 to 1850. Although they might suffer in comparison with the smarter barometers of 50 years earlier, when situated on their own in and amongst other possessions they do indeed look elegant and give considerable pleasure, as well as doing the job they were made for.

Perhaps the most obvious example of change in the Victorian period was the influence of Admiral Fitzroy, a Victorian eccentric who developed a barometer with more information, accrued as a Naval Admiral, and which he extended when he became the first Meteorological Officer to the Board of Trade. Fitzroy Barometers were made under licence and continued to be popular long after his death in 1865. Fitzroy could be considered the father of our modern forecasting system. Today prices depend to some extent on the elaboration of the case, simple examples at about £500–£700 ($750–1,000), and more Gothic and carved barometer upwards of £850 ($1,200). As such they can be considered an interesting scientific barometer and a good investment in the longer term.

The aneroid barometer, which was invented in 1845, also became very popular as the 19th century progressed, some examples being very sought after today. They were made in vast quantities so it is possible to get such a barometer at a sensible price. In fact, the fun of collecting aneroids, whether they be small pocket barometers, or slightly larger and carved Victorian examples, is that they are readily available and relatively inexpensive. It is possible to build a collection of small items which do not take up much space, even over 100. Though this is a very brief résumé of the barometer as an item of furniture, it shows that there are many styles available to fit in with most tastes, the bonus being of course that provided they are restored by specialists and are in working order, they will carry out the function for which they were invented. If not actually replacing television and the weather forecast, at least they give more local indications of the expected changes in the weather – traditionally a pre-occupation of most inhabitants of the British Isles!　**Derek and Tina Rayment**

Stick Barometers

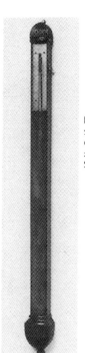

◄ **A mahogany bowfronted stick barometer,** by Adie, Edinburgh, with silvered scale, the case with reeded pediment and cistern cover, c1810, 41in (104cm) high.
£7,350–8,800
$10,600–12,000 ✦ Bea

► **A rosewood barometer,** signed Adie & Son, Edinburgh, c1830, 41½in (105.5cm) high.
£2,900–3,500
$4,200–5,000 ✦ S(S)

◄ **A mahogany crossbanded stick barometer,** the silvered scale signed Sharp, Faversham, 19thC, 38in (97cm) high.
£500–600
$720–870 ✦ P

A late Victorian carved oak stick barometer, signed E. W. Bachmann, Guernsey, with bone scales, twin verniers, trunk set with thermometer, carved pediment and cistern cover, 45in (114.5cm) high.
£750–900
$1,100–1,300 ✦ Bon

A mahogany stick barometer, by Baddely, Albrighton, with round top and hemispherical cistern cover, c1790.
£1,800–2,200
$2,600–3,200 ⊞ W&W

◄ **A walnut stick barometer,** by Bennett, London, with bone register plates, c1850.
£1,600–1,800
$2,300–2,600 ⊞ PAO

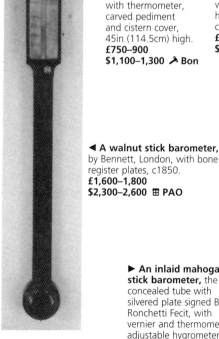

A Georgian mahogany stick barometer, by Thos. Blunt & Son, London, c1810.
£3,000–3,500
$4,400–5,000 ⊞ W&W

◄ **A French provincial stick barometer,** the polychrome pine board painted with a scale and flowers, the domed top inscribed Baromètre Simple, mercury tube replaced, late 18thC, 37in (94cm) high.
£1,200–1,500
$1,700–2,200 ✦ CSK

► **An inlaid mahogany stick barometer,** the concealed tube with silvered plate signed Bapst. Ronchetti Fecit, with vernier and thermometer, adjustable hygrometer above, the case with broken architectural pediment and urn finial, inlaid at the front with stars and bordered with ropetwist stringing, c1800, 46in (117cm) high.
£2,900–3,700
$4,200–5,400 ✦ S

◀ A mahogany barometer, inscribed Fraser, Bond Street, London, with silvered dial, c1800.
£1,300–1,800
$1,900–2,600 ⚒ WW

▶ A mahogany stick barometer, by D. Bolongaro, Manchester, c1820, 37½in (95cm) high.
£1,200–1,300
$1,750–1,900 ⚒ P(M)

◀ An ebony-veneered mercurial barometer, by Samuel Chave, Taunton, the ivory scales engraved and incorporating 2 setting verniers with a thermometer set into the front of the case, c1850.
£3,500–4,500
$5,000–6,500 ⊞ PAO

▶ A mahogany and ebony-strung bowfronted stick barometer, concealed tube with silvered plates and vernier signed Cary, London, inset at the front with thermometer, with urn cistern cover, c1820, 40in (101.5cm) high.
£4,400–5,900
$6,400–8,600 ⚒ S

A mahogany stick barometer, the ivory plates signed Chadburn Brothers, Sheffield, Registered Oct 14th 1851, No. 2980, No. 168, mercury thermometer, replaced cistern cover, c1855, 38in (96.5cm) high.
£300–500
$440–720 ⚒ S(S)

A mahogany stick barometer, the silvered plates signed Cary, 181 Strand, London, mid-19thC, 38½in (98cm) high.
£2,050–2,500
$3,000–3,600 ⚒ S(S)

◀ A stick barometer, with silvered register plates, by Cary, London, c1820, 37in (94cm) high.
£5,150–5,900
$7,500–8,500 ⚒ McC

A mahogany stick barometer, signed Cary, London, c1820.
£1,100–1,300
$1,600–1,900 ⚒ LT

A figured walnut stick barometer, by W. Cox, Devonport, with silvered dial plates, c1870.
£1,300–1,500
$1,900–2,200 ⊞ MGM

A carved oak stick barometer, by Chamberlain, London, c1865.
£2,000–2,400
$2,900–3,500 ⊞ W&W

A stick barometer, by Darcy of London, c1830.
£650–800
$870–1,150 ⊞ SO

◄ **A Regency mahogany bowfronted stick barometer,** with ogee top, glazed vernier scale signed G. & C. Dixey, London, with moulded ebonized cistern cover to shaped base, restored, 38½in (98cm) high.
£3,500–4,500
$5,000–6,500 ⚒ C

A Georgian mahogany stick barometer, with silvered and engraved dial marked Joseph Tory & Co, London.
£1,850–2,000
$2,700–3,000
⊞ MGM

A walnut stick barometer, with architectural top, silvered and engraved dial plates, by John Patrick, Old Bailey, London, 18thC.
£8,000–10,000
$11,500–14,500 ⊞ MGM

A Georgian mahogany stick barometer, the silvered brass plate signed J. Search, London, with brass cantilever fine adjustment, domed cistern cover, brass tap and rounded top, 38in (96.5cm) high.
£4,100–5,150
$6,000–7,500 ⚒ CSK

◄ **A mahogany stick barometer,** with silvered scale, early 19thC, 37in (94cm) high.
£1,500–1,750
$2,200–2,500 ⊞ SBA

A George III mahogany stick barometer, signed B. Cole, London, with vernier and thermometer, c1770, 44½in (113cm) high.
£3,700–5,150
$4,500–7,500 ⚒ S

► **A mahogany bowfronted stick barometer,** signed G. & C. Dixey, Opticians to the King, 3 New Bond St, London, bone scales, vernier and trunk set thermometer, case with moulded pediment, cistern cover missing, c1830, 39in (99cm) high.
£1,750–2,500
$2,500–3,600 ⚒ Bon

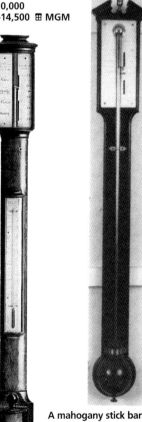

A mahogany stick barometer, by Dollond of London, c1810.
£3,700–4,400
$5,400–6,400 ⊞ SBA

An ebony-strung stick barometer, by Gilbert & Wright of London, with silvered dial, c1800, 41in (104cm) high.
£1,900–2,200
$2,750–3,200 ⊞ SBA

A mahogany stick barometer, by Dollond, London, the swan-neck pediment with ivory paterae and finial, silvered brass scale, and lockable glazed door, c1800.
£2,800–3,000
$4,000–4,400 ⊞ PAO

◀ **A mahogany bowfronted barometer,** by Dollond, London, with ogee top moulding, ebonized cistern cover, and silvered brass scale, the centrally mounted thermometer with both Fahrenheit and Réaumur scales, maker's name engraved with cross-hatching, c1825.
£7,500–9,000
$11,000–13,000 ⊞ PAO

▶ **A mahogany stick barometer,** the silvered register plate inscribed with maker's name Egerton Smith & Co, Liverpool, enclosed by a glazed hinged door below a break-arch pediment centred by a brass finial, 1820, 38in (96.5cm) high.
£1,050–1,300
$1,500–1,900 ⚒ HSS

▶ **A feathered mahogany stick barometer,** signed Ezekiel, Exeter, with engraved silvered plate, incorporating a thermometer, turned cistern cover, arched pediment top, c1830, 39½in (101cm) high.
£2,650–2,900
$3,850–4,200 ⚒ WL

Condition

The condition is absolutely vital when assessing the value of an antique. Damaged pieces on the whole appreciate much less than perfect examples. However a rare desirable piece may command a high price even when damaged.

◀ **A mahogany and chequer-banded stick barometer,** by P. Gally, Cambridge, c1820, 38½in (98cm) high.
£1,200–1,500
$1,750–2,200 ⚒ CSK

A Victorian rosewood mercury stick barometer, by J. Gargory, Bull Street, Birmingham, with ivorine inner plates, thermometer, vernier reading scale, c1860, 36in (92cm) high.
£1,100–1,250
$1,600–1,800 ⊞ GH

A mahogany stick barometer, the silvered scales signed J. Finlayson, London, the case with exposed tube and turned cistern cover, c1810, 38½in (97cm) high.
£900–1,000
$1,300–1,500 ⚒ S

◄ A mahogany flame-veneered stick barometer, by J. Jenkins, Swansea, signed under bone scales Tagliabue & Casella, London, the thermometer showing both Fahrenheit and centigrade scales, c1860.
£1,300–1,500
$1,900–2,200 ⊞ PAO

► An inlaid mahogany stick barometer, by Lock, Oxford, c1800.
£2,000–2,500
$2,900–3,600 ⊞ W&W

► A Georgian mahogany and ebonized stick barometer, the bowfronted case with swan-neck pediment and ivory urn finial above a silvered dial, the trunk with thermometer, the base with urn-shaped reservoir, signed Thos. Harris & Sons, British Museum, London, 41in (104cm) high.
£4,000–5,150
$5,800–7,500 ⚖ CSK

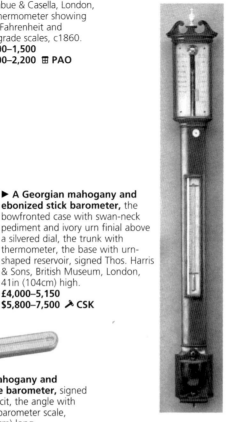

A mahogany and ebony-strung stick barometer, signed W. & S. Jones, London, c1805, 39in (99cm) high.
£2,650–3,200
$3,850–4,600 ⚖ P

A George III mahogany and boxwood angle barometer, signed Josho. Knight Fecit, the angle with rubbed silvered barometer scale, c1810, 32in (81cm) long.
£5,900–8,100
$8,500–11,700 ⚖ C

► A walnut stick barometer, with silvered dial and vernier, signed J. King & Son, Bristol, with glazed door and turned cistern cover, c1850.
£450–750
$650–1,100 ⚖ Bon

◄ A mahogany stick barometer, the bone plates signed H. Hughes, 59 Fenchurch Street, London, with mercury thermometer, the case with arched top and turned cistern cover, c1840, 36½in (92.5cm) high.
£1,050–1,300
$1,500–1,900 ⚖ S(S)

◄ **A mahogany stick barometer,** the paper plates signed Manticha Fecit, the case with exposed tube, fluted corners and rectangular cistern cover, c1800, 38½in (98cm) high.
£900–1,050
$1,300–1,500 ⚒ S(S)

A Dutch walnut and chequer-inlaid barometer, the pewter plate inscribed J. Stopanni Fecit, Amsterd.', with thermometer and mercury U-tube, the architectural pediment surmounted by a wood urn finial, c1810, 50in (127cm) high.
£1,750–2,650
$2,500–3,500 ⚒ C

◄ **A mahogany stick barometer,** by Nairne & Blunt, London, with silvered scales signed by the maker, with vernier, enclosed mercury tube, boxed cistern, restored, c1790, 37½in (95cm) high.
£1,500–2,200
$2,200–3,200 ⚒ CSK

► A mahogany stick barometer, by F. Molton, Norwich, with glazed door and swan-neck pediment, c1815.
£2,500–3,500
$3,600–5,000 ⊞ W&W

A mahogany stick barometer, by Edward Nairne, London, c1765.
£2,600–2,800
$3,800–4,000 ⊞ PAO

A mahogany stick barometer, the engraved silvered dial signed D. Ortelly & Co, Bath, damaged, 19thC, 37in (94cm) high.
£650–900
$950–1,300 ⚒ P

► **A George III mahogany, crossbanded and marquetry-inlaid stick barometer,** by T. Naylor, Halifax, with flower-painted plates, scrolled pediment, glazed door, and oval cover with paterae, c1810, 38½in (98cm) high.
£1,750–2,050
$2,550–3,000 ⚒ AH

A mahogany stick barometer, the exposed tube with silvered plates and vernier signed Nairne, London, the case veneered with well-figured wood, moulded edge and hemispherical cistern cover, c1780, 38½in (98cm) high.
£1,900–2,500
$2,750–3,600 ⚒ S

A walnut stick barometer, by Nairne & Son, London, with engraved brass dial and silvered thermometer, c1780.
£1,900–2,500
$2,750–3,600 ⚒ RBB

◀ **A mahogany bowfronted mercury stick barometer, t**he silvered dial with vernier inscribed J. Pastorelli, Gable St, Liverpool, boxed thermometer with silvered scale, c1850, 37½in (95cm) high.
£3,200–3,700
$4,700–5,500
🔨 CSK

▶ **A mahogany stick barometer,** with boxwood and ebony herringbone inlay, with visible tube and plain turned cistern cover, the silvered dial with thermometer and vernier, signed F. Pellegrino Fecit, c1800, 39in (99cm) high.
£2,200–2,900
$3,200–4,200
🔨 CSK

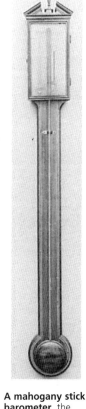

A George III mahogany barometer, the break-arch pediment above a chequerbanded shaft with brass dial signed Josh. Pastorele & Co, London, above replaced domed reservoir, c1820, 37½in (95.5cm) high.
£800–1,100
$1,150–1,600 🔨 C

A mahogany stick barometer, the brass register signed Fra Pinni & Co, Holborn, No. 81, London, c1820, 38½in (98cm) high.
£600–750
$870–1,100 🔨 DN

A mahogany stick barometer, by B. Peverelly, London, c1820.
£1,300–2,050
$1,900–3,000 🔨 Mit

◀ **A mahogany stick barometer,** with domed cistern and broken pediment, the register signed Rizzi Fecit, with thermometer and pressure scales, c1840, 37in (94cm) high.
£650–750
$950–1,100 🎟 P(Re)

▶ **A mahogany stick barometer,** the plates signed Polti-Exon, the case with hemispherical cistern cover, 39in (99cm) high.
£750–800
$1,100–1,200 🔨 S

A George III bow-fronted mahogany stick barometer, with ebony stringing, by J. Ramsden, London, with engraved silvered dial, c1780, 38in (96.5cm) high.
£5,150–5,900
$7,450–9,000 🔨 Bea

A George III mahogany stick barometer, the concealed tube with silvered plates and vernier, the case with swan-neck cresting, cistern cover, bordered with ebony stringing and inset with a mercury thermometer, signed Jas. Powell, Worcester, c1820, 39in (99cm) high.
£1,500–2,200
$2,200–3,200 🔨 S

A Dutch inlaid walnut barometer, the pewter plates signed Joseph Brenta fec: Amsterd, with mercury U-tube, late 18thC, 49½in (125.5cm) high.
£3,500–4,500
$5,000–6,500 🔨 S

◀ **A mahogany ballooning barometer,** the detachable ivory thermometer signed G. & C. Dixey, Opticians to the King, 3 New Bond Street, London, c1825, 36½in (93cm) high.
£1,300–1,500
$1,900–2,200 ↗ CSK

▶ **A Victorian mahogany stick barometer,** the ivory plate signed M. Sadler, Aston St, Birmingham, with sliding verniers for barometer and thermometer, the trunk with turned cistern cover.
£600–900
$870–1,300 ↗ Bon

A mahogany angle barometer, by E. Scarlet, London, the frame with broken pediment centred by a ball and spire finial, the visible angled tube with silvered scale from 28in (71cm) to 31in (78.5cm) above a silvered hygrometer and with a signed alcohol thermometer to the side with spirally turned knopped cistern covers and mirror, the glazed centre engraved 'A Perpetual Regulation of Time' with apertures for high water at London Bridge, equation of time, fixed feasts, sunrise/sunset, length and break of day, declination of the sun and day of the month, with further tables for the Year of the Lord with dominical letter from 1753–1852, 18thC, 40in (101.5cm) high.
£35,000–45,000
$50,750–65,000 ↗ P

A George III mahogany and chequerbanded stick barometer, dial signed J. M. Ronketti, c1800, 38in (96.5cm) high.
£1,300–1,500
$1,900–2,200 ↗ CSK

◀ **A provincial mahogany stick barometer,** by Smith, Kington, the case with fan and star inlay and boxwood string edging, brass silvered scale, c1800.
£2,100–2,300
$3,000–3,400 ⊞ PAO

◀ **A rosewood stick barometer,** with 2-day bone plates and verniers signed Josh. Somalvico & Co, 2 Hatton Garden, London, the case with leaf-carved cresting, applied at the front with a spiral reservoir thermometer, carved corbels to the side and urn cistern cover with carved lid, c1850, 44in (112cm) high.
£4,400–5,150
$6,400–7,500 ↗ S

◀ **A Scottish mahogany stick barometer,** the silver plate signed N. Tarra, Louth, with vernier and thermometer, the broken-arch case with a shaped cistern cover and set with a hygrometer, early 19thC, 38in (96.5cm) high.
£1,200–1,750
$1,750–2,500 ↗ S

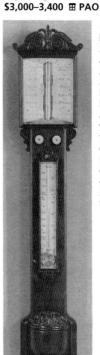

◀ **A mahogany stick barometer,** the register with vernier scale and signed Jo. Smith, Royal Exchange, London, the case with inset thermometer, ebonized moulded edge, shallow domed cistern cover and surmounted by later scroll crestings, register plate originally silvered, c1800.
£1,600–2,500
$2,300–3,600 ↗ L

▶ **An oak stick barometer,** signed J. H. Steward, 457 West Strand, London, with flat top, above ivory scales with vernier, 1860, 36½in (92.5cm) high.
£650–800
$950–1,200 ↗ CSK

◀ **A George III mahogany stick barometer and thermometer,** the silvered scale plate inscribed Tagliabue Torre and Co, 294 Holborn, London, with break-arch pediment, c1810, 38in (96.5cm) high.
£900–1,000
$1,300–1,500
⚒ HSS

A mahogany bowfronted barometer, by Stebbing, Southampton, the silvered brass register plates with vernier, c1840.
£6,000–8,000
$8,700–11,600 ⊞ PAO

▶ **A flame mahogany bowfronted stick barometer,** with silvered plate and inset thermometer, by G. Tickell, Dublin, c1830.
£4,500–6,500
$6,500–9,400
⊞ W&W

An oak stick barometer, the bone scales signed Steward, Strand & Cornhill, London, twin verniers, the case with thermometer on trunk, c1880, 39in (99cm) high.
£750–900
$1,100–1,300 ⚒ Bon

▶ **A mahogany and chequer-strung stick barometer,** inscribed J. Vitory Zaneta, 98 Market St Lane, Manchester, c1830, 39in (99cm) high.
£1,100–1,250
$1,600–2,000 ⚒ CSK

An oak fishery or sea-coast stock barometer, by J. C. West, 92 & 93 Fleet Street, London, with twin glazed ceramic scales, c1870, 40½in (103cm) high.
£650–750
$950–1,100 ⚒ P

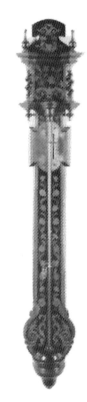

A Queen Anne walnut stick barometer, with concealed tube, brass register signed John Williamson, adjustable pointer, shaped base, turned cistern cover, c1700, 49in (124.5cm) high.
£5,900–7,350
$8,500–10,500 ⚒ S

◄ **A walnut and floral marquetry stick barometer,** with silvered scales, the case with oak carcase, c1700, 49½in (125.5cm) high.
£3,700–5,150
$5,350–7,450 ⚒ P

► **A walnut stick barometer,** the concealed tube with silvered plates and simple vernier, the case with broken-arch cresting, brass ball and spire finials and turned cistern cover, case altered, c1730, 39½in (100cm) high.
£3,700–5,150
$5,350–7,450 ⚒ S(S)

◄ **A mahogany stick barometer,** with silvered register plates, flanked by carved beading and scrolls, fluted trunk, convex fluted cistern cover, 18thC, 40in (101.5cm) high.
£1,300–1,750
$1,900–2,500 ⚒ Bon

◄ **A George II mahogany stick barometer,** with later wood finial to cavetto arched top, the dial with foliate border engraving, 38in (97cm) high.
£850–1,000
$1,250–1,500 ⚒ C

► **A mahogany stick barometer,** with shaped brass plates, adjustable pointer, concealed tube with turned cistern cover, on a moulded backboard with broken-arch top and base, late 18thC, 38in (96.5cm) high.
£600–900
$870–1,300 ⚒ S

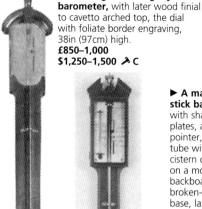

A mahogany stick barometer, by W. S. Jones, London, with silvered brass dials and thermometer, c1790.
£3,300–4,000
$4,800–5,800 ⊞ W&W

◄ **A mahogany stick barometer,** with break-arch pediment, thermometer to main dial and exposed mercury tube to front of case, with original round cistern cover, c1800.
£1,700–2,100
$2,500–3,000 ⊞ W&W

A mahogany bowfronted stick barometer, with original ebony urn cistern cover, c1790.
£6,000–8,000
$8,700–11,600 ⊞ W&W

◀ A mahogany
bowfronted stick
barometer,
early 19thC.
£4,400–5,900
$6,400–8,500 ➶ P(S)

▶ A mahogany
bowfronted stick
barometer, with step
pediment and bow-
fronted thermometer to
main trunk, with original
ebony urn cistern cover
to the base, c1835.
£3,600–4,600
$5,200–6,700 ⊞ W&W

**A mahogany
stick barometer,**
with round top,
exposed tube
and hemi-
spherical cistern
cover, c1800.
**£2,400–3,000
$3,500–4,400
⊞ W&W**

**A mahogany
stick barometer,**
early 20thC,
37in (94cm) high.
**£800–950
$1,150–1,400 ⊞ SBA**

▶ **A Scottish
mahogany stick
barometer,** in the
style of Knie, c1820.
**£1,500–2,000
$2,200–2,900 ⊞ SO**

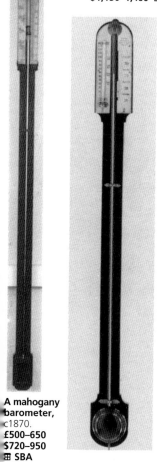

**A carved oak stick
barometer,** c1870,
46in (116.5cm) high.
**£750–800
$1,100–1,500 ⊞ SBA**

**A brass-cased Fortin
stick barometer,**
on a mahogany
backboard, c1890.
**£1,000–1,400
$1,500–2,000 ⊞ W&W**

**A walnut double-angle stick
barometer,** with wooden and
paper scales, the cistern
adjusted by a screw to give
weather indications, in a plain
case with carved pediment,
c1900, 41½in (105.5cm) high.
**£7,500–8,500
$10,500–12,500 ➶ S(S)**

**A mahogany
barometer,**
c1870.
**£500–650
$720–950
⊞ SBA**

◀ **A mahogany model barometer,**
with ivory plates, c1870.
**£900–1,400
$1,300–2,000 ⊞ W&W**

Marine Barometers

◄ **A rosewood marine barometer,** the concealed tube with angled bone plates and vernier signed W. Murphy, Anchor & Hope Alley, Wapping, made by A. Colomba, the case with ring handle, gimballed wall bracket, inset with a thermometer and brass cistern cover, c1870, 37½in (95cm) high.
£2,400–2,850
$3,500–4,100 ⚒ S

A mahogany ship's barometer, by Agusti of Falmouth, the case in original polish with large brass cistern cover at base, restored, gimbal replaced, c1860.
£3,600–3,850
$5,200–5,600 ⊞ MERT

◄ **A rosewood marine barometer,** with ivory main dial and silvered brass sympiesometer to the trunk, original brass cistern, replacement gimbals, c1840.
£2,300–2,700
$3,350–3,900 ⊞ W&W

► **A walnut fishery or sea-coast stick barometer,** with twin-glazed ceramic scales, by R. & J. Beck, 31 Cornhill, London, c1880, 39in (99cm) high.
£600–650
$870–950 ⚒ P

A rosewood ship's barometer, by J. Bassnett of Liverpool, gimbal missing, c1840.
£2,150–2,850
$3,100–4,100 ⚒ Mit

► **A mahogany ship's barometer,** the bone plates stamped J. Blair, 45 Prince Street, Bristol, behind a bevelled glass plate, c1870, 36in (91.5cm) high.
£2,150–2,850
$3,100–4,100 ⚒ CSK

◄ **A Victorian rosewood marine barometer,** the bone plates with vernier, signed B. Biggs, Cardiff, the case with a brass cistern cover, later gimbals and set with a thermometer, later brass mount and wood shield, c1860, 34in (86.5cm) high.
£1,300–1,700
$1,900–2,500 ⚒ S

► **A rosewood marine barometer,** by Cameron, Glasgow, with ivory register, the trunk with sympiesometer, thermometer and hygrometer scales, with brass cistern cover and shell pediment, gimbals missing, 19thC, 40in (101.5cm) high.
£2,850–3,600
$4,100–5,200 ⚒ P(M)

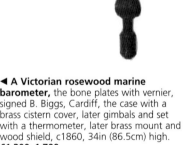

A ship's barometer, c1860.
£800–1,000
$1,150–1,500 ⚒ Mit

◄ **A mahogany marine barometer,** by Spencer Browning, London, with brass-trimmed ivory plates, replaced gimbals, c1835.
£2,300–2,800
$3,500–4,000 ⊞ W&W

Admiral Fitzroy Barometers

An Admiral Fitzroy oak barometer, with arched carved top, fitted interior with Victorian lozenge marked No. 367815, 19thC, 42in (106.5cm) high.
£300–400
$440–600 ⊞ **GH**

A Polytechnic barometer, in an oak Gothic-style case, with thermometer, with paper plates, c1890.
£450–520
$650–900 ↗ **GAK**

An Admiral Fitzroy barometer, in a carved oak case, c1890.
£520–580
$750–900 ⊞ **GD**

An Admiral Fitzroy barometer, in an oak frame, c1920, 40in (101.5cm) high.
£300–370
$440–540 ⊞ **JMW**

Admiral Fitzroy Barometers

Admiral Robert Fitzroy (1805–65), formerly captain of Darwin's ship, *Beagle*, is perhaps best known for developing and then popularizing techniques in weather forecasting through his highly popular *Weather Book*, published in 1862.

The type of barometer associated with his name is contained in a long, broad case, usually of oak but sometimes in mahogany, walnut or beech, in styles ranging from plain to highly decorated cases with carved pediments. The scales are almost invariably of paper, bearing a synopsis of the Admiral's remarks on weather forecasting. Under the headings 'Rising' and 'Falling', Fitzroy stressed the importance of studying changes in air pressure rather than simply the actual height of the mercury.

Fitzroy barometers generally contain, in addition to a syphon-tube barometer with twin register pointers, a mercury thermometer and – of rather spurious accuracy – a 'storm-glass'. An interesting variant is the Royal Polytechnic Barometer, produced in significant numbers by Joseph Davis of London.

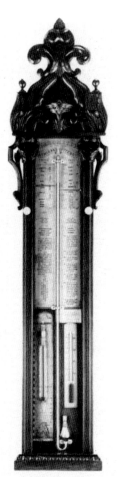

An Admiral Fitzroy Improved barometer, with paper register, storm-glass and thermometer, in an oak case carved with foliage, c1890, 47½in (120.5cm) high.
£650–750
$950–1,200 ↗ **DN**

▶ **An early Admiral Fitzroy barometer,** in an elaborately carved walnut case, c1865.
£1,100–1,400
$1,600–2,000 ⊞ **W&W**

Wheel Barometers

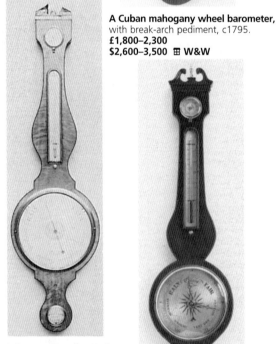

A mahogany wheel barometer, by Josh. Somalvico, London, c1790.
£2,200–2,700
$3,200–3,900 ⊞ **W&W**

A Cuban mahogany wheel barometer, with break-arch pediment, c1795.
£1,800–2,300
$2,600–3,500 ⊞ **W&W**

A Georgian mahogany and fruitwood inlaid wheel barometer, with alcohol thermometer, the break-arch pediment and acorn finial, the silvered dial signed Lione Somalvico & Co, 125 Holbn. Hill, London, c1810.
£650–700
$950–1,500 ⚒ **Bon**

An inlaid mahogany wheel barometer, with satinwood and ebony stringing, c1815.
£850–1,100
$1,250–2,000 ⊞ **W&W**

A George III satinwood wheel barometer, signed D. Poncia, with 10in (25.5cm) silvered register, thermometer and hygrometer in a shaped case, pediment lacking, in need of restoration, c1820, 42in (106.5cm) high.
£900–1,000
$1,300–1,500 ⚒ **DN**

A mahogany four-dial wheel barometer, with ebony and boxwood stringing, c1830.
£900–1,200
$1,300–1,750 ⊞ **W&W**

A mahogany wheel barometer, by A. Tacchi, Bedford, the case with ebony stringing, crossbanded sides, the thermometer with engraved brass scale, 1830.
£850–1,000
$1,250–1,500 ⊞ **PAO**

A mahogany wheel barometer, the dial inscribed Rowe, Cambridge, c1840, 42in (107cm) high.
£750–900
$1,100–1,300 ⚒ **CSK**

A mahogany wheel barometer, by A. Aiano, Northgate, Canterbury, with 8in (20cm) silvered dial, the case inlaid with shell and leaf ornament, c1830, 38in (96.5cm) high.
£600–650
$870–950 ⊞ GA(W)

A brass-inlaid rosewood wheel barometer, the 8in (20cm) silvered dial signed F. Amadio & Son, 118 St John St, London, with hygrometer, alcohol thermometer and spirit level, the case with swan-neck cresting, c1830, 39in (99cm) high.
£1,150–1,500
$1,650–2,200 ⚒ S

A rosewood wheel barometer, the level plate signed Abraham, Optician, Bath, silvered dial, hygrometer and thermometer scales, c1840, 43in (109cm) high.
£500–750
$720–1,100 ⚒ CSK

A rosewood wheel barometer, by Adshead & Son, Dudley, with white enamel dial, temperature gauge, shaped case, c1870, 39in (99cm) high.
£200–250
$300–500 ⊞ GH

A rosewood wheel barometer and thermometer, by Aronsberg & Co, with silvered register plate, the case with C-scroll carving to the borders, c1860, 44in (112cm) high.
£500–650
$720–950 ⚒ HSS

A mahogany shell-inlaid wheel barometer, signed M. E. Bianchi, c1815.
£1,100–1,200
$1,600–2,000 ⊞ GIB

A walnut wheel barometer, the silvered dial signed L. Casartelli, 20 Duke St, Liverpool, the trunk with thermometer, with a raised carved border, c1870, 45in (114.5cm) high.
£500–750
$720–1,100 ⚒ Bon

l. A mahogany wheel barometer, signed G. Croce, York, with 8in (20cm) silvered dial, thermometer, hygrometer, level and convex mirror, c1830, 40in (101.5cm) high.
£450–550 $650–800
r. A mahogany wheel barometer, signed G. Bregazzi, Derby, with 8in (20cm) silvered dial, thermometer, level and convex mirror, c1830, 40in (101.5cm) high.
£480–600 $700–1,000 ⚒ WL

A mahogany barometer, by Camble of Oswestry, with thermometer in the dial, c1840, 36in (91.5cm) high.
£850–1,100
$1,250–1,600 ⊞ SBA

A mahogany barometer, by Corti & Son, London, the 8in (20cm) scale reading from 28in (71cm) to 31in (78.5cm), c1820.
£1,100–1,400
$1,600–2,000 ⊞ PAO

A mahogany and boxwood-strung wheel barometer, signed E. Cetti & Co, No. 11 Brook Strt, Holbn, London, with thermometer, hygrometer and mirror, 19thC, 49in (124.5cm) high.
£750–900
$1,100–1,300 ⚒ C

A flight of 3 walnut barometers, by C. H. Chadburn & Son, with 8, 10 and 12in (20, 25 and 31cm) dials, with patented rack and pinion movement, dated 1861.
£5,100–5,750
$7,400–8,350 ⊞ MERT

▶ **A mahogany wheel barometer,** the 8in (20cm) silvered dial signed Bullocech, Bradford, with thermometer, the case inlaid and outlined in ebony and boxwood stringing, c1825, 38in (97cm) high.
£650–800
$950–1,200 ⚒ S

A mahogany and boxwood-strung wheel barometer, the 8in (20cm) dial inscribed A. Corti Fecit, the thermometer with silvered scale in Fahrenheit, c1830, 38in (97cm) high.
£600–650
$870–1,000 ⚒ CSK

A carved oak wheel barometer, by Cremonini, Wolverhampton, with temperature gauge, c1860, 45in (113cm) high.
£320–380
$460–600 ⊞ GH

A mahogany wheel barometer, by Dollond, London, c1840, dial 10in (25.5cm) diam.
£1,400–1,800 $2,000–2,600 ⊞ W&W

A mahogany wheel barometer, by F. Faverio & Co, Lincoln, with silvered register plates to the dry/damp dial, thermometer and spirit level, verge watch escapement, ivory turner, the case crossbanded and strung with ebony and boxwood, bezel missing, c1820, 46in (117cm) high.
£1,500–2,200
$2,200–3,200 ⚒ HSS

A bird's-eye wheel barometer, by Evans, Carmarthen, c1850.
£800–1,200
$1,150–1,750 ⊞ W&W

An inlaid mahogany wheel barometer, signed Josh. Frigerio, 281 High Holborn, with 8in (20cm) dial, alcohol thermometer, the case with architectural pediment inlaid with shells and stringing, c1820, 38½in (98cm) high.
£600–650
$870–950 ⚒ S(S)

A wheel barometer, signed Gally Tarone & Co, Grevil St, Holborn, London, the thermometer with engraved and silvered scale, early 19thC, 39in (99cm) high.
£1,200–1,400
$1,750–2,000 ⊞ DRA

A rosewood wheel barometer timepiece, the 12in (30.5cm) scales inscribed D. Fagioli & Son, 3 Gt Warner St, Clerkenwell, c1830, 51in (130cm) high.
£1,800–2,050
$2,600–3,000 ⚒ S(S)

A fan-inlaid mahogany barometer, by J. Gatty, London, c1800.
£1,900–2,300
$2,750–3,350 ⊞ **W&W**

A mahogany wheel barometer, the 8in (20cm) silvered dial signed Thos Jones, 62 Charing Cross, the case with swan-neck cresting, outlined with ebony stringing, c1845, 41in (104cm) high.
£750–900
$1,100–1,300 ⚒ **S**

A Victorian rosewood and mother-of-pearl inlaid wheel barometer, by Laffrancho, Ludlow, with temperature gauge, 39in (99cm) high.
£250–300
$360–500 ⊞ **GH**

A mahogany and fruitwood-strung wheel barometer, signed Lione & Co, 7 Charles Str, Hatton Garden, with 10in (25.5cm) silvered dial, mirror, thermometer and hygrometer above, and level below, c1835.
£400–500
$580–800 ⚒ **Bon**

A George III wheel barometer, the silvered scale plates inscribed Manticha Fecit, with thermometer, c1780, 39in (99cm) high.
£2,500–3,200
$3,600–4,700 ⚒ **HSS**

▶ **A mahogany and ebony-strung wheel barometer,** by P. L. D. Martinelli, London, c1790.
£1,800–2,200
$2,600–3,200 ⊞ **W&W**

A rosewood wheel barometer, by R. Mears, Boston, with silvered register plate, thermometer, dry/damp dial, and spirit level, the case inlaid with bands of leaves in mother-of-pearl, c1860, 42½in (108cm) high.
£500–750
$720–1,100 ⚒ **HSS**

A Sheraton-style inlaid mahogany wheel barometer, by Mojana, Edinburgh, with thermometer, c1820.
£1,300–1,600
$1,900–2,300 ⊞ **W&W**

A mahogany barometer, by Nicholson, Kirkcudbright, c1860.
£700–850
$1,000–1,250 ⊞ **SBA**

A mahogany wheel barometer, by Northen, Hull, c1830, dial 6in (15cm) diam.
£1,500–2,050
$2,200–3,000 ⊞ **W&W**

A George III inlaid mahogany wheel barometer, the 8in (20cm) dial signed J. Pastorelli, Bowling St, Westminster, c1810, 39in (99cm) high.
£700–900
$1,000–1,300 ⚷ **S**

A Louis XVI parcel-gilt wheel barometer, with painted dial and register signed Philippe, Opticien, 59 Rue des Crois Cailloux, Amiens, c1780, 41in (104cm) high.
£1,300–1,650
$1,900–2,400 ⚷ **S**

A mahogany and fruitwood-strung wheel barometer, the 8½in (21.5cm) silvered dial signed Piotti, Hull, the case with floral and shell paterae and break-arch pediment, c1820.
£450–650
$650–950 ⚷ **Bon**

A mahogany wheel barometer, the 8in (20cm) register signed Rivolta, Chester, with thermometer, 1830, 38in (96.5cm) high.
£450–650
$650–950 ⚷ **S(C)**

◀ **A carved giltwood barometer,** signed Watt, London, c1870, 36in (91.5cm) high.
£2,550–3,200 $3,700–4,700 ⊞ ARE

▶ **A satinwood wheel barometer,** by Saltery, with thermometer and spirit level, London, 1825.
£1,100–1,400 $1,600–2,000 ⊞ W&W

A mahogany wheel barometer, by Rossiter, Bridgwater, with 6in (15cm) dial, square base, c1845.
£1,400–1,800 $2,000–2,600 ⊞ W&W

A Regency mahogany clock barometer, by G. Rossi, Norwich, with hygrometer dial, c1815, 51in (129.5cm) high.
£3,800–5,100 $5,500–7,400 ⚒ C

An inlaid mahogany wheel barometer, by V. Zanetti, Manchester, with 12in (30.5cm) scales, c1830, 50in (127cm).
£2,800–3,300 $4,000–4,800 ⚒ S(S)

An inlaid mahogany wheel barometer, by Stampa, London, c1815.
£850–1,000 $1,250–1,500 ⊞ W&W

◀ Λ **giltwood barometer,** signed Ronquette G. de rue du Faubg St Antoine, plate signed Paris, 1754, 41in (104cm) high.
£2,550–3,200 $3,700–4,700 ⚒ C

A mahogany barometer, by Stanislao Catteli, London, with 8in (20cm) silvered brass dial, fan inlay and triple boxwood and ebony stringing, c1790.
£1,850–2,000 $2,700–2,900 ⊞ PAO

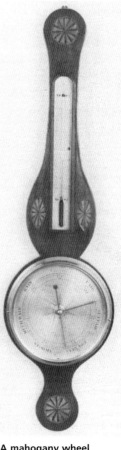

A mahogany wheel barometer, c1785.
£2,400–2,900 $3,500–4,200 ⊞ W&W

A mahogany wheel barometer, with silvered brass 10in (25.5cm) dial and thermometer scale, c1830.
£1,300–1,500
$1,900–2,200 ⊞ PAO

A mahogany wheel barometer, with hygrometer, thermometer, with 6in (15cm) dial, signed on spirit level, square base, c1840.
£1,200–1,800
$1,750–2,600 ⊞ W&W

A flame mahogany wheel barometer, with 8in (20cm) dial, hygrometer, thermometer, signed on round level, the case with a swan-neck pediment, c1840.
£850–1,100
$1,250–1,600 ⊞ W&W

A mahogany five-dial wheel barometer, with ebony and boxwood stringing, c1845.
£700–900
$1,000–1,300 ⊞ W&W

A mahogany wheel barometer, with 10in (25.5cm) silvered dial, c1850, 42in (106.5cm) high.
£250–400
$360–600 ⊞ GH

A rosewood barometer, with 10in (25.5cm) silvered dial, shaped case with thermometer and inlaid with mother-of-pearl bird and leaf motifs, c1860, 42in (106.5cm) high.
£500–650
$720–1,000 ⚒ S

A wheel barometer, c1860.
£500–550
$720–1,000 ⊞ GIB

A Victorian rosewood and inlaid mother-of-pearl wheel barometer, 8in (20cm) register and level, hygrometer, thermometer, 38in (96.5cm) high.
£450–600
$650–1,000 ⚒ P(M)

A rosewood wheel barometer, by Bellairs, Spalding, decorated with simulated brass inlay, c1870, 41in (104cm) high.
£250–320
$360–500 ↗ WHB

A rosewood and brass-inlaid wheel barometer, by M. Barnascone of Leeds, with silvered humidity, temperature, and leveling dials, convex mirror, c1870, 37in (94cm) high.
£380–480
$550–700 ↗ DA

A mahogany wheel barometer, signed L. Biaggini, Uckfield Warranted, inlaid with boxwood and ebony, with thermometer, c1830.
£700–850
$1,000–1,250 ↗ CSK

A mahogany wheel barometer, by Girletti of Glasgow.
£700–900
$1,000–1,300 ⊞ SBA

An inlaid mahogany wheel barometer, by J. Somalvico, Hatton Garden, with silvered dials, c1815.
£500–600
$720–870 ⊞ MGM

A mahogany wheel barometer, by A. Maspoli of Hull, with silvered humidity, barometer, levelling and thermometer dials, c1840.
£400–500
$580–720 ↗ DA

A mahogany and boxwood-strung five-dial wheel barometer, by P. Soldini, Hull, c1840.
£320–450
$460–650 ↗ TM

▶ **A Sheraton-style inlaid mahogany wheel barometer,** by Catelly & Co, Hereford, c1810.
£900–1,150
$1,300–1,650 ↗ LRG

◀ **An inlaid mahogany wheel barometer and thermometer,** by Tacchi, Bedford, with broken pediment, c1830.
£450–650
$650–1,000 ⚒ HSS

▶ **A mercury wheel barometer,** by J. Stopan of Aberdeen, the case inlaid with shells, with ebony and boxwood stringing, c1820, 38in (96.5cm) high.
£600–700
$870–1,000 ⊞ SBA

▶ **A mahogany wheel barometer,** with swan-neck pediment, edged in boxwood and ebony stringing, c1830, 39in (99cm) high.
£750–900
$1,100–1,300 ⊞ SBA

A mahogany wheel barometer, with 11in (28cm) silvered dial, mercury thermometer, convex mirror, bubble level signed L. Martinelli, Brighton, the case with swan-neck pediment and rounded base, c1840, 42½in (108cm) high.
£700–900
$1,000–1,300 ⚒ S(S)

A wheel barometer and thermometer, with inset small convex mirror, ivory turning handle, c1840.
£400–450
$580–800 PC

◀ **An oak clock barometer,** c1870, 39in (99cm) high.
£1,300–1,900
$1,900–3,000 ⊞ SBA

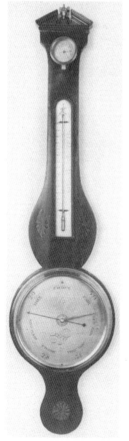

◀ **A mahogany wheel barometer,** with 8in (20cm) silvered dial, convex mirror and spirit level, signed A. Terrati, Newcastle, with mercury thermometer, c1840, 37in (94cm) high.
£600–650
$870–1,000 ⚒ S(S)

A mahogany wheel barometer, with 8in (20cm) dial, hygrometer, thermometer, the case with break-arch pediment, inlaid with fan motifs, c1800.
£1,100–1,500
$1,600–2,200 ⊞ W&W

A mahogany wheel barometer, c1840, 39in (99cm) high.
£700–850 $1,000–1,250 ⊞ SBA

A Georgian mahogany wheel barometer, inscribed G. C. Ross, York, 39in (99cm) high.
£400–450
$580–650 ⚒ HSS

Aneroid Barometers

An oak aneroid barometer, with 4½in (11.5cm) card dial, c1875, 26in (66cm) high.
£200–300
$290–440 ⊞ MERT

A carved oak aneroid barometer, by Coombes of Davenport, with printed 8in (20cm) dial, c1910, 33in (84cm) high.
£150–200
$225–290 ⊞ MERT

An ebonized and brass-mounted aneroid barometer, by J. H. Steward, 46 Strand, London, with silvered dial, each day with individual recording stylus, underside stamped 138, late 19thC, 9in (23cm) high.
£400–500
$580–720 ⚒ CSK

► A Continental-style oak combination 8-day clock and aneroid barometer, with 6in (15cm) barometer dial and porcelain thermometer scale, clock with enamel face, c1875, 28in (71cm) high.
£450–600
$650–870 ⊞ MERT

A lacquered brass aneroid barometer, by J. Goldschmid, Zurich, early 20thC.
£500–550
$720–800 ⚒ CSK

► A Victorian oak aneroid barometer.
£250–300
$360–440 ⚒ DaD

◄ A Regency-style mahogany aneroid wall barometer, by J. Lucking & Co, Birmingham, with 8in (20cm) silvered dial, crossbanded with satinwood, with thermometer box, early 20thC, 34in (86.5cm) high.
£400–500
$580–720 ⊞ GH

Glossary

Aneroid barometer: Invented c1843, a barometer which uses an evacuated sealed chamber instead of mercury to measure air pressure. (Aneroid = without liquid.)

Angle barometer: A barometer in which the recording section of the tube is turned almost to the horizontal to extend the scale in the 27in (68.5cm) to 31in (78.5cm) range.

Banjo barometer: A wheel barometer, so-called on account of its shape.

Marine barometer: A stick barometer fitted with gimbals and a constricted tube to minimize oscillations in the mercury.

Réaumur scale: Thermometer with a freezing point of zero and boiling point of 80°.

Stick barometer: A cistern or syphon-tube barometer housed in a slender case. It records air pressure by the height of the mercury column.

Sympiesometer: An instrument that uses a gas and coloured oil or other liquid to record air pressure.

Wheel barometer: A barometer with a round register plate and siphon tube, in which the mercury movement is measured by a weight attached to a pulley whose wheel turns the pointer on the dial.

An Art Nouveau aneroid barometer, by Negretti & Zambra, London, c1920, 11½in (29cm) wide.
£100–175
$145–255 ⊞ MERT

A Victorian moulded copper-mounted aneroid barometer, with 5in (12.5cm) dial, c1890.
£75–110
$110–160 ⊞ MERT

A French bronze aneroid barometer, with foliage and ribbon decoration, castings marked FW, 33in (84cm) high.
£800–1,050
$1,150–1,500 ⊞ MERT

An aneroid ship's barometer, with 5in (12.5cm) white glass dial, printed in fine filigree pattern, cast iron case, c1880.
£150–250
$220–360 ⊞ MERT

◄ **An oak combination clock and barometer,** in anchor design with rope-carved pattern around bezels, 8-day clock movement, 21in (53cm) high.
£375–500
$560–720 ⊞ MERT

An oak aneroid barometer, with thermometer, white glass dial, c1930, 33in (84cm) high.
£100–150
$145–220 ⊞ MERT

A clock barometer, the dial inscribed Harrods & Co, a compass set above the barometer dial, early 20thC, 6in (15cm) wide.
£600–650
$870–950 ⏶ MJB

A miniature aneroid barometer and thermometer, 7in (18cm) high.
£60–100
$90–145 ⏶ PCh

Glossary

Act of Parliament clock: An alternative term for the wall-hanging tavern clock of the 18thC, so-called because an Act passed by Parliament in 1797 placed a tax on all privately owned clocks, causing a need for more public timepieces.

Anchor escapement: Said to have been invented c1670 by Robert Hooke or William Clement. A type of escape mechanism shaped like an anchor, which engages at precise intervals with the toothed escape wheel. The anchor permits the use of a pendulum (either long or short) and gives greater accuracy than was possible with the verge escapement.

Arbor: The round steel spindle or shaft on which a wheel, pinion, lever or anchor is mounted.

Architectural top: A decorative hood in the form of a classical pediment.

Automaton clock: A clock with figures or mechanical devices that move or strike at predetermined times, activated by the striking or going train of the clock.

Backplate: The rear of the two vertically aligned plates between which the clock movement is supported.

Balance: A wheel which oscillates to and fro at a constant rate and controls, via the escapement, the timekeeping of a watch or clock.

Balloon clock: A type of bracket clock, the upper part of which is shaped like a balloon.

Banjo clock: A type of American wall clock, shaped like a banjo, first made by the Willard family during the early 19thC. Can also refer to some tavern clocks, usually with lacquered cases.

Barrel: A cylindrical brass box containing the mainspring in spring-driven clocks. In weight-driven clocks, the line on which the weight is hung is wound around the barrel.

Basket top: An ornamental top made of gilt-metal or silver and usually elaborately pierced. Used mainly on late 17thC- and early 18thC-English bracket clocks.

Beat: A clock is 'in beat' when the escape wheel produces a regular and even 'tick-tock'. This is essential for the correct running of the clock.

Beat scale: A graduated scale behind the tip of the pendulum, which is needed to measure the arc or swing to see if the clock is 'in beat'.

Bell top: The concave-shaped top of a bracket or longcase clock, used from 1740–1800.

Bezel: The ring, usually brass, surrounding the dial and securing the glass dial cover.

Bob: The disc-shaped or cylindrical weight at the bottom of the pendulum rod, usually made of lead, with an outer casing of brass.

Bolt and shutter: A type of maintaining power used in early longcase clocks to keep the clock going during winding. Shutters covering the winding holes are pulled away, and at the same time a small spring is activated to keep the clock going.

Boulle (or Buhl) case: A form of marquetry combining metal, usually brass, with tortoiseshell, named after the French maker André-Charles Boulle (1642–1732).

Bracket clock: A type of spring-driven clock designed to stand on a bracket or table.

Break-arch (or broken arch): Semi-circular arch at the top of a clock case, or dial, on bracket and longcase clocks.

Bull's-eye: Glass pane, usually of thickened glass, fitted to a longcase clock opposite and exposing the pendulum bob.

Caddy top: Convex shape like a tea container, used on the top of many early longcase and bracket clocks.

Calendar aperture: An opening in the surface of the dial, through which the date can be seen.

Capital: The ends of a column, usually made of brass, on the hood or trunk of a longcase clock.

Carriage clock: A small spring-driven portable clock, usually with a brass frame and glazed sides and back, produced mainly by French makers during the 19thC.

Cartel clock: A French spring-driven wall clock, of fire-gilt bronze, or finely chased and decorated gilt brass, first produced during the 18thC, continuing until WWI. English versions had wooden cases.

Cartouche: A decorative panel containing an inscription.

Cast and chased: Clock ornaments such as spandrels were cast in metal, then chased to improve the detail before gilding.

Chapter ring: The circular ring on the dial on which the hours and minutes are engraved, attached or painted.

Chiming clock: A clock which sounds the quarters as well as the hours.

Chinoiserie: Oriental-style decoration, usually found on lacquered and painted cases.

Chronometers: Very precise portable timekeepers, designed for use at sea.

Clepsydra: A time movement regulated by the flow of water (see **water clock**).

Cock: A single-ended bracket used on clocks and watches.

Collet: A dome-shaped ring, or washer, used to secure the clock hands and held in place by a tapered steel pin. Also refers to the stepped collar used to attach a wheel to an arbor.

Compensated: Designed to eliminate the effect of changing temperature on the pendulum or balance wheel of a clock.

Comtoise clocks: Longcase and wall clocks produced by provincial French makers, mainly during 19thC. Cases, when provided, are usually pine, with a bulbous trunk.

Count wheel: A wheel with segments cut out of the edge or with pins fitted to one face, which controls the striking of a clock. Also known as a locking plate.

Crazing: A network of fine cracks found on enamel or painted metal dials.

Cresting: Applied ornament, such as pierced wood or repoussé metal, fixed to the top of the clock case.

Cromwellian clock: A colloquial term for a lantern clock.

Crossbanding: Small pieces of veneer at right angles to the main veneer, or grain of the wood.

Crossings: A term used by clockmakers for the spokes of wheels. Five or more crossings are usually a sign of good quality.

Crown wheel: The horizontally mounted escape wheel used in a verge escapement.

Crutch: A rod attached at the top to the pallet arbor and with a fork, slot or pin which engages with the pendulum.

Cushion top: A rounded top on many early English bracket clocks. Also known as caddy top.

Cylinder escapement: A form of escapement, invented in 1695 by Thomas Tompion, fitted to many watches and carriage clocks in the 19thC.

Deadbeat escapement: A type of anchor escapement, possibly invented by George Graham, but without a recoil. Used in precision pendulum clocks.

Dial clock: A type of English wall clock with a round dial of engraved brass, painted wood or painted iron. All are spring-driven and usually have a fusee movement. Most are timepieces.

Dial plate: The visible dial to which the chapter ring and spandrels are attached.

Drum: The barrel on to which the cord of a weight-driven clock is wound.

Duration: The period for which a clock runs between windings.

Dutch striking: A striking system in which the hour is struck on a large bell and then repeated at the half hour on a smaller higher pitched bell.

Ebonized case: A clock case that has been stained black and polished to resemble ebony.

Endless rope: A type of winding mechanism, used typically on clocks of 30-hour duration. It consists of a loop of rope or chain running through a series of pulleys connected to the train, with a single weight to provide power.

Engine-turned: Decorative patterns, usually on or around the dial, created by being turned and inscribed on a machine.

Equation clock: A clock designed to show the difference between solar and mean time.

Escapement: That part of the clock that regulates it and transmits the impulse of the wheel train to the pendulum or balance.

Escape wheel: The wheel which engages with the pallets.

Falseplate: A metal plate, with pillars, used on painted dial longcase clocks to secure the dial to the frontplate.

Finial: A brass or wooden ornament, applied to the top of a clock.

Foliot: A bar with small adjustable weights attached, which acts as a balance in a verge escapement. It appears only on the very earliest domestic clocks.

Fret: A pierced-out section of the hood of a longcase clock, or the case of a bracket and lantern clock, usually in wood or brass, to let the sound out.

Frontplate: The plate nearest to the dial encasing a clock movement.

Fusee: A conical spool that compensates for the uneven pull of a mainspring as it unwinds. The fusee is used to ensure accurate timekeeping, commonly used on English bracket clocks, dial clocks and marine chronometers.

Gimbals: The pivoted rings used to keep marine chronometers level in their boxes.

Going barrel: A cylindrical brass drum containing the mainspring. Toothed on its periphery, it transmits power directly to the wheels of the train. Used in clocks which do not have a fusee movement.

Gong: Usually a coiled steel wire, used in place of a bell for the striking mechanism of many 19thC-clocks, especially carriage clocks.

Grande sonnerie: Striking system that repeats the last hour after each quarter has been chimed.

Great wheel: The first and largest wheel in a clock train.

Gothic clock: A name applied to medieval clocks of German, Swiss or Italian origin.

Gridiron pendulum: A type of pendulum rod used on very accurate clocks such as regulators. The gridiron consists of up to nine rods of alternating brass and steel. The rods expand or contract in different directions with changes in temperature, ensuring that the effective length of the pendulum remains the same and that the timekeeping of the clock is not affected.

Halifax clocks: Clocks made by Thomas Ogden of Halifax (1692–1769), containing moonphases in the arch.

Helical spring: A balance spring formed by winding a spring round a rod and used in marine chronometers.

Hood: The upper portion of a longcase clock, removed by pulling it forward. Before 1700 longcases had a rising hood.

Impulse: One of the phases in the action of the escapement, during which the train imparts impulse to the pendulum.

Inverted bell top: The opposite of the bell top, featuring a convex centre, used on bracket clocks from c1715.

Lancet clock: A bracket clock with a pointed Gothic-style top, popular 1790–1830.

Lantern clock: An early English domestic 30-hour clock, made 1600–1730, with all-brass case and dial, weight-driven, with striking mechanism and sometimes an alarm.

Leaves: The teeth of a pinion.

Lenticle: Also known as 'bull's-eye', the round section in the trunk door of a longcase clock through which the pendulum bob can be seen.

Lever escapement: A type of escape mechanism, invented in 1757, which uses a pivoted lever to connect the pallets and the balance wheel. Generally used on travelling clocks, and watches.

Locking plate striking: A method of controlled striking where a plate has notches cut at increasing intervals in its circumference, allowing the train to strike until a locking arm falls into a notch.

Longcase clock: A floor-standing clock, the weight-driven movement contained in the hood, with anchor escapement, long pendulum, of 30-hour or 8-day duration. Also known as a grandfather clock, a grandmother clock being a smaller version.

Mainspring: A coiled steel spring that, when wound, provides the power for the wheels of the going and striking trains in a spring-driven clock.

Maintaining power: Mostly found in regulators and chronometers. A simple device to ensure that power continues to be applied to the going train, by means of a spring-loaded lever, while the clock is being wound. The clock therefore does not stop or need to have the time adjusted after winding.

Mantel clock: A small bracket or table clock, typically in a rosewood, mahogany, ebonized or gilded case, produced mainly in the 19thC.

Marine chronometer: Very accurate spring-driven portable timepiece, for use at sea, usually of 1, 2, or 8-day duration.

Matting: A distinctive hammered finish found on the dial centre of many English longcase and bracket clocks.

Mean time: The time usually shown by clocks. The mean day is the average of all the solar days.

Mercury jar: A type of pendulum bob used on very accurate clocks and intended to compensate for changes in temperature that can affect timekeeping. The mercury in the jar rises as temperature increases, raising the centre of oscillation of the pendulum as the length of the rod increases.

Mock pendulum aperture: An opening in the dial of some bracket clocks showing the motion of the pendulum.

Month clock: The addition of a wheel to some movements allows it to go for 32 days.

Moon dial: A subsidiary dial, usually fitted in the arch of a longcase clock, to show the phases of the moon.

Motion work: The wheels and pinions that interconnect and drive the hands of a clock.

Movement: The mechanism of a clock, usually made of brass with some steel parts. Early American clocks were often made with wooden plates and wheels. Wood was also used in German, Swiss and Austrian clocks.

Musical clock: A clock that plays a tune at set times or often at will.

Mystery clock: A clock whose way of working is deliberately kept obscure.

Night clock: A clock showing the time at night, often by means of a light shining through a pierced dial.

Ormolu: Metal which has been fire gilded.

Pallet: An arm in the escape mechanism that checks the motion of the escape wheel by intermittently engaging with the teeth of the wheel.

Passing strike: A striking mechanism operated directly from the going train, causing a hammer to strike the bell once every hour.

Pedestal clock: A large bracket clock mounted on a matching floor-standing pedestal, produced in France from late 17thC to mid-18thC.

Pendule d'officier: A small portable spring-driven timepiece, made in France during the 18thC.

Pendule religieuse: A bracket clock produced in France during the late 17thC, named after the resemblance of the case to religious architecture.

Pendulum: A swinging rod with a bob on the end which regulates the timekeeping of the clock by releasing the clock's train at set intervals.

Perpetual calendar work: A mechanism which automatically corrects for the short months and leap years.

Petite sonnerie: A type of striking mechanism in which the clock strikes the hours and quarter hours, but usually repeats grande sonnerie.

Pillar: The rods, usually brass, which hold the two plates of the movement together.

Pinion: A small, toothed steel wheel which engages with a larger wheel.

Pinwheel escapement: A type of escape mechanism in which the pallets of a narrow anchor arm engage semi-circular pins on the side of the escape wheel, rather than the usual teeth. Commonly used on 18thC French clocks.

Pivot: The fine ends of an arbor, which run in pivot holes in the plates.

Plates: The flat metal pieces that contain the movement.

Platform: Common in carriage clocks, consisting of a horizontally mounted plate with the lever escapement mounted on it.

Plinth: The base of a clock case, particularly longcase clocks.

Posted movement: A clock movement, the top and bottom plates attached by four corner pillars or 'posts'.

Pull repeat: A striking train in which the last hour may be repeated by pulling a cord.

Quarter rack: The rack in a clock which controls the quarter chiming.

Quarter strike or chime: A form of striking mechanism in which each quarter hour is struck on a number of bells or gongs.

Rack striking: A device comprising a curved toothed bar which determines, by the amount to which it falls at the hour, the number of blows struck by the hammer.

Rating nut: The nut beneath a pendulum bob used to regulate the position of the bob on the pendulum staff to adjust the timekeeping.

Recoil escapement: A type of anchor escapement in which the escape wheel recoils slightly as each tooth escapes from the pallets.

Regulation dial: A subsidiary dial which permits adjustments to be made to the length of the pendulum, thus the timekeeping.

Regulator: An extremely accurate clock, used as a standard by which other clocks may be set. Most regulators have a deadbeat anchor escapement, maintaining power, and are weight-driven.

Repeater: A clock or watch which repeats the last hour, and sometimes the last quarter, five minutes or even minute, when a cord is pulled or a lever activated.

Reversed fusee: A movement in which the fusee chain is crossed so that the fusee and spring barrel rotate in opposite directions.

Rise and fall dial: A small dial for regulating the pendulum length and thus the timekeeping.

Sedan clock: A watch/clock contained in a wooden frame, usually with a handle.

Set-up: The residual tension in a spring when a clock has run down.

Sidereal: A sidereal day is 23 hours 56 minutes 4 seconds of mean time.

Spade hands: A 19thC-type of clock hands.

Spandrels: The ornate decoration in the corners of the dial.

Stop work: A device to prevent the overwinding of a clock.

Strike/Silent: Usually a lever to control the clock striking, either on the dial, or by a subsidiary dial.

Stringing: Fine inlay of brass or wood found on decorative clock cases.

Suspension: Method used to support the pendulum.

Sweep seconds: A movement in which the seconds hand is mounted in the centre of the dial.

Tabernacle clock: A German domestic clock of architectural form, manufactured 1570–1670.

Tallcase clock: The American term for a longcase clock.

Tavern clock: Also known as an Act of Parliament clock, a large timepiece hung in a public place such as an inn.

Tidal dial: A dial indicating the time of high water at a certain sea port.

Timepiece: A clock which does not strike or chime.

Ting-tang striking: A strike in which the quarters sound on two bells or gongs of different tones.

Torsion pendulum: The pendulum bob rotates by the twisting and untwisting of a long suspension spring.

Train: An interconnected series of wheels and pinions which make up the moving parts of a clock, used to transmit power from the spring or weight to the going or striking mechanism.

Turkish numerals: The dials of some clocks which were made for the foreign market have Turkish numerals.

Veneer: Early clock cases were made of oak and often veneered with another wood such as ebony, kingwood, olivewood, lignum vitae, mahogany or walnut.

Verge: A rod with two pallets.

Verge escapement: A mechanism used from c1500 to regulate the movement.

Verre eglomisé: Reverse-painted glass, commonly used by makers in the US and elsewhere, often featuring animals, plants, geometric patterns or historical and patriotic motifs.

Vienna regulator: Very precise and finely made weight-driven clocks, wall-hanging or floor-standing, produced in Austria during the first half of the 19thC.

Wagon spring: A wide spring made up of steel leaves. Provides the motive power in some American shelf clocks.

Warning piece: The striking train is activated momentarily just before it is due to strike and instantly stopped again on the warning piece. It is finally released at the correct point in time by the minute-hand wheel and striking takes place.

Water clock, or clepsydra: A timepiece activated by running water.

Weights: The masses providing power in a clock. They are usually made of iron, lead, or lead encased in brass.

Winding square: The square end of the winding arbor on which the key is placed.

Year clock: A rare type of movement designed to continue for a year with a single winding.

Year sidereal: The time taken for the earth to make a complete revolution around the sun.

Index to Advertisers

Directory of Specialists

If you would like to contact any of the following dealers, we would advise readers to make contact by telephone before a visit, thereby avoiding a wasted journey.

London

Aubrey Brocklehurst,
124 Cromwell Road,
SW7 4ET
Tel: 020 7373 0319

Patric Capon, 350 Upper St,
Islington, N1 0PD
Tel: 020 7354 0487

John Carlton-Smith,
17 Ryder St, St James's,
SW1Y 6PY
Tel: 020 7930 6622

City Clocks, 31 Amwell
St, EC1R 1UN
Tel: 020 7278 1154

The Clock Clinic Ltd,
85 Lower Richmond Road,
Putney, SW15 1EU
Tel: 020 8788 1407
clockclinic@btconnect.com
www.clockclinic.co.uk

C. R. Frost & Son Ltd,
60–62 Clerkenwell Road,
EC1M 5PX
Tel: 020 7253 0315
www.crfrost.com

Gutlin Clocks & Antiques,
616 King's Road, SW6 2DY
Tel: 020 7384 2439

North London Clock Shop,
Rear of 60 Saxon Road,
SE25 5EH
Tel: 020 8664 8089

Old Father Time Clock Centre,
101 Portobello Road,
W11 2QB
Tel: 020 8546 6299
Mobile: 07836 712088
www.oldfathertime.net

Pendulum of Mayfair Ltd,
51 Maddox St, W1
Tel: 020 7629 6606

Raffety & Walwyn Ltd
34 Kensington Church St,
W8 4HA
Tel: 020 7938 1100

Roderick Antique Clocks,
23 Vicarage Gate,
Kensington, W8 4AA
Tel: 020 7937 8517

R. E. Rose,
731 Sidcup Road,
Eltham, SE9 3SA
Tel: 020 8859 4754

Strike One Ltd,
48a Highbury Hill, N5 1AP
Tel: 020 7224 9719

W. F. Turk
Tel/Fax: 020 8543 3231
By appointment only

Avon

Antique Corner – A & C
Antiques, 86 Bryants Hill,
Hanham, Bristol, BS5 8QT
Tel: 0117 947 6141

The Barometer Shop,
2 Lower Park Row,
Bristol, BS1 5BJ
Tel: 0117 927 2565

Bath Galleries,
33 Broad St,
Bath, BA1 5LP
Tel: 01225 462946

David Gibson,
4 Wood St, Queen Square,
Bath, BA1 1SH
Tel: 01225 446646

Kembury Antique Clocks,
Bartlett St Antique Centre,
Bath, BA1 2QZ
Tel: 0117 956 5281

Winter's Antiques,
62 Severn Road, Weston-super-Mare, BS23 1DT
Tel: 01934 620118

Bedfordshire

Ampthill Antiques, Market
Square, Ampthill, MK45 2EH
Tel: 01525 403344

Berkshire

The Clock Workshop,
17 Prospect St,
Reading, RG4 8JB
Tel: 0118 9470741
theclockworkshop@supanet.com

P. D. Leatherland Antiques,
68 London St,
Reading, RG1 4SQ
Tel: 0118 9581960

Medalcrest Ltd, Charnham
House, 29/30 Charnham St,
Hungerford, RG17 0EJ
Tel: 01488 684157

The Old Malthouse,
Hungerford, RG17 0EG
Tel: 01488 682209

Times Past Antiques,
59 High St, Eton, SL4 6BL
Tel: 01753 857018

Alan Walker, Halfway Manor,
Halfway, Nr Newbury,
RG20 8NR
Tel: 01488 657670

Buckinghamshire

Chess Antiques, 85 Broad St,
Chesham, HP5 3EF
Tel: 01494 783043

Robin Unsworth Antiques,
1 Weston Road,
Olney, MK46 5BD
Tel: 01234 711210

Cambridgeshire

John Beazor & Sons Ltd,
78–80 Regent St,
Cambridge, CB2 1DP
Tel: 01223 355178

Doddington House Antiques,
2 Benwick Rd,
Doddington, PE15 0TG
Tel: 01354 740755

T. W. Pawson, 31a High St,
Somersham, PE17 3JA
Tel: 01487 841537

Cheshire

Adams Antiques, 65 Watergate
Row, Chester, CH1 2LE
Tel: 01244 319421

Antiques Etc,
Shepcroft House, London Rd,
Stretton, WA4 5PJ
Tel: 01925 730431

Anthony Baker Antiques,
14 London Rd,
Alderley Edge, SK9 7JS
Tel: 01625 582674

The Clock House, 14 Buxton
Road, Hazel Grove, Stockport
Tel: 0161 456 5752
www.clock-house.com

J.D Luffman,
Bank House,13 Bradeley
Road, Haslington, CW1 5PW
Tel: 01270 500199
Mobile: 07836 592898

Derek & Tina Rayment
Antiques, Orchard House,
Barton Road, Barton,
Nr Malpas, SY14 7HT
Tel: 01829 270429

Cornwall

Cremyll Antiques,
The Cottage, Cremyll Beach,
Torpoint, PL10 1HX
Tel: 01752 823490

A. W. Glasby & Son Antiques,
Leedstown, Nr Hayle,
TR27 6DA Tel: 01736 850303

Cumbria

Antiques of Penrith,
4 Corney Square,
Penrith, CA11 7PX
Tel: 01768 862801

Saint Nicholas Galleries Ltd,
39 Bank St, Carlisle, CA3 8HJ
Tel: 01228 544459

Derbyshire

Derbyshire Clocks,
104 High St West,
Glossop, SK13 8BB
Tel: 01457 862677

Devon

Atropos Antiques,
Watersmeet, Lymebridge,
Hartland, EX39 6EA
Tel: 01237 441205

Barometer World,
Quicksilver Barn, Merton,
Nr Okehampton, EX20 3DS
Tel: 01805 603443

Leigh Extence, 49 Fore St,
Shaldon, TQ14 0EA
Tel: 01626 872636
Mobile: 07967 802160
clocks@extence.co.uk
www.extence.co.uk

Dorset

D. J. Burgess,
116–116a Ashley Road,
Parkstone, BH14 9BN
Tel: 01202 730542

M. C. Taylor,
995 Christchurch Road,
Boscombe, BH7 6DJ
Tel: 01202 429718
www.taylorclocks.com

Tom Tribe & Son,
Bridge St, Sturminster
Newton, DT10 1BZ
Tel: 01258 472311

Durham

Weardale Clocks
Tel: 01388 528350
Mobile: 07808 727366
www.weardaleclocks.com

Essex

Bellhouse Antiques
Tel: 01268 710364

It's About Time,
863 London Road,
Westcliff-on-Sea, SS0 9SZ
Tel: 01702 472574
IAT@clocking-in.demon.co.uk
www.clocking-in.demon.co.uk

Littlebury Antiques,
58–60 Fairycroft Road,
Saffron Walden, CB10 1LZ
Tel: 01799 527961

Gloucestershire

Grandfather Clock Shop,
The Little House,
Sheep St, Stow-on-
the-Wold GL54 1JS
Tel: 01451 830455
info@stylesofstow.co.uk
www.stylesofstow.co.uk

Jeffrey Formby,
Orchard Cottage,
East St, Moreton-in-Marsh
GL56 0LQ
Tel: 01608 650558
www.formby-clocks.co.uk

Jillings Antique Clocks,
Croft House, 17 Church
St,Newent,GL18 1PU
Tel: 01531 822100
www.jillings.com

Montpellier Clocks,
13 Rotunda Terrace,
Montpelier,
Cheltenham GL50 1SW
Tel: 01242 242178

Greater Manchester

Northern Clocks,
Boothsbank Farm,
Worsley M28 1LL
Tel: 0161 790 8414
www.northernclocks.co.uk

Hampshire

Bryan Clisby Antique Clocks,
Andwells Antiques,
High St, Hartley Wintney
Tel: 01252 716436

The Clock-Work-Shop,
6A Parchment St,
Winchester, SO23 8AT
Tel: 01962 842331
Mobile: 07973 736155

Gerald E. Marsh, 32a The
Square, Winchester, SO23 9EX
Tel: 01962 844443

Herefordshire

Barometer Shop, New St,
Leominster HR6 8DP
Tel: 01568 613652

Hertfordshire

The Clock Shop,
161 Victoria St,
St Albans, AL1 3TA
Tel: 01727 856633

Country Clocks,
3 Pendley Bridge Cottages,
Tring Station, HP23 5QU
Tel: 01442 825090

David Harriman Antiques
Tel: 01923 776919
GALLIARDI@aol.com
Consultant:
richardgooderham@compuserve.com

Howards, 33 Whitehorse St,
Baldock, SG7 6QF
Tel: 01462 892385

Humberside

Time & Motion, 1 Beckside,
Beverley, HU17 0PB
Tel: 01482 881574

Kent

Campbell & Archard Ltd,
Lychgate House, Church
St, Seal, TN15 0AR
Tel: 01732 761153
pnarchard@aol.com
www.campbellandarchard.co.uk

Gem Antiques,
10 Gabriels Hill,
Maidstone, ME15 6JG
Tel: 01622 763344

Gem Antiques,
28 London Road,
Sevenoaks, TN13 1AP
Tel: 01732 743540

Gaby Gunst, 140 High St,
Tenterden, TN30 6HT
Tel: 01580 765818

The Old Clock Shop,
63 High St,
West Malling, ME19 6NA
Tel: 01732 843246

Derek Roberts Antiques,
25 Shipbourne Rd,
Tonbridge, TN10 3DN
Tel: 01732 358986
drclocks@clara.net
www.qualityantiqueclocks.com

Lancashire

Drop Dial Antiques, Last Drop
Village, Bromley Cross, BL7 9PZ
Tel: 01204 307186

Harrop Fold Clocks,
Lane Ends, BB7 4PJ
Tel: 01200 447665

Lincolnshire
Robin Fowler (Period Clocks),
Washing Dales, Washing Dales
Lane, Aylesby, DN37 7LH
Tel: 01472 751335

Grantham Clocks,
30 Lodge Way, NG31 8DD
Tel: 01476 561784

Second Time Around,
Hemswell Antique Centre,
Caenby Corner Estates,
Hemswell Cliff, Gainsborough,
DN21 5TJ
Tel: 01427 668389
Mobile: 07860 679495
info@hemswell-antiques.com

Merseyside
The Clock Shop, The Quadrant,
Hoylake, CH47 2EE
Tel: 0151 632 1888

Middlesex
Rita Shenton, 142 Percy Road,
Twickenham, TW2 6JG
Tel: 020 8894 6888
rita@shentonbooks.demon.co.uk

Norfolk
David Bates, Church Cottage,
Church Lane, Cawston,
Norwich, NR10 4AJ
Tel: 01603 871687

Keith Lawson Antique Clocks,
Scratby Garden Centre,
Beach Road, Scratby,
NR29 3AJ
Tel: 01493 730950
www.antiqueclocks.co.uk

Village Clocks, High St,
Coltishall, Norwich, NR12 7AA
Tel: 01603 736047
Mdarley@Excite.co.uk
www.Village-Clocks.co.uk

R. C. Woodhouse,
10 Westgate,
Hunstanton, PE36 5AL
Tel: 01485 532903

Northamptonshire
M. C. Chapman,
11–25 Bell Hill,
Finedon, NN9 5NA
Tel: 01933 681260

Northumberland
Gordon Caris, 16 Market
Place, Hexham, NE46 1XQ
Tel: 01434 602106

Oxfordshire
Craig Barfoot, Tudor House,
East Hagbourne, OX11 9LR
Tel: 01235 818968

Jonathan Howard,
21 Market Place,
Chipping Norton, OX7 5NA
Tel: 01608 643065

Rosemary and Time, 42 Park
St, Thame, OX9 3HR
Tel: 01844 216923

Republic of Ireland
Jonathan Beech,
Westport, Co Mayo
Tel: 00 353 98 28688
www.antiqueclocks-
ireland.com

Scotland
Ian Burton Antique Clocks at
John Whitelaw & Sons,
125 High St, Auchterarder,
Perthshire, PH3 1AA
Tel: 01334 471426
Mobile: 07785 114800
ian@ianburton.com
www.ianburton.com

John Mann, The Clock
Showrooms, Canonbie,
Nr Carlisle, DG14 0SY
Tel: 013873 71337/71827
Mobile: 07850 606 147
www.johnmannantiqueclocks.
co.uk

Shropshire
The Clock Shop,
7 The Parade,
St Mary's Place,
Shrewsbury, SY1 1DL
Tel: 01743 361388
clockshopshrewsbury@hotmail.
com

Somerset
Bernard G. House,
13 Market Place,
Wells, BA5 2RF
Tel: 01749 672607

Staffordshire
The Essence of Time,
Unit 2 Curborough Farm
Antiques & Craft Centre,
Watery Lane, Off Eastern
Avenue Bypass, Lichfield,
WS13 8ES
Mobile: 07944 245064

Grosvenor Clocks,
71 St Edward St,
Leek, ST13 5DN
Tel: 01538 385669

R. A. James, 1 High St,
Tutbury, Nr Burton-on-Trent,
DE13 9LP
Tel:01283 814596
www.antique-clocks-
watches.co.uk

James A. Jordan,
7 The Corn Exchange,
Lichfield, WS13 6JR
Tel: 01543 416221

Manor Court Antiques,
4 Manor Court St,
Penkhull, Stoke-on-Trent
Tel: 01782 410140

Suffolk
Clock House, Locks Lane,
Leavenheath, CO6 4PF
Tel: 01206 262187

Patrick Marney,
The Gate House, Melford Hall,
Long Melford, CO10 9AA
Tel: 01787 880533

Suthburgh Antiques,
Red House, Hall St,
Long Melford, CO10 9JQ
Tel: 01787 374818

Village Clocks,
Little St Mary's,
Long Melford, CO10 9LQ
Tel: 01787 375896

Surrey
Abbott Antiques,
75 Bridge Road,
East Molesey, KT8 9HH
Tel: 020 8941 6398

The Clock Shop,
64 Church St,
Weybridge, KT13 8DL
Tel: 01932 840407

Roger A. Davis Antiquarian
Horologist, 19 Dorking Road,
Great Bookham,
KT23 4PU
Tel: 01372 457655

Horological Workshops,
204 Worplesdon Road,
Guildford, GU2 9UY
Tel: 01483 576496
enquiries@horologicalworkshops.
com

B. M. & E. Newlove,
139–141 Ewell Road,
Surbiton, KT6 6AL
Tel: 020 8399 8857

Surrey Clock Centre,
3 Lower St,
Haslemere, GU27 2NY
Tel: 01428 651313

Sussex
Arundel Clocks,
Lasseters Corner,
High St, Arundel,
BN18 9AE
Tel: 01903 884525
www.arundelclockman
@btinternet.com

Churchill Clocks,
Rumbolds Hill,
Midhurst, GU29 9BZ
Tel: 01730 813891
www.churchillclocks.co.uk

Hove Antique Clocks,
68 Western Road,
Hove, BN3 2JQ
Tel: 01273 722123

Sam Orr, 36 High St,
Hurstpierpoint, BN6 9RG
Tel: 01273 83208

Anthony Woodburn,
PO Box 2669, Lewes,
BN7 3JE
Tel: 01273 486606
www.anthonywoodburn.com

Tyne & Wear
Peter Smith Antiques,
12–14 Borough Rd,
Sunderland, SR1 1EP
Tel: 0191 567 3537

Warwickshire
The Grandfather Clock Shop,
2 Bondgate House, West
St, Granville Court,
Shipston-on-Stour, CV36 4HD
Tel: 01608 662144

Summersons,
172 Emscote Road,
Warwick, CV34 5QN
Tel: 01926 400630
clocks@summersons.com
www.summersons.com

West Midlands
R. Collyer, 185 New Road,
Rubery, B45 9JP
Tel: 0121 453 2332

F. Meeks & Co,
197 Warstone Lane,
Hockley, B18
Tel: 0121 236 9058

Osborne Antiques,
91 Chester Road,
New Oscott, B73 5BA
Tel: 0121 355 6667

Wiltshire
Inglenook Antiques,
59 High St,
Ramsbury, SN8 2QN
Tel: 01672 520261

P. A. Oxley,
The Old Rectory,
Main Road,
Cherhill, SN11 8UX
Tel: 01249 816227
info@paoxley.com
www.allan-smith-antique-
clocks.co.uk

Allan Smith, Amity Cottage,
162 Beechcroft Rd,
Upper Stratton,
Swindon, SN2 6QE
Tel: 01793 822977
allansmithclocks@lineone.net
www.allan-smith-antique-
clocks.co.uk

Trevor Waddington,
5 Trowbridge Road,
Bradford on Avon,
BA15 1EE
Tel: 01225 862351.
www.antiques-
uk.co.uk/waddington

Chris Wadge,
83 Fisherton St, Salisbury
Tel: 01722 334467

Worcestershire
Broadway Clocks,
5 Keil Close, High St,
Broadway, WR12 7AL
Tel: 01386 852458

Hansen Chard Antiques,
126 High St,
Pershore, WR10 1EA
Tel: 01386 553423

Yorkshire
John Pearson Antique Clocks,
Church Cottage, Birstwith,
HG3 2NG
Tel: 01423 770828

Brian Loomes,
Calf Haugh Farm,
Pateley Bridge,
HG3 5HW
Tel: 01423 711163
www.brianloomes.com

Keith Stones Grandfather
Clocks, 5 Ellers Drive,
Bessacarr, DN4 7DL
Tel: 01302 535258

Time & Motion, 1 Beckside,
Beverley, HU17 0PB

Weather House Antiques,
Kym S. Walker,
Foster Clough,
Hebden Bridge, HX7 5QZ
Tel: 01422 882808/886961
Mobile: 07889 750711
www.kymwalker@btinternet.com

USA
Classical Clock Company,
1086 East Stanley Blvd,
Livermore, CA 94550
Tel: 925 371 8342
info@classicalclock.com
www.classicalclock.com

Conneticut Clocks,
80 Wood End Drive,
Easton, CT 06612
ctclock@optonline.net
www.pricelessads.com/ctclocks/

Gordon S. Converse & Co,
503 W. Lancaster Avenue,
Strafford, PA 19087
Tel: 800 789 1001
www.converseclocks.com

Kirtland H. Crump Antique
Clocks, 387 Boston Post Road,
Madison, Conneticut 06443
Tel: 203 245 7573
www.crumpclocks.com

Charles Edwin Inc,
PO Box 1340, Louisa
VA 23093-1340
Tel: 540 967 0416
info@charles-edwin.com
www.charles-edwin.com

Fred Hansen Antiques Inc,
27 North Chestnut St,
New Paltz, NY 12561
Tel: 845 255 1333
www.fredhansen.com/

Mark of Time Inc,
1128 8th Avenue West,
Palmetto, Florida 34221
Tel: 800 277 5275
www.markoftime.com

Michael's Antique Clocks.
PO Box 721361,
Oklahoma City,
Oklahoma 73172
Tel: 405 722 3300
oldclocks@home.com
www.michaelsclocks.com

Old Timers Antique Clocks,
Box 392, Camp Hill,
PA 17001
Tel: 717 761 1908
anytime@prodigy.net
www.antiqnet.com/oldtimers

R. O. Schmitt, Box 1941,
Salem, NH 03079
Tel: 001 603 893 5915
www.antiqueclockauction.com

The Barometer Shop,
C. Neville Lewis,
576 Pleasant Pt. Road,
Cushing, ME 04563
Tel: 207 354 8055
barometershop@earthlink.net
www.barometershop.net

Dennis A. Ward's Clock
Workshop, 11475 Rugby Hill
Drive, Redding, CA96003
Tel: 530 243 2809
info@dawclocks.com
www.dawclocks.com

Index

Italic page numbers denote colour pages; **bold** numbers refer to information and pointer boxes